THE WORLD OF K'UNG SHANG-JEN

Studies in Oriental Culture, Number 17
  Columbia University

尚狂的世界

宣立敦 著

孔德成 署

THE WORLD OF

K'UNG SHANG-JEN

A Man of Letters in
Early Ch'ing China

RICHARD E. STRASSBERG

Columbia University Press
New York 1983

The author and publisher gratefully acknowledge the
generous support toward publication given them by the
National Endowment for the Humanities.

Library of Congress Cataloging in Publication Data

Strassberg, Richard E.   1948-
  The world of K'ung Shang-jen.

  (Studies in Oriental Culture; no. 17)
  Bibliography: p.
  Includes index.
  1. K'ung, Shang-jen, 1648-1718. 2. Dramatists,
Chinese--Biography. I. Title. II. Series.
PL2717.U47Z88 1983   895.1'24   [B]   83-1838
ISBN 0-231-05530-7

Columbia University Press
New York   Guildford, Surrey

TO MY PARENTS

Studies in Oriental Culture
Edited at Columbia University

Board of Editors
Pierre Cachia, Professor of Arabic Language and Literature
Wm. Theodore de Bary, John Mitchell Mason Professor
 of the University
Ainslie T. Embree, Professor of History
Donald Keene, Professor of Japanese
Barbara Stoler Miller, Professor of Oriental Studies

CONTENTS

Foreword, by Cyril Birch   ix

Preface   xi

Acknowledgments   xv

List of Illustrations   xvii

Abbreviations   xxiii

Map   xxiv

1. Ch'ü-fu, the Sacred Precinct   1

2. Down from the Mountain   71

3. By Southern Lakes and Seas   117

4. Below the Palanquin   217

Epilogue   291

Notes   295

Bibliography   419

Glossary-Index   441

K'ung Shang-jen was born in 1648, four years after the native Chinese ruling house of the Ming had yielded place to the Ch'ing dynasty of the alien Manchus. He died in 1718, the fifty-seventh year of reign of the remarkable K'ang-hsi Emperor, whom K'ung had not only met but deeply impressed. K'ung's circle of acquaintance was wide, and varied from royal princes and scholar-officials to painters and collectors, actors and musicians. He is a splendid subject for biography, for the interests and activities reflected in his writings take us into the heart of the high civilization of China in its late flowering, a century and a half before the influences of the Western world began their irreversible flood.

K'ung had two great advantages. He was a lineal descendant of Confucius in the sixty-fourth generation, and he had outstanding poetic talent. He approached the study of past tradition and ritual in the spirit of a keeper of the flame, a transmitter of the esoteric mysteries. Even after three decades of Marxist attack on Confucius and the structure of values associated with his name, the Sacred Precinct of the Master is still today a site of pilgrimage. It is at Ch'ü-fu in Shantung, and since it was the backdrop to so much of K'ung's life, Richard Strassberg begins his book with a vivid evocation of its quiet groves, paved courts, and gleaming tiles. To the Precinct came the Emperor, on a visit which Strassberg describes in detail, citing the lecture K'ung composed for this august occasion. K'ung himself probably regarded the composition of this lecture as the greatest challenge of his literary career, but we will find his talent more vigorously displayed in a piece such as his travel essay on the subject of nearby Stonegate Mountain. This is a tour de force, both in the original and in Strassberg's rendering, an example of a genre much cherished by Chinese tradition but sadly underrepresented in available English translation.

As a lover of calligraphy and painting with a particular penchant for esthetic theory, K'ung Shang-jen engaged in some of the central intellectual movements of his time and was closely associated with the arbiters of thought and taste. Richard Strassberg has spent years exploring the world of art and intellect in which K'ung moves, and his book opens up new avenues of understanding for us.

None of K'ung's acquaintances, not even the actors or singing-girls whose milieu of the pleasure quarters is brought before us in chapter three, could possibly have predicted that he would be remembered first and foremost as a playwright. It is fascinating to follow the description of K'ung, late in life and ignorant of the rules, seeking the help of professional composers in the attempt to spin a dramatic romance around the subject of an antique stringed instrument that had come into his possession. But at last everything came together: K'ung's gift for lyrical verse, his passion for history and for the poignancy of the Ming collapse which still seared the memories of old men he knew, his love of the theater and his new command of dramaturgy. The result was <u>The Peach Blossom Fan</u>, the most celebrated of all Chinese historical dramas, whose fabric is woven form the bygone splendors of Ming romanticism. Strassberg's extensive and searching critique of this fine play makes a fitting coping stone to his book, just as the play itself did to its author's life and career.

It is always a pleasure to see the highest scholarly standards combine with a sense of what is both appealing and revealing in a culture as exotic as that of seventeenth century China. Richard Strassberg has written an unusual account of an unusual life, and the result is an unusually attractive book.

PREFACE

K'ung Shang-jen is most readily remembered as the author of China's greatest historical drama, The Peach Blossom Fan, but he is also one of those emblematic figures through whom we can see an age. A latter-day descendant of Confucius, he was heir to the central mysteries of Chinese civilization as maintained by his clan at the Confucian shrine of Ch'ü-fu. K'ung himself became an expert in the staging of ritual ceremonies dating back some two thousand years, and when the K'ang-hsi Emperor visited the shrine on one of his tours of inspection, K'ung was fortuitously chosen as lecturer and guide. Through imperial favor, he was meteorically propelled into the highest levels of capital society in Peking and began his close friendships with the leading figures of the early Ch'ing. He was an enthusiastic literatus, official, scholar, connoisseur, and socialite, and his wide-ranging activities provide us with a fascinating view of the artistic, political, and intellectual life of his time.

The seventeenth century in China was a turbulent era of transition. It began in the late Ming in a deceptive atmosphere of cultural romanticism set amidst deepening economic and political contradictions. By the mid-century, the triple threat of peasant rebellion, Manchu invasion, and court factionalism culminated in national catastrophe and the collapse of the Ming. To the Chinese elite, this cataclysmic change was not just another episode in the rise and fall of dynasties. The Ming order, as the successor to the hated Mongols, had represented the greatest flowering of the literati vision and its dismal performance in its final years led to a soul-searching inquiry into the core values of the native civilization. K'ung's own era witnessed the establishment of a new dynasty after decades of suffering and disorder. Yet, the early Ch'ing was pervaded by a fundamental irony. It was not merely that the world's oldest literary civilization had been ignominiously overwhelmed by a nomadic tribe that had barely adopted an alphabet a generation before. Rather, it was that the Manchus, unlike the Mongols, governed astutely and soon gained the support of most of the Chinese ruling class. By restoring stability based on a reintegration of traditional continuities, the Ch'ing Emperors succeeded according to the very standards by which the Chinese themselves judged sagely rulers. Toward the last decades of the century, the turmoil of the transition had largely become a memory and the permanence of the new dynasty was accepted as fact.

Despite this, not all Chinese truly welcomed the foreign Manchus as their rulers. Ming loyalism continued to be a force among "survivors" who lived on, tolerated by the Ch'ing as long as their resistance remained moral rather than military. K'ung met many such figures in his youth and his later career as a river control official took him to the heart of Ming loyalism in the southern cities of the lower Yangtze. There, he sought out leading "survivors" and joined their circle, a subculture of poets, painters, intellectuals, and recluses who continued to practice the styles and embody the values of late Ming romanticism.

K'ung thus personified the contradictions of his time. As a public symbol of Confucian orthodoxy, his service to K'ang-hsi and the Ch'ing symbolized native Chinese acceptance and legitimization of alien rule. Yet he maintained an emotional and aesthetic allegiance to the core values of Chinese civilization which he nostalgically associated with the bygone ethos of the late Ming. His life appears as one strongly mediated by a creative consciousness, for he perceived his world in terms of a rich literary tradition. In his poetry, he explored man's relationship to historical place and to cultural memory, seeking to chart the present through the many senses of the past. Later in his life, he found in drama the ideal vehicle for representing the conflict between romance and history which he realized was the essential cultural tension of his era. In his monumental work, The Peach Blossom Fan, K'ung recreated a panoramic view of the events and characters involved in the fall of the Ming, summing up a long artistic tradition with the realism, tragedy, and irony which were the hallmarks of his style.

In this literary biography, I have attempted to present K'ung close to the way he presented himself. In part, this was a stylistic choice, a desire to envisage a Chinese literatus in terms of his own culture's image of the self. Yet this was also determined, to a certain extent, by the kinds of data available. The Chinese literati were highly conscious of posterity's judgment and saw literature as a means of creating an idealized public personality. As a man of the early Ch'ing, K'ung reflected the growing self-consciousness of that age. He tells us much about his career, his experiences in nature, attitudes toward the past, toward literature, and toward art, and also about his extensive social circle. Yet, due to the conventions of Confucian decorum, we know little of his intimate family life and of his love affairs, while his deeper anxieties were disguised in poetic imagery. The inner psychological elements which we in the post-Strachey era have come to expect of a rounded biographical portrait are more obliquely present in the life of a Chinese literatus, if only because the existence of such elements was less defined in their own awareness. Were it not for the expressiveness of K'ung's great drama and the confirming evidence of his poetry and prose, we might be left, as in the case of lesser figures, with merely the history of a reputation instead of the evolution of a personal mythology.

A noted Western biographer described his task as that of "a storyteller who may not invent his facts but who is allowed to imagine his form."[1] The form of this book I would liken to that of an archaeological reconstruction. Important parts are selected fragments unearthed from K'ung's collected works; in these, I serve merely as his translator. Into the lacunae, I have offered interpretations of the meaning of his words and sought to restore the texture and patina of the early Ch'ing. In sum, I have tried to recreate the complexity of a lost world, in some respects exotic and remote from our own, but in others familiar, in that the same questions about man and the fate of his civilization are still pondered today.

Richard E. Strassberg

Los Angeles
Fall 1982

ACKNOWLEDGMENTS

This book has had a somewhat extended odyssey. My interest in K'ung Shang-jen began a decade ago when I was a graduate student. A fellow-student presented me with a musty, Chinese-bound edition of The Peach Blossom Fan. The fascinating recreation of the era of late Ming romanticism which I found in K'ung's great drama inspired me over the years to attempt a similar pursuit--that of evoking the world which K'ung Shang-jen himself moved in during the early Ch'ing. In expressing gratitude to those who helped me along the way, I should perhaps begin at the beginning by thanking my first teacher of Chinese, Prof. Bernard Solomon of Queens College, CUNY, for setting me on the path of a life of scholarship. Prof. Yu-kung Kao of Princeton University was inspiring and supportive during my graduate study when this book was in its embryonic form as a doctoral dissertation. In Taiwan, Mr. Hsu Yen-chih and his wife, the late Ms. Chang Shan-hsiang, generously taught me the art of performing K'un-ch'ü. Although I did not realize at first what I was getting into when I asked Mr. Hsu to teach me the Chinese flute, both he and Ms. Chang initiated me into a rich dramatic tradition through which I have experienced many moments of creative enjoyment and encountered many extraordinary personalities. To Mr. Ch'en Wan-nai of the National Palace Museum (Taipei), one of the leading scholars on K'ung, my thanks for supplying me with his publications and friendly encouragement. Profs. Cheng Ch'ien and Tseng Yung-i of National Taiwan University were also most generous with their expertise, as were Profs. Tanaka Kenji and Iriya Yoshitaka of Kyoto University. Mr. K'ung Te-ch'eng, 76th Generation Duke of the Sagely Posterity and himself a scholar of his ancestor was kind enough to provide me with valuable memories and insights into the world of the K'ung

K'ung clan. His excellent seal-style calligraphy graces this volume. In Ch'ü-fu, Mr. K'ung Hsiang-lin of the Ch'ü-fu Bureau of Cultural Properties kindly spent an afternoon with me providing information on the present state of the Confucian Shrine.

The friendship of my colleagues, Prof. Hans Frankel and his talented wife Ms. Chang Ch'ung-ho, made the years I spent teaching at Yale a memorable experience. Yet another benefit of that period was the friendship of Prof. Jonathan Spence, whose knowledge of the seventeenth century and whose literary skill were most helpful in providing comments on early versions of several chapters. Prof. Marsha Wagner of Columbia University offered enthusiastic reception to the book and helpful editorial suggestions. Prof. Cyril Birch of the University of California, Berkeley, whose excellent translation of The Peach Blossom Fan helped pave the way for a biography of K'ung, has been continually encouraging. He has generously contributed an introduction, and this book can only hope to approach the high standard which he has set in the art of translation as well as in drama scholarship. Mr. William Bernhardt, Associate Executive Editor of Columbia University Press, patiently guided the manuscript through the various stages of its acceptance with professional expertise. The final version was typed by Mrs. Irene Chow. Ms. Yenna Wu and Ms. Yang Su-hsiang, graduate students at UCLA, helped proofread the translations, all of which are my own unless otherwise noted, and for which I take full responsibility.

Finally, I would like to thank the members of my family, who have wondered over the years what this book was all about, for their curiosity, concern, and support.

LIST OF ILLUSTRATIONS

Frontispiece   The World of K'ung Shang-jen written in seal-style calligraphy by K'ung Te-ch'eng, Duke of the Sagely Posterity in the 76th generation.

pp.8-9   Map of the Chü-fu Area. The city of Ch'ü-fu containing the Confucian Temple and the Ducal Mansion is located within the crenellated inner walls on the left and surrounded by the remains of the old wall of Lu. Directly to the north is the Confucian Grove and beyond that, Mt. T'ai. The two parallel rivers to the north and west are the Ssu and Shu Rivers with the I River to the south. All three converge before the city of Yen-chou. Stonegate Mt., site of K'ung's retreat, is located in the upper right. From Ch'en, Ch'ueh-li-chih.

p.13   Portrait of Confucius as Minister of Justice in Lu. The woodblock print is based on a stone engraving in the Hall of the Sage's Life which itself was taken from a Ming painting formerly conserved in the Confucian Temple. From Ch'en, Ch'ueh-li-chih.

p.25   An acolyte at the Confucian Shrine formally attired and standing in a ceremonial pose with feathered staff and baton. From Ch'en, Chueh-li-chih.

p.26   A set of bells in the Confucian Temple modeled on Chou dynasty forms used in ceremonial music. From P'an, Chü-fu.

p.35   A fan with the calligraphy and seal of Chia Fu-hsi. Discovered in Shantung in 1931, it identifies Chia as "The 'Wood-and-Leather' Wanderer." From Liu, Mu-p'i.

p.61   Traveling in the Mt. T'ai range, slightly to the northwest of Stonegate. Detail from Wang Hui and assistants, K'ang-hsi Emperor's Second Southern Tour of the South. The Metropolitan Museum of Art, Purchase, The Dillon Fund, 1979.

p.83   Portrait of the K'ang-hsi Emperor at the age of forty-five. National Palace Museum, Peking.

pp.84-5   K'ang-hsi enters the city of Tsinan. Detail from Wang Hui and assistants, K'ang-hsi Emperor's Second Southern Tour of the South. The Metropolitan Museum of Art, Purchase, The Dillon Fund, 1979.

pp.96-7   Map of the Confucian Temple. The pilgrim entered through the arch at the bottom and proceeded through the file of gates and buildings to reach the Hall of Accomplishment in the compound at the top which also contains the Apricot Terrace and the juniper planted by Confucius. In the courtyards alongside the central file are pavilions housing famous steles. The Ducal Mansion is located outside the Temple to the upper right and the gate announcing the "Tower District" where Confucius dwelled stands over the street in the lower right. From Ch'en, Chueh-li-chih.

pp.106-7 Map of the Confucian Grove. The grave mounds of Confucius, his son Po-yü and grandson Tzu-ssu are located within the walled compound in the upper middle portion. In accordance with Chinese geomancy, the path was laid out on an indirect axis proceeding from the outer gate below along a file of funerary statues through the Sacrificial Pavilion. This was done to inhibit the movement of evil spirits. The other mounds in the grove are the graves of leading descendants and clan heads. From P'an, Ch'ü-fu.

p.129 A typical outdoor commercial theater. Such stages were often set up temporarily by traveling troupes who would attract large audiences at festivals. The scene is from a Ch'ing palace copy of the famous Sung scroll by Chang Tse-tuan, Scenes Along the River During the Ch'ing-Ming Festival, National Palace Museum, Taipei. However, this scene does not appear in the original painting and the details of the performers' costumes as well as the musical instruments reflect the Ch'ing theater.

p.130 A formal performance of literati drama held in an official's mansion. The host is seated in the upper center and the guests arraigned in order along both sides. The performers stage a dance on the carpet in the middle. From a late Ming edition of the drama Water Margin by Yang Ting-chien.

pp.142-3   Fang Shih-shu and Yeh Fang-lin, The Literary Gathering at a Yangchow Garden (detail). The Cleveland Musuem of Art, The Severence & Greta Milliken Purchase Fund. A pictorial record of an actual literary gathering of members of a poetry society held next to the Temple of Heavenly Peace where K'ung himself often stayed.

p.153   A poem by K'ung Shang-jen written in his own hand. It was originally a colophon to a painting of falconry by his older relative in Ch'ü-fu, Yen Kuang-min (Hsiu-lai). Photo courtesy Renditions.

p.154   Part of an informal letter by K'ung Shang-jen praising a landscape painting he received. Chao-tai ming-jen chih-tu, reprinted in Ch'en, yen-chiu.

p.181   Kung Hsien, A Thousand Peaks and Myriad Ravines. Museum Rietberg, Zurich, C. Drenowatz Collection.

p.182   Cha Shih-piao, Old Man Boating on a River. The Metropolitan Museum of Art, Purchase, The Sackler Fund, 1969. 242.7.

p.203   Tao-chi, Reminiscences of Ch'in-huai River. The Cleveland Museum, Purchase, John L. Severance Fund.

p.204   The Tomb of Ming T'ai-tsu in Nanking, based on a Ming woodblock print by Ling Ta-te. The tomb is located in the left-hand portion while the complex of buildings on the right is the Temple of the Valley of Souls. Wang, Ming-hsiao-ling-chih.

p.213　　　The K'ang-hsi Emperor inspects river control projects in P'ei-chou, Kiangsu. From Wang Hui and assistants, <u>K'ang-hsi Emperor's Southern Tour</u>, Musée Guimet, Paris.

p.231　　　The T'ang dynasty instrument "Little Thunderclap" rediscovered and restored by K'ung Shang-jen. The original drawing was done in the early 20th century by the artist Lin Shu for the collector and bibliophile Liu Shih-heng. K'ung, <u>Hsiao-hu-lei</u>.

p.237　　　The heroine Cheng Ying-ying performs on "Little Thunderclap" accompanied by the T'ang Emperor Wen-tsung on the flute and the Emperor's younger brother, Prince Chin, on the drums. The villain Ch'ou Shih-liang attends them. Woodblock print by Li Shih-tien from scene 28, "A Courtesan Ennobled" in <u>"Little Thunderclap"</u>. K'ung, <u>Hsiao-hu-lei</u>.

p.253　　　Yang Wen-tsung paints Fragrant Lady's bloodstains on the fan into peach blossoms as Su K'un-sheng looks on and the heroine herself languishes in her chamber. From scene 23, "The Message on the Fan" in <u>The Peach Blossom Fan</u>. K'ung, <u>Tao-hua-shan</u> (Nuan-hung-shih ed.).

p.287　　　Tai Pen-hsiao, <u>Landscape</u>. Ching-yuan-chai, Berkeley.

ABBREVIATIONS

CTS	Ch'üan-t'ang-shih
K	K'ung, K'ung shang-jen shih-wen-chi
SPPY	Ssu-pu pei-yao
SPTK	Ssu-pu ts'ung-k'an
TSCC	Ts'ung-shu chi-ch'eng
T	K'ung, T'ao-hua-shan (Wang and Su, eds.)
P	K'ung, The Peach Blossom Fan (Ch'en, Acton, and Birch, trans.)

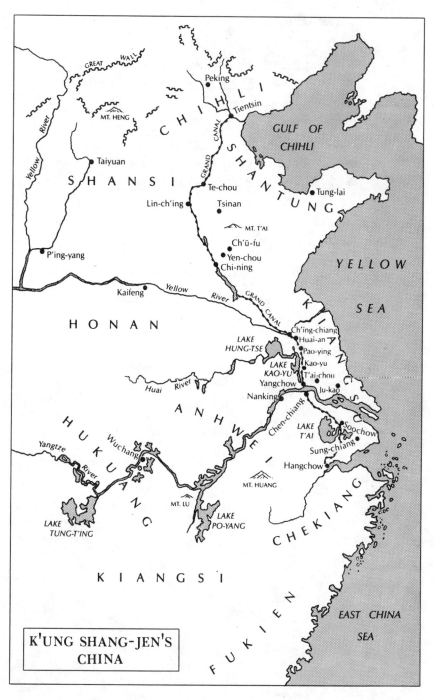

Map: K'ung Shang-jen's China

Chapter One
CH'Ü-FU, THE SACRED PRECINCT

*Je suis venu au monde tres jeune dans un
temps très vieux.--Erik Satie*

The pilgrim to Ch'ü-fu[1] in the early Ch'ing passed
through successive scenes of sandy plains framed by cloud-
wrapped mountains before coming to one such expanse more
favored through time. Screened by Mt. Ni to the southeast
and Stonegate[2] to the northeast with the shadows of Mt.
T'ai beyond, the high, flat area of some 1,400 square miles
was approached from the west after passing through
scattered, somnolent villages. Whether traveling by
horseback, sedan chair, oxcart, or a local mode of
transportation called a "gentlemen's ox" (in fact, a
wheelbarrow propelled by man), the immediate view upon
entering was of a vista not much different from those which
preceded save for a cluster of yellow-tiled roofs
glistening through evergreens in the distance.

The first landmark to be noticed as the dirt road
became paved was the Sluice Bridge across the Ssu River,
forming a deceptively pastoral tableau. Women pounded
their wash against the stones, bamboo-hatted muleteers
paused to drink. In summer, naked children bathed off the
clinging dust. The Ssu often altered its course since
first mention of it in the Water Classic,[3] and in its less
benevolent moments, it could innundate the entire western

part of the city. Its silty yellow flow was enlarged by a major dredging during the Chia-ching reign (1522-67) of the Ming but this did little to alter the regular occurrence of disasters. In gazetteers recording the Shun-chih (1644-62) and early K'ang-hsi (1662-1723) reigns alone, barely five years pass without an entry of some major flood setting off ripples of famines and banditry.[4] A counterpoint of earthquakes, locusts, droughts, and hailstorms composes endless permutations of suffering interrupted only by the brief hiatus which, one assumes, denotes peaceful times. Then, the river meandered westwards out of the mountains three miles northeast of Ch'ü-fu. It circled around the Confucian Grove turning south to parallel the city wall and then southwest on to the prefectural capital of Yen-chou twelve miles away. Beyond that, it disappeared meekly into the Yellow River. Though reduced to a shallow trickle in the hot summer months, the Ssu and its confluents, the Shu and I, wet the fields alongside in the rainy season providing irrigation for rice, sorghum, millet, and a variety of vegetables. These gave the area a reputation for producing, if not agricultural rarities, at least quantities of the eternal staples to keep most of the population fed.

Across the bridge, the yellow-green landscape was splattered with patches of deep sand, requiring wooden planks to be laid down in some places. Once negotiated and the narrow Shu river crossed, the wall of Ch'ü-fu appeared directly east. It was completed during the Chia-ching reign to guard against a recurrence of the bandit raid of 1511. On February 24 of that year, marauders who had already overrun other parts of Yen-chou reached the city. Several hundred inhabitants died, undefended by the frightened soldiers that provincial authorities had ordered to the rescue. Miraculously, the extensive pillaging spared the Confucian Temple and Grove. In 1513, the Surveillance Commissioner P'an Chen commenced the building of the wall, using 10,000 corvee laborers off the fields. After nine years and some 35,800 tales, the wall was finished, encircling the city nearly three miles around.[5]

The road markedly improved again as the pilgrim approached to the point where he could clearly view the wall standing 24 feet high and half again as wide. Yet after passing through one of the five gates, there was a frequent sense of surprise at the spartan appearance of the city, especially for those who harbored grand visions inspired by the hyperbole of Confucian letters or expected a scale similar to Peking some 430 miles away. The outer neighborhoods of the town reflected the bare simplicity of Shantung. Many houses were thatched or roofed in common grey tile and the streets were but dirt-packed alleyways. Few stores, restaurants, or inns existed in this basically agrarian community where every two or three days a market was held by one of the city gates. The only ready refreshments for the weary were outdoor snack counters selling sorghum dumplings and salted noodle soup. The official visitor might have been royally lodged in the Ducal Mansion or the Temporary Palace, but others were hard-put to find accommodations and often preferred to stay in Yen-chou. The atmosphere was one of an inbred serenity sustained by the ritualized manners of small-town life. A more recent observer noted, not unadmiringly, that

Ch'ü-fu has a benevolent character where people observe the proprieties and yield to their elders. Even now, when men's minds are slowly becoming more crafty, their respect for poetry and history as well as their occupation with farming and silk producing has not changed. They are still content with whatever is and avoid traveling any distance, preferring to stay at home and tend to their affairs rather than venture far. So few have ever gained great profit or risen to high positions as officials.[6]

Yet its past is filled with vicissitudes. First mention of it is as the capital of the Sage-king, Shen Nung.[7] Two miles northeast is the birthplace of the Yellow Emperor[8] whose son, Shao-hao,[9] also made it his capital. In the time of Yü, it fell within the province of Hsu-chou; during the Shang, it was the capital of Yen. The Duke of Chou was enfeoffed in Ch'ü-fu, which, with the surrounding area, was named Lu.[10] Lu was conquered by Ch'u during the Warring States period. Ch'in placed it in Hsueh-chün, Ch'u recaptured it and then it fell to the Han which made it part of Yü-chou. During the T'ang, it was incorporated into Yen-chou within the Honan Circuit. Briefly renamed "Hsien-yuan" or "Source of the Immortals" under the Sung, it regained its name in the Chin. Finally, in the Ming, it was designated Ch'ü-fu District, Yen-chou Prefecture in Shantung Province. The rise and fall of sage-kings, feudal lords, emperors, and bandits had destroyed the city numerous times. By the Han, though, it had attained its present location slightly west of the ancient site.

Only upon entering the Temple itself did the style turn imperial. With the gradual elevation of the Confucian cult to the role of state orthodoxy, the places and objects associated with Confucius were incorporated into a national shrine. Supported over the centuries through successive acts of imperial patronage, the shrine grew into a vast complex centered principally on the Confucian Temple (covering some 49 acres in the western section of the city) and the Confucian Grove (about a mile outside the northern wall and containing the Sage's tomb). In addition, there were numerous secondary temples to lesser divinities scattered throughout the area as well as sacred sites and academies. This sprawling mecca was maintained by the K'ung clan, whose hereditary leaders had been raised to the rank of dukes and dwelled in a palatial mansion just east of the Temple.[11]

The paved walk to the Temple formed the main north-south axis of the city and led into a grandiose establishment, the model for all others throughout China. Ancient evergreens backgrounded by a low wall defined the long outer compound across which a small stream intervened. Three slightly arched marble bridges spanned it and placed the pilgrim before a series of gates. The third one opened into a courtyard dotted with small pavilions protecting the most valuable of the more than 1,000 steles. Of these, 16 dated from the Han--the earliest from A.D. 153[12]--making it the largest such collection extant. After yet another gate, the first major building appeared, its three-tiered roof rising some 85 feet high. Erected in 1190, the Hall of the Literary Constellation[13] housed the clan library with its priceless rare editions specializing in works on ceremonial form. More steles stood about it arranged by dynasties, like clusters of lesser stars.

Upon passing through the Gate of Accomplishment into the inner compound, the area was divided into three sections. On the left was a series of halls including the Hall of Chimes and Strings, where the historic drums, gongs, zithers, and flutes used in sacrifices were stored.[14] To the right was a similar file of structures including the Hall of Poetry and Ritual, where the Analects records Confucius as having advised his son Po-yü on the value of studying these subjects.[15] Just behind this were two noted sites--the old well of Confucius' mansion and the "Wall of Lu," the latter containing the hollow where the classics were hid during the Ch'in persecution.[16] Nearby, a stele identified this as "Ch'ueh-li," the "Tower District" mentioned in the Tso Commentary.[17]

The central area, marked off by galleries on all sides, contained the main Hall of Accomplishment, in front of which was the Apricot Terrace. Protected by the ubiquitous yellow tiles and supported by flowered columns festooned with gold and vermilion plaques, the stone terrace marked the location of Confucius' academy, a site which apparently originated from a legend in Chuang-tzu.[18] Also of mythical status was the petrified juniper said to have been planted by Confucius himself standing on the right side of the courtyard.[19]

The main hall rested imposingly on a stone platform and stood 84 feet high and 153 feet wide (or 9 chien according to traditional Chinese measurement). In a truly palatial style dating from the 1499 renovation, its huge double-tiered roof was supported outside by ten marble columns front and back, each carved from a single block in the form of dragons grasping pearls while twelve nan-mu pillars, each from a single tree, provided interior support.

Inside, Confucius as the "Throneless King" dominated the somber chamber. He wore the "Crown of Heavenly Rule" and twelve emblems of rank, and he held the jade "Scepter of Pacification."[20] The Attendant Spirits of Yen Hui, Tzu-ssu, Tseng-tzu, and Mencius flanked him while before him was an array of bronze vessels modeled on Shang and Chou forms.[21] A small hall dedicated to Confucius' wife was in back, and beyond that was another containing over a hundred stone tablets mounted along the vermillion walls on which were engraved scenes from the life of the Sage.

Not to be neglected by the pilgrim was the Confucian Grove. Chang Tai,[22] a noted observer of seventeenth century scenes, once visited it and recalled:

About two or three miles beyond Ch'ü-fu's northern
gate is the Confucian Grove, surrounded by an
imperial-style brown wall with yellow tiles. A
tower stands above the gate, from which a small
speck of a mountain can be viewed to the southeast-
-Mt. I. Turning to the west, one comes across
several stone tigers and rams in the tall grass.
Then a bridge is crossed. There are two rivers
which flow into the Ssu. Behind the Sacrificial
Pavilion are junipers planted by Tzu-kung. There
are about a thousand of these large and small,
which the people of Lu use to make chessboards and
scales. Just opposite the Sacrificial Pavilion is
the tomb of Po-yü. Confucius buried his son there
so that he could obtain the most central
influences. To the right of Po-yü's tomb stands
that of the Sage, a few yards from which a small
mound has been built. South of this mound is the
tomb of Tzu-ssu. Thus within about a hundred steps
of each other, father, son, and grandson and
buried. Ch'iao Chou[23] records, "After Confucius'
death, more than 100 local households settled
around his grave and were known as the 'Confucian
Village.'" The Discourses of the Confucian School[24]
says: "Confucius' grave is a third of a mile in
circumference and is located some two to three
miles north of the city, beyond the Ssu River."
More than fifty houses were given to members of the
K'ung family as fiefs, each located according to
their genealogical relationship to Confucius; but
there is no longer any record of this. There are
three steles and also round tablets in the shape of
animals which remain. The Imperial Encyclopedia[25]
says: "Each of the disciples planted trees from

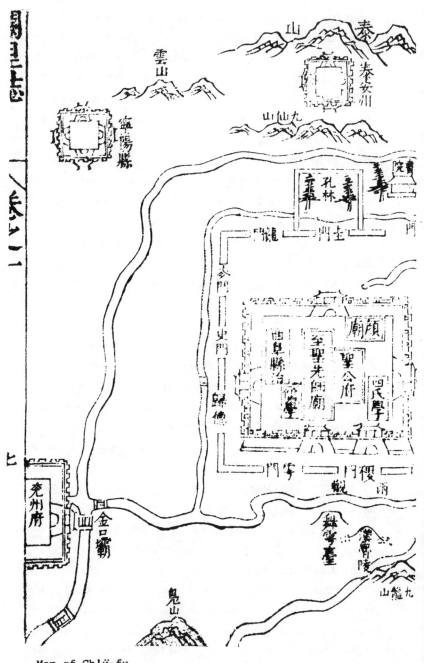

Map of Ch'ü-fu

every area so there are many exotic varieties which cannot be named; within the grove, thorns and brambles have never grown." Beyond the wall, there are graves of several thousand families. For over three millenia his descendants have not deserted him and are all buried about, something no emperor or king has ever matched. . . .[26]

Not far from the Sage's tomb is the grave of a particularly noteworthy descendant. Incised dragons surrounding the words "Great Ch'ing" cap the erect stone slab on which is engraved his posthumous and official titles: "Great Officer with Direct Access to the Throne" and "Assistant Director of the Kwangtung Department of the Board of Revenue."

K'ung Shang-jen,[27] was born in Ch'ü-fu on November 1, 1648, four years after the establishment of the Ch'ing dynasty. In the genealogy which he later compiled, K'ung recorded his membership in the 12th branch, 41st subbranch of the K'ung clan, placing himself in the 64th generation of descent from Confucius.[28] As with many literati who only achieved prominence in their later years, few events of his youth and early maturity were noted. A local gazetteer printed a year after his death contains a hagiographical incident about him when he was four years old, designed to presage his lifelong sensitivity to injustice and suffering.[29] A short biography appended to selections of his poetry conventionally records him as a child prodigy who could produce rhymed couplets at the age of five and who had mastered the major forms of poetry and prose by the time he was twelve.[30]

The biographer is thus faced with a considerable gap in K'ung's early years; he can either pass over them as if nothing much of interest occurred, or attempt to sketch the formative contours of his mature imagination. Until his discovery by the K'ang-hsi Emperor, K'ung spent the first 36 years of his life in obscurity in Ch'ü-fu. It was the continuity with the past sustained by the K'ung clan in this capsule environment which stimulated his creative interests and gave them their particularly dualistic character. His exploration of the scenic beauty of the area, encounters with "survivors" of the late Ming, and mastery of the ceremonial forms of the Confucian Shrine all contribute to define the poles of romanticism and historicism which constitute the essential tension in his artistic vision. In his later years, despite the fame his writings attracted, his prestige among the literati continued to rest on the aura of his K'ung heritage. He himself frequently referred to it and later, in casting his persona in The Peach Blossom Fan as an aged master of Confucian ceremony from the late Ming, he revealed how central the self-image he developed during this period remained for him. In his time, the K'ung clan numbered more than 10,000 members. The perspective of this unique world, not only towards its own traditions but towards its role in an age of conquest and dynastic transition, endowed K'ung Shang-jen with a passionate concern over the fate of his civilization.

THE K'UNGS OF CH'Ü-FU

Few great families can rival the continuity of the K'ung clan, which extends beyond the eightieth generation today. Its ability not only to survive but to attain a central position in the mind of traditional China must be accounted one of the rareties of human history. To trace its lineage is to follow a single thread through three millenia, during which it grew from a minor military family into a powerful gentry, becoming the living embodiment of the national cult of Confucianism and the purveyor of legitimacy to emperors and dynasties.

While it is difficult to find reliable evidence for the beginnings of the clan prior to the eighth century B.C., their own mythology posits an origin 47 generations before Confucius. Similar to the reference in the Tso Commentary, upon which the account in the Historical Records is largely based, it claims descent from the Yellow Emperor and a series of other legendary sage-kings down through T'ang, founder of the Shang dynasty.[31] Thus they connected themselves with a royal house and believed that they were enfeoffed as dukes in the state of Sung by the succeeding Chou dynasty in order to carry on their ancestral sacrifices. While in Sung, the legitimate line was usurped several generations later when the rightful heir, Ho,[32] yeilded the dukedom and accepted a lesser position as High Minister. Five generations after that, his descendants had slipped to the rank of Great Officer in the person of Chia, whose courtesy name was K'ung-fu.[33] The first character of his courtesy name was adopted as a surname in order to distinguish this lesser branch from its ducal cousins; but it did not protect K'ung-fu from assassination in 709 B.C. for being too closely connected to Duke Shang.[34] His son fled from Sung to Lu where he settled, still as a Great Officer.[35]

Confucius[36] was born in Ch'ang-p'ing-hsiang (modern Tsou-hsien) just south of Ch'ü-fu in 551 B.C., in the fifth generation after the migration from Sung. His father, Ko,[37] had hastily taken a concubine from the neighboring Yen clan in order to produce a healthy heir and died when Confucius was but four. This left him without a powerful protector in an age of decline when the bonds of Chou feudalism were fragmenting. It would hardly be possible

像寇司

Portrait of Confucius

here to chronicle Confucius' life of wandering in search of an enlightened sovereign, or survey his philosophy, which was to become so central to later Chinese civilization. From the point of view of the K'ung clan, he was considered the progenitive ancestor in relation to whom all later generations were enumerated. Their carefully charted blood lineage, proprietorship of his shrine, and maintenance of the Shang and Chou ceremonies he espoused, constituted the basis for their claim to being the authentic vehicle of the Confucian tradition. Through political pragmatism, favorable events, and the mystique of their ancestor, they were able to weather centuries of upheavals around them and prosper.

Despite bequeathing a corpus of classics and a coterie of disciples, Confucius did not notably increase the position of his clan during his lifetime. When he died in 470 B.C., his disciple Tseng-tzu was heard to remark that the lavish burial belied the reality of his powerlessness.[38] Yet, around his grave a small community grew. Family, loyal disciples, and neighbors settled on about 15 acres of land forming a hamlet of some 100 houses known as the "Confucian Village." There, they privately supported sacrifices to his memory and housed his memorabilia in a small building which marked the beginning of the shrine complex.

A series of early descendants were somewhat more successful than their ancestor in the world of politics.[39] But in the ninth generation, with the rise of Ch'in Shih-huang (r. 221-209 B.C.), the fortunes of the K'ung clan underwent a reversal. The head, K'ung Fu,[40] had initially been honored with the office of Junior Guardian and the title, "Lord of Literary Understanding in Lu." Moreover, in 219 B.C., the Emperor had visited the locality and met with local Confucians who advised him on the proper ceremonies to be held on nearby Mt. T'ai.[41] In 213 B.C. however, the notorious policies of the prime minister, Li Ssu, which led to the execution of Confucians and the burning of most of the classics, forced K'ung Fu and his disciples into hiding. Before fleeing to Mt. Sung, he secreted copies of some of the classics inside the wall of the ancestral mansion to be recovered in better times.

With the rise of opposition to the Ch'in, the K'ungs threw their support to the contender Ch'en She, who assumed the title "King of Ch'u." K'ung Fu briefly accepted the rank of Grand Guardian and the clan continued their allegiance when the leadership of the cause passed to Hsiang Yü, who was enfeoffed as Duke of Lu in 207 B.C.[42] This exceptional devotion was an example of the loyalist sympathies which would surface again at later points in history. Lu was the last area to resist the victorious Han Kao-tsu (r. 206-194 B.C.) who personally led an army in 202 B.C. to slaughter the resisters in the city. It is recorded that upon his arrival, he was much impressed by the sentiments of the people, whose leaders only surrendered when he displayed Hsiang Yü's severed head.[43] In all probability though, the crime of Lu's defiance was lessened considerably by the mediation of K'ung Chü.[44] A nephew of K'ung Fu, he served as a general under Han Hsin and commanded the left flank in the final defeat of Hsiang Yü at Kai-hsia. The following year, he was enfeoffed as Marquis of Liao, the first K'ung to be ennobled by the Han. It thus tended to be true that even when the majority of the clan maintained loyalist sympathies with a fallen cause, there were always leading members closely involved with the other side, so that in the end the K'ungs were able to avoid the consequences of their moral stance.[45]

Han Kao-tsu, a man of action from peasant origins, hardly bothered to conceal his low opinion of Confucians.

Yet, as the years of ruling an empire wore on, he learned to appreciate them as administrators and arbiters of court ceremony.[46] This acceptance was symbolized by a pilgrimage to Ch'ü-fu towards the end of his reign in 195 B.C.,[47] marking the first such visit by a ruler and the beginning of the clan's enduring relationship with the imperial state. On this occasion, K'ung T'eng,[48] brother of K'ung Fu, was enfeoffed as Lord of Ancestral Sacrifices. The Emperor, in paying homage to Confucius, demonstrated the growing ideological and religious function which the Sage's philosophy was attaining; and the K'ungs, for their part, graciously purveyed the seal of moral authority.

The ultimate triumph of Confucianism in the Han was actually a slow process hampered by the Taoist and occultist leanings of the court. The K'ungs continued to receive occasional benefits depending on the inclinations of the emperors. However, they not only had to compete with more fashionable religions but with other spokesmen for Confucianism as well.[49] With the accession of Han Wu-ti (r. 140-86 B.C.), an ideological version was promoted as a state cult. This enunciated the Sage's moral ideals although the court's motivation was actually to employ the literary skills of the Confucians to centralize the bureaucracy. Faculties in the five classics were instituted in 136 B.C. and two clan members, K'ung An-kuo and K'ung Yen-nien,[50] were appointed to chairs as Erudites. Six years later, a quota of fifty students, mostly from Lu, was established with state support. This began the association of the clan with what later developed into the Imperial Academy, one of the important conduits of talented K'ungs into government.

It could be said that the clan reached the apogee of its national influence in the Han. K'ung An-kuo's transcriptions of K'ung Fu's "ancient texts" and his commentaries on the classics were among the major intellectual achievements of the period. Official recognition of these versions over the "recent texts" was motivated largely by the administrative need to promote a uniform script, but the result was to recognize the K'ungs as authoritative interpreters.[51] Clan members frequently served with high rank both at court and in the provinces; and towards the end of the dynasty, the royal house became increasingly dependent on the military power of officials such as K'ung Jung[52] for defense against usurpers. In subsequent centuries, though, the K'ungs became more and more peripheral in national life. Their numbers increased, their lands became more extensive and honors were heaped upon them; but they did not often venture into court politics or maintain a constant military force. Nor did they remain in the forefront of the major philosophical trends. A rare exception to this was K'ung Ying-ta,[53] a key proponent of the revival of Confucianism in the early T'ang; but he seems a lone figure towering over the later generations. Inevitably, the clan became preoccupied with preserving its growing fiefdom in Ch'ü-fu. Particularly in periods of disorder, the external activities of the K'ungs were largely diplomatic necessities arising from this conservative policy, rather than a continuation of their ancestor's sense of historic mission.

In the early centuries, the economic mainstay of the clan was the private wealth of its leading members derived from their estates and supplemented by their earnings as officials. In addition, there were occasional benefits granted by the emperors, such as individual gifts, contributions for building construction, stipends, and honorary titles. As early as 153 B.C., military forces were stationed in Ch'ü-fu at government expense to protect the shrine. Later, tenants were bestowed. Some were attached to the land, producing income, and others moved en masse to the site of the Shrine in order to maintain it. The K'ungs were also exempted from corvée labor and assorted taxes. That these privileges were periodically reconfirmed, however, suggests that they were not constant and that the K'ungs may have found it difficult to maintain them during times when imperial support was less certain.[54]

Fixed land endowments, which later became the basis of the clan's wealth, only began in the Sung when Chen-tsung (r. 998-1023) donated 100 ch'ing (one ch'ing is about 15 acres) in 1008, designated for support of sacrifices. This land was given by Che-tsung (r. 1086-1101) in 1086 to clan members to freely administer. Seven years later, another 100 ch'ing were donated, the income from which was to be used as follows: 20 ch'ing for student scholarships; 20 ch'ing to support sacrifices; 10 ch'ing for interior refurbishing of the shrine; 50 ch'ing for new buildings and exterior maintenance.[55]

A major endowment occurred upon the founding of the Ming when T'ai-tsu (r. 1368-99) donated land from 5 military encampments as well as 2,000 ch'ing located in 27 areas around Ch'ü-fu. This continued to be supplemented in succeeding reigns and represented an immense expansion of the clan's assets. Not all this land was productive or even under the control of its nominal owners though. In the seventeenth century, banditry, squatters, natural disasters, inefficiency, tenant abandonment, and litigation combined to reduce the property so that by the early Ch'ing it was estimated that only about 60 percent of the original Ming endowment was still in the K'ungs' possession.[56]

With the establishment of the Ch'ing, all existing privileges accumulated under the Ming were reconfirmed and another large-scale land grant was made, bringing the total up to 2,157 ch'ing. Other property in Ch'ü-fu was reckoned as follows: Confucian Grove, 18 ch'ing; Confucian Temple, 3 ch'ing; agricultural tenants, 500 families; labor and maintainence tenants, 115 families; school property, 50 ch'ing.[57] There were modest increments to this and in one case another 11 ch'ing was added to the Confucian Grove by the K'ang-hsi Emperor through K'ung Shang-jen's personal request.[58] By the seventeenth century, the K'ungs had expanded to such an extent that it was difficult to add on new lands without displacing legitimate owners; and there were always the competing needs of the neghboring clans descended from Mencius, Yen-tzu, and Tseng-tzu.[59] Consequently, they developed their other holdings in five nearby counties as well as in Peking and Chekiang.

The wealth of the K'ungs was protected through a political network whereby leading members administered clan affairs, served in local government, and maintained a liaison with the capital. This too developed with imperial patronage dating back to A..D. 221, when the first clan academy was founded.[60] Such schools developed an elite pool of talent and sustained it through hereditary ranks and government appointments. In the early Ch'ing, a promising K'ung would probably have been trained in one of these academies, which were supported by endowed land and staffed by highly educated relatives. The main institution was the Academy of the Four Clans, attached to the Confucian Temple. Others were the Mt. Ni. Shu-ssu, Spring and Autumn, and Stonegate Academies, located in the countryside.[61] Modeled on Chu Hsi's Grotto Academy, they taught a special curriculum emphasizing Confucian studies. Among the texts employed were the imperial editions of the Four Books and the Thirteen Classics, the Twenty-two Dynastic Histories, the Three Comprehensive Histories, the Compendium on the Principle of Human Nature, and readings in ancient prose and poetry. Interestingly, a local gazette sternly notes that all "unsagely" subjects were to be expunged.   Teachers were forbidden to lecture on contemporary writings and popular literature while any who perused erotic plays and novels were to be censured.[62] Such proscriptions, however, do not seem to have deterred the young K'ung Shang-jen from an early fascination with storytellers, ballads, and, in in his later years, drama.

From the academies, candidates were examined by the District Magistrate, who since the T'ang had always been a K'ung. This certified them as Students, enabling them to take further examinations on the prefectural level. After being tested by the Literary Chancellor of the province in calligraphy, classics poetry, and composition, they attained the first degree of Licentiate. Each Licentiate was then expected to major in a particular classic and was retested yearly as he began the arduous climb towards the higher degrees of Provincial Graduate and Metropolitan Graduate.   Every twelve years, the best of these Licentiates were further examined by the Provincial Governor and the top few became Senior Licentiates of the First Class to be presented at court and given government posts.   The others who passed were able to enter the Imperial Academy and complete a course which might also lead to office.   In addition, there were a number of subcategories of Licentiates who were able to study in the capital.   Every year, an outstanding Student became a Senior Licentiate by Imperial Favor.   Stipendiary, Licentiate of the Second and Third Class, appointments by hereditary right and by purchase were alternate avenues of mobility.[63]   These K'ungs who entered the bureaucracy and served as magistrates or in board positions represented the furthest extension of clan influence.

At the pinnacle of power within the clan were those members who had inherited ranks. This practice is traced back to Han Kao-tsu's enfeoffment of K'ung Chü. In addition to the appointment of a K'ung as District Magistrate,[64] the second son of the head of the clan was appointed Erudite of the Five Classics in the Han-lin Academy and the third son became Erudite at the Court of Imperial Sacrifices.[65] Both had ceremonial duties in the Ch'ü-fu area and traveled frequently to the capital, serving as liaisons with the court. K'ungs held the offices of Registrar and Sub-Registrar in local academies[66] and members, including some of K'ung Shang-jen's direct forebears, were active in education in neighboring prefectures.

Overseeing this vast establishment was the head of the clan who had been given the title of "Duke of the Sagely Posterity" by Sung Hui-tsung (r. 1101-26) in 1104. In the early Ch'ing, this position was upgraded with the honorary title of Great Officer of the Banqueting Court of the Regular First Rank, with protocol accorded board presidents. The Duke presided over major sacrifices at the Confucian Temple in Ch'ü-fu as well as at the Confucian Temple and Han-lin Academy in Peking. He hosted the Emperor on imperial visits and escorted Licentiates to the capital to enter the Imperial Academy. More importantly, in his daily responsibilities, he was a combination of administrator, aristocrat, cult priest, scholar, lobbyist, and sometimes imperial confidant.[67] To be in charge of such extensive resources and patronage was a considerable position which led to intense vying for the succession. Primogeniture was not a frequent practice and occasionally the strife resulted in breaks in the legitimte line.

One such hiatus began in the year 912 during the Posterior Liang dynasty. The head of the clan in the 42nd generation, K'ung Kuang-ssu, was assassinated by a usurper, K'ung Mo, who headed a rival branch.[68] K'uang-ssu's infant son, Jen-yü,[69] was secretly saved by his mother, who sought refuge with her family and waged a political campaign at court demanding revenge. In 930, the succeeding Posterior T'ang dynasty reversed the situation, ordering the execution of K'ung Mo and reestablishing the line with Jen-yu. In the genealogy which K'ung Shang-jen compiled, this is termed the "Restoration" and each of the twenty branches existing in the seventeenth century were traced back to one of two sons of Jen-yü.[70]

An even more serious split occurred after the fall of the Northern Sung when many loyalists migrated south to establish the Southern Sung in Hangchow. K'ung Tuan-yu,[71] head of the clan in the 48th generation, fled in 1131 and set up a clan-in-exile in San-ch'ü, Chekiang. There, he was succeeded by his nephew in 1132.[72] Meanwhile, Tuan-yu's brother, Tuan-ts'ao,[73] remained in Ch'ü-fu and was confirmed as Duke by the new Chin dynasty. He proceeded to propagate his line in the north and the split continued for a hundred and fifty years until the Southern Sung fell. After five generations, the southern line yielded its claims in 1282 but a final reconcilation was not effected until the reign of Ch'eng-tsung (r. 1295-1308) in the Yuan after much confusion and contention.[74]

Subsequently, the internecine struggles subsided and the transmission of the dukedom during the Ming and Ch'ing periods became more orderly. In both the Restoration and the reunification of the northern and southern branches, the power of the imperial court was a key factor in regulating the succession. The emperors, who had originally been looked to for military protection or economic largesse, came to play a greater role in the internal politics of the clan through the power of enfeoffment; and, with the gradual expansion of privileges over the years, they increased their political leverage on the K'ungs, a development which tended to have a stabilizing effect on clan rivalries.

If the K'ung's themselves had been asked what they considered their role in the civilization to be, they probably would have replied that it was to maintain the forms of ritual (li) which their ancestor had espoused. While abandoning Confucius' political activism, they emphasized instead his belief that the world could be brought to perfection if the ceremonies of the golden age of the sage-kings were revived in the present.[75]

For Confucius, ritual was an encompassing concept which enabled man to define the key relations of his existence. It was as well the primary tool for regulating these relations in accordance with Tao. As a method of personal cultivation, the practice of universalized patterns of behavior enabled the self to overcome the isolating tendencies of the ego and develop a role in concert with others.[76] In the public sphere, the conduct of ceremonies was synonymous with statecraft.[77] They ordered society hierarchically and achieved an equilibrium of inner emotions. By comparing their performance with the ancient forms, the state of a nation could be monitored, the quality of its government judged, and the collective fate predicted.[78] Furthermore, on the spiritual level, sacrifices provided the context for a religious communication with the unseen, enabling the participant to achieve an attitude of transcendental harmony. "Ch'ü-fu is the sacred precinct and the environs within which ritual is maintained," declared the K'ang-hsi Emperor on the occasion of his visit, pronouncing the sentiments felt by most other pilgrims to the shrine.[79] The K'ungs dedicated themselves to this priestly mission of conservation and, as the eternal arbiters of form, saw themselves as the moral gyroscope of the nation.

Over the centuries, a repository of texts, bronze vessels, costumes, and musical instruments was built up and a regular series of sacrifices conducted throughout the year. The most important of these were those held on the first day (denoted "ting") in the second month of every new season. There were, in addition, less regular but more lavish spectacles such as the Imperial Grand Oblation and, the grandest of all, imperial visits.[80] The emperors maintained a Confucian temple in the palace and one in the capital modeled on those at Ch'ü-fu. During the Sung and Chin periods the performers were all K'ungs but, beginning in the Yuan, others were also trained. A quota of 60 acolytes was established in 1374 and continued under the Ch'ing. In that same year, 120 dancers and musicians were maintained at the court with the privileges of Stipendiaries. The number of performers was eventually doubled in the Ch'ing, most of them coming from Ch'ü-fu and trained by K'ung specialists.[81]

The continuity of ceremonial forms derived both from traditional practice at the shrine and from various textual authorities. Confucius was credited with the editorship of a number of the classics, and his own revision of the court music of his time served as a model of public activity for the clan.[82] In particular, his search for authentic forms of the Hsia and Shang dynasties sanctioned the kind of scholarly investigation of the liturgy which had begun to interest literati in the later dynasties.[83] As early as the beginning of the Ming, it began to be recognized that the ceremonies in Confucian temples were not in strict accord with ancient texts. Scholars such as Sung Lien and, later, Ch'ü Chiu-ssu, noted significant differences in the staging, choice of programs, and musical forms when compared to those in Han and earlier classical sources.[84] As the movement towards historical authenticity in culture

A Confucian Acolyte

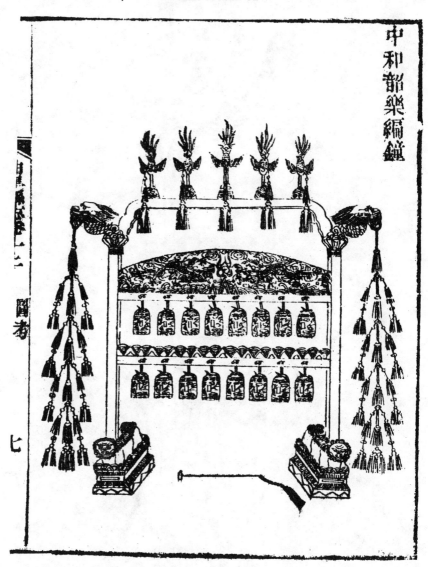

A Set of Ceremonial Bells

grew and became increasingly scholarly in focus, the K'ungs looked back into their archives to redesign many of their ceremonies so as to achieve a greater fidelity. It was precisely in this area that the young K'ung Shang-jen developed a reputation for expertise within his clan and, through his activities, gained imperial favor.

EARLY YEARS

K'ung Shang-jen was born into the upper stratum of the K'ung clan, and while he was not so fortunate as to inherit any ranks or offices, he could count among his forebears degree-holders, education officials, and men of local distinction.

K'ung's great-great-grandfather, Ch'eng-tz'u,[85] was a Confucian teacher who held the position of Sub-Registrar of the Academy of the Three Clans. His great-grandfather, Hung-chieh,[86] perhaps the most notable of his direct ancestors, was a man of recognized moral stature whose spartan and unadorned prose style was influential throughout the clan and later used as a model for students. He held the degree of Senior Licentiate, Second Class, and a series of administrative posts in education from that of Sub-Director of Schools in Shang-ho-hsien to District Director in Hsien-ning-hsien and Prefectural Director in T'ai-p'ing-fu.

In contrast to both Ch'eng-tz'u and Hung-chieh was Ch'eng-tz'u's brother, Ch'eng-t'i.[87] He was, in his own way, equally noted but more for his cultural accomplishments. Ch'eng-t'i was a man of broad learning and a voluminous writer. A poet and master of Yen Chen-ch'ing's style of calligraphy, he was often called to write inscriptions for the shrine. Moreover, he was also highly successful in government for over three decades. Most significant, however, was his fervent devotion to Wang

Yang-ming's interpretation of Confucianism. Wherever he served, he would open a school and gather students, instructing them in Wang's doctrine of the "innate goodness of the mind" and the popular sycretism emphasizing the unity of the Three Teachings. His prolific writings on the classics enunciated a point of view which, while not banned as heterodox, was definitely in contrast to the central tendency of the clan to espouse Chu Hsi's orthodoxy. These poles of orthodox Confucian and literatus-aesthete were so apparent in K'ung Shang-jen's own character that, while he never met either Ch'eng-tz'u or Ch'eng-t'i, he seemed to have inherited their diverse temperaments. Yet another aspect of K'ung Shang-jen's imagination—that of eremitism— is represented by his grandfather, Wen-na.[88] Although Wen-na held the degree of Stipendiary he rarely ventured out into society, and maintained well on into his old age that enviable innocence and purity of character which often results from a lifetime of cultivation uncompromised by politics.

K'ung's father, Chen-fan[89] was, on the other hand, quite committed in his youth and his activist opinions on public issues made a considerable impression on his elders. Chen-fan was successful in the examinations, earning the Provincial Graduate degree in 1633; but like many of the outstanding talents of his generation, his ambitions were curtailed by the alarming disintegration of the Ming dynasty. In the year that Chen-fan earned his degree—the fifth of the Ch'ung-chen Emperor's reign (1628-44)—the scattered peasant rebellions which had arisen from famine and burdensome taxation entered a fatal phase. The various forces became consolidated into swollen armies under determined leaders now bent on plans of national conquest. Arising in Shansi and Szechuan, they eventually overran much of the populated sections of the country. Ch'ü-fu was not in the direct path of the major armies of Li Tzu-ch'eng and Chang Hsien-chung, yet it too suffered on the periphery.   Hoards of disaffected and defeated soldiers roamed at will while smaller bands of starving peasants frequently raided the granaries and markets.   Only a unified gentry such as the K'ungs maintained local order and Chen-fan, as a clan notable, found himself engaged in famine relief, organizing military defenses, and refugee settlement.   Such preoccupations with protecting his family's interests made government service away from home impossible. With the conquest of Peking by the Manchus in 1644, Chen-fan refused to serve the new dynasty.   He retired to a lakeside setting in the hills where he turned to farming and studied the Confucian texts which earned him the nickname, "Mr. Orthodox Learning." There he died in 1653 at the age of 72, when K'ung Shang-jen was only six.[90]

The early death of K'ung's father affected the course of his life in several ways. His only memories of Chen-fan were from this period of "compulsory eremitism" and it rendered Chen-fan somewhat larger in K'ung's eyes than he had perhaps been in life. It may also have contributed to his inordinate admiration for those he later met whose virtues resembled his father's. It seems remarkable that most of K'ung's closest friends, particularly in Yangchow, were much older than him and many fit the category of "heroic loyalist." While evidence does not allow us to make too much of this psychologically, it is not impossible that these figures formed a composite image of the father he hardly knew. Politically, Chen-fan's death also deprived him of a patron who could ease his way into official life; for although his father did not serve the Ch'ing, he was still a man of considerable local prestige and would have had little difficulty in arranging the social mechanics to facilitate his son's rise. K'ung was to suffer from this handicap in his early years. Although he later gained prominence and rose to a high government position, his career was unconventional, propelled by influential friends and imperial favor rather than by examination success and a step-by-step progress through the ranks.

Of K'ung's mother as well as the other women in his life such as his wife, daughter, and whatever courtesans he may have met along the way, we regretfully know little. Such omission of the private and sensual sides is not uncommon among Chinese literati and K'ung's orthodox background may have made him especially reticent. From a poem to his mother on her 80th birthday,[91] and from references elsewhere to collateral relatives, it is clear that she was born Ch'in-shih in 1623, which would make her 39 years younger than her husband--she being 26 and he 64 at the time of their son's birth. Thus K'ung Shang-jen, like Confucius, was probably the son of a concubine, for he was closer in age to his cousin in the 65th generation than to his two elder brothers in the 64th.

An anecdote of his youth later recorded in a local gazetteer states:

> Once, when he was still young enough to be carried, a neighbor tied up a sow to be sold. The sow kept looking back at her piglets and the piglets continued to suckle, refusing to let go. Though the seller beat them, they would not leave. Shang-jen put aside his dates and pears and started wailing so that the neighbor relented and untied the sow. His father picked him up and said to the others, "Someday, this child will help save the world."[92]

There is in this story a myth of loss, prefiguring the tragic artist who seeks to rectify a disruption of the natural order with his outcries. It is commonly maintained that the origin of K'ung's sensibility lay in his response to the effects of Manchu conquest and rule. But if we can accept the conventions of traditional Chinese biography, it would indicate that such sensitivity to injustice was at an early point essential to his awareness of the world. The fortuitous conjunction of this nature and the historical situation made him a voice of the age, at least as much as the age molded him.

Throughout his life, K'ung does not seem to have suffered any material hardship and the laments of poverty which occasionally appear in his poems should be read as a conventional pose of the artiste or, at least, within the context of the resources of his class. His friends noted that he did not enrich himself while an official; and his lavish entertaining, particularly during the Yangchow years, may well have constrained his budget at times. Yet his primary income, probably derived from inherited land, was enough to allow him to indulge a lifelong passion for collecting art. While still a child, he obtained a curio in the shape of a gourd[93] and later, on a trip to Tsinan, a scroll by Chao Meng-fu of a T'ang poem. This he described as being "in characters larger than the palm of one's hand, written with an untrammeled feeling."[94] The collection eventually numbered more than 157 items including paintings, calligraphy, jade, musical instruments, rubbings, bronzes, inkstones, porcelain, seals, and mirrors.[95] Several of his antiques were a source of literary inspiration and led to his earliest efforts in drama. Through his collecting, he later came into contact with some of the leading painters of his time and gained a reputation among literati as a connoisseur.

Although the Ch'ing was formally proclaimed in Peking in 1644, it took several decades to consolidate control

over the entire country. In the year that K'ung was born,
Ming resistance was strong in Kwangsi under Prince Kwei, in
Fukien under Prince Lu, and in Taiwan and coastal areas
under Cheng Ch'eng-kung. Major insurrections occurred in
Kiangsi, Fukien, and Kwangtung; in the Ch'ü-fu area,
loyalists allied with peasant rebels to plague the new
administration through guerrilla tactics.[96] Although the
K'ung clan had immediately reached an accommodation with
the new rulers, the hopes of the population as well as
individual clan members were decidedly for a restoration of
the Ming. The contemporary writer P'u Sung-ling noted this
situation in nearby T'eng-i-hsien somewhat facetiously when
he wrote:

> During the Shun-chih period, seven out of ten
> people in T'eng-i were Ming loyalists and the
> Ch'ing officials were afraid to arrest them.
> Later, when the area was pacified, the magistrates
> used to distinguish them from others and
> deliberately decided cases in their favor for fear
> that they might revolt again.[97]

There was thus considerable continuity with the late Ming
throughout K'ung's youth. A variety of figures--eremites,
underground resisters, former officials--were in the area
and he met many of them. Through these acquaintances, he
began to accumulate the wealth of narrative incident and
historical detail that he later incorporated into his drama
of the period.

Among his close relatives, there were two who were
closely involved in the Nanking Restoration of the Ming in
1644-45. One was K'ung Shang-tse.[98] This cousin, of the
same generation as K'ung Shang-jen, was considerably older,
having earned the Metropolitan Graduate Degree in 1640. He
served as County Magistrate of Lo-yang and Ch'üan-chiao,
Nan-chihli, during the Ch'ung-chen reign, later becoming

Director of the Kiangsi Bureau in the Board of Justice in Nanking. Noted for his hard-line policy against the peasant rebels, he joined the Nanking Restoration when the Ming collapsed in the north and was a valuable eyewitness to the events and personalities of Prince Fu's Southern Court.

Another relative, Ch'in Kuang-i, was an uncle of K'ung Shang-jen on his mother's side and was also related to K'ung Shang-tse by marriage. Ch'in sought refuge with his kinsman in Nanking and remained with him for three years, during which he heard many tales of the events of 1644-45. When Ch'in returned to Ch'ü-fu, he related these to the young K'ung Shang-jen, who later wrote:

I checked these facts against the existing histories and they agreed at every point, so they must have been true accounts. However, the incidents where Li Hsiang-chün drips blood from her facial injury onto the fan and where these spots are transformed into a painting by Yang Wen-ts'ung were anecdotes which Yang told K'ung Shang-tse. Although not to be found in any other source, they were unique events worthy of transmitting and they were the inspiration for <u>The Peach Blossom Fan</u>.[99]

Another figure in Ch'ü-fu who influenced K'ung Shang-jen, both as an example of a late Ming personality and as the prototype for his characterization of the storyteller Liu Ching-t'ing, was Chia Fu-hsi, alias "The 'Wood-and-Leather' Wanderer (<u>Mu-p'i san-k'o</u>)."[100] Chia was born in the area in 1589 and became a Senior Licentiate by Imperial Favor in 1624. Thereafter, he held several posts during the T'ien-ch'i (r. 1620-27) and Ch'ung-chen reigns. In 1639, he served as County Magistrate of Ku-an, Chihli, becoming a Secretary in the Board of Justice in 1640 and Director of the Kiangsi Bureau in the same board in 1641.

He resigned the following year, apparently in disagreement with the policies at the time. Upon returning to Ch'ü-fu, he began his avocation of reciting ballads on current issues in which he voiced his discontent, becoming even more vocal in the early Ch'ing.

Chia's loyalist sympathies reflected the ambivalent emotions felt by many who were active in office in the last years of the Ming. On the one hand, he opposed the peasant uprisings, the Manchu invasion, and the subjugation of his native Han race; but on the other hand, personal experience made him acutely aware of the corruption and ineffectiveness of the Ming in its last days. He typified the postconquest dilemma of being suspended in a moral and political limbo--between commitment to a futile resistance and the even more distasteful choice of serving the new overlords. When K'ung visited him in 1657, he had already gained notoriety as an outspoken critic, which forced him to move away from Ch'ü-fu to nearby Tzu-yang. Most of his outrage was directed not against the Manchus, for prudent reasons, but rather against his fellow literati who he felt had failed in their public responsibility. The collapse of native values, the weakening of the Confucian moral fabric, and the decline of a heroic spirit of sacrifice were frequent themes in his stories.

Among the surviving ballads is a lengthy ku-tz'u[101] containing a variety of philosophical views and revaluations of the major historical figures in Confucian mythology. It expresses a tragic view of heroic action, and pessimism over the meaning of human events in the light of chronic injustice and the obliterations of time. Another piece is a set of arias in the I-yang style then popular titled "Pity the South (Ai-chiang-nan)." This is a lament about the Nanking Restoration, which was included by K'ung in the final act of The Peach Blossom Fan. Here the

木皮散客遺墨興印記

Calligraphy by Chia Fu-hsi

opera teacher Su K'un-sheng sings it as a nostalgic
conclusion to the play. There is no evidence to suggest
that Chia ever visited Nanking, even though the ballad
contains poetic descriptions of famous sites connected with
the Ming. Perhaps his source was the same as K'ung Shan-
jen's, that is, K'ung Shang-tse, with whom Chia was
friendly in Ch'ü-fu.[102]   Several shorter ku-tz'u are
derived from anecdotes from the classics. The Music Master
Departs for Ch'i (T'ai-shih-chih shih-ch'i)[103] is based on
Analects 18:9 and narrates an upright official's refusal to
serve the usurping ducal house in Lu. K'ung also included
this in his play, in which Liu Ching-t'ing recites it to
explain why he rejected the patronage of the villian, Juan
Ta-ch'eng. It appears that Chia's original motivation,
though, was to defend his resignation under Ch'ung-chen and
his subsequent eremitism under the Ch'ing. A third ballad,
The Man of Ch'i (Ch'i-jen-chang) is based on Mencius 4b:33
but in Chia's version is actually a comic story about
domestic disharmony caused by an overly ambitious wife.[104]

Chia died around 1670 when he was well over eighty. As
a personality, he is remembered solely through K'ung Shang-
jen's insightful and sympathetic biography of him written
some years after they met:

THE "WOOD-AND-LEATHER" WANDERER
The "Wood-and-Leather" wanderer took his pleasure
in reciting ballads--"Wood-and-Leather" referring
to clappers and drum, the very instruments of joy,
laughter, anger, and scorn. He would appear before
students in school, before high ministers in their
chambers, and before bureaucrats in their offices,
"wood" and "leather" ever by his side. Any
audience was an opportunity to perform and no
matter whether rich or poor, he was inseparable

from these tools of his trade. Whenever he spoke
to officials of loyalty or to sons of filial piety,
he always employed the discourse of storytelling
with scant regard for proper quotation from the
classics and histories. His opinions of the
emperors, kings, generals, and ministers mentioned
there were, in fact, quite unique and differed from
those held by most other Confucians. His listeners
were aghast and thought him a weird eccentric; in
the end, though, they were never able to find the
words to refute him.

He appeared to espouse the style of a Taoist
yet he married, held office, and acquired
property--fine land, a large residence, fat oxen,
sturdy horses, vegetables, fruits, chickens, and
pigs, all of the most uncommon sort. He used to
say, "How I love profit!--for I can create it
myself without stealing from others. (Such
stealing would make one no better than a robber.)
And how I love power!--but when I use it, I don't
pretend to any false humility nor do I latch on to
powerful people. (Such false humility is
prostitution and latching on to others, worthy of a
dog.)"

Towards the end of the Ch'ung-chen reign, he
began his rise by passing the examinations in
classical exposition, becoming a county magistrate,
whence he rose further to a board position. After
the dynastic change, though, he maintained a lofty
dignity and refused to serve. A magistrate
pressured him on several occasions so that he
turned around and accepted his old office once
more; but under the pretext of official business,
he took great pleasure in ordering that same

magistrate publicly beaten in front of the county office. Several months afterwards, he tried to resign on grounds of illness but was refused. He secretly told his superior of this affair and asked, "Why not impeach me?" The latter said, "But you haven't committed any crime," to which he replied, "I engage in story-telling to the neglect of my official duties--that would be a good charge. If you can free a King Wen, why worry over how to phrase it?"[105] Thus, he was able to retire. At home in his village, he often wore his official robes when he called on his neighbors; and when the tax collector came to his door, he made him kneel, saying, "Otherwise, I won't pay." Yet he would meet his old colleagues casually attired, abandoning all formal greetings.

When I was about ten years old, I called on him at his home. He placed me in the seat of honor and served me fish and meat, saying, "I treat myself sparingly but think nothing of offering you these because you are quick-witted. I am getting old now and may need you in some way--it's not because I think of you as your late father's son." He pointed to someone who was shoveling manure outside over by the corner of a wall. "That one is also the son of a late acquaintance but since he has the ability of a slave, I treat him like one." He also said, "Behind the parlor of your house is some captivating green bamboo. Is the red-mouthed parrot which used to be hung there still well? I often remember it in my dreams. I cannot remember, though, how often your father liked to invite me there."

Before I left, he recited several stories based on the Analects, all of which were completely contrary to the meaning of the original. He habitually chose the Analects as his text, sitting erect in the marketplace as he recited it to the drum and clappers. His general theme was that throughout time the sages did not speak against profit, while their actions did not shrink from involvement in power; it is those who violate their hearts as they deceive others who are the "carping villagers" condemned by Confucius.[106] (How much were his own resentments contained in the emotions summoned up by his "wood-and-leather"!) Up until his eighties, he never ceased his laughter and scorn. But people who laugh and scorn others invariably find themselves treated likewise, so he could no longer remain at home and had to move from Ch'ü-fu to Tzu-yang. He shut his door to the world and composed a score of volumes which he titled Enduring Words from Placidity Patch.[107] His style mixed elegance and vulgarity, the serious and the satirical, much like Li Chih, Hsu Wei, and Yuan Hung-tao[108] of the late Ming. Hardly anyone among the local people understood it. Yen Ku-ku of P'ei-hsien and Ting Yeh-ho of Chu-ch'eng[109] had his papers bound and presented them to his son. (In all probability, they had been visitors to his house around the time that they were in hiding.)

The Hermit of the Pavilion of the Solitary Cloud remarks: "The Way of Heaven is a turbid blend wherein the Sage ferments his character. Master 'Wood-and-Leather' expressed such in his cutting views. Confucius said, 'My followers are a hasty

lot . . . who know not how to trim their
passions'[110] but when they do, then they
can dwell in loyalty and trustworthiness,
acting with modesty and purity. And did he
not also state that 'if unable to join
those along the middle path, I would prefer
the headstrong and the cautious'?[111] So
'the headstrong and the cautious' are also
disciples of the Sage!" (K/495-97)

K'ung probably underwent the traditional education of
clan members through the academy system and, sometime in
his teens, earned the first degree of Licentiate. This was
the highest degree he was ever to attain despite several
attempts at the examinations. This obstacle considerably
delayed his entry into the official world and gave his
early years the appearance of frustrated ambition. One
cannot underestimate the effect which years of fruitless
studying must have had on K'ung. Obliged to spend the most
energetic period of his life mastering the artificial
fashions of the eight-legged essay, he could but hope
against statistical odds to climb the only legitimate
ladder of success in the imperial state. It must have
sharpened his keen sense of irony that, as a scion of the
canonical literatus, and schooled in his civilization's
oldest tradition, he should regularly have had his
abilities found unacceptable by a foreign dynasty. Like
many literati whose talents did not quite fit the mold
decreed by the state bureaucracy, K'ung developed an
antipathy to the examination system and came to view it as
a distortion of the true spirit of learning. In an address
to an educational conference years later, he remarked:

Experts in examination essays all know how to
follow Chu Hsi. But when asked why, they reply,

"Because he wrote commentaries to the classics."
And they all know one is supposed to attack Lu
Hsiang-shan and Wang Yang-ming. But when asked
why, they reply, "Because they didn't write
commentaries." Now, how could the commentaries
cover the entire range of Chu Hsi's learning or Lu
and Wang be considered insufficient since they
didn't write any? What these people revere and
attack is just for the purpose of writing
examination essays.[112]

K'ung may have engaged in some form of teaching during
this period but there is little evidence about his other
activities.[113] He considered himself, of course, a true
Confucian--at the very least, society expected it of anyone
with his background. When public occasions called for it,
he was capable of enuciating orthodox sentiments with the
proper rectitude and authority. This derived in part from
an aristocratic conviction that he and his clan were the
conservators of the genuine tradition. Yet his personal
understanding of Confucianism was neither the speculation
of a moral philosopher nor the ideology of a politician.
He wrote no commentaries to the classics, underwent no
startling spiritual rebirths, and was as ambivalent as many
other K'ungs were at the evident enthusiasm with which the
Ch'ing dynasty was promoting his ancestor's teachings. An
examination of his doctrinal beliefs indicate that they
were fairly conventional, although he did display an
admiration for certain activist thinkers of the late Ming
who advocated practical involvement in human affairs.[114]

It was rather the ritual forms maintained by the clan
and their concrete manifestations in Ch'ü-fu which engaged
his lifelong interest. In addition to the Book of Poetry,
the only other classic he seems to have studied in any
depth beyond his formal education was the Book of Ritual

and particularly the Treatise on Music. Mastery of these during his early years must have preceded his later service at the Confucian Temple and led to two treatises on ceremonial form and theory of pitch.[115] K'ung's Confucianism thus evolved along two related lines-- aesthetic and scholarly. He enjoyed the theatrical nature of the temple ceremonies and aspired to direct their actual performance. At the same time, he was heir to the Empirical Studies Movement of the seventeenth century with its concern for historical authenticity and the use of data derived from empirical research.

K'ung defined his interest in empirical studies some years later when he recalled a discussion he had with fellow scholars:

Upon my return, I thought over what you had said and it centered around "textual authority (tsun- ching)," which is the bridge leading to the study of sagehood. Chih-nan's views were based on "making the will sincere (ch'eng-i)," which is the pillar of the mind. I, however, advocated the "investigation of things (ko-wu)". . . . One must not shrink from the coarsest and lowest phenomena but rather confront them directly and thereby comprehend related things, seeking to dispel doubt in order to gain contentment. This is the process of studying from below and rising to achievement, gaining knowledge through hardship as one struggles to act. Moreover, in The Great Learning, "regulating the family" and "pacifying the world" all begin with "the investigation of things." (K/570)

In May 1669, the new Duke, K'ung Yü-ch'i[116] escorted qualified Licentiates of the K'ung clan to Peking. In accordance with privilege, the students were inspected by the young K'ang-hsi Emperor in an elaborate ceremony and admitted to the Imperial Academy. K'ung seems to have been in this group and henceforth referred to himself as "Senior Licentiate" and as "Student of the Imperial Academy." Assuming he finished the full prescribed course, he would have graduated three years later in 1672. It was common for some students to directly enter government while others remained on a waiting list; but no offices opened up for K'ung and he subsequently disappeared from notice. For the next few years, there is no record of his activities at all until September 1678. Now 31, he traveled to Tsinan, Shantung's provincial capital and the major city in proximity to Ch'ü-fu. Perhaps he went to try his luck again at the examinations as well as buy antiques and sightsee. He fared no better in accomplishing the first object but the trip did result in a group of poems. These are his earliest surviving works and begin to chart the territory of his poetic sensibility.

Tsinan Verses[117]

Sept.--Oct. 1678

1.

When Yung-lo breached Tsinan's eastern wall[118]
Drums and trumpets filled the skies,
    the forest became an army.
Memorial placards feel no sensation
    of the eternal sorrow--
Before the Temple of T'ieh Hsuan[119]
    I utter a choked sob. (K/4)

K'ung's loyalist sympathies surface in this historical poem commemorating an early Ming martyr cruelly executed for defending the legitimate emperor, Chien-wen (r. 1399-1403). By K'ung's time, some 250 years after the actual event, T'ieh Hsuan's memory had already been revived by the Nanking Restoration which posthumously enfeoffed him in

1645; in addition, he had been transformed into a popular hero by such dramas as <u>The Rude Scholar</u> and <u>The Daughters of T'ieh Hsuan</u>.[120] The poem is neatly bisected. In the first two lines, the poet draws on his historical imagination to suggest the horror of battle. The second section shifts to an ironized present. It is not so much the physical temple but literary memory which is the source of the poet's feeling and which is the vehicle of a timeless sympathy. Indeed, the temple, though providing the stimulus for the poet's reflections, conspires by its very conventions of commemoration against any intense identification with the pain of T'ieh's sacrifice. This introduces one dimension of K'ung's irony--the disparity between a secure, insensate present and a more vivid albeit terrifying past. Only the poet's capacity for supersensory perception can bridge the gap of time and ethical consciousness to experience the powerful emotional truth of heroic sacrifice.

     2.

Fragrance exudes from lotuses
   to waft through every household.
Along the moat, bramble gates
   open to the water's flow.
Having pointed out the painted boats,
   I'm left without a care.
And the girls, opposite me,
   wash their silvery gauze. (K/4)

Although K'ung revealed little of his love life, there are many poetic references to courtesans and the life of the pleasure quarters. Such poems always have a certain impersonality to them; the women are rarely identified or given any individuality. Nor are there dedications to particular favorites. The poet usually remains at a distance, as here, where he scans a panorama containing these beauties caught in a delicate view. The scene is probably Lake Ming. Clogged with giant lotuses and mazes of tall reeds through which narrow channels weave, the boats appear to linger discretely, half-hidden. The sequence of "fragrance," "lotuses," opening water-gates, and "painted boats" provides an erotic tint intensified in the final line. There is a fine contrast between the artifice of the boats, whose exquisite indolence connotes a literati fantasy of feminine beauty, and the natural toil of the women as they perform their regular tasks. Such realism only enhances the poet's sensual pleasure as he steals an intimate view of them in their simplicity and innocence. The line contains an ambiguity further relating the poem to the concrete. The "girls (nü-lang)" may also be a nearby peak, Mt. Nü-lang, some ten miles to the west.[121] The conceit may derive from K'ung's imagining that the mountain is facing him and its gleaming reflection in the lake is the washed gauze.

    3.

  Smoke and mist impose upon the hill;
      chickens and dogs strut about.
  The market is filled with fish and salt
      for a new tide flowed in.
  Local kids cunningly boast
      now as in the past,
  Demanding highest prices
      for lotus roots and pears. (K/4)

Poems such as these comprise that portion of K'ung's oeuvre which has led some recent critics to categorize him as a "materialist" in the Marxist sense.[122] To be sure, a number of his pieces reveal a strong social awareness. Many in this vein deal with the effects of natural disasters, and his reactions to human suffering and bureaucratic indifference. Here, there is a sardonic

observation of the surface prosperity he witnessed in
Tsinan.   In the light of the chronic afflictions of the
region, there is a suggestion that this sudden plenitude,
like the mist, is ephemeral and that expectations about the
good life are hubristic.   The upward turn in the economic
situation has its social costs as well, with the haughty
atmosphere and puffed-up animals symbolizing the nouveau
riche profiting from the change.   Actually, there was a
serious drought in Tsinan that year[123] which may account
for the high price of agricultural produce.   This fact is
introduced by K'ung to cast a final shadow on the general
euphoria, implying that truer values lie beyond the
momentary ups and downs of the economy.

4.

I travel alone across the lake;
    the lake is also where I sleep.
Reeds and rushes fill my eyes
    stirring up the chilly mist.
The people here raise lotus roots,
    as if it were millet grain.
Women bring food to their men
    working in the fields.   (K/4)

The loneliness of the traveler is evoked, as a bleak
image of rootlessness is juxtaposed against the constant
normalcy of the peasants.   There is in this the
characteristic literati attitude of social and agricultural
primitivism.   Obliged by the realities of public service to
lead peripatetic lives reinforced by the isolating elitism
of an educated class, poets often expressed envy of the
unselfconscious simplicity of those tied to the land.
There is no thought of their suffering, exploitation, and
hopelessness.   Rather, it is the yearning of the outsider
who sees in their engagement with the fundamentals of life
a brief mooring in a floating existence.

5.

From Tse-hua Bridge[124] I gaze at Mt. Li[125]

Across scattered trees and clumps of reeds

Where pavilions stretch on without a break.

Beyond twilight shadows,

    a herd-boy and his ox returns. (K/4)

The natural scene was a prime ground for K'ung's expression of his transcendental yearnings, reflecting his admiration for the Wang Wei style of landscape poetry. Here, the view from the southern part of Lake Ming locates the poet looking across the major portion of the city, in which numerous temples appear among trees and behind which Mt. Li stretches horizontally forming a misty screen. The mountain, also known as Thousand Buddha Hill since the Sui Dynasty when numerous statues were carved in it, prompts K'ung's borrowing of a Buddhist-Taoist motif--that of the herd-boy and ox. Ch'an Buddhism in particular employed these figures to chart the stages of spiritual cultivation. In the series of pictures traditionally ascribed to the monk Kuo-an, the herd-boy riding home on the back of an ox depicts the sixth stage when the mind has been disciplined to proceed freely with a minimum of conscious control.[126] If the poems are read as a sequence, they present a cycle of self-cultivation. The poet begins, enmeshed in the tragedy of history, then gains refuge and relief in aesthetic moments, observes the inequities of the present material world, and suffers the weariness of his journey. Finally, he achieves release from all mental anxieties, transforming his mind into one of smooth-running equilibrium through spiritual contemplation. The assumption behind this progress is a central one throughout Chinese thought, that the solution to the problems of the external world lies in the internal rectification of the individual and a return to a fundamental awareness of the Tao.

Upon returning from Tsinan, K'ung immediately set out upon another journey, this time to nearby Stonegate Mountain, which he adopted as his retreat. There, he built his studio and took the artistic name, "Hermit of the Pavilion of the Solitary Cloud." He was to visit it frequently throughout his life and when away from Ch'ü-fu, reminisced about it. Stonegate was not only an escape world but a vantage point from which to contemplate his ambitions and assess his strategies in life. It was filled with an extraordinary, awesome beauty and was rich in ancient literary associations. His travel essay weitten around this time is perhaps his finest prose work, deftly weaving several levels of experience. In its physical description of the mountain, it adopts the objective, reportorial viewpoint found in the diaries of the late Ming traveler, Hsu Hsia-k'o.[127] But K'ung is inclined to voice his aesthetic judgements and is thus more indebted to the poetic travel essays of the T'ang literatus Liu Tsung-yuan.[128] Not only are the scenes he describes infused with symbolic meanings but throughout there is an allegory of the wandering sage set apart from the world who seeks solace and meaning in nature. Even more than Liu, K'ung's forays into the sublime are a function of literary experience, triggered by a poetic allusion, a mythical name, or the metaphorical quality of a scene. As an autobiographical document, the essay indicates something of K'ung's state of mind at this point in his life when he divines the hexagram, "Ch'ien: Obstruction." Having reached the age of 31 and still without any major accomplishment or definite prospects, he must have felt considerably frustrated. This was compounded by the apparent delay of his plan to build an academy on the mountain, which he hints was due to the lack of financial support from local temples.

Beyond its vivid descriptive power and resonant meanings, there is another characteristic element in K'ung's work. It is illustrated by the final paragraph, in which his confessions about the actual problems of living on the mountain create a destructive opposition to the predominately romantic mood of the piece. The presence of this paragraph indicates a fundamental tendency found in his poetry and drama to explore and then reject escapist moods. At the end of his lengthy journey, he summarily brings the reader down to earth with an ironic admission, creating an ambivalent aftertaste in his attempt to reflect on the total meaning of an experience.

WANDERING ON STONEGATE MOUNTAIN

Stonegate Mountain[129] is a fistlike rock which possesses the majesty of the Five Alps.[130] Travelers cannot catch sight of every view nor can their feet cover even that which they can see. So they compare it to the Five Alps as a fantastic sight without parallel. None among the preent generation, however, has bothered to inquire about it though it is barely fifteen miles from Ch'ü-fu. I can well understand how the fisherman's tale may have fallen on deaf ears, but Peach Blossom Spring[131] lies not in Heaven nor need it be sought along a forgotten path.

I entered the world of the mountain with Mei-yuan and Ching-ssu[132] on October 27, 1678, three days after the Ch'ung-yang Festival. We climbed up hills and peered down into valleys in what was the most enjoyable trip of my entire life--brothers together along with Stonegate. Wine was poured on the earth and a pledge made: "If any of us should someday forsake this mountain, may he sink like this wine into the ground." That evening, we stayed at Mei-yuan's cottage and determined to retire to these hills. Mei-yuan had to return home the next morning to take care of some matters but Ching-ssu persuaded me to journey further. After circulating around Mt. Hua-pu-chu three times, every aspect of the mountain's vitality unfolded before us.

By the Terrace of the Chinned Pearl,[133] we awaited the moon. Autumn had well advanced through the depths of the mountain; and realizing that our bedding would not protect us, we made our way beneath the moonlight shadows for about ten miles before reaching an inn where we ordered wine as a reward for our efforts. Though there were a variety of side dishes provided, it was the surrounding peaks and streams which we munched on. We chatted and laughed, laughed some more and then hooted, our boisterousness awakening the other sleepers. We two, however, stayed up all night long. When we got back, we told Mei-yuan all about it and it made a grand tale indeed. After this, scarcely a day went by when we didn't meet for intimate conversation along with the resolute Stonegate. Standing there before us in its imposing grandeur, its pavilions, terraces, trees, and rocks seemed to continually change in appearance.

A few weeks later, Ching-ssu went insane and died, babbling about Stonegate on the very eve of his death. Mei-yuan wept with grief and said that the mountain was a "stele of falling tears"[134]

which we should never visit again. But I replied
that the spirit of Ching-ssu would flow through the
mountain for a thousand autumns--to cut ourselves
off from Stonegate would be to cut ourselves off
from Ching-ssu. So I sorted out the famous spots,
arranging images of the land and the trees.
Although I can mention only one out of a hundred,
still, certain high places, remote spots, things
old, rustic, grand, and imposing appear like
mirages rising out of the sea or worlds fabricated
out of thin air. Of these, I made a record and had
my nephew, Yen-shih[135] illustrate it. Should
anyone come and ask about the mountain and my
awkward reply prove unsatisfying, I would show him
these comments and illustrations. Then he could
understand Stonegate as though he had been there.

Stonegate seems a continuation of the Mountain
of the Nine Immortals but it is, in fact, separate.
As soon as I set out from the northern section of
Ch'ü-fu, I began to feel invigorated and crossed
the Shu and Ssu Rivers, winding on toward the
northeast. After traversing a number of hills and
plateaus, I came across a mountain. It is shaped
like a thin-waisted gourd and has three ridges, all
of which look alike--what one would call "from the
same mold." Now, I tend to dislike all objects
which are identical and how much truer this is when
it comes to scenery. Known as "Commonplace
Mountain," there is little that can be done to
improve it. Still, it is a loyal retainer of
Stonegate (though more like the ugly counterpart of
the beauty, Hsi Shih).[136]

After this, I entered a large ravine whose
depth strengthens the majesty of the mountains

where shadows flicker and dazzle the eyes; already, I could see the true face of the land. A peak appears from the east. Fiercely precipitous, it lies athwart and is the first barrier before Stonegate itself. It can be entered, however, via the southwest by slipping through a break, for such virgin beauty could not remain completely concealed. Fording the Asarum River, I climbed up along the crisscrossed field paths as vapors rose from the ripening millet. Here, one can drop the reins and relax as if not ascending a mountain at all. A glance back at the city reveals that it is already enveloped in smoke and mist; truly one feels that one has entered a place of scenic beauty. To the side of the road is a buff-colored cliff with luxuriant verdure, graceful and alluring. How absolutely marvelous: one can just imagine what everything else around it is like. From here on, the rocks all appear to be painted in the "ancient style" and every tree seems delineated by an uncommon brush. One continues up along a stepped path, craning one's neck all about, rather like being a puppet on a stage with no control over the strings. Here, I would like to pile up some rocks and build a gate off to the right, inscribing "The Aesthetic Scene." That way one could avoid becoming a gawking tourist.

The road runs around the peaks and I crossed a small stone bridge named "Bridge to Scenic Wonders." Suddenly a vista opens up and I focused on a miniature azure pond. This is where Tu Fu, Judge Liu Chiu, and Mr. Cheng, who was posted in Hsia-ch'iu, held a banquet. Tu Fu's poem went:

The autumnal water's unfathomable purity

   lies somber, cleansing a traveler's heart.

Your Honors, seeking reclusive delights

   have galloped over to this tangled forest;

Two worthies meeting like the halves of a

   jade tally at this banquet worth a tael

   of gold.

Night approaches to an exotic tune

   and the "Dragon March" sounds from the

   watery depths.[137]

So I named the pond "Autumnal Waters" and the
pavilion "Somberness," not knowing when I should
ever be able to reach the source of the spring.

Further ahead is situated the Monastery of
Absolute Truth.   There is a stele from the Yuan
dynasty worth noticing and monks have long flocked
there.   Should I follow the hedonistic egotism of
Master Yang?   Or the ascetic activism of Master
Mo?[138]   Their neighbor is the Temple of the Jade
Spring.   During the Yung-lo reign, a Ch'an master
named Tsu-yung sought refuge and then died here.
The temple reached its height in the late Ming when
such local illuminates as Kuo Lu-ch'uan and Li Lan-
kuo wrote essays about it; but now its roof tiles
are broken and covered with a thorny overgrowth,
like that on the Lucerne Hall owned by my clan.
Still further is where Confucius studied the
hexagrams.[139]   Legend has it that just prior to the
Ting Sacrifice,[140] a member of the clan, K'ung
Sheng-yu,[141] asked, "What offering shall be made to
the spirits?" and the diviner replied, "They will
enjoy pine fragrances offered up by children."
Later, at the expected time, he saw a number of
herd-boys gather pine-flowers and juniper seeds and

offer them up in this spot, thus convincing him of the diviner's powers.   (At present, I am planning to establish an academy someplace supported by these two venerable institutions; there ought to be such a place amidst the mountains and streams of this realm of Lu.)

Suddenly, I stood face-to-face with Yellowstone Mountain--he who had angrily blocked me before. But now that I have entered his domain, how could we not help looking at each other with laughing faces?   Stonegate flourishes with an abundance of birds and animals while Yellowstone is of indigo rock streaked with yellow patterns without a trace of growth.   Yellowstone by no means imitates Stonegate.   In many ways, Yellowstone looks as if it has been painted with the brush-strokes of Huang Kung-wang.[142] The more one looks, the more one falls in love with it and it held me transfixed for a long while.   A monk said, "further on is the Grotto of Banners.   When the Huang Ch'ao Rebellion[143] broke out in Lu, the rebels occupied this very ridge."   But I had no time to investigate it.

The site for the academy is flat and wide: in front it overlooks the Terrace of the Chinned Pearl, and in back it shoulders Emerald Jade Peak. Surrounded by pearls; encircled by jade--all this lies here for our enjoyment.   On the left-hand side is the central peak, an interweave of rocks and trees whose dense vendure pulsates with energy. The curved things are the trees; the straight things, the rocks.   Rocks fill in the cracks of the trees; trees plug up the fissures in the rocks. Halfway up the peak, two cliffs issue forth exposed beyond the tips of the trees. They resemble two upended bolts of Goose Creek silk[144] which can be seen for miles. I would like to polish these cliffs and engrave the characters "Stonegate Mountain" but perhaps it would seem boastful.

The traveler who climbs this far sighs deeply in full satisfaction, not knowing that this is only the first peak of the mountain. One proceeds along the ridge, passing the Hill of the Singing Phoenixes where, during the Han dynasty in 68 B.C., a pair of phoenixes sang. There are many sterculia trees on its southern slope. Clambering on, there is the Peak of Dwarfed Lu[145] from which the realm of Lu below looks like an anthill. And still further is the Peak of Jade Bamboo Shoots--a thicket of swords and halbards; a ranking of bayonets and a salute of knives--all of which is overwhelming. It is quite different from the ethereal scene by the River Wei.[146] It is also called "Tiger Peak" and I avoided climbing to the top for fear that there might be some crouching there.

Below lies the Ridge of the Forked Springs where the water flows out like milk from nipples, following an undulating path from Peach Blossom Valley to a point facing the Fishing Terrace. And just like sweat streaming down one's back, all the springs, streams, ponds, and water falls in the mountain gushed--"ts'ung-ts'ung se-se"--down myriad courses. Their source, it seems, could only be Heaven itself. Continuing onwards and turning north is the Peak Which Strokes the Azure Sky. To climb to the top is to reach the ultimate but the servants hesitated. They even feared to breathe, saying that they dare not proceed for fear of trespassing on the Jade Emperor's throne.[147]   I looked off to the east at the boundless blue sea into which silver flowed down across embossed emerald interwoven with magenta and turquoise; and I stared transfixed beyond the gleaming white rays, unable to tell if it was the ocean or not, for all became an amorphous expanse of cosmic energy.   I had reached the Isles of the Immortals!

In front there is a flat slope known as "The Palace of the White Clouds," where sacrifices used to be made to the Jade Emperor.   Right in the middle of the path is a rock shaped like an incense burner and I regretted that I could not officiate at some kind of ceremony there.   Turning northwest, there is a small peak called "Crag of the Spirit of the Earth"[148]--I suspect it refers to the Spirit of the Earth God of Lu.   Descending through Pure Wind Gorge, I came across the site of a temple to the Green Ruler[149] and continued upwards to the west where stands the Peak Saluting the Mountain.   It bows respectfully to the northwest as if circling about an old man in hope of gaining some pears and chestnuts.   By descending westwards, I came to the site of the ancient stone gate which forms the back door to the mountain and is the actual boundary of the capital of Lu.   People passed through here bound north and south along what was considered a thoroughfare.   Proceeding along the route from the Stream of Parting to the Bridge of Scenic Wonder, one can reach Lu by going westward and Pien by going eastward.   It is one road which forks in front and thus there are actually three gates, the middle one acting as the junction.   In Biographies

of Eremite Scholars,[150] written during the Han, a
native of Lu known as the Morning Gatekeeper is
described as being in charge of guarding the stone
gate to Lu--where the disciple Tzu-lu[151] carried
rice to sustain his parents and shouldered his
satchel of books while he followed his teacher.
For those who are vexed by life in Lu or Pien,
where else should they dwell but here? Taoist
priests seek out the stone gate in order to
sacrifice to the constellation Hsuan-wu.[152] It is
also an excellent location for divination, since
its western side is particularly broad, firm, and
sloping. The Twin Cinnabar Peaks of ancient rocks
and hoary trees contrast with the gleaming white
clouds, imperceptibly exuding an atmosphere of the
immortals. Some year in the future, I would like
to come here with just a gourd-bowl and a bamboo
hat and practice meditation. While I might not
attain immortality, at least I won't die as soon as
I might otherwise.

If one were to start out from the central peak
and tread along the ridge for about three miles,
one would crosss over thirteen other peaks before
arriving here at the end whereupon one would find
oneself back within a foot of the central peak
again. Mei-yuan called it, "like two jade tallies
joined together." Ching-ssu said, "like a string
of pearls." But I cried out, "It's unquestionably
like a coiled dragon." The nostrils touch the tail
as it breathes in and out and the surface of Twin
Cinnabar Peaks resembles reptile scales with a
bristling mane.

Cultivation Peak is surrounded by Cage Peak;
viridian and emerald jade rocks stick up like

points around a solitary face of stone suspended
high.   A study belonging to an ancient scholar lay
in ruins and I built another in the same place on a
spot which Ching-ssu had selected.   I consulted the
hexagrams and drew "The secluded person perseveres
and enjoys good fortune."[153]   So I looked up Tu
Fu's poem entitled "The Secluded Person"[154] and
took the phrase "Solitary Cloud" as my studio name.
Within the studio itself I've placed a wooden
couch, cloth curtains, tea-bowls, and an incense
burner.   I consider myself to have had my share of
good luck--only I regret Ching-ssu's cruel fate.
Often I would point out the distant city to Mei-
yuan and laughingly say, "Those who strive for fame
and are lured on by profit, entangled in endless
lawsuits, are but a speck there in the white mist.
They cannot see me and I cannot see them.   Compared
to them we are far more than just a hundred feet
high."

T'ao Yuan-ming wrote:

From this lofty tower a hundred feet high,
I see clearly the four corners of the earth.
At night, an abode for returning clouds;
By day, a hall for flying birds.
Mountains and rivers fill my eyes
But the flat plain alone stretches
    without bounds.
Famous warriors in an ancient time
Bravely struggled over this land.
On a single day, their lives simply ended
And together they returned to the northern
    hills. . . .[155]

I wish I could raise a tower with high rafters
so I could recite this poem day and night.   There

is another pleasurable aspect of this place: my studio is a hundred steps from water, so I had to trouble a servant to go out and fetch some for my inkstone or to brew tea with. But closer by, I used a bamboo staff to part the grass and found a spring by the west of the house. The water soon flowed out like milk from nipples into every crevice of the land. When the sun's rays strike the sandy soil, they highlight its golden color so I named the spring "Golden Powder" as a perfect complement for the jade liquid. With great care, I removed the rocks from about the spring so it could bubble up for a couple of inches. A Buddhist monk came to view it and said, "It was blocked up since the dynastic chaos and has been unable to flow freely for decades. If it had not been for your staff today, its sorrow would have destroyed the mountain."

In back of the site is Cultivation Peak. The more one looks at it, the more vital it seems. The middle is wrapped in luxuriant emerald vapors and, because it contains a mountain spring, it is even more emerald and even more vaporous; it could not possibly lack a Pavilion of Luxuriant Emerald Jade. At the foot of Twin Cinnabar Peaks is a rocky slope which can accommodate one thousand men. I squatted there, gazing up at the entire aspect of Cultivation Peak, which resembles a lotus pod in the midst of louts petals. Fragrant dew glistens fresh with a delicate moisture most extraordinary; none of the other peaks can match it, for all of its skills have been perfected. This is the fourteenth peak of Stonegate. I particularly counted them as I crossed their ridges. To spy out

Traveling in the Mt. T'ai Range near Stonegate

their "treasure-house," enter circuitously where the head and tail meet. I went on, floating over on a boat, then crossed a bridge and clambered up the mountain by grasping the branches. There, I drew the hexagram "Chien: Obstruction,"[156] which said that my every wish would ultimately be granted but it did not indicate the precise route of my return.

The entrance to the ravine was narrow. A waterfall cascades down to where the oncoming water meets it, only to flow away. Crossing the stream and turning westward, I saw a curtain of wisteria vines entwined like a basket trellis over the rocks at the foot of Twin Cinnabar Peaks. The rocks appeared softened by its trunk and branches; the wisteria, hardened by the bones of the rocks. Both wisteria and rocks fused to become indistinguishable. Proceeding halfway along a cliff, I came across the old path to Golden Powder Spring. Following it up northwest led to my cottage on Cultivation Peak and, feeling my way eastwards down the circuitous stone steps, I reentered the ravine. In the middle, there is a spring which is unfathomable, a fitting complement for Golden Powder. The water runs down the north and creates a powerful scene at this point. I gazed up towards the east at a peak a thousand yards high--a solitary wall of rock stroking the void. To look through the myriad flora which forms an umbrageous interweave around it reveals a line of greened sky. The water flows below through the earth while man stands above alongside the water. He cannot merge with it but neither can he take leave of it. Although this is called the "Ch'i-lu Throughfare," it is as difficult to pass through as the road to Shu.

When I finally exited from the ravine, another world appeared. Directly facing is a large creek which has been blocked up, beyond which stand peaks, trees, and dwellings. Add some fallen petals and the inhabitants would certainly have been "those who had fled from Ch'in."[157] It had long been clogged up by marsh weeds and Mei-yuan wanted to clear it up. We thought it ought to be named "Mei-berry Creek." Continuing along to the east, the woodcutter's path narrows and deepens, branching off like unraveling threads which then wind back together again, leading to all the peaks on the southeast. I would like to toss pinecones all about the valley to produce myriad trees of freshening shade whose emerald cool would drench one's clothes. This could not be accomplished for years, though, so what can I do? I'll just have to use peach and apricot pits as a substitute!

Northwards, I crossed the Bridge of Karma and entered Lingering Valley. It resembles Wang Wei's Wang-ch'uan Villa or Cheng Tzu-chen's Mouth of the Vale[158] and is part of the eastern road of Stonegate. To the side is where Tzu-lu passed the night. One should sacrifice to him along with the Morning Gatekeeper, appropriately uniting warm enthusiasm with cool-tempered words. To the west is the Ridge of Horizontal Clouds; to the east, the Cave of the Slain Tiger. Because of Confucius' remark about "he who would beat a tiger with his bare hands," Tzu-lu went on to achieve a heroic reputation for filial piety.[159] It rather makes one laugh. I exited from the valley and turned eastwards, where a waterfall dribbles through rocky teeth--now visible, now hidden--as it soaks down along the veins of the mountain into a cyan stillness for which it is called "Blue Dragon."[160] Further upwards I reached the Spring Where Three Friends Gargled. We three once purified ourselves here and some monks from the mountain came by and joined us. Li Po's

> They axe the ice to gargle the frigid stream;
> Three gentlemen matched like a pair of
>   clogs[161]

is a better source for a description, though. West of the spring are the ruins of Duke Lü's[162] mansion, which has become the Hall of Dreaming Cranes. There are statues of cranes sleeping there, of children sleeping there, and of immortals also sleeping there, so upon arrival I felt extremely fatigued and likewise lay down to nap opposite them. One feels tranquilized and the mountains seem vacant; water flows by as flowers fade. Is it because they cannot bear this world of flesh that they slumber for a thousand years?

I climbed to the east where there is a Snow Veil Precipice with water cascading over the edge like pearls and crystals. The common sort of traveler inevitably calls it "The Cave of Watery Curtains" yet on a clear day the "curtains" cannot be seen. So where are the immortals then? To the south, a pagoda has been placed which subdues the tail of Tiger Peak. It seems unquestionably real and yet it is just rock, so when I arrived alongside it, I could not pet it. If one wishes to view the peaks on the northeast, choose the path which turns north; to view the peaks on the northwest, choose the path which turns west. But both have no place to rest one's feet. Only below Dragon Peak is there a small "Peach Blossom Spring" called the Valley of the Leaping Dragon. It is blocked up by a group of peaks and to enter it is not easy. Years ago, it was filled with peach blossoms long since swept away so one need not enter it at all. Besides traveling throughout the mountain, I also noted its spiritual character, discerned its physical appearance, and gathered information from all whom I met; for though I could not cover every inch of the mountain, how could it conceal its real self from me?

Then I crossed the Bridge to Scenic Wonders and ascended the Terrace of the Chinned Pearl to the south. The rocky terrace is about an acre wide. Its sinews and bones protrude grotesquely. Seated here, the precipitously high and flattened distance seems strewn about like one's robe and sash. The scene is suitable on a clear day, in the rain, and especially under the moonlight. At the end of the terrace is a single rock standing erect like a stele and occupying the "throne" of the mountain. The mountain's spirit must indeed desire recognition, for it awaits someone to carve "Stonegate Mountain" on it. In the shady part of the terrace hangs an ancient wisteria, below which I saw a shrine to a Buddhist priest. It is where Tsu-yung experienced enlightenment. East of it is the Pavilion for Cleansing Ears,[163] where the waterfall crashes against the rocks as it flows down, roaring as if locked in an endless struggle against death. It hastens toward some urgent business like a speeding comet, impossible to slow

down. It bewilders the five senses while the body
remains agile like the man whose ax-handle slowly
rotted away.[164] And there is, in fact, a studio
located off to one side called the Lodge of the
Rotted Ax-Handle.

I crossed the waterfall and visited the
quarters of the Monastery of the King of the
Underworld. Looking out over the water through an
open window, I titled the scene "Snowy Waves." Ah,
the water! How can one not feel sad at the passing
of things? In back of the monastery is the eastern
road leading to the front of the temple; it turns
south toward the gate formed by a pass. Engraved
in stone is "The True Landscape" which mirrors "The
Aesthetic Scene," for this is on the left side of
the road and one of the so-called "Three Gates of
Stonegate." I opened it and gazed eastward at the
road, so solid and durable that it can accommodate
two carts abreast. The scenic power of the western
road lies in its circuitous ups and downs; that of
the eastern road in its level straightness. (It is
quite a rare thing to find a level, straight road
in the mountains.) I rested for a while under the
shade of the trees and faced Yellowstone Mountain
again, gazing at him with a sense of familiarity.
He looked like a spotted tiger whose tail stretched
out straight from his arched back while a pair of
eyes glared. Then I suddenly realized that while
Stonegate was a coiled dragon, he was a crouching
tiger. Together with the accumulation of wind and
clouds, both serve those sages and worthies who
have dwelled in the southwest--how could this scene
exist by mere chance?

I circled the central peak and continued northwards, entering Sterculia Valley where the Shao-t'ung Divinity attained the Way. Now it is dedicated to the Tzu-t'ung Divinity.[165] Though they are two spirits, they are identified here as one. At the mouth of the valley is a small field of mulberry and hemp where smoke and mist delicately waver about the dwellings. I inquired of a villager and learned that this was where Mr. Chang[166] lived in seclusion. Mr. Chang, whose courtesy name was Shu-ming, was an eremite at Bamboo Brook and also a Licentiate of Lu. Tu Fu became friends with him through Li Po and visited him twice, writing poems on each occasion. One goes:

> The Spring mountain is without a companion;
>> alone, I seek you out.
> Sounds from a woodcutter--"cheng-cheng"
>> and the forest further deepens.
> The stream clings to the end of winter
>> as I cross over the snow;
> On Stonegate Mountain, sunset rays
>> arrive at the wooded hills.
> I seek not emanations of gold and silver
>> which appear in the night;
> And distance such harm by observing
>> the deers at their morning play.
> Moved by the spirit, things blur,
>> I forget whence I came.
> I gaze at you--can we be floating
>> on a boat through the limitless void?

and the others:

> I often come by to see you
> And you invite me to relax and stay late.

The sturgeon teem in the azure pond;

Deer frolic amongst the spring grass.

Tu brings the wine, insisting they drink:

Chang supplies the pears, no need to search
beyond.

The road is steep to the village ahead

But I'm always carefree when returning
drunk. [167]

Such friendship among the ancients seems hardly attainable today. I would sacrifice to all three of them, each a leg of the tripod which is this mountain.

Eastwards, I crossed over Leopard Ridge and gazed off at Solitary Mountain and Wild Beast Mountain, all projecting like claws from Stonegate. Then I reached Peach Blossom Valley, where there is a Cave of the Queen Mother of the West. [168] The stepped road goes straight on to the Temple of the White Clouds which is not the entrance via the stone gate. It is called the Eastern Temple. I exited northwards through the mouth of Horizontal Ridge, which parallels the back of the mountain. The road was high and level, like the top of a lofty rampart; and it exuded a spiritual power like the mansion of a noble whose vermilion gates, even when tightly locked, possess a solemnity which inspires fearful respect. Proceeding westwards, I came across Dogteeth Mountain, which is a throng of lesser peaks lacking any true affinity with the rest of the mountain. Someone characterized them as "in-laws," and Stonegate does not deign to recognize them. I left them behind and continued downhill to the south. The landforms which connect with peaks arise while those which connect with gorges submit; arising, they become a range, submitting, they become valleys. They all have names, but it is not necessary to know them. To the southwest is a valley called Thatch Valley where the giant rocks are multitudinous and the smaller ones, adamantine, making it hard on the sandals. Climbing up halfway, one can enter the Hall of the Sagely Monks and view Lao-tzu's Furnace. The valley ends where one enters the Temple of the Moon's Reflection. This is called the Western Temple and is likewise not entered via the stone gate. Now the stone gate stands on the main road between Ch'i and Lu, so it has always been possible to enter the Eastern and Western Temples from it. They must have their private entrances as well, though the public gentleman would not care to know them.

I then passed between two peaks and saw the Valley of Bubbling Cinnabar blocked off by firey mountains where it is narrowest. When I traveled by here, I could not tell what realm of existence it was. Expansive clouds severed a ridge and suddenly I came upon an old acquaintance, for I had finally reached the western road of Stonegate. I had mounted it, descended it, gone inside and outside it, zigzagged and encircled it, wearing out ten pairs of sandals before I was able to encompass the entire mountain in my heart. For the flushed blossoms and extraordinary birds do not constitute its fascination--its fascination lies in its pristine form; dense trees and thickened clouds do not constitute its mystery--its mystery lies in its energies; reddening leaves and clear streams do not constitute its purity--its purity lies in its structure; withered trees and awesome rocks do not constitute its cool detachment--its cool detachment lies in its spirit. Those who arrive are unable to leave it, while those who have left cannot forget it. It is like meeting a beauty who, from a few words, understands one's heart and pleases in every way. How could one not want to engage her affections with a gift of fine hair oil? Or, it is like encountering a polished gentleman whose lofty brilliance transcends the vulgar and whose steady warmth can be relied on. How could one not want to share one's inkstone and couch with him?

But when there is a year of famine on Stonegate, the bandits are no longer pacified and it is difficult to protect one's home. If one dwells in an isolated place, then the brave and worthy do not come by and it becomes difficult to gain recognition. The monks are lazy and make no effort to raise funds, so it is difficult to erect new buildings. The government is far away, offering little protection or support, so it is difficult to produce anything. Once, when I had finished talking about the mountain with Mei-yuan, I opened my eyes and gazed around, letting out a great sigh at how truly difficult things can be here."[169] (K/416-22)

Chapter Two
DOWN FROM THE MOUNTAIN

It profits one to meet the
Great Man.--The Book of Changes

By 1681, K'ung Shang-jen was still so devoid of prospects that he returned to Stonegate for what he thought would be an extended, if not permanent retreat. Several years later, he reminisced about this brief idyll in a poem. Here is an excerpt:

I diverted a small stream
to create a garden
And had just built a studio
but had no chance to hang up my lute.
In the autumn nights, unending rain
easily ruined the windows.
The woodcutter's path ran close by
so the trees never did grow thick. (K/113)

From this confession, it appears that his attempt to live the ideal life of a recluse was not particularly successful. Ambition and the intrusive difficulties of rural living conspired against his adopting self-imposed exile as a meaningful existence, however beautiful the surroundings. K'ung's admiration for the many unconventional figures he befriended during his life appears more compre-hensible in the light of this inability to dwell apart

from the world very long. His highly social personality,
wide cultural interests and Confucian sense of public
service relegated his yearnings for gentlemanly reclusion
to the realm of imagination, to be explored in his poetry,
his travels, and vicariously through friendships with those
he regarded as living more purely than he could.
Recognizing that isolation was no solution to the age-old
problem of literati weltschmerz, he needed little
persuading when, barely a year later, the Duke summoned him
back to Ch'ü-fu. With considerable financial inducement,
K'ung was invited to undertake several projects which soon
led to a dramatic change in his fortunes.

Initially, it was his expertise in ceremonial forms
which was needed in directing the funeral of the Duke's
wife, née Chang. Afterwards, perhaps as a reward, he was
made the editor of the bureau which compiled the Genealogy
of the K'ung Clan.[1] The work involved a massive effort at
census-taking, scholarly research into ancestries, and
revision of the clan organization. Of prime importance as
an early example of Ch'ing scholarship, it was praised by
Liang Ch'i-ch'ao, who wrote that

> it sets strict standards for collecting material
> and completely eliminates divinations, false
> genealogies, and unreliable clan accounts. It also
> corrects many errors in the "Genealogy of
> Confucius" in the Historical Records. One seldom
> finds a work so clear and precise before the height
> of the School of Empirical Studies.[2]

Its contents include charts of the clan organization, a
chronicle of pre-Confucian origins, biographies of leading
figures of each generation, and a list of living members
arranged in sub-branches.

Of particular interest are the large number of prefaces
which contain detailed information on the process of

compilation. One preface reprints the various instructions issued by the bureau regarding security arrangement, rules for inclusion of names, and the monetary contribution of .08 taels for each person recorded. Another lists twenty-eight editorial principles. For purposes of convenience, the living members of the clan were divided into twenty branches and sixty sub-branches. The various stages and dates whereby material was submitted by each sub-branch, copied, checked, recopied, and printed is also recorded. Yet another preface lists the number of characters and sheets in each chüan making a total of 841 sheets and 265,321 characters. Altogether, the clan members donated 874.97 taels, with leading members making extraordinary contributions. Following the income is a list of disbursements for office equipment and supplies, employee wages, food, entertainment, printing, and even such minutinae as the tobacco used by the staff (nine boxes costing .216 taels). The entire project lasted from September 18, 1682, when K'ung joined the bureau, until February 24, 1684, when the work was published. It expended 762.527 taels, of which 300 taels were used to support a concurrent project which K'ung also edited. The local gazetteer of Ch'ü-fu, last compiled by Ch'en Hao during the Hung-chih reign (1488-1506), was in need of extensive revision. K'ung issued an expanded version under the title A New Gazetteer of Ch'ü-fu[3] in 24 chuan. It was published in conjunction with the Genealogy and designed, in part, to supplement the short biographies in the latter work.

By this time, K'ung had already fathered two sons. Both were given names commemorating the editorial projects--the elder, Yen-p'u, after the Genealogy and the younger, Yen-chih, after the Gazetteer.[4] Yen-p'u inherited his father's interests in education and art. He went on to serve as Registrar of Tan-yang-hsien and was noted for his paintings, which were classified in the highest category, "untrammeled (i-p'in)." A poet as well, he gained recognition as one of the "Eight Masters of the Mountains and Lakes Poetry Society." Yen-chih inherited his father's bureaucratic ambitions and remained in Ch'ü-fu where the court appointed him Controller of the Confucian Shrine.

While engaged in these editorial projects, K'ung also found time to train over seven hundred students from Ch'ü-fu and neighboring districts in ceremonial forms to be used in sacrifices at the Confucian Temple. These involved not only directing the actual services at the altar but choreographing accompanying dances and orchestrating musical accompaniment as well. Artisans were hired by him to cast new bronze vessels and create instruments which he designed to more closely resemble classical sources. The climax of these activities was in the fall of 1684, when an Oblation of Legumes[5] was held in the Temple, attended by over 10,000 clan members. This particular form was an abbreviated version of the Grand Oblation[6] using vegetable rather than animal offerings and seems to have been revived by K'ung after many years of neglect.

Thereafter, there followed an unexpected series of events which propelled K'ung from obscurity onto the national stage. This surprising change in his fortunes brought upon by the visit of the K'ang-hsi Emperor was much celebrated, due in part to his own widely-read account. It is a compelling and incisive narrative, written in a style ranging from high Confucian rhetoric to personal confession. Entitled The Extraordinary Events Whereby I Came Down from the Mountain,[7] it is not only a rare autobiographical document, but describes the details of an imperial visit, the personality of K'ang-hsi and the politics of the K'ung clan.

I had planned to return to the mountain after the ceremony when news was received of the Emperor's Eastward Progress,[8] during the course of which he would visit Ch'ü-fu. So the Duke and my fellow clansmen kept me on to assist with the sacrificial ceremonies and I continued to train students in the Confucian Temple. On November 13, the Emperor dispatched Chang Liang-hsing, Councillor at the Court of Sacrificial Workship, and Han Pu, Herald at the Court of State Ceremonial, to Ch'ü-fu bearing incense and silk. They came to inspect the ritual vessels and I worked together with them for more than a month.

On December 21, we received news that His Imperial Majesty was returning from the south and had already reached Fei-hsien. I was racing all around the Temple and didn't return home until late that night. No sooner had I fallen asleep than I heard a sharp rapping at the gate. The gatekeeper said, "An Imperial Envoy has come east with a proclamation mentioning your name. Hasten to receive him--do not delay!" I threw on my formal clothes and, with only a servant-boy to help me along, ran to the Eastern Library of the Duke's mansion where the lanterns were blazing. Two Excellencies looking quite imposing in their regalia came forward to grasp my hands and said, "So you've arrived. Bow down to receive the proclamation." I was still panting for breath but dropped to the floor and prostrated myself in order to hear the imperial instructions:

"PROCLAIMED THAT Ch'ü-fu is the Sacred Precinct and the environs within which ritual is maintained. We are journeying to the realm of Lu to sacrifice to the Foremost Preceptor, endeavoring to disseminate his refined teachings and thereby encourage Confucianism. When such sacrifices are completed, let there be illuminating discourse on the meaning of the classics. Search exhaustively for the central essence so as to accord with this grand occasion. Choose from amongst the descendants of Confucius those of extensive learning much capable of such discourse and let them prepare lectures on those passages suitable, submitting them to Us in advance."

The officials kowtowed and rose. The two Excellencies were Ch'ang-shu, Chancellor of the Han-lin Academy, and Chu Ma-t'ai, Reader of the Han-lin Academy, while the receiving officials were Chang P'eng,[9] Governor of Shantung, and the Duke. I came forward, saluted, and said, "I am but a stripling scholar filled with trepidation at having been chosen to lecture. I dare not refuse yet I know not which passages would accord with this grand occasion."

His Excellency Ch'ang-shu displayed two yellow folios: one with the preface to The Great Learning and the other with the first passage of the "Commentary on the Appended Judgements" from The Book of Changes. Then a table and chairs were dusted off as a brush and paper were prepared. The two Excellencies sat facing west, the Governor and Duke faced east, while I was ordered to sit facing north. The candle had already burned down to the fifth mark but I was still unable to write anything down. His Excellency, Ch'ang-shu, laughed and said, "With two candles burning and four pairs of eyes staring, even 'a genius who could write a poem within seven paces'[10] would find it hard to collect his thoughts." The Duke then had another table set up for me. In a flicker, "A Lecture on The Great Learning" was completed. His Excellency, Ch'ang-shu, glanced about and said, "This lecture is quite correct but we must not neglect the latter part which should glorify the Emperor." I quickly agreed and amended it. He also urged me to write the one on The Book of Changes but I declined, saying, "I am a specialist on The Book of Poetry but have not mastered The Book of Changes." His Excellency, Chu, sneered and said, "How can anyone be considered knowledgeable who hasn't mastered the Five Classics?" Ashamed, I forced myself to write on The Book of Changes. It was finished before the candles went out. His Excellency, Chu, read it through and slapped me on the back saying, "Clearly your reputation is well-deserved." He then recopied them and sealed the folios. The water-clock indicated 2 a.m. and the Excellencies saddled up and galloped off to complete their mission.

On December 22 around four in the afternoon, His Imperial Majesty arrived in Ch'ü-fu. I stood with a group of other Licentiates and bowed in greeting. That night, he was to be accommodated in the Temporary Palace[11] south of the city. Towards dark, two mounted pages came to the Temple and ordered me to proceed to the Palace where I was to kneel down under a canopy outside the wall and offer greetings to His Imperial Majesty. His Excellency, Sun Tsai-feng,[12] Chancellor of the Han-lin Academy, related that the Emperor remarked, "The lectures were quite fine but there are a few words which are inappropriate so I would have you change them." He pointed out one by one the places where changes should be made. The text bore faint impressions of fingernail marks, no doubt reflections of the clear mirror of the imperial mind. I thus added a few more words, resubmitted it, and it was accepted. It was also made known that there were supposed to be two student lecturers at the ceremony and I recommended my elder cousin, K'ung Shang-li,[13] who was a Provincial Graduate. After this proposal was accepted, we entered His Excellency Sun's quarters. He wrote out copies of the lectures and said, "This is to be placed on His Imperial Majesty's desk." Then he ordered a Secretary in the Grand Secretariat to make two more copies saying, "This is for the desk of the lecturers." I did not wait for the final two copies to be made but took leave of His Excellency and reentered the city. It was already midnight.

There was a Sub-Director of the Court of State Ceremonial, His Excellency Hsi-an, who summoned me to the Hall of Poetry and Ritual to rehearse the formal motions of the lecture. After a while, the two mounted pages from before came in with the copies of the lectures and solemnly placed them on His Imperial Majesty's desk and on the lecturer's desk. They looked up and saw a painted screen in the Hall and one of the pages said, "I know this painting—its 'Two Yellow Orioles Sing Amongst Emerald Willows; A Line of White Egrets Ascends to the Blue Heavens.'"[14] I nudged my cousin Shang-li and said, "Both of us are bound to enter the Court." The two pages were Clerks in the Imperial Academy: one was Mr. Ya Ssu-t'ai and the other Mr. Chao T'e-pa. Both had achieved some literary fame and had served in connection with other official lectures. They spent all night teaching us the proper tone of voice when speaking and also about deportment.

On the next day, the twenty-third, His Imperial Majesty entered the city by Palanquin and proceeded to the Temple of the Perfect Sage[15] where he alighted in front of the Hall of the Literary Constellation and rested under a marquee. Then he went on foot into the Hall where he knelt and read the annunciation. Three oblations were made with three bows and nine kowtows--something utterly unprecedented. An ox, goat, and pig were used as sacrifices and there were ten vessels filled with offerings as well as six rows of dancers. The students who participated in the ceremony were those whom I had trained myself. I, however, was waiting in the Hall of Poetry and Ritual in preparation for the lecture and so did not get to accompany the entourage. After the ceremony, His Imperial Majesty returned to the marquee to rest again and change his regalia, putting on a falcon-white robe with a jacket of azurite blue. When the clock struck 8 a.m., Silda,[16] Sub-Chancellor of the Grand-Secretariat, and Gestei, Director of the Court of Sacrificial Worship, escorted His Imperial Majesty from the Hall of the Literary Constellation eastward through the Gate of Inherited Sagacity into the Hall of Poetry and Ritual, where he sat down on the throne.

Numerous officials attended the lecture. On the left were the Grand Secretaries Mingju[17] and Wang Hsi,[18] President of the Board of Civil Appointments Isangga,[19] President of the Board of Rites Chieh-shan,[20] President of the Board of Works Samha,[21] Sub-Chancellors of the Grand Secretariat Maltu and Silda, Chancellors of the Han-lin Academy Ch'ang-shu and Sun Tsai-feng, Reader of the Grand Secretariat Hsu T'ing-hsi,[22] Chancellors of the Han-lin Academy Chu Ma-t'ai and Kao Shih-ch'i,[23] Senior Vice-President of the Censorate Sun Kuo, Libationer at the Imperial Academy A-li-hu, Director of the Court of Sacrificial Workship Gestei, Sub-Director of the Court of the Imperial Stud Yang-shu, Sub-Director of the Court of State Ceremonial Hsi-an, Sub-Director of the Banqueting Court Hu Shih-t'u, Senior Metropolitan Keeper of the Seal of the Personnel Section Fiyanggū,[24] Provincial Censor of the Shansi Circuit Lajan, and Governor of Shantung and President of the Censorate Chang P'eng.

And on the right were Duke of the Sagely Posterity K'ung Yü-ch'i, Hereditary Erudite of the Classics and Members of the Han-lin Academy K'ung Yü-t'ing,[25] Yen Mao-heng, Tseng Chen-yu, Meng Chen-jen, Chung Ping-chen, Emeritus Erudite of the Classics K'ung Yü-ying, Assistant Secretary of the Chihli Intendant K'ung Hsing-hung, Hereditary Magistrate of Ch'u-fu K'ung Hsing-jen, Registrar of the Imperial Academy K'ung Shang-k'an, Sub-Registrar of the Ni-shan Academy K'ung Yü-hsi, Sub-Registrar of the Shu-Ssu Academy K'ung Chen-cho,[26] and thirty-five expectant candidates from the other four clans.   Officials in the departments, circuits, prefectures, and districts were all in attendance outside.

When the groups had arrayed themselves, there was an imperial proclamation: "The Prefect of Yen-chou, Chang P'eng-ko,[27] is a pure and upright official and is permitted to hear the lecture." He was subsequently ordered to enter and was placed below the Governor. The Herald from the Court of State Ceremonial intoned "Bow Down!" and the Duke of the Sagely Posterity led us members of the Five Clans in the customary three bows and nine kowtows. The Herald then intoned "Let the lecture begin!" whereupon I and K'ung Shang-li ascended the platform from the western side. We kowtowed thrice and then stood to the west of the lecturer's desk. I was the first to walk over to the desk, positioning myself facing north, whereupon I opened up the texts and arranged two silver rulers as paperweights. On His Imperial Majesty's desk, the text was also opened and fixed with two gold paperweights. The two tables were placed within a foot of each other. His Imperial Majesty sat solemn and erect as I began to speak on the preface to the sacred classic, The Great Learning:

"'The Way of the Great Learning lies in illuminating bright Virtue, in renewing the people, and in resting in the ultimate good.'[28] This preface discourses on the crucial process of cultivating one's self so as to rule others, activating inner sageliness and outer kingliness. It is the principle of the entire classic, while this phrase is the principle of the preface. Confucius meant that when the Great Man rules the

world in order to thereby establish perfection,
three ways must be learned:

One way is 'Illuminating Bright Virtue.' That
nature which is decreed by Heaven and bestowed upon
man, extremely abstract and responsive to all
situations, is fundamentally bright. It may become
obsessed and obscured by vitalistic forces and
material desires such that its brightness is
beclouded. Nevertheless, its fundamental state is
to be bright and it has never ceased to be so.
What is necessary to restore its original state is
to illuminate its sprouting of goodness. This is
how The Great Learning presents the substance of
the matter.

Another way is 'Renewing the People.' Virtue
is what all men may achieve in concert, while it is
the Great Man who can illuminate virtue by himself.
He thereby, of necessity, extends it toward others
as he encourages them to attain it. He causes all
who realize this virtue to expunge contaminations
from the past and encourage reform. This is how
The Great Learning presents effective functioning.

Yet another way is "Resting in the Ultimate
Good." "Bright Virtue" and "Renovating the People"
are the most proper and unshakable of standards--
pure heavenly principles without a trace of human
desire, what is called the ultimate good. The
Great Man, as regards his own virtue, must not fail
to comprehend even a single principle; as regards
the virtue of the people, he must not fail to renew
even one person. Both these acts of construction
lie in the realm of the ultimate good, where he
maintains an affirmative attitude without change.
This is how The Great Learning presents the

Portrait of K'ang-hsi

K'ang-hsi on Tour in Shantung (a)

K'ang-hsı on Tour in Shantung (b)

achievements of the Sage and the proper treading of the kingly Way.

When Confucius illuminated these central ideas, he sought their fount in those transmissions from the minds of a thousand sages and opened the means of ruling for a hundred kings. His general principles and procedures were gloriously set forth in their entirety: and therein is the method of ruling the mind and the people complete. May His Imperial Majesty perceptively practice it and luminously reflect the sagely teachings in His bright countenance. Achieve a concentration of its essential qualities proceeding back to Yao and Shun. Personally receive that learning which arose by the rivers Shu and Ssu.

Now, on this Southern Tour heralded by kingfisher banners, joy has surged upwards in the hearts of the people. The jade-rolled scrolls have been opened, the meaning of the classics is perspicuously manifest. Thus is His Imperial Majesty's cultivation and virtue widely diffused, graciously enriching the grand dynastic enterprise. Your servant is but of simple mind. His humble wish is that Heaven may protect You and reward Your perseverance, that all may advance to an exalted prosperity. As all deficiencies are removed without exception, the people will gaze up at the glory of the four dragon pillars and the laws will be emblazoned, a mirror which will forever illuminate through a thousand autumns. May this flourishing dynastic enterprise join Heaven and Earth; and its policies surpass those of all former sovereigns."

The lecture completed, I withdrew. The Heavenly Countenance radiated clear joy and, turning towards his attendant officials, he said, "Our official lecturers cannot compare with this one." K'ung Shang-li then stepped forward to lecture on the first passage of the "Commentary on the Appended Judgements" from The Book of Changes. He said:

"'Heaven is lofty and Earth is lowly and thus are the male and female principles established. High and low are manifest and thus are noble and humble positioned. Activity and repose have their constancy and thus is the fixed and the pliable defined. Directions associate according to kind; phenomena are distinguished by categories. Thus does the fortunate and the calamitous arise. What in Heaven are abstract symbols become on Earth concrete forms. Thus is transformation made visible.'[29]

This passage reflects how Confucius, after The Book of Changes came to be written, looked back to the state before this was achieved and realized that Heaven and Earth do proceed through natural changes of their own accord. His intention was to state that though such changes contain the male and female principles and these principles contain the noble and the humble, the fixed and the pliable, fortune and calamity, how could transformation itself have only begun with the creation of The Book of Changes? Heaven maintains yang as superior; Earth maintains yin as inferior. One, exalted, the other, lowly. Therein lies the principle of regulated sequence whereby male and female are established. It thus follows that Earth

and the lesser myriad phenomena are unfolded from
below while Heaven and the greater myriad phenomena
are unfolded above; and likewise, those lines of
the hexagrams which are highest are most exalted
while those which are lowest are most humble
indeed. Heaven and the myriad phenomena which are
yang are by nature predominantly active, while
Earth and those myriad phenomena which are yin are
by nature predominantly quiescent. Thus, those
lines in the hexagrams denoted as yang are fixed,
while those which are yin are pliable and are
judged accordingly.

When man's mind desires to do good, all kinds
of goodness may be accumulated; when his mind
desires to do evil, then he will attract all kinds
of evil.   This is because things "associate
according to kind."   In human affairs, good
associates with goodness and does not join with
evil; evil associates with evil and does not become
good. This is because things are "distinguished by
categories." If the accumulation within a category
is good, then fortune will reflect it. If evil,
then calamity will arise from this and thus is
derived the principles of fortune and calamity. In
Heaven, the sun, moon, and stars are abstract
symbols. On Earth, the mountains, rivers, animals,
and plants are concrete forms, so that in The Book
of Changes the transformations from yin to yang and
from yang to yin can be seen therein. The changes
behind natural creation are likewise perceived. So
the sixty-four hexagrams can be reduced to one pair
of Ch'ien and K'un and these two compose the simple
principle of all change. Association, achievement,

continuity, and expansion all derive from this. Thus does change coordinate Heaven and Earth.

Our Gracious Majesty, who has perfected virtue and personifies the principle Ch'ien has, through sagely achievement, encouraged prosperity, touring the land and observing the people so as to spread good government and effect moral transformation. With His beatific countenance, He seeks tranquility in himself so that his vast movements range to the limitless. To that extent, He takes Heaven as a model and follows the patterns of Earth. These are the symbols of a great peace enabling the grand ambition to expand things and accomplish construction. Your servant is ignorant and but wishes that You achieve the essence and integrate the three forces of Heaven, Earth, and Man through steadfestness. Imitate heavenly temporality; grasp the reins of the grand transformation. Allow the clouds to fructify and lead the land to receptivity so that zephyrs may waft under the luminary brilliance of perfect government. May China and the Lands-Across-the-Oceans ever expand into the cosmos. Thus may Your position beneficently participate in the creativity of Ch'ien and K'un."

After the lecture, he withdrew and we both descended the staircase, returning to our group. An official from the Court of State Ceremonial announced the reading of the imperial proclamation and the Duke led us members of the Five Clans in kneeling down as the Grand Secretary Wang Hsi read:

"PROCLAIMED THAT The Way of the Perfect Sage proceeds along with the movements of the sun and moon, flowing together with Heaven and Earth. Sovereigns for myriad generations have all been guided by it down to nobles, gentry, and commoners--there are none who lack such motivation. All of you have long received the Sage's enriching legacy maintained by your clan from generation to generation. May you concretize benevolence and avow righteousness. Stride along the middle path and tread that of harmony. Maintain loyalty and forgiveness in establishing your minds. Benevolently exercise filiality and brotherly love in cultivating your conduct. Do not neglect this in order to carry out the sagely teachings, so as to merit Our compassionate expectations. May all of you but obey this completely and never forget it."

The Duke led us descendents in kowtowing our gratitude. Then we all emerged and waited for His Imperial Majesty outside the Gate of Cherished Values. His Imperial Majesty issued a command to the Grand Secretaries Mingju and Wang Hsi: "The lectures of K'ung Shang-jen and the other one have completely fulfilled Our expectations. We are not to be restricted by the conventional regulations and have decided to employ them outside the usual quotas." And he also commanded, "This is Our first visit to the Sagely Precinct. Now that the sacrificial ceremonies have been completed, We wish to tour the various monuments to the Sage. Have the Duke of the Sagely Posterity, the Governor of Shantung, and the lecturers guide Us."

Before long, His Imperial Majesty's entourage proceeded through the Gate of Inherited Sagacity. A eunuch walked in advance holding a bamboo tube covered with imperial yellow damask while I and others guided the entourage back through the Gate of Accomplishment and up into the Hall of Accomplishment where we reached the altar before the image of the Foremost Preceptor.

The bodyguards were ordered to lift open the curtains and sweep away the dust, whereupon His Imperial Majesty solemnly gazed upon the statue of the Sage. He turned and commanded me, "Inform Us abut this" as an attendant tugged at my robe and then pressed me down into a kneeling position. I answered, "In the year 540, during the Eastern Wei dynasty, the Prefect of Yen-chou, Li T'ing, was the first to have a statue of the Sage cast." Having finished, I was pulled to my feet again. Next we proceeded to the statues of the Four Attendant Spirits[30] and looked them all over. Also viewed were the sacrificial vessels on the altar table, where there were three tsun[31] pieces decorated with images of the constellations, clouds, and thunder. I was asked, "What dynasty do these date from?" and I answered, "These were given in the year 85 when the Emperor Chang-ti of the Han dynasty sacrificed at Ch'ü-fu." We also inspected the picture of Confucius as the Minister of Justice of Lu, painted by Wu Tao-tzu,[32] which had been engraved in stone. Exiting via a door to the north, we went through the Hall of the Sagely Consort, into the Hall of the Sage's Life where all the stone-cut engravings of events in the life of Confucius were displayed. There were portraits of him seated and standing, and a small picture of him teaching Yen-hui. His Imperial Majesty asked "Which portrait is the most authentic?" and I answered, "Only the small picture of him teaching Yen-hui and the other disciples is really authentic. Legend has it that it was painted by Tzu-kung and recopied by Ku K'ai-chih[33] of the Chin dynasty." His Imperial Majesty dusted it off and stared at it intently for a long time.

We exited down the left stairs and he asked, "What lies on the left?" I answered, "In front stands the Hall of Chimes and Strings, and in back The Temple to the Patriarch Liang, Uncle of the Sage." His Imperial Majesty put on a serious expression and stopped to gaze off at it. Then we entered the Hall of Accomplishment where he stood in front of the left door, facing south. The descendants of the Five Ancestors who were officials had all entered and were kneeling on the platform. They were personally addressed as follows:

"The virtue of the Perfect Sage is lofty, luminescent, vast, and as great as Heaven, Earth, the sun, and the moon--nothing can adequately express it. We have always endeavored to comprehend the meaning of the classics, personifying it through contemplating the perfect Way. While it is our desire to bestow a laudation, no words seem adequate. Thus we have written the characters "The Veritable Teacher of Myriad Generations"[34] to be hung high in the center of the Hall. Not only is it to exalt the sagely teachings but to serve as an admonition to all in the future."

He ordered a bodyguard to bring forward the bamboo tube. On top was a lock which, when opened, revealed the imperial calligraphy inside. The sun and stars illuminated each other; clouds and the Milky Way glistened. All the officials were overjoyed and in one shout offered praise. The

Duke of the Sagely Posterity then came forward to receive it, reverently placing it in the middle of the Hall. His Imperial Majesty further announced, "Sovereigns through the ages have come to sacrifice within the Sagely Precinct, bestowing gold and silver vessels. Today, We have personally visited and carried out the ceremonies expressing Our reverence for the Perfect Sage in a manner far different from those before. Henceforth, all yellow canopies[35] will remain in the Temple, thereby indicating Our intention to respect the Sage."

The canopies were those often carried before the Emperor. Erudite of the Five Classics K'ung Yü-t'ing received and placed them reverently in the center of the Hall. The Duke led us descendents in expressing our thanks as all the officials cried out, "Long Live Your Majesty!" He then proceeded out of the Hall to the outer terrace where he surveyed the grand layout and asked about the tablet above the Hall of Accomplishment. I answered, "This is the 'Flying White' style calligraphy of the Sung Emperor Hui-tsung." His Imperial Majesty stood under one of the pillars and touched the coiled dragon carved in stone, briefly praising it. Then he descended the stairs. He asked, "What is your age?" and I answered, "Your servant is thirty-six years old." "How many generations removed are you from the Foremost Teacher?" "Your servant is of the sixty-fourth generation." "What generation is the Duke of the Sagely Posterity?" The Duke replied, "I am of the sixty-seventh generation."

His Imperial Majesty was then conducted to the Apricot Terrace where I explained, "This is where the Foremost Teacher discoursed on the Way." He inspected the stele with the seal-style characters "Apricot Terrace" engraved on it, written by the Chin dynasty official Tang Huai-ying, and also he enjoyed the dragon incised on the stone incense burners. I explained, "This was carved in the reign of the Emperor Chang-tsung of the Chin dynasty" and His Imperial Majesty praised its intricate beauty. The procession moved on to the pavilion which housed the imperial inscription from the Sung dynasty. We viewed the stele by the Sung official Mi Fei[36] "In Praise of the Juniper" and that with the inscription "Confucius and His Seventy-two Disciples" erected by the Sung Emperor Chen-tsung together with his officials.

Within the Gate of Accomplishment in the east, we inspected the juniper which the Foremost Teacher had planted himself.[37] His Imperial Majesty asked, "This tree has not yet withered, so why are there no branches?" I replied, "In 1499, both the Gate and the Hall caught fire and this tree was located right between them. The branches and leaves were scorched and fell off; the trunk alone remains. It has been almost two hundred years and it has neither withered nor flourished, remaining firm as iron, so it is popularly called the 'Iron Tree.'" His Imperial Majesty ordered the bodyguards to help him cross over the railing where he rubbed his hands along the trunk for a long while and pronounced it a marvelous rarity. We then went out through the Gate of Accomplishment again and I was asked, "Where are the Han steles?" "The Han steles

are before the Hall of the Literary Constellation,"
I replied and conducted him past the Pavilion of
the T'ang Steles, where he looked at the one
erected by a T'ang emperor, and then on into the
Hall of the Literary Constellation. I explained,
"In this Hall are stored books and records from the
past. Imperial commentaries on the classics are
also preserved here." We exited via the western
side-door, looking at steles from the Yung-lo and
Hung-chih reigns,[38] and proceeded to the Gate of
Unified Script[39] where we viewed the Han Stele on
the right.

"This is the 'Officer's Stele'[40] which the
Prime Minister of Lu, I Ying, erected in 153 during
the Han dynasty. Now it is called the 'Stele of
the Hundred Households,' I explained." "Why is it
called that?" "Historically, the Court privileged
us by establishing four officials: Archivist, to
oversee ritual and ceremony; Music Master, to
regulate music and dance; Controller, to control
military lands; and the Head of the Hundred
Households,[41] to administer the Temple and Tomb
areas. Thus they are called the Four Offices:
Ritual, Music, Military, and Agriculture.
Nowadays, Archivist, Music Master, and Controller
are all selected by the Court. Only the Head of
the Hundred Households is designated by the Duke of
the Sagely Posterity. Yet this is not quite in
accordance with past practice and we therefore look
upward to special imperial grace, whereby the
complete set of personnel would be selected by the
Court." His Majesty approved this recommendation
and passed the matter on to the Board of Civil
Personnel to deliberate.

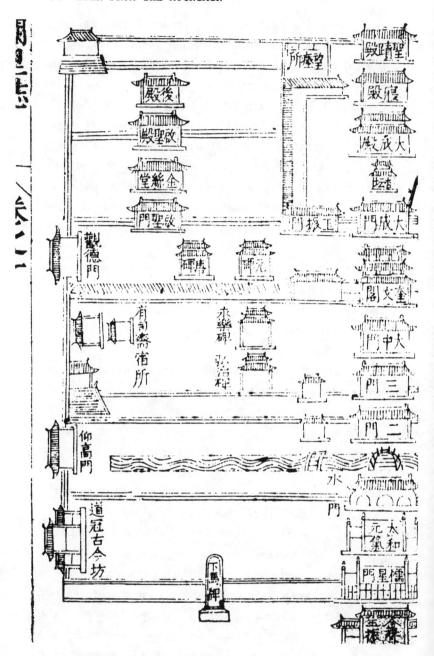

Map of the Confucian Temple

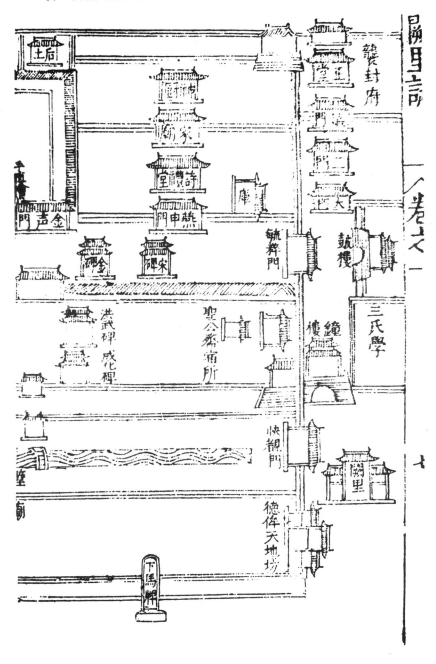

Next we viewed the "Stele of the Ritual Vessels"[42] which Han Ch'ih had erected in 156, the stele of the Provincial Inspector K'ung Ch'ien[43] dating from 155, and the stele erected in 220 which records the enfeoffment of K'ung Hsien as the Marquis of the Sagely Lineage.[44] We also passed to the left of the Gate where we viewed the stele erected in 169 recording Shih Ch'en's sacrifice,[45] the stele erected by Han Ch'ih in 157 upon restoring the Tomb, the Stele of the Commandant of Mt. T'ai, K'ung Miao,[46] and the stele of the Prefect of Po-ling, K'ung P'iao.[47]

When His Imperial Majesty had finished reading these inscriptions, he asked, "Do any famous sites still exist outside the Gate?" I replied, "In front of the Gate of Lofty Inclinations there is a winding stream which often dries up for lack of a source. If the Spring of Literary Contributions east of the city were to be led into the Temple confines to replenish it, then this stream would always be full and the grass would find succor. But we have never received permission to do this and we dare not act hastily." His Imperial Majesty said "What possible harm could there be in this?" and turned to the Grand Secretary Wang Hsi, saying, "As the Duke of the Sagely Posterity and others have memorialized, the stream outside the wall of Ch'ü-fu may be diverted into the city limits, inasmuch as it does not adversely affect the flow of the Grand Canal. This matter is remanded to the attention of the Governor to carry out."

His Imperial Majesty returned via the Gate of Unified Script, viewing the steles from the Hung-wu and Ch'eng-hua eras,[48] and entered the eastern

side-door of the Hall of the Literary Constellation
compound. He gazed at the steles which recorded
the restorations of the Temple in the Sung, Chin,
and Yuan dynasties. Then he asked me "How many
children have you at the age of thirty-six?" "Your
servant has two sons," I replied. His Imperial
Majesty's face became relaxed as he expressed his
compassionate interest. Proceeding north a bit, he
asked again, "The Temple's domains are quite
extensive. Wherein lies the original dwelling of
the Foremost Teacher?" I explained, "In back of
where Your Majesty attended the lecture is the site
of the Wall of Lu,[49] which is where the dwelling of
the Foremost Teacher was." We went back through
the Gate of Inherited Sagacity and, in front of the
Hall of Poetry and Ritual, viewed the Stone of the
Dawn of Creation, the T'ang dynasty ash tree, and
the T'ang dynasty ginko. Then we entered the Hall
by the central staircase. I said, "This is where
the Master stood and stopped Po-yü, who was
hurrying across the court, in order to admonish him
to study poetry and ritual.[50] His Imperial Majesty
went back to the back of the chamber and looked at
the remaining well of Confucius' home.[51] He leaned
across the bannister with a wistful air of
admiration, tasting some of the water drawn from
it. His Imperial Majesty then asked about the
remains of the Wall of Lu. I explained, "Of old,
when the First Emperor of the Ch'in ordered the
burning of books, your servant's ancestor in the
ninth generation, K'ung Fu,[52] took precautions by
secreting the Book of History, the Analects, and
the Book of Filial Piety in the hollows of the
wall. During the Han dynasty, when Prince Kung of

Lu decided to raze the home of the Ancestor in order to expand his palace, he heard the sounds of chimes, strings, and pipes. After investigating, he obtained the ancient texts written on bamboo strips. Thus, later generations called his palace 'Chimes and Strings' and called this the 'Wall of Lu.'"

His Imperial Majesty ordered me to show him the place and he looked over every part of it. He also asked me, "Have We seen all the relics of your clan?" I replied, "Many of the relics of the Foremost Sage have disappeared and the rest are not worthy of your Majesty's cognizance. Having received this brief gaze of Your sagely benevolence, from here on the ancestral shrine will magnify in glory. It will be written into history and throughout the world for myriad generations, people will seek to know of this fragrant visitation in which Your Imperial Majesty manifested esteem of the Teacher and concern for the Way. It will not merely be your servant's clan who will spread this."

The Grand Secretary Wang Hsi, Chancellor Sun Tsai-feng, and the Expositor of the Han-lin Academy Kao Shih-ch'i all knelt and said, "What K'ung Shang-jen has said is indeed true." His Imperial Majesty smiled and nodded. He then ascended the Hall of Poetry and Ritual and entered the special imperial canopy. The Duke led myself and others outside, where we awaited him beyond the Gate of Inherited Sagacity. His Imperial Majesty fetched his "Poem on a Visitation to the Sagely Precinct" and handed it to the Grand Secretary Wang Hsi, who

bestowed it on the Duke. I was ordered to kneel
and read it:

> The belled palanquin came to Eastern Lu
> And forthwith did We ascend to the Hall of
>   the Master.
> By the paired pillars, sacrifices were made;
> Before lofty Mt. T'ai, the Duke's palace
>   appeared.
> The tradition is inherited from Yao and Shun:
> Confucianism nurtured by the banks of the
>   Shu and Ssu.
> Within the gates, We felt the pines and
>   junipers
> And paid Our respects in formal regalia.

After the reading the Duke and everyone else
bowed, expressing gratitude, and I said:

"Since ancient times, when sovereigns visited
Ch'ü-fu, only Emperor Hsuan-tsung of the T'ang[53]
wrote a poem. It merely lamented that the Sage had
been born during the decline of the Chou--that he
had virtue but was without office. It lacked
completely andy statement of reverential joy or
aesthetic appreciation. Your Imperial Majesty's
new composition surpassed the present and
transcends the past. It evokes a longing for the
sagely Way like that of the worthy successor Shun
for the Sage-king Yao. Fortune indeed has devolved
upon Your servant's clan to thus receive this
gracious favor. It will be diligently preserved
from generation to generation and accepted as a
model."

The imperial entourage exited through the Gate
of Inherited Sagacity and the Grand Secretary Wang
Hsi read an announcement: "His Imperial Majesty

will now proceed to the Confucian Grove[54] and
commands the Duke of the Sagely Posterity and the
lecturer K'ung Shang-jen to accompany him." Before
long, His Imperial Majesty exited via the Gate of
Cherished Values and entered a summer palanquin
which was preceded by the imperial standard. We
passed the gate of the Duke's palace, before which
we stopped, gazing at it for a while, then moved
eastward through the Drumtower Gate, northward
through neighborhood streets and out via the
northern gate of Ch'ü-fu. The common people filled
the streets, falling prostrate on the ground, each
nudging the other in order to get a better view of
the heavenly countenance.

There was a descendent of the Duke of Chou
named Tung-yeh P'ei-jan. He was supporting his
father, an old man who grasped a staff as he knelt
on the left side of the street, holding up a
memorial in both hands. The memorial beseeched
that he be enfeoffed as a hereditary official and
that his ancestral shrine be elevated alongside
those of the Four Ancestors. (It was I who had
written out his supplication for him.) His
Imperial Majesty read it and asked, "The Duke of
Chou was surnamed Chi. Why is your surname Tung-
yeh?" P'ei-jan replied, "In ancient times, the
youngest son of Po-ch'in was named Yu. He was
enfeoffed in Tung-yeh and took this for a
surname.[55] His Imperial Majesty asked, "Where is
the Temple to the Duke of Chou?" P'ei-jan pointed
and replied, "To the East by the high hill where
the pines and cypresses thickly grow, there lies
the Temple to the Duke of Lu." His Imperial
Majesty craned his neck to get a glimpse of it,

then he turned to the old man with the cane. "Who
is this old man?" P'ei-jan replied, "It is your
servant's father, Tung-yeh Yun-p'eng, who is now in
his seventy-fourth year." "How many members are
there in your clan?" "There are not even a hundred
men." His Majesty read the supplication and passed
it on to an attendant to give to the proper office
for discussion.

We proceeded less than a mile before arriving
at the Gate to the Sagely Grove.[56] The three
imperial escorts were ordered to dismount and we
proceeded a bit further as His Imperial Majesty
passed through the Towerview Gate. There, the Duke
led myself and others in kneeling by the left side
of the road. His Imperial Majesty looked about and
laughed, "You've all arrived here first." When he
reached the Shu River Bridge,[57] he ordered the
palanquin set down but the Duke and others
memorialized, "This place is yet some distance from
the Tomb" and led the palanquin to the gate where
he then disembarked and entered. He reverently
walked up to the Tomb of the Foremost Teacher[58] and
knelt facing north. The Grand Secretary Mingju
held up a golden basin from which His Imperial
Majesty thrice poured libations of wine and then
kowtowed. The Duke led myself and others in
accompanying him behind. I noticed that the lining
of the imperial kingfisher robe had been mended
after having been scorched and I looked up with
admiration at our Sovereign's frugality and perfect
virtue, qualities that matched those of the Sage-
King Yü.

His Imperial Majesty turned towards the stele
on the Tomb and asked, "What trees are growing

above the Tomb?" I replied, "The trees in the
Confucian Grove are those from every area
represented by his disciples. They have been
transplanted baside the Tomb and there are so many
kinds that it is difficult to distinguish them.
However, the pistacia tree[59] and the milfoil plant
are the two most plentiful." "What uses are there
for the pistacia tree?" "Its wood is fit for
making staves and chessboards while the knots on
the trunk can be made into gourds. Its leaves can
be eaten as vegetables and also dried for tea; its
seeds can be pressed for their oil and also used
for candles." His Imperial Majesty also asked, "Is
there any milfoil? Fetch some to show Us."
Whereupon the Duke picked some milfoil from the
side of the Tomb and presented it. His Imperial
Majesty looked it over and said, "'The Numbers of
the Great Expansion make fifty, of which forty-nine
are employed in divination.'[60] Those bunches of
milfoil which contain fifty stalks are thus fit-
test for divination. Do such kind exist nowadays?"
I answered, "Within the Grove are many kinds of
milfoil but those whoch contain fifty stalks are
guarded below by a divine tortoise. They are
called 'Auspicious Legumes' and do not occur often.
But with this visitation of the belled palanquin,
some will, of course, appear. Your servant will be
obliged to present them."

His Imperial Majesty then proceeded along the
western side of the Tomb to the site of the
Foremost Worthy Tzu-kung's home and tomb[61] where
the acolytes Tuan-mu Chin and Tuan-mu Ch'ien were
kneeling outside the house. They submitted a
memorial requesting that, as in the case of the

descendants of Confucius, they too be allowed to sacrifice to their ancestor with the rank of Hereditary Erudite. His Imperial Majesty asked, "Why are the descendants of Tzu-kung here?" The Duke replied, "They are indeed descendants of the Tuan-mu clan and burn incense to him here."

After His Imperial Majesty read the memorial, he handed it over to attendants and went eastward past the Dismounting Pavilion[62] which commemorates the Emperor Chen-tsung of the Sung dynasty. He pondered it for a long time and then ordered the attendants to accompany him as he ascended to the top and gazed far around. His Imperial Majesty saw a tree with a wild vine growing up it and he grabbed a leaf asking "What is the name of this plant?" I replied, "This is called the 'Literary Florescent.' It does not wither in either winter or summer; and the stalks, leaves, flowers, and fruits are all multicolored with a profusion of aromas." Southward, we passed by the Juniper Pavilion.[63] I explained, "This is the juniper which Tzu-kung planted himself. It is petrified and thus has not decayed. Later, a pavilion was built beside it." His Imperial Majesty asked, "If there is a clump of milfoil growing, We should like to view it." I led him to a steep hill west of the pavilion which was overgrown with thorns and brush and parted some of the undergrowth, saying, "Here is a milfoil plant." He picked a stalk himself and toyed with its stem and branches. He also picked its seeds so that it filled his hands, sniffing it; then he turned to give these to me, saying, "They have an unusual fragrance when sniffed closely." He also asked, "What is the name of this tree?" I answered, "It

Map of the Confucian Grove

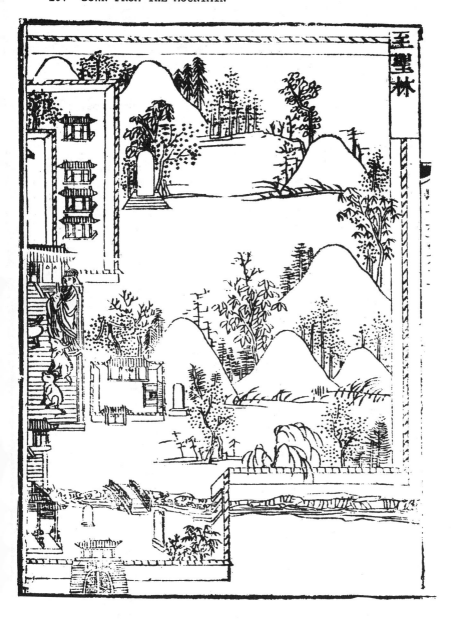

is popularly called the 'chestnut tree.'"   His
Imperial Majesty laughed.   "Its real name is the
'hu-oak'--'hu'--written with the wood radical next
to the phonetic 'hu' which means 'a measure of
corn.'"   He enjoyed the scene past noontime, then
went out of the Sacrificial Pavilion,[64] down the
steps where he turned south.

The Duke led myself and others in kowtowing and
expressing our graitude, stating:

"Hitherto, visits of our soveriegns have only
designed to grace the Temple.   Only the Emperor
Chen-tsung of the Sung dynasty has likewise
alighted from the palanquin and graced our Grove,
such an event having been transmitted as an act
virtually unprecedented in history.   Our Present
Sovereign, having sacrificed at the shrine, has
gazed upon the ancestor's tomb, pouring libations
in a proper ceremony, viewing the ancient relics
and expressing compassion for plants and trees.
Nothing more could be added to such sincerity in
reverencing the Teacher and emphasizing the Way.
Your servant and all of us are but the remnants of
the Sage's descendants, yet ever will we endeavor
to record this lofty beneficence."

The Grand Secretaries Mingju and Wang Hsi knelt
and said:

"Since sovereigns first graced Ch'ü-fu with
visits, never has there been so perfect a ceremony
as that occasioned by our Present August Emperor.
Your servants and all who have attended You express
their endless joy."

The Chancellor of the Han-lin Academy Sun Tsai-
feng and the Expositor Kao Shih-ch'i knelt and
said:

"None who are human can fail to be affected by the grand ceremony occasioned by Our Gracious Majesty's visit to Ch'ü-fu. Rendering sincere the yearnings of the land; fortifying peace for a thousand years. It will not merely be the K'ung clan who will celebrate this act of imperial favor."

The two descendants of Tzu-kung also came near the steps and performed three bows and nine kowtows. His Imperial Majesty then proceeded along the avenue leading from the Tomb,[65] noticing the stone altars, ornamented pillars, and statues of guardians, unicorns, and leopards. He gazed at the gate to the Tomb and looked westward, asking, "What building is that?" I replied, "This is where your servant's clan gathers to perform the Spring and Autumn Sacrifices. It is called 'Commemoration Hall.'" Its door had been barred and all the officials went ahead to clear the way. Only I remained by His Imperial Majesty's side, thinking to myself, "I am just a blade of grass. How can I be standing here alone beside him?" His Imperial Majesty read the stone inscription on the western wall and read the poem "On a Visit to the Grove" by the Ming official, Pi Mao-k'ang.[66] When finished, he asked me, "Are you indeed thirty-six years old?" I replied, "Your servant is." "Can you write poetry?" "I did study some poetry." Then I knelt to receive the imperial command but his heavenly countenance smiled with delight and ordered me to rise several times. He dispersed the awesome air of the surroundings; sovereign and minister became like father and son. That in one day he should have thrice inquired after my age is truly an experience of a lifetime.

I then conducted His Imperial Majesty into Commemoration Hall and he asked, "What famous inscriptions are there on the walls?" I answered, "They are all inscriptions by people of the Sung and Yuan dynasties." He looked at all of them, then sat down in the middle of the Hall facing south and asked, "How large is the Grove?" I said, "In all, about two hundred and seventy acres. During the past two thousand years, the clan has multiplied and there is little room left for gravesites." "What do you plan to do in the future?" "We have no choice but to bury people closer to each other." "Why not expand the area?" "Your Imperial Majesty's concern would be fortunate for the myriad generations of descendants in your servant's clan. Yet outside the Grove is registered land belonging to others. Though we wish to expand, we cannot. We longingly await Your Majesty's blessings."

His Imperial Majesty turned to an attending official and uttered a few words with a smile, then turned and said, "You may petition this matter." The Duke led myself and others in kowtowing our gratitude. He then proceeded out of Commemoration Hall, entered the palanquin, and exited through the gate, turning westward toward Yen-chou as the Duke led myself and others in kneeling by the left side of the road. A eunuch Libationer came over and asked me, "Do you know what His Imperial Majesty said in the Commemoration Hall?" I answered, "No." "He said, 'What cheek this Licentiate has! He knows how We reverence the Foremost Teacher so he keeps on making all these requests. But since We are visiting his home, We have granted whatever he asks.'" I felt grateful for His Imperial Majesty's genial and forgiving grace and wept as I followed him along the road. I related this incident to whomever I met.

We returned to the city around 4 p.m. and went right into the Hall of Poetry and Ritual to await the announcements, by the President of the Board of rites, of the imperial gifts. To the Duke of the Sagely Posterity, the Erudite of the Classics, and the Magistrate of Ch'ü-fu went copies of the lectures on The Great Learning and The Book of Changes. The Duke was given a fox-trimmed formal robe embroidered with pythons, a black sable jacket, and five bolts each of silk for outer shell and lining. The Erudite, Magistrate, and the descendants of the Four Ancestors who were listed in the records of the gentry--in all thirty-five people--received a sheepskin robe each with embroidered pythons and a cotton jacket with embroidered pythons. To those descendants of Confucius who held the Metropolitan Graduate, Provincial Graduate, and Senior Licentiate degrees--in all eleven people--were given cotton-lined damask robes with edged collars and sleeves and cotton-lined jackets. To those who were students in the Imperial Academy or held the Licentiate degree--in all three hundred people-- were given five silver taels. The people of Ch'ü-fu were exempted from corvée labor and land taxes for the following year. My place was with the latter group of students and so I also received five taels. All kowtowed at the Temporary Palace to express their gratitude.   Then the Duke departed for Yen-chou first in order to arrange the farewell.

That night, I returned home, bathed, and then lit incense in a ceremonial announcement to the ancestors.   I knelt beside my elderly mother and related the day's events.   She was so moved by the kindness of His Imperial Majesty that she suddenly began to weep.   Dinner was being served when two messengers arrived from the prefectural capital bringing an order from the Duke: "His Imperial Majesty is in the Western District outside Yen-chou and has asked for K'ung Shang-jen.   Hurry!"   I spurred on my horse and galloped off, arriving at the Temporary Palace at about 10 p.m.   His Imperial Majesty had not yet retired and was commanding the Grand Secretaries Mingju and Wang Hsi to look up the proper ceremony and prepare a formal announcement and ritual sacrifices, dispatching Prince Kung[67] and President of the Board of Rites Chieh-shan to return to Ch'ü-fu in order to sacrifice at the Temple of the Duke of Chou.   The Duke led myself and others present in expressing thanks.

From outside, I could see into the Palace where there was a table with candles over four feet high. His Imperial Majesty took off his headdress and leaned on the table to write a commemorative placard for the eightieth birthday celebration of the Duke's grandmother, Lady T'ao of the First Rank.   The Duke and others were kneeling at the bottom of the steps.   In a short while, the inscription "Her Virtue Matches That of the Immortal Pine" was completed.   Attendants held it up for all the officials to view. The calligraphy ascended like a dragon and soared like a phoenix; the ink was suffused with fragrance. I was ordered to read it aloud as the Duke and his younger brother knelt and received it, performing three kowtows. By the time it was all over, the drumtower had struck 1 a.m. That night, when I returned home, I had barely fallen asleep when I had to rise again. At dawn the next day, which was December 24, we escorted His Imperial Majesty on his journey northward. As we proceeded along the road, all the accompanying officials pointed to me, saying, "This is the Licentiate who lectured'; and each evening I joined the Duke in attendance at the various Temporary Palaces, where we were rewarded with gifts of tea.

We set out early on the morning of the 26th, stopping to rest at an ancient temple along the way. His Imperial Majesty looked up and ordered a mounted escort to come over and ask, "Who is this group of people?" "The Duke of the Sagely Posterity K'ung Yü-ch'i and others, here to escort His Imperial Majesty," we replied. He also asked, "Is the lecturer K'ung Shang-jen here?" "Yes, Sir, he is." The escort reported back and in a while attendants brought each of us a present of a cup of tea. That day, I met various officials in the Board of Personnel who were sitting about on the side of the road. They saw me and said, "We were just about to call you here. Today we are deliberating on who to appoint as Head of the Hundred Households. Who would be suitable?" I consulted with the Duke and wrote down the present incumbent Ch'en Chih-shih's name on the document. Then I submitted it to the officials of the Board.

The following evening, I went by the tent of the Grand Secretary Wang Hsi. He received me with proper hospitality, treating me quite warmly. Soon he clasped his hands in a polite salute and said, "Your great genius has attracted the beneficent notice of our sovereign to a degree beyond that of other officials. Today we were discussing appointments on his Imperial Majesty's orders. Your ability and your future is most promising. Truly, you are to be congratulated." I replied, "Our sovereign is the Son of Heaven ruling over myriad lands who has sacrificed to the Sage of myriad ages. This had been an unprecedented occasion. That I, a mere blade of grass, should have been able to participate in this grandeur is itself a thing of matchless glory. How dare I harbor such reckless thoughts that a deliberation of official position might result from imperial grace?" At this, His Excellency Wang displayed a solemn respect.

A day later on the journey, I saw the officials of the Board of Personnel seated about again as before and they called out in loud voices, "Today we are discussing K'ung Shang-jen's official position." I got down from my horse and clasped my hands in a salute, thanking them without saying a word. That night I met the Grand Secretary Wang Hsi, who told me, "It's already been decided. Before long, you'll be an Erudite in the Imperial Academy." I was overjoyed with gratitude and said, "In the Han and T'ang dynasties, Confucian scholars who were employed because of their knowledge of the classics were all granted the title of Erudite. Although my talent and learning scarcely deserve mention, our sovereign's method of granting office may be said to accord with tradition."

On the 28th we spent the night at Te-chou, and the next morning His Imperial Majesty boarded a boat to enter the capital. The Duke led myself and others in kneeling to bid farewell on the western bank as His Imperial Majesty, leaning against a window, stroked his whiskers and ordered us to return home. On January 3rd, we arrived back in Ch'ü-fu.

An official announcement arrived on January 5th:

"The Ministry of Personnel on Instructions from His Imperial Majesty Has Deliberated and Issues the Following: That on this Southern Tour, during which a visit was made to the Sagely Precinct and the Foremost Teacher was sacrificed to in the Temple in a grand ceremony, there were ordered lectures on the classics to exalt the sagely teachings and encourage Confucianism in order that this occasion, so rare in history, may indeed be distinguished as a grand celebration of Our flourishing dynasty. K'ung Shang-jen and K'ung Shang-li have expounded the texts and fulfilled their sovereign's expectations. It is right and proper that they should not be bound by the conventional practices, but rather be appointed Erudites of the Imperial Academy outside the usual quotas. This matter has been submitted and approved."

On February 20, 1685, I left for Peking and on March 1st I was installed as an Erudite. On March

11th I was assigned to the examinations, where I temporarily became an official in the Bureau of Copying. After my service in the examination halls was finished, the Libationer Weng Shu-yuan[68] assumed office. He knew that I had personally lectured to His Imperial Majesty and set up a lectern in the western part of the Hall of Moral Relationships. Striking bells and beating drums, he assembled several hundred students from the Eight Banners and fifteen provinces, who sat down around me and formally bowed thrice while I sat under a yellow canopy in front of indigo fans and lectured on the classics. I held three such lectures a month, and when it was over I distributed the texts to the students. At that time, everyone was praising it as a grand event.

The Duke of Sagely Posterity was just then in the capital to thank His Imperial Majesty and I joined the lower ranks of his entourage. At a banquet given him by the Board of Rites where the President, Chang Shih-chen,[69] was host, I enjoyed the wine and feast of high officials and viewed the entertainment of their professional actors.

Such rare experiences encountered by a bookworm seem to me to be beyond my destiny. I can only hope to render the service of a dog or horse until my teeth fall out. Yet, somewhere in my dreams is the memory of the mountains; as yet unforeseen is the time when I can hug the pine trees again. If Stonegate has a spirit, has it forgotten me? Or is it calling to me? (K/425-37)

Chapter Three

BY SOUTHERN LAKES AND SEAS

You bid farewell
  at Yellow Crane Terrace
And sailed down to Yangchow
  in the month of misted blossoms.
The distant shadow of your sail
  vanished with the green hills,
Leaving only the river
  flowing into the horizon.--Li Po, "Seeing Off
Meng Hao-jen on his Journey to Yangchow"

K'ung's mood abruptly shifted after he settled down in
Peking. The initial euphoria subsided and he found himself
tied to a routine which was less challenging than he had
anticipated. Though flattered by the Emperor's attentions
and the warm welcome given him by his colleagues, he
gradually realized that he was more venerated as a living
symbol of the Confucian tradition than empowered as a man
of action. Little further contact with K'ang-hsi and the
light, bureaucratic duties he was assigned as an Erudite
left him unoccupied and restless; but he did not remain
idle for long. The following year, he was asked to join
the staff of Sun Tsai-feng[1] who had been placed in charge
of an important river control project. Sun, a Chancellor
in the Han-lin Academy, was the one who advised K'ung on
his lecture to K'ang-hsi and he had been much impressed by

his talents. Now promoted to Vice-President of the Board of Works, he was to become K'ung's principle political patron for the next few years. From late 1685 through 1689, K'ung traveled south, journeying extensively along the rivers, lakes, and deltas in the Huai-yang area of Kiangsu. In what he regarded as the most stimulating and fecund period of his creative life, he visited numerous historic sites, met a cross section of literati society, and produced his most famous poetry collection--all while energetically involved in the complexities of river control.

The Ch'ing inherited awesome problems with the river system for the dikes not only were extensively damaged from the conquest but were also suffering from a half century of poor maintainence by late Ming administrations.[2] With the drastic shift of the Yellow River back to an earlier path in 1644, Shun-chih officials found themselves plagued with severe floods every few years. The situation only worsened during the early K'ang-hsi reign with a particularly severe flood in 1662. More followed nearly every year after that, with the most catastrophic one in 1676. Thirty dams were destroyed at Kao-yu and the river overflowed into the Grand Canal, Lake Hung-tse, and the Huai River. The damage from this flood spread as far as Yangchow, seriously affecting economic activity.

Ch'ing experts recognized, to a greater extent than their predecessors, that the perennial flooding was a comprehensive problem involving the entire system formed by the Yellow and Huai Rivers, the Grand Canal, interlocking tributaries, and the large lakes in central Kiangsu.[3] Ever since the Yellow River had dramatically shifted its course southwards over five hundred miles in the Sung, the huge amounts of silt deposited in its lower reaches increasingly affected the hitherto placid Huai. This silt, comprising as much as 70 percent of the current, reduced the depths of the waterways joining the two rivers, causing overflows, back-ups, and diversions. Under one of the late Ming plans, the clear water of the Huai was to meet the Yellow River at Ch'ing-k'ou near Ch'ing-chiang (modern Huai-yin) and help flush the silt out to sea via Yun-t'i-kuan. But the extensive hydraulic system had never operated properly. Every rainy season brought new damage, rendering the entire effort of river control a Sisyphean labor. K'ang-hsi himself took great interest in the various projects, not only because of their vital importance to the shipment of food supplies to the capital but because of their staggering expense, which he once estimated as running over three million taels.[4] On each of his southern tours, he made it a point to inspect specific construction sites so as to gain a first-hand view of the problems which politicians endlessly debated at court.

In 1676, the year of the most severe flooding, a special commission under Isangga[5] presented recommendations to K'ang-hsi resulting in the appointment of Chin Fu,[6] then Governor of Anhwei, as Director-General of the Conservation of the Yellow River. Chin Fu took office in May 1677 and emphasized the comprehensive nature of the problem, urging construction not only in areas crucial to shipping but wherever required in an overall plan. The hundred-mile stretch from Ch'ing-chiang to the sea was identified by him as the critical area and he shifted headquarters to that city from Chi-ning in Shantung. Chin found that decades of silting at Ch'ing-k'ou had backed up the waters and raised Lake Hung-tse so that the city of Huai-an lay below water-level. In some places, the river's depth was a precarious 2 to 3 feet, threatening the Grand Canal and, ultimately, the middle reaches of the Yellow River in Honan and Shantung. To alleviate this, Chin Fu proposed a set of eight policies which, despite occasional political reversals, remained the basic approach through the rest of the K'ang-hsi reign.[7]

Chin enjoyed the Emperor's confidence until 1681 when, after three years of massive construction, the Yellow River had still not returned to its pre-1644 path. Under criticism, he offered his resignation but was allowed to continue supervising construction. The following year, however, further breaks in the dike system led a Lieutenant Governor, Ts'ui Wei-ya,[8] to submit a 24-point plan which called for a reversal of Chin's policies. Isangga was again asked to investigate and submitted a report critical of Chin's faulty construction, voicing little confidence in his proposals. Then, in 1683, the river suddenly returned to its earlier course enabling Chin to defend his programs and gain reappointment. On the 1684 Southern Tour, K'ang-hsi was generally pleased with what he witnessed at Kao-chia-yen and publicly praised Chin Fu.

While inspecting the sites, the Emperor became aware of the suffering of the people in the seven districts around the lakes in central Kiangsu. This led him to appoint Yü Ch'eng-lung,[9] then Prefect of Nanking, to drain the area in 1685. Yü, promoted to Judicial Commissioner of Anhwei, ran headlong into his nominal superior, Chin, and the conflict was aired at a lengthy debate in Peking in December. Yü advocated dredging the waterways and widening the river mouth; Chin, believing the area was below the water-level, was for construction of dikes and water gates to divert the flow out to sea via Hsing-hua. Others at the conference voiced a variety of differing views. President of the Board of Works, Samha,[10] and Governor of Kiangsu, T'ang Pin,[11] ascertained local sentiments, reporting that the people in the Kao-yu and Hsing-hua areas feared further flooding might result and were opposed to both plans.

Later, T'ang Pin, in an audience with K'ang-hsi, came out
in support of Yü Ch'eng-lung and blamed Samha for the
negative report. The displeased Emperor demoted Samha and
budgeted 200,000 taels for Yü's plan.

It was this particular project which Sun Tsai-feng was
put in charge of.[12] Like Yü, he advocated dredging rather
than dike construction, working on existing river paths
rather than opening up new ones, and concentration on the
lower reaches of the river. K'ung was given leave from the
Imperial Academy to serve on Sun's personal staff. His
duties would send him traveling to the various construction
sites acting as liaison man from headquarters and as a
front-line inspector, reporting back directly to Sun. With
a renewed sense of mission, K'ung set out for the south in
August 1685, bound for Yangchow, which was to be his
headquarters for much of the next four years. The
following month, he reached the banks of the Yellow River
and expressed his thoughts on the eve of the enterprise:

> Crossing the Yellow River
> I waver anxiously -- which plan
>   will save this cultivation? --
> As I stop my horse at the edge of the bank
>   and call to the ferryboat man.
> White geese fly over the September marsh;
> Yellow silt glows by the lonely sunset town.
> Widen the river south at Ch'ing-k'ou
>   and divert the Huai?--ineffective.
> Build dams at Yun-t'i-kuan to the east,
>   flushing it out to sea? -- expensive.
> Who can control the onrushing flow
>   which passes through this place?
> For when autumn winds begin to rise
>   we river officials grieve. (K/8)

THE CITY OF MISTED BLOSSOMS

The Yangchow which K'ung sailed to was unquestionably the most vibrant city in China at that time. Divided into two walled parts comprising old and new cities, it was encircled on three sides by the Ts'ao river; along the fourth side, to the southeast, ran the Grand Canal. Thus, favored by geography, and embellished with a rich, historic past, it had made a striking recovery from the effects of the Manchu conquest, continuing its rise to unprecedented heights of prosperity and cultural distinction. Barely three decades before, the city lay in ruins as it suffered the brunt of the conquerors' revenge for its stiff resistance. Shih K'o-fa,[13] as Govenor-General, had shifted his headquarters there in 1645 to coordinate the final defense of the Nanking Restoration. Beginning on May 9th, the city held out against attack for almsot two weeks only to finally fall in a panic resulting in Shih's martyrdom. Then, from the 20th to the 29th, the fury of the Manchu soldiers was unleashed against the defenseless population.[14] Yangchow remained a center of loyalist sentiment for years afterwards. Many survivors, some of whom lived to the end of the century, bore bitter memories of their suffering and maintained only a surface tolerance for the new order. The depth of anti-Manchu feeling among such people may well have persuaded the K'ang-hsi Emperor to avoid the city on his first Southern Tour. Among the younger generations, however, the Yangchow holocaust was a historical event which people heard tales of or read about in memoirs. By K'ung's time, Shih K'o-fa's memorial on Plum Blossom Hill had become a popular scenic spot where sightseers returned for the lighthearted pursuit of money, beauty, and pleasure.

This other image of Yangchow--as the center of southern sensuality--was rooted in the city's long history of

prosperity antedating such rivals in the area as Hangchow,
Nanking, and Soochow.   In the late Spring and Autumn Period
(722-481 B.C.), King Fu-ch'ai of Wu (r. 496-73 B.C.) took
note of the favorable location of the area, crisscrossed by
small, navigable streams between the Yangtze and the Huai.
Upon gaining control of the territory in 487 B.C., he
extended the Han Canal linking these two large rivers.
Thus began the Grand Canal, and the city of Wu on its banks
became the commercial hub of the area.[15]

It was under the viceroyship of Yang Kuang, later Sui
Yang-ti (r. 604-18), that the city was transformed from a
frontier outpost of the empire into an important economic
and political center.   Aided by the further extension of
the canal system in 587 and the shifting of the Buddhist
establishment from the Ch'en dynasty capital of Chien-k'ang
(modern Nanking), Yangchow reached a new level of
importance as one of the three capitals of the Sui.[16] Yang-
ti was truly the founding spirit of the city.   The events
of his life and the places he built were immortalized in
popular mythology and his image endowed the city with
several characteristic themes in literature: the conversion
of the northern conqueror to southern culture; the extravagant decadence of a "bad-last" ruler; and the tragic fall
of aristocratic taste and beauty.[17]

By the T'ang, Yangchow was already the economic center
of the south and a required stop for officials on their
journeys.   Few poets who passed through failed to avail
themselves of its famed sources of inspiration and its
pleasures, flocking to be near influential patrons.   The
young Tu Mu was celebrated for his sojourn in 833 when he
came to serve as a Secretary to the Imperial Commissioner,
Niu Seng-ju.[18]   Tu Mu's nighttime exploits were later the
subject of Ch'iao Meng-fu's tsa-chü, A Yangchow Dream,
which dramatizes his love affair with the courtesan Chang

Hao-hao. The aria which Tu sings upon arriving in the city captures the impressions which visitors have felt through the ages:

> (To the pattern of "The Roiling River Dragon")
> The scene remains unchanged
> As songs and sounds by the western bamboo[19]
>   Waft through old Yangchow.
> A crescent moon above
> And miles of pleasure houses.
> With verdant water
>   In fragrant ponds
>   Where jade skiffs float;
> With pearl curtains
>   And embroidered drapes,
>   fastened by golden hooks.
> Where a hundred twenty merchant firms
>   are headquartered;
> And eighty-four thousand romantics
>   add luster.
> The Hall Level with the Peaks[20]
> And the Pavilion of Kuan-yin--[21]
> Where idle blossoms grow amid rustic grass.
> The Pool of Nine Turns[22]
> Little Gold Mountain--[23]
> Where egrets bathe and terns nap.
> Horse Market Street
> Rice Market Street
> With crowds like herds of dragonish stallions.
> The Temple of Heavenly Peace,[24]
> The Temple of Universal Peace--
> Where people congregate thick as ants.
> Within the tea houses
> Breezes waft
> Through the pines
> And spicy, crisp "phoenix marrow" is served.

Upstairs in the winehouses

"The Cassia Moon" is sung

By oriole voices to sandalwood clappers.

From front-hall parlors

To the back chambers

Are lined stairs shaped like horse-hoofs.

I approach the carved balustrades,

Enter jade doors

See windows shaped like tortoise shells.

Dewdrops from gold basins,

Dewdrops from hortensia flowers

Are fermented into fine wines.

Mandarin mutton,

Willow-steamed mutton--

Are caterings of rare delicacies.

Gaze at the football game

Where they keep their sleeves dropping

As they stand stiff-shouldered kicking.

I love the entertainment quarters

Where they have a talent for singing

And marvelous dancers, comedians, and musicians.

They have come from the capital each wearing

   light gauze wrapped up in rare brocades.

All arranged by age

As they tune up the strings and play lively pipes.

Night and day, the party carries on

As patrons dispense ten thousand taels of gold

   to purchase a woman's smiles,

Throw away a hundred lengths of red brocade

   to coif a courtesan.[25]

In the late fifteenth century, Yangchow entered its greatest period of preeminence, lasting some four hundred years until the T'ai-p'ing rebellion. The breakup of the old salt-grain exchange system led to the rise of a new

breed of capitalists composed of local producers together
with Shansi bankers and Huichow merchants. These groups
formed the salt-monopoly system where, under close imperial
control, some thirty large families presided over several
hundred smaller ones in the exploitation and shipping of
this vital commodity.[26] By the early Ch'ing, the merchants
had accumulated an immense amount of wealth, second only to
the imperial household. In the characteristic style of the
city, they dispensed it with an unrivaled talent for
extravagance. This grew, in part, from a sense of
inferiority to the literati. Although the salt merchants
did not suffer from official discrimination as did other
merchants, they were well aware of the traditional attitude
which ranked those who engage in trade with the lowest
social orders. Like many newly rich, they set out to
achieve by display the virtues which established families
cultivated over generations.

Li Tou, who surveyed the Yangchow scene during the
first half of the Ch'ing, wrote:

> The Yangchow salt merchants used to compete
> with each other in extravagance. They gave
> funerals and weddings where they spent several
> hundred thousand taels for the food, decorations,
> gowns, and carriages . . . there was the one who
> wanted to dispose of 10,000 taels of gold all at
> once. A guest of his spent the money on pieces of
> gold foil which he carried up to the top of the
> pagoda on Gold Mountain. These he threw to the
> wind, and in an instant they were dispersed among
> the grass and trees, impossible to recover.[27]

But this amusing stereotype of vulgar eccentricity has
perhaps been overstated.[28] Yangchow could boast of
possessing the same elements on which neighboring cities
based their claims to aristocracy--an old, landed gentry, a

long, distinguished history, and the commitment of leading
families to the support of cultural life. Among the
merchants were numerous discerning bibliophiles who over
generations built up libraries and published major
anthologies. Others were discriminating patrons of the
arts who assembled painting collections and hosted poetry
gatherings. The city abounded in tasteful mansions such as
the Rainbow Bridge Garden,[29] an important salon where the
talented from all over the nation could associate, and a
lively literary life centered around independent poetry
societies.

The effect which the rise of the merchants had on
Yangchow society was less a case of a nouveau riche
achieving dominance over former elites than a blending of
the traditional stratifications. Aristocrats, officials,
gentry, scholars, soldiers, merchants, artisans, and
performers crossed economic, political, philosophical, and
class lines to a greater extent than ever before. This was
particularly true after the Manchu conquest when the
dislocation of war encouraged new alliances. The old
elite, anxious to preserve its privileges, entered into
symbiotic relationships with those who had come to the
forefront under the new dynasty. It was no longer unusual
for official families to develop ancillary commercial
operations, nor was it outlandish for merchants to adopt
literati tastes and purchase degrees. This process of
expansion and overlapping of legitimate social roles was
more pronounced in Yangchow than anywhere else. It stamped
the city with a particular brand of individualism, upward
mobility, and hedonism catalyzed by a high-velocity social
life.

In such an environment, the theater flourished. There
were actually several kinds in the south but it was the
literati and commercial theaters which K'ung came into

contact with most often.[30]   A number of his friends were
wealthy enough to maintain their own troupes, as elite
society expected them to do, for not only were dramas
essential to private banquets but a well-trained troupe was
a standard of cultural distinction.   One such friend, a
former Secretary in the Grand Secretaiat named Yü Chin-
ch'üan, maintained a troupe of female actresses.   They
performed both dance and drama and on one occasion, Yü
contributed them to a gathering hosted by K'ung.[31]   Not
only leading individuals but institutions such as the
Liang-huai Salt Merchants Guild also supported troupes.[32]
There were frequent opportunities to view performances.
These were held on red carpets spread out in the villas of
the great, at famous sights about the city, in government
office compounds and in one of the four major temples which
contained fixed stages.[33]   K'ung Shang-jen left a number of
poems in which he mentions attending both official and
private performances; and he frequently stayed at the
Temple of Heavenly Peace which had the most active public
stage.

The commercial theater represented a far more diverse
situation, composed of independent troupes presenting a
variety of forms.   Some stayed in the city, others toured
the area or migrated from the hinterland.   These were
contracted to perform for the general public, largely in
teahouse theaters, on open-air stages, in the temples, and
at private affairs.   The performers of commercial troupes,
like their counterparts in the literati theater, were
segregated into all-male and all-female troupes, ostensibly
for moral purposes.[34]   However, they were considered less
accomplished; most were purchased young from poor families
and were dependent on their masters for their well-being
and training.   The most talented might hope to own their
own troupes someday or be purchased by literati patrons;

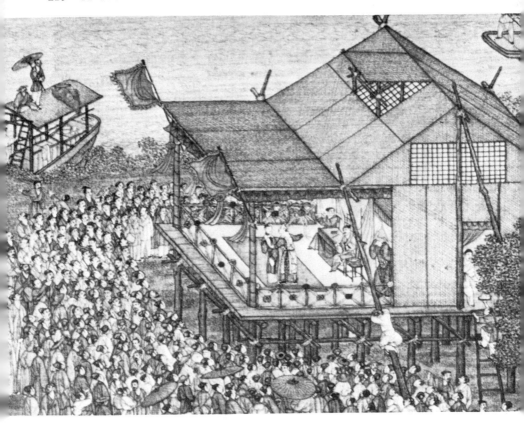

An Outdoor Commercial Theatre

A Formal Performance of Literati Drama

the others were condemned to a hard life of economic exploitation and, not infrequently, ill-treatment.[35]

In addition to the social distinction, there was a considerable stylistic difference between commercial and literati troupes. The literati, in general, preferred the K'un-ch'ü style, which had gained popularity during the late Ming. First developed in the mid-sixteenth century by Wei Liang-fu in K'un-shan, Kiangsu, it synthesized several local forms into a musical system characterized by soft, flowing melodies and subtle intricacies of breath control in singing.[36] By the Wan-li period, K'un-ch'ü had attained the status of the "elegant sound (ya-yin)" in the south and in such major northern cities as Peking, becoming the preferred choice among elite entertainments.[37] During the first decades of the Ch'ing, the style suffered a setback in popularity due to the destruction of theatrical centers such as Yangchow and the disruption of the patronage system. K'un-ch'ü was only beginning to recover by K'ung's time, a trend which his own play was considered to have facilitated.[38]

The commercial theater offered a cruder version of K'un-ch'ü with few of the fine points which interested connoisseurs. The bulk of their repertoire consisted of a variety of local forms, of which the most important was the I-yang[39] style. I-yang had stepped into the vacuum created by the temporary decline of K'un-ch'ü. It gained a large measure of acceptance and eventually came to coexist with it in some theater programs. Kiangsi was its geographic center, from which it spread along the trading routes of merchants from that area who enjoyed patronizing it on their travels. More percussive musically than K'un-ch'ü, it came to be associated with traditionally "northern" aesthetic characteristics—robustness, speed, military virtue, simplicity. It was possible to perform the texts of K'un-ch'ü plays to I-yang melodies, the differences being primarily musical and linguistic; however, commercial I-yang largely used texts from oral literature, or stories based on contemporary events in society, rather than elite literary sources. Despite its growth in influence, it continued to be regarded as "popular singing (su-ch'ang)" by many southern literati who not only appreciated the superior artistry of K'un-ch'ü but relished the nostalgic association of it with late Ming romanticism.

Because I-yang had already spread north by the late Ming, it was one of the first forms of drama which the Manchus came into contact with. They generally preferred it, finding it more entertaining and comprehensible than other styles. The story is frequently recorded of the dramatist Juan Ta-ch'eng performing I-yang rather than K'un-ch'ü for the Ch'ing soldiers in Fukien during the conquest.[40] By the first decades of the early Ch'ing, it became acceptable to perform I-yang at literati gatherings, at least in Peking, where Manchu taste was most influential.[41]

Linking both literati and commercial theaters was the courtesan world. Accomplished beauties formed the natural pool of talent from which young performers were purchased for both kinds of troupes. The finest were thought to come from Soochow, the center of K'un-ch'ü, while Yangchow also had a reputation for its alluring women. The ability to sing arias or play an instrument was part of a courtesan's training on the middle and upper levels of the profession. At the very top, some of the elite courtesans were as famous as noted household performers. They were the companions of the literati and were unwilling to sing for the general public, appearing only at intimate gatherings. A few achieved the ideal goal of being redeemed by their wealthy lovers to become concubines. The majority of courtesans were less exclusive and entertained a wider clientele on the pleasure boats, in the garden restaurants, and in the houses of the gay quarters. The latter neighborhoods were the real home of the theater where a cross section of society gathered. The houses functioned as important institutions, supporting performers, engaging teachers to train them, and presenting them to the client-audience. In Yangchow, the largest gay quarters were in the western part of the New City, along the Little Ch'in-huai Canal, named after its more renowned counterpart in Nanking.[42] This and such areas as Peony Alley and Twenty-four Bridges[43] were year-round centers not only of pleasure but of artistry.

Chang Tai, the inveterate observer of such scenes, recalled:

> The romantic scene by Twenty-four Bridges in Yangchow is still unchanged beside the Han Canal. About a quarter of a mile beyond the long wall at Ch'ao-kuan are nine alleys where about a thousand people weave in and out along the right and left. The entrances to the alleys are narrow and winding. Standing neatly alongside each other are intricate, secluded houses where famous courtesans and prostitutes dwell. The famous courtesans within never appeared themselves and one required the services of a guide in order to gain entry. Then, there were about five or six hundred prostitutes. Every day towards evening they would come out to the entries of the alleys, all perfumed and made-up, and loiter and squat by the teahouses or taverns. This was called "manning the gates."[44]

Upon arriving in Yangchow, K'ung enthusiastically plunged into the social whirl. No place could have been more different from the provincial, introverted world of

Ch'ü-fu.   Long starved for recognition and anxious for artistic stimulation, he was dazzled by the opportunities to meet the leading lights of the time and set about announcing his presence.   Not long after arriving, he paid tribute to the <u>genius loci</u> in a poem:

<u>Yangchow</u>

It's fitting that Wang Shih-chen[45] served
 in Yangchow,
A worthy follower of the romantic Tu Mu.
The winehouses have multiplied by
 Twenty-four Bridges
But their names are still mentioned before
 the Hall of Thirteen Chambers.
No willowy beauty stands idle in the
 painted boats they knew:
And their oriole voices would seem familiar
 if they passed their windows once more.
Then there was the talented hand
 who composed a <u>fu</u> on Wu-ch'eng[47]
And those fine lines on "misted blossoms"[48]
 which even romantics must acknowledge.   (K/10)

It is worth noticing that, as the poem indicates, K'ung chose Wang Shih-chen as one of the models for his social identity.   Although the two were not destined to meet for several more years, Wang's reputation appealed to K'ung as one of the most successful literatus-officials of the age. Both men were from Shantung and talented poets.   In Yangchow, twenty years earlier, Wang had gained fame while serving as a police magistrate and went on to a meteoric career in the capital.   He became a great patron of talent and through his poetry and criticism exercised a major influence on the literary scene for over half a century. Yangchow well remembered Wang for his famous gathering at the Rainbow Bridge Garden in 1662, a site which K'ung frequently visited and later chose for one of his own gatherings in conscious imitation.[49] While K'ung's background and official position gave him entrée to old Yangchow society, it was his talent, enthusiasm as a host, and capacity for sympathetic friendship with Ming loyalists which enabled him to quickly attract the leading artistic lights of the city. His social circle, evident from an active correspondence and from the attendance at his frequent parties, shared a commitment to the aesthetic values of late Ming romanticism and cemented their bonds in poetic expression.

POETIC ACTIVITIES

Toward the end of 1686, K'ung hosted his first soirée in his official residence.

A Poem Written at a Gathering at My Yangchow
Villa in December, 1686 at Which We Wrote Poems
Listening to the Rain . . .[50]

The notables at this elegant affair
    were all in scholar's caps.
From north and south of the Yangtze River
    my intimate friends have gathered.
We wrote poems for each other to the drips
    and drops as the rain made its entrée;
Then the candle was trimmed, all became quiet,
    watergreens were served.
Hearty drinking urged us on
    to reveal our innermost selves
And prolong the moment
    for only our sensibilities are real.
Their pouches filled with jeweled phrases,
    all sailed off with the wind.
Henceforth people will want to take note
    of what we wrote at Han-kuan. (K/18)

Preeminent among the guests was Mao Hsiang. Few people
in the south better symbolized the late Ming than the
75-year-old survivor. His official career thwarted by the
peasant rebellions during the Ch'ung-chen reign, he went to
Nanking where he became active in Fu-she circles. He and
three other friends--Hou Fang-yü, Ch'en Chen-hui, and Fang
I-chih--became known as the "Four Esquires"[51] for their
cultural and political leadership in the city. They were
particularly influential during the final years of the Ming
as leaders of the opposition to Juan Ta-ch'eng and Ma Shih-
ying[52] and were victims of a bloody purge when the latter
faction gained power at court. With the conquest, Mao and
his family were forced to flee their estate in Ju-kao, and
lost a considerable part of their property, an escapade
described in his widely read memoir, <u>Reminiscences of the
Studio of Shadowy Plum-blossoms</u>.[53] After the establishment
of the Ch'ing, Mao's refusal to associate with the new
dynasty increased his prestige among loyalists. In later
years, his economic fortunes revived and he spent his time
in travel, entertainment, and aesthetic pursuits. He
excelled in poetry and calligraphy, and maintained an opera
troupe in Ju-kao. Despite his advanced age, he continued
to be active in literati circles and eagerly sought the
acquaintance of younger friends.

K'ung regarded the senior Mao with awed reverence and
at the beginning of their friendship wrote to him in a
letter:

> You are an elder from the fallen dynasty, of a
> constantly lofty and placid demeanor. Knowing you
> is like facing a statue engraved by the ancients,
> like gazing at a bronze vessel from an earlier age.
> (K/506)

A passion for collecting art was one of the bonds the
two men shared. In his youth Mao's patron had been Tung

Ch'i-ch'ang and he had assembled a vast collection housed in his library, The Hall Infused with Fragrance. This building had tragically burned in 1679 but a painting by the late Ming artist Kuan Chiu-ssu was among those saved. It was presented to K'ung by Mao Hsiang's son, Tan-shu, bearing a colophon written by his father in praise of K'ung's connoisseurship.[54] Mao relished the role of living legend and enjoyed indulging in recollections of the late Ming days. The two must have had many conversations about the past, especially during the month when Mao accepted K'ung's hospitality at Chao-yang.[55] Perhaps Mao informed K'ung about the character of Hou Fang-yü, whom K'ung recreated as the hero of The Peach Blossom Fan, as well as about details of the key events in the rise and fall of the Nanking Restoration. Mao died in 1693, six years before the completion of the play, but K'ung obliquely mentions him in Scene 4. Based on an actual incident, Mao, along with his fellow "Esquires" Fang I-chih and Ch'en Chen-hui, is reported as criticizing a performance of a play written by the villain, Juan Ta-ch'eng.[56]

Also present at this gathering were the poets Huang Yun and Teng Han-i, two of K'ung's closest friends in Yangchow. Huang was another of those who fit the personality type of the "heroic loyalist" which K'ung found so appealing. He was politically reclusive, having rejected government service under the Ch'ing. Somewhat impoverished, notoriously eccentric, yet extremely erudite and dynamic, he expressed a proud, defiant attitude towards life's vicissitudes. K'ung went out of his way to pay him a visit even before arriving in the city and remained lifelong friends with him and his two sons. Among poetry circles, Huang was quite active. He claimed influence from Wang Shih-chen when the latter was in Yangchow and his two poetry collections were widely read in the area. K'ung, in his poems and letters to him, often alludes to Huang in terms ordinarily need to describe unrecognized sages and regarded him as typifying a southern tradition of tragic fate and mystical transcendence going back to Ch'ü Yuan. We may assume that Huang's poetic style absorbed something of Wang's metaphysical theory; K'ung praised his works as displaying "a method beyond methods, and a flavor beyond flavors."[57]   Here is one of Huang's most widely read poems:

Upon Hearing a Wu Song While Spending the Night on a Boat at Liang-ch'i[58]

A rooster crows through the mist--
sounds of clanging oars.
I roused myself from wine-laden dreams
before the dawn appeared.
Only after the southern scene faded
Did I hear the first strains of a Wu Song.[59]

The recreation of poetic experience to suggest spiritual enlightenment, identification of the poet's intuitive being with an impressionistic view of nature, and a mood of inspired encounter with mystical truth are characteristic techniques of the metaphysical approach. Huang combines this with an allusion to the dynastic change in the fading of the southern scene, positing an ironic release from both history and nature.

Teng Han-i was also from T'ai-chou, a place which seems to have produced more than its share of strong individualists. Although he refused to attend the Po-hsueh hung-tz'u examination of 1679, Teng later accepted a nominal position in the Grand Secretariat.   He was a central figure in Yangchow poetry circles for several decades, tirelessly traveling about to attend gatherings. In addition to producing seven collections of his own, he edited an influential series of four anthologies, Poetic Perspectives, which remains an excellent source of

early Ch'ing poetry in the south. While staying at
Yangchow, Teng frequently put up at the Tung Chung-shu
Temple in Little Ch'in-huai where K'ung visited him on one
occasion, bearing a sheaf of his poems for inclusion.[60]
Teng's friendship was important in easing K'ung's way into
artistic circles and he printed 15 of K'ung's poems in the
third series of Poetic Perspectives, which appeared in
1689. The two had an easygoing relationship, as can be
seen from several of K'ung's informal and humorous letters.
Teng, was, in fact, mortally ill at the time. Kung only
saw him for half a year in Yangchow and when Teng returned
to the city in October 1688. He died later that year,
before K'ung could secure some rare medicines for him from
a salt-official.

Huang and Teng, together with a third poet-friend,
Tsung Yuan-ting,[61] jointly edited K'ung's first and most
famous collection, Poems from the Lakes and Seas. The
work, in 13 chüan, contains 644 poems, 46 essays, and 222
letters, covering the Yangchow years from 1686 to 1689.
Well over a hundred friends are mentioned. The title
probably derives from K'ung's transient life during these
years, when his inspection duties required frequent travel
along the waterways and long periods of residence on
boats.[62] In their prefaces dated 1688, Huang and Tsung
make much of the public K'ung--his Confucian background,
study of ceremonial forms, lecturing to K'ang-hsi; the
river control work; and Tsung gave some indication of how
he regarded K'ung's style by describing it as "having the
quality of far-off antiquity and a clean elegance,
somewhere between Wang Wei and Kao Shih."[63]

But what were K'ung's own ideas about poetry? Like
most Chinese poets, he presented his work to stand on its
own, rather than as examples of a particular theoretical
program. He lacked the modern artist's enthusiasm for

endless self-reflection and rarely adopted polemical stances. A cross section of his closest poet-friends reveal many who did not share K'ung's ideas. This not only suggests a lack of missionary zeal on his part but indicates that he did not define his poetic circle in terms of a uniform style. In part, this may be due to his emphasis on character in poetry. K'ung read other poems primarily as expressive communications rather than as texts to be critically analyzed. What remarks he did make are scattered in the prefaces to collections of fellow poets, written during these years in Yangchow. They were the random reflections of a practitioner designed to guide others onto the proper path in their own work; they focus on attitude rather than on product, on meaning rather than on technique.

K'ung did live in a period, though, which saw the growth of criticism. Leading literati such as Wang Shih-chen were prolific in publishing comments on poetry to be read by their inner circle as well as the widening amateur public.[64] The latter group in particular formed a readership in need of authoritative methodologies and devoured works by congnoscenti. This trend was aided by the highly social nature of Chinese poetry, centered on poetry clubs which encouraged theoretical debates and definitions of style.[65]

K'ung was somewhat skeptical of an independent criticism which was not based on the experience of creativity. He suspected that pure speculation would lead to proliferating discussants rather than producers of poems. Later writers, overawed by prestigious theories, not only would fail to measure up to the ideals of the original proponents but would neglect to explore the true range of their own talents:

I seem to notice how people nowadays prefer
discussing poetry to reading poetry and, moreover,
steal what others have said in making their own
remarks. After a while of this, even those who
enjoy readiang poems will believe their ears
instead of their eyes if a poem is not highly
regarded by contemporary criticism. A pity!
(K/474)

Since he was a noted figure who enthusiastically
participated in the social aspect of poetry, it may seem
surprising that K'ung voiced strong opinions about the
nonartistic motivations of many whom he encountered. He
had ample opportunity to survey the variety of poets of his
time on many levels--from the intimate circle to the formal
poetry clubs to official occasions. His reaction to what
he observed in the two major cities he resided in suggests
that K'ung's sense of artistic purpose was, fundamentally,
intimate and elitist. He viewed poetic motivation as a
delicate maiden easily compromised by diversions towards
inauthentic goals:

Peking and Yangchow contain the most poetry critics
in the world, yet in the time I have spent in these
places I have never seen a single poem from them.
In poetry, the aim is to attain a correct
expression of one's natural sensibility (hsing-
ch'ing). If one's intention is diverted by common
concerns, then the entire principle of the thing is
lost. All in the world, as soon as they learn a
little something about poetry, decide to visit
Peking and Yangchow. Why? They say, "to be nearer
nobility" and "to be closer to wealth." The nobles
of Peking ride in palanquins surrounded by giant
fans; every day servants front and rear call out to
clear the road for them. Visitors from all corners

Fang Shih-shu and Yeh Fang-lin,
The Literary Gathering at a Yangchow Garden

of the empire try to attract their attention so that they can advance as high as the clouds. How could anyone who sees this not admire and seek to serve them? So the poems they write are mostly in praise of these nobles. Is this a perfect expression of their natural sensibilities?

The wealthy of Yangchow have amassed an immense amount of property and they live in grand mansions. Even their accountants, clerks, slaves and servants dress up in flashy clothes, putting on airs in order to snub others. If one waits around at their gate, one may be able to beg a few droplets to feed wife and children. How could anyone who sees them not feel envy and thus try to befriend them? So the poetry they write is mostly in praise of wealth, and they are even less concerned with natural sensibility. (K/476-77)

The key phrase in these remarks is hsing-ch'ing, which has also been translated as "nature and emotions," "personality," and "innate sensibility." As with many terms in Chinese poetics, the meaning is often determined as much by contextual usage as by its lexical components. An early appearance of the expression occurs in the late-fifth-century work, The Literary Mind and the Carving of Dragons. In the chapter titled "Emotion and Style," the author, Liu Hsieh, writes of hsing-ch'ing as meaning the inner feeling which gives rise to expression and he gives it priority over verbal ornamentation both in the process of composition and in critical value. Elsewhere in the same work, in the chapter on "Style and Nature," hsing-ch'ing indicates the essential personality of the writer as the determining factor in stylistic orientation.[66]

K'ung was heir to both senses but, being closer to the influence of late Ming romanticism, emphasized hsing-ch'ing as the essential qualities of an individual nature revealed in a state of inspired feeling. In this, he is close to Yuan Hung-tao, whose related concept of hsing-ling (personal nature) denoted the authentic self of the writer.[67] If we could draw a fine distinction between the two poets it would be in the greater ethical content of the concept for K'ung. Yuan associated hsing-ling with pien (transformation) and felt that artistic truth was revealed in the differentiating qualities of a poet and his style.

The emphasis on the communicative aspect of poetry was an important part of K'ung's understanding and explains why, despite his criticisms above, he remained a very social artist himself. A considerable portion of his output was written for a specific coterie of readers and he found a variety of group occasions suitable for expression:

There are many ways to find friendship but poetry is the most immediate, for it is the sound of our emotions. If we join in together chanting, we can distinguish each other's natural sensibilities (hsing-ch'ing). By contrast, presenting gifts of cloth to show one's esteem is as far removed from it as the momentary from the enduring. Although I have but recently made the acquaintance of gentlemen in Yangchow, everyone communicates through poetry. Whenever a poem reaches my house, I look for the person it reveals even before considering its technique. Many are the differences between worthy and unworthy characters; were it not for poetry, how could we arrange each according to kind? Technique or the lack of it are also far removed from each other; without poetry how could we sum up their conduct? In the past, when people read poems or books, they emphasized the character of the writer. Isn't it true, though, that it is easier to discuss the work than understand the person? (K/473)

From the point of view of the poet's inner experience, the emphasis on hsing-ch'ing appears as a theory of pure expressivism in which fundamental value is placed on the act of verbalizing interior states; from this perspective, the communicative function almost vanishes as a source of meaning in the ecstasy of the moment:

Nowadays, people who write poems do not write them in order to be sung in temples, the court, or at formal banquets. Though distinguished formally as "ancient style" and "recent style," they are all "airs." By "airs" I mean that they express one's innermost feelings and intentions rather than praise great deeds or laud virtue. Personae such as a man at toil, a lonesome wife, a survivor of a fallen dynasty, or a misunderstood official can be invoked at will. They are no more than subjects fit for conveying one's feelings. Whether or not the poem is passed on by later generations is of little concern, let alone whether or not contemporaries read it. (K/473-74)

Here, K'ung further reveals his affinities with the late Ming program of authenticity in literature. The precedence given personal values over public, or formal ones, the spontaneity of creation and catholicity of subject matter reflect the kind of romantic ideals of the Kung-an school and those influenced by them. K'ung equated hsing-ch'ing with chen (authenticity) and contrasted this to excessive technique, relegating the latter to the realm of externals:

In prose before 1684. the "outer skin" was dominant but such skin, being false, depended on powdery embellishment. There was hardly time left for

other efforts. In prose after this date, natural
sensibility (hsing-ch'ing) triumphed. For natural
sensibility is authentic (chen) and, being
authentic, the Hundred Philosophers and the Six
Arts can aid the writer; there are no principles
which cannot be incorporated. Poetry is
particularly close to prose in this respect.
(K/478)

K'ung is nowhere too specific as to what constitutes
external inauthenticity: nonartistic motivations as well as
imitation of archaic styles are seen as inhibiting factors
in poetic realization. K'ung was quite aware, however, of
the need for an external correlative to balance the inner
focus and he does not, in any final sense, advocate an
expressivism devoid of the universe beyond the self. In
this regard, a natural scene serves as the proper
correlative, the evocator of response and source of images:

Painters are classified into northern and southern
schools and poetry is similar. Northern poetry has
the quality of enduring profundity but its flaw
lies in its exaggeration; southern poetry is supple
and sensual but its defect lies in its
extravagance. Although one may master these
styles, he would not be able to completely capture
the vital energy of natural scenery. For scenery
is the root of a poet's natural sensibility. He
gains spirituality from the clouds and mists,
refinement from the flow of the springs, solidity
from the hills, vigor from the forests, mists and
fires in the marsh. If a man can't write poetry
then there's nothing more to be said, but if he
can, then he will have to obtain these things. If
he writes a poem and is still unable to attain
them, then it is because he doesn't express his own

ideas but imitates others. If this becomes a habit he will never find his way back, and though he may encounter a natural scene, it would not aid him. This is what I mean by defects of "exaggeration" and "extravagance." (K/475-6)

What finally places K'ung's views on poetry in a wider perspective and prevents his expressivism from becoming too inward is his belief in the Tao as underlying poetic experience. From the point of view of the ultimate value of poetic experience, the poet's identification with the Tao is given precedence over critical values which derive from the text. At the same time, as a practical matter of interpretation, the poet's demonstrated understanding of the Tao and the objective elements which constitute style are granted a coequal status and are actually indivisible in the reader's comprehension of the poem.

The most regrettable thing in life is not to have understood the Tao--far more regrettable than not succeeding as a writer. One should read the classics of the ancients in order to study their Tao; even if one doesn't master their literary style, the Tao will still be apparent. Nowadays, some just study style and do not bother to inquire about the Tao or think that the Tao will be realized if they only imitate a style to perfection. This is how Tao and style have become two different things. After a while, style will no longer be based on Tao. The Tao will decline and style will be unable to function on its own. Even if a forest of literati produce a hoard of poems in rivalry, knowledgeable readers will proclaim them unworthy of attention. . . . If the Tao is present, then style will be present. Is not the mastery which comes from studying the Tao the same as that which comes from studying poetry, and he who understands the Tao the same as he who understands poetry? (K/472)

K'ung's discussion of Tao in literature requires some clarification in the context of early Ch'ing literary theory, particularly with regard to whether or not he was primarily a "pragmatist." The K'ang-hsi period witnessed a growing emphasis on literature as a vehicle of ethical values. Citing the orthodox Confucian interpretation of The Book of Poetry, these writers read symbolic content as a didactic guide to human relationships and a referent of good and evil. The function of literature, in their view, was to influence the readership towards moral cultivation and positive social action.[68] Although this movement did not reach full maturity until the T'ung-ch'eng School of the eighteenth century, it already possessed spokesmen in K'ung's time. He was familiar with the work of some of them, such as Shen Han-kuang, and was especially close friends with a student of Shen's, T'ien Wen.[69] Certain recent mainland critics have tended to overemphasize the above passage and attempt to classify him in the "Pragmatist Movement (Tsai-tao-p'ai)," reinforcing this by citing certain realistic and materialistic tendencies in his poetry and drama.[70]

To be sure, K'ung's concept of Tao included pragmatic considerations just as his appreciation of character blended individualism with moral stances such as Ming loyalism. But the range of his poetic oeuvre and critical remarks do not support this as the sole center of his poetic consciousness. The Tao he speaks of is deeply spiritual as well and denotes an awareness of the entire universal process, a process perceived as much in nature as in society or history. That he maintained associations with poets of pragmatic views is no more definitive of his own standpoint than his connections with metaphysical intuitionists such as Wang Shih-chen, who in some respects stood at the opposite theoretical pole. To limit the significance of K'ung's poetry to pragmatism is to overlook the essential ambivalence of his nature, which comprehended a range of dualities. The territory he charted overlapped the borders of pragmatism and maintained affinities with the metaphysical position while its real domain was the expressiveness of his romantic sensibility as he sought to comprehend the meaning of historical events. It is in the light of this expressiveness that such distinctive tendencies as his realism and his sense of tragedy and irony should be viewed, as we shall see when considering some of the poems themselves.

These remarks of K'ung's indicate some of his theoretical orientations but they do not reveal much about the distinctive qualities of his own style. We can begin to point out some of these by focusing on his attitude towards scene. As he stated above, K'ung believed that the conjunction of scene and a poet's natural sensibility were the essential elements leading to the expression of emotion. Moreover, he felt that this communion was largely beyond will or predetermination, being a chance occurrence arising during the poet's lifelong exploration of the world:

Yangchow possesses the best of northern and southern scenery. Worthies wander by, choose a garden, and organize a gathering in the manner of the ancients, believing that what they write will certainly be passed on. Yet how quickly it fades into the void. On the other hand, one or two bohemians happened to encounter the moon and mist and produced some poems which they thought hardly worth saving. Yet it seems these are still remembered today. So I know that when man encounters a scene, whether the result is worth transmitting or not depends on chance. (K/439)

A cycle of 24 chueh-chü poems has been preserved, reflecting K'ung's varied emotions upon viewing Yangchow's famous sites. They were written towards the end of his stay in 1689 and are like album-leaves, mininature perspectives reflecting a particular mood upon contemplating some aspect of the past. These may well have been connected with the work of a close poet-friend, Wu Ch'i,[71] whose Prefaces to Songs on Scenic Spots in Yangchow contains prose descriptions of many of the same places. Fourteen of the more significant ones are translated here, along with the brief prose descriptions which K'ung himself prefaced to them. As a group, these poems reveal a sense of place suffused with the presence of time and events. It could be said that the central tendency of K'ung's literary oeuvre is to explore the various relationships between these elements and the self-in-the-present. On the broadest level, this is charted in mythic dimensions where time's boundaries are extended to the hoariest antiquity and the event is a cataclysm of cosmic proportions. In the first poem of the series, K'ung seeks guidance from the spirit of the Sage-king Yü.

Floating Mountain

Located within the city of Yangchow, the mountain appears to be level with the plain; thus, legend has it that it is the very heart of Heaven and Earth. On top, a temple to the Sage-king Yü has been built.

Again I worship at the Temple of Yü

There is no trace of his divine success.

How can one grasp this convulse of nature

Where Earth engulfs the mountain's crest? (K/166)

Yü was traditionally considered the founder of the Hsia dynasty (c. 2205-1600 B.C.) and is an appropriate spirit for a river-control official, for he was credited with the first successful efforts to regulate the Yellow River. Yü thus represents the ability to understand and control the Tao of nature, surely the most difficult of man's aspirations. The problem is presented in terms of the archetypal duality of Heaven and Earth basic to the Book of Changes' view of cosmic transformation. The implicit question is how to achieve a lasting equivalence between the two, hence the significance of Floating Mountain. The scene resembles hexagram eleven, T'ai (Harmony), where Earth is rising upward and Heaven moving downward, forming a harmonious bond. Underlying this strange equilibrium is a sense of the terrible moment which forged this unique scene. The poet's response to such magnitude is largely beyond intellect and, seemingly, even human understanding. Yet the scene itself is a symbol of hope and inspiration confirming that, among the 64 possible permutations of change, such a balance is indeed possible.

The remainder of the poems are concerned with human events in historical time. Some deal with events of political, social, and moral significance, others with events of aesthetic or literary moment. The relationship of the poet to each of these scenes is more problematical and ranges from a sense of isolation to identification with the living spirit of the past. In the first group of poems, his emotions are weighed with tragedy as he observes the disparity between an idealized world and a concrete present.

黃河縈塞天山路玉勒金貂侍獵年風骨乍傳新照夜鬚眉不數

舊凌煙誰知學士嫻鞍馬卻許將軍愛賦篇好績蜀機三丈錦揮

鞭直肯射鵰還　　近體應

修翁先生教　　　　　里弟孔尚任

A Poem by K'ung Shang-jen

大華山水居然大癈電煙
兄動神韵獨究宇宙者卧榻
可省登嶠筋力感〻

尚任頓首

An Informal Letter by K'ung Shang-jen

The Yangchow Tide

It is referred to in Mei Ch'eng's _fu_, Seven
Inducements. There is no record of its earlier
path but legend has it that it ran east of
the old city wall of Kuang-ling.

Day and night the River Han flows on,
Its former banks no one can remember.
The music ceases on the official barge:
A sudden cold sweat
As I huddle in my cover. (K/166)

The Eastern Hall

Where Ho Hsun wrote his praise of the plum
blossoms; now part of the prefectural
office.

When did such inspiration fade
From the Hall stacked with accounts of
    revenue?
Where the moon shines on the plum blossom
    trees
Ho Hsun now collects taxes due. (K/166)

The Pavilion West of the Bamboo

In old Yangchow, the place where music and
song were performed, located west of the
Temple of Ch'an Awareness.

The courtesans of Yangchow
Were upstairs every day.
It's empty now, the music and song are over--
Not even a soul to hear the
    bamboo sway. (K/167)

The Hortensia Temple
It is the old Temple of Prosperity, where
the hortensia flower withered long ago.

The hortensia is a flower of misfortune,
A treasured symbol of Yangchow's fate.
It died and the Sui Palace burnt,
Gazing at it leaves one agape.   (K/167)

Twenty-four Bridges
Where Sui Yang-ti often visited, now gone.

The old bridge can no longer be seen,
Though I search for the moon of that date.
Where is the flute sound coming from?
In the middle of the night,
   so desolate.   (K/168)

Thunder Pool
Where Sui Yang-ti is buried, located in the
Encircling Citadel.

Flowers fill up Thunder Pool.
In the ample Spring rain, frogs sound croaky.
For ages, those who grabbed for fish
Have latched onto white bones
   with algae.   (K/168)

The Hall Level with the Peaks
Where   Ou-yang   Hsiu   and   Su   Tung-p'o
entertained.

The old Hall still looks out on the scene
But those venerables are no longer about.
Just the roaming city kids
Seeking a place to hang out.   (K/169)

Plum Blossom Hill

Magistrate Wu P'ing-shan built the hill and
planted plum blossoms on it.   Grand
Councillor Shih K'o-fa's official uniform
is buried there.

The blossoms have withered
    and the hill crumbles.
I come to stand and utter sighs.
The water flows on down the hill
As the general's uniform putrifies. (K/170)

In several poems, the mood is one of desolation caused
by the perception of discontinuity. This is a function, in
"The Yangchow Tide," of a loss of memory. As the preface
indicates, the River Han exists in the literary mind of the
elite but most other people have forgotten the path of this
earliest of Yangchow's recorded landmarks. The poet rooted
in the concrete world experiences an acute sense of anxiety
over this irony: if the patternings of literature are
designed to correspond to reality, should he not find the
two to be in closer conjunction within the Tao?   The
ceasing of music is a frequent motif in K'ung's poems and
its interpolation into the middle of the scene is a
dramatic touch, at once positing the existence and
extinction of ongoing life.   The relationship of the
components in this scene are somewhat reversed in "Twenty-
four Bridges" but the mood remains the same. An initial
absence is evoked by the complete disappearance of the
original bridge where courtesans used to gather.   The
continuous flow of sounds here gives definition to this
space and underscores the theme of the impermanence of
beauty and taste.

In "The Pavilion West of the Bamboo," even the physical
survival of a building and human memory are not enough to
counter the sense of absence. The pavilion was still well-

known in K'ung's day and was frequently used as a site for poetry gatherings. But it appears to K'ung as a shell devoid of the gaiety which he imagines characterized Tu Mu's day a thousand years before. Even the knowledge of past pleasures cannot make up for the melancholy of the solitary poet. In the preface, the term "Ch'an Awareness" in the name of the nearby temple offers more than a factual context. It expands the mood to the borders of Buddhist contemplation and implies the potentiality of a spiritual solution beyond the lines of the poem itself in the extinction of desire.

K'ung expresses his pervasive sense of irony about a grander past and a reduced present with sardonic humor in "The Eastern Hall." The poet Ho Hsun's love of plum blossoms represents the finest inclinations of man's spirit. He wrote a poem on these flowers near his residence in Yangchow which gave rise to a number of legends. According to one of these, so attached to them was he that when later posted to Loyang, he requested transfer back so he could continue to enjoy them. Upon his return, they were just in bloom and he hosted a gathering at the Eastern Hall in celebration.[72] The conceit of Ho transformed into an accountant is K'ung's wry comment on human progress, whereby human creativity is seen as dulled by the mechanical demands of economics.

"The Hall Level with the Peaks" is a similar statement of time's diminishing effect on man, here perceived in terms of the present void of artists of stature. The Hall is an appropriate site from which to contemplate grandeur. The distant mountains to the south appear level with the Hall when viewed from the terrace, thus giving visitors a sense of ascension and an encompassing vision. As Confucius himself stated, journeying to a lofty place impelled one to create. The power of this scene is

heightened by the meeting there of Ou Yang-hsiu and Su
Tung-p'o, two towering spirits of the literary pantheon.
When K'ung visits it, however, his realism impels him to
confess his disappointment and punctuate it by the contrast
between the aura of the two great writers and the crass,
lazy indifference of the younger generations.

If time's flow erodes great events and drains a place
of its accumulated meanings, it can also be a cruel force
exacting an eternal, merciless revenge. The sight of
fishermen latching onto Sui Yang-ti's bones in "Thunder
Pool" is a gruesome view impressed upon the reader by the
contrast with images of amplitude and fulfillment in the
first two lines. Here the scene wears two faces: the
surface mask of the seasonal renewer of life; and the
darker visage of natural decay and revenge. The latter is
revealed in a gothic manner, as Yang-ti is unknowingly
dismembered by the descendents of those he ruled in a place
which he often journeyed to with his favorites.

The fall of the Sui is a frequent subject of K'ung's
reflections; Yang-ti could hardly fail to appear in poems
on a city he so impressed with his personality as builder,
Emperor, sybarite and, finally, failed hero. No doubt, his
figure suggested to K'ung vainglory--that of a man who,
after conquering the known world, watched it crumble
quickly with fatalistic amazement. Though Yang-ti's self-
indulgence is implicit in the moral significance of his
fall, K'ung seems more fascinated with him as a towering
example of the impersonal workings of destiny.

A correspondence between nature and the Sui dynasty's
fate is suggested in "The Hortensia Temple," which K'ung
was later to choose as a site for one of his most important
gatherings. It was a neglected place in his day, somewhat
off the beaten track for visitors. The legend that the
flower died simultaneously with the fall of the Sui

intrigued him as a mysterious example of the conjunction of
nature and history.   The simple compounding of the two
levels of events in line three presents a blunt fact which,
when contemplated, leaves the poet with an ineffable
reaction.

The fall of the Sui, of course, is a convenient
substitute for the fate of the Ming as well.   However,
K'ung was not reticent about expressing loyalist sympathies
on acceptable topics.   In "Plum Blossom Hill," K'ung writes
of Shih K'o-fa, who, as the city's defender in 1645, had
become the most celebrated of Ming loyalists in Yangchow.
Local legend had it that he had heroically jumped into the
Yangtze after the battle and died uncompromised, by his own
hand.   The Ch'ing did not go to any great lengths to
discourage local reverence for Shih, even though he was
actually captured and killed for refusing to surrender to
the Manchus after the city fell.   Though his body was never
found, his uniform was interred on Plum Blossom Hill.
K'ung shared the local feeling for Shih and led a
charitable effort to erect a Confucian academy near the
memorial.   The poem, written around the same time, seems to
strongly lament the slipping away of Shih's memory among
the local inhabitants forty years afterward.   Here, water
symbolizes the natural Tao eroding the moral Tao as the
man-made hill suffers the fate of change.

If historical scenes are largely a source of tragedy,
K'ung is not without the literatus' traditional
consolation.   In the second group of poems, the immortality
of letters and the imagination's visionary power enable man
to find a bulwark against the effects of time.

The Tower of the Literary Anthology
Where Prince Chao-ming edited the Literary
Anthology, located in the Temple of the

Banner of Loyalty.   I heard that there is
another such place in Hsiang-yang.
Poetry and prose issued forth
From this very tower, rising a
  hundred feet.
Where stood the palace of the
  Liang Dynasty?
All that remains
  is the Prince's seat.   (K/167)

The Winehouse at Red Bridge
Located along the Little Ch'in-huai Canal.
Wang Shih-chen often partied here when he
was a police magistrate.   He wrote a tz'u,
"Seductive Spring," which many recite.

Red Bridge's fame is quite recent,
Attracting revelers out beyond the
  city wall.
Wang's poem is fine
And the local wine,
  not bad at all.   (K/170)

Tung Chung-shu's Well
In the former residence of Master Tung, now
the Salt Bureau.

The great Confucian never had time to taste
The spring which bathes the vegetables.
Now it belongs to a salt official
But its flavor remains
  mild and venerable.   (K/167)

Jadehook Slope

It lies west of the city, where beauties of
the Sui Palace are buried.
Wild plum trees shade neglected tombs.
No human sounds,
   just the autumn hoppers' cries.
Those powdered, perfumed
   beauties underground
Have become fragrances
   which from the grass arise.   (K/168)

Peony Hall

Located   west   of   the   Temple   of   Ch'an
Awareness, where Magistrate Han Wei one day
gathered with Wang Ch'i, Wang Ching, and
Ch'en Hsiu to enjoy the "golden cinctures"
peonies.

Some guests happened to be served some wine
And it became a feast of ministers.
Where the flattering peony flower
Stepped forward to offer
   "golden cinctures."   (K/169)

Ch'un-yü's Residence

Located west of the Monastery of Heavenly
Serenity, it is where Ch'un-yü Fen dreamt
of the realm of Nan-k'o.

Autumn's rain splatters
   the ancient dwelling,
Fallen leaves cover the oak root.
The Grand Illusion is hard to dispel
And lesser dreams,
   unworthy of dispute.   (K/166)

In 'The Tower of the Literary Anthology," the well-known
collection of Han and Six Dynasties literature edited by
Prince Chao-ming is a far greater monument to human
civilization than a dynasty.   The irony in this case is
reassuring to the poet, validating his own efforts and
including him in the company of the true survivors.   "The
Winehouse at Red Bridge" is a lighthearted celebration of
life's pleasures and the satisfactions of society.   Once
again, K'ung pays homage to Wang Shih-chen and in doing so
consciously participates in Yangchow's ethos as he gains
for himself a place in the city's mythology.   "Tung Chung-
shu's Well," relates literary immortality more closely to
character.   Water is here equated with the enduring moral
Tao--that of the Confucian tradition of Tung Chung-shu as a
canonical saint; commerce, in the form of the flamboyant
salt merchants, is unable to alter his essential qualities
of purity and understatement.

   Beyond even the enduring existence of words is the
power of the mind.   "Jadehook Slope" and "Peony Hall" are
both pure realms of the poet's vision in which he
celebrates his imagination's control over reality.   The
mood of the former, on a potentially tragic Sui theme, is
sublime in the resurrection of the palace favorites as
fragrances.   The image of plum blossoms, with their
associations of beauty, perfume, and the survival of
winter, frames the poet's solitude and dissolves death in
the aromas of life's process of transformation.   Time is
overcome in another manner in the latter poem, which stands
at the opposite pole from his poems of tragic irony.   Here,
the past event is fully reexperienced as the simple act of
drinking wine establishes contact with a moment of literary
glory.   The wealth of cultural consciousness is unlocked as
it expands to occupy the full space of the present moment.

Transcendental sentiment is voiced in "Ch'un-yü's Residence." Though the place has no historical authenticity, it was well-known through both fiction and drama as the setting for his dream on the vanity of worldly ambition. It prompts K'ung to express his escapist longings in the language of Taoist poetry. Leaves now cover the roots of the tree, obscuring the route by which Ch'un-yü journeyed and gained enlightenment. Thus, K'ung notes the tendency of time to draw the quester further into complexity and away from the simple intuition into universal truth. Though himself imprisoned by desire, there is a certain solace gained even as he recognizes the continuing gap between the human condition and spiritual attainment.

In K'ung's poems, there is an inescapable impingement on the poet's consciousness of the actuality of a scene—its concrete detail as well as its traditional meanings. In many of the tragic poems, this is something which the imagination cannot totally deny or overcome. It immobilizes the poet within a set of painful recognitions for which there is no clear solution on the same level of representation. This focus can be seen to constitute a basis for the realism of his work. But unlike those writers who may be more absolutely defined in this way, it does not reflect a firm conviction on K'ung's part as to the sole truth of this perspective. Rather, it tends to suspend him in ambivalent attitudes both towards this state and towards the alternatives—romanticism and the classicism of Confucian ethics. In his search to resolve the dilemma of an existence which seems devoid of a genuine spiritual structure, he is more inclined to create composite visions incorporating all three levels.

Another aspect of realism, that of the representation of a set of social or material conditions of life, has been applied to K'ung's poetry.[73] This has created a misinterpretation of the role which such poems actually play in his oeuvre. As a river control official, he was deeply committed to humanitarianism and public welfare, but in his role as a poet, such concerns were overshadowed by his historical meditations. Moreover, the motivation for such works is less one of active protest than the expression of sympathy, detachment, or bemusement. The following poem, for example, treats the subject of the arrogance of officialdom. But what emerges is less an indictment of the ruling class than a certain irony in the poet's suggestion that it is the extremity of the beggar's suffering that enables him to endure oppression and maintain a shred of self-respect.

The Posthouse Beggar

A high mandarin is ensconced in the
    imperial posthouse
Sputtering at a lesser one who fails
    to bow quickly.
Thousands swarm just to get a glimpse.
A path must be cleared in front of him.
Assistants stand in embroidered robes,
    at attention
While a beggar in rags is arrested.
He sees the mandarin but does not bow.
The mandarin glares at him, furiously.
How could he know that the beggar
    was starving?
For the beggar accepts poverty
    but will not suffer shame;
Innocent, why should he bother with
    mandarin protocol? (K/83)

An unusual event which was the source of a long poem was a local murder of passion. The poet here adopts the

tone of a balladeer as he describes, step by step, the
events leading to the gruesome crime. The first two lines
contain three characters each while the rest are in five
characters and rhyme every other line. Thus it has the
rhythm of oral literature. Such devices as the day-by-day
enumeration of a sequence of actions and the interpolation
of a poetic interjection on peach blossoms give the piece a
strong narrative character. In fact, the subject matter
and its treatment are reminiscent of some of the short
stories in the collections of Feng Meng-lung. There is a
similarity in the revelation of human desires, the
representation of the world of ordinary people, and the
"dual-allegiance" of the writer to both the individual
psyche and the moral code.[74] K'ung perceives the irony in
the situation--the name "Ch'ing-chiang," meaning "Pure
Stream," stands in contrast to the pollution of adultery;
and yet he also expresses a covert sympathy for the woman,
implicitly recognizing, like Feng, the legitimacy of human
needs and the tragedy of being trapped by the social order.

The Woman of Ch'ing-chiang

The woman of Ch'ing-chiang

had been cast into the bushes.

Did anyone sigh out of pity for her?

"She should have died sooner," they cursed.

Her door stood opposite the Buddhist temple.

The monk was her husband's close friend.

The two often visited

And the woman seemed like a sister-in-law.

But she was a young duckling from southern waters;

He, a Kalaninka bird from the Western Seas.

They spent the nights and even the days

Until gradually, everyone heard of it.

Her husband chased her out.

Her brother was vexed in secret.

The first day, the wife stopped eating.
Early she rose the next day.
On the third, she finished washing
And then slipped out the door.
Her brother searched for her at her husband's.
Her husband inquired at the temple
Where, deep in the winding recesses,
He found her stretched out on a couch.
Husband and brother, speechless,
Bound and cast her into the watery depths.
Oh, those beautiful floating peach blossoms
Which a fisherman found by luck.
But the husband had revenge in his heart,
Dragged her back home and cut off her head.
The bushes could not conceal her body.
No one removed the blood stains.
Everyone who passes by asks about it
Annoying the old woman next door.   (K/125-26)

FRIENDS-IN-PAINTING

In addition to poets, another important group of
friends with whom K'ung associated during this period were
painters. The connection between painting and literature,
particularly poetry, has always been close in China.[75] Not
only were both considered forms of artistic patterning
(wen) in the broader sense but each, in its own sphere,
often attempted to capture the values particular to the
other. Through the centuries, poets have often appended
colophons to paintings they admired, while painters have
been inspired by the verbal scenes in poems. In rare
cases, both talents have appeared in a single individual to
a high degree as in Wang Wei, one of the great T'ang
landscape poets and the traditional founder of the orthodox
school of southern literati painting. Su Tung-po's well-

known phrase about Wang, that there was poetry in his
painting and painting in his poetry, expresses the ideal
conjunction of the two arts. Socially, both writers and
painters often mixed, the spontaneous creation of painting
being as much a part of a literati gathering as the writing
of verse, opera singing, or musical performances.[76]

The area bounded by Mt. Lu to the west, the Yangtze and
Yangchow to the north, Hangchow to the south, and the sea
coast to the east, has been termed the "eye-area" of
Chinese painting.[77] Overlapping the provinces of Kiangsu,
Chekiang, and Anhwei, it contained many of the inspiring
scenes which served as subject matter in landscape painting
and had nurtured most of the major artists since the
Southern Sung. During the Wan-li period (1573-1620), a
fundamental redefinition of literati painting occurred
through Tung Ch'i-ch'ang which was to influence painters
throughout the seventeenth century.[78] Tung's theory and
stylistic innovations revived the fatigue which had begun
to pervade the traditional painting centers of Soochow (Wu)
and Hangchow (Che) by the late Ming. Following the
practice in Ch'an Buddhism of distinguishing between
northern and southern schools, Tung and his associates
defined a southern tradition going back through the Wu
school through the Yuan masters, to Chü Jan and Tung Yuan
of the Five Dynasties and finally Wang Wei as patriarch.
This was contrasted to a northern tradition which Tung saw
as represented by the rival Che school whose style had
largely descended from the academic painters of the Sung.
He articulated again such basic ideals of literati painting
as the kinesthetic representation of Nature's vital spirit
(ch'i-yun sheng-tung), the attitude of learned amateurism,
and most importantly, the calligraphic basis of
brushstroke. The decorative, mimetic, and descriptive
values of academic painting were disparaged by him as

characteristic of the professional craftsman. On the highest creative level, painting was a representation of the inner self, executed in an effortless, spontaneous attitude of freedom.

Through his teaching and his works, Tung's vision of southern painting influenced succeeding generations of artists. A number of individualists interpreted his traditionalism in a highly intuitive and personal sense while a school of orthodox masters arose which more closely reinterpreted past models. The cultural conditions of the early Ch'ing encouraged a kind of painter which has been termed the "professional amateur,"[79] that is, someone who maintained a philosophical allegiance to the literati ideal of art as self-cultivation while producing works on a commercial basis. Such artists were most at home in Yang-chow, with its wealthy patrons. The newly rich with their exhuberant tastes supported certain nontraditional values in painting, such as brilliant colors, striking compositions, rapid execution, simple subject matter, large and miniature formats--in general, works which were more stimulating visually than intellectually. Almost all the major artists of the period passed through the city at some point in their careers. Even those who were more conservatively schooled often adapted to popular taste, leading to an admixture of styles and a wealth of cross influences.

K'ung, as river official and as private traveler, visited many of the creative centers in the "eye-area" and had more opportunities to meet artists while residing in Yangchow. He himself did not paint and, though accomplished in small-scale, regular, and seal-style scripts, did not seek renown as a calligrapher either. But as a life-long collector, a scholar of ancient bronzes, and a social poet, K'ung found painters convivial acquaintances.   Several were among his closest friends. The twenty-eight figures who are mentioned in his poems and letters ranged from orthodox masters to individualists, further attesting to his catholicity of taste.[80]   They not only shared insights on connoisseurship and exchanged poems but also accepted commissions from him.

Among some of the notable artists with whom he came into contact were Wang Hui, Tao-chi, Cha Shih-piao, Tai Pen-hsiao, and Kung Hsien.   K'ung's connection with Wang Hui,[81] perhaps the greatest of the orthodox masters of the seventeenth century, seems to have been primarily a sharing of interest in connoisseurship.   During the two decades that he was under the tutelege of Wang Shih-min, another great master and follower of Tung Ch'i-ch'ang, Wang Hui traveled widely through the area, viewing and copying works in private collections.   By the time he and K'ung met, Wang Hui not only had achieved his "great synthesis" which was to make him a favorite painter of K'ang-hsi, but had developed one of the most discriminating eyes.   In the catalog of his collection, K'ung mentions a blue-and-green landscape by Chao Meng-fu which his "friend-in-painting," Wang Hui, borrowed to enjoy for a number of months.[82]

There is a bit more evidence of K'ung's relationship with Tao-chi,[83] whom he greatly admired.   Tao-chi was a member of the Ming imperial family, the son of the Prince of Ching-chiang whose fief was in Kwangsi.   He was but four when Peking fell, and shortly after he was orphaned when his father was murdered by rival loyalists.   Through the help of a family servant, he managed to escape and subsequently entered the Buddhist faith for safety.   During the next few decades, Tao-chi wandered throughout the "eye-area," engaging in "journeying 10,000 li and perusing 10,000 volumes" as was recommended for the education of a painter.   Famous sites along the artistic routes were absorbed into his memory and he came into contact with many Anhwei and Nanking masters. The early 1680s were spent in the former Ming capital, largely in seclusion; however, there too he met such leading artists as Tai Pen-hsiao and K'un-ts'an and was also introduced to the K'ang-hsi Emperor on the latter's 1684 tour. By the late 1680s, Tao-chi had gravitated to Yangchow, which was to become his base for most of his remaining eyars. This period, during which he met K'ung, marked the beginning of a new phase in his development, for his increased social activity led to important contacts with influential patrons, both Chinese and Manchu.[84] The opening up of opportunity later resulted in a long visit to Peking and, upon his return to Yangchow, in such important turning points as his renunciation of Buddhism, the turn to professionalism, and his acceptance of Ch'ing rule.

Tao-chi was the greatest of the individualists, with a forceful artistic personality transcending the confines of imitation and conventional allusion. His command of a wide range of subject matter included not only landscapes but bamboo, orchids, plum blossoms, and the kind of colorful vegetable and flower compositions popular in Yangchow. Both the more meticulous modes and the spontaneous "free-style (hsieh-i)" were practiced by him and he mastered clerical, regular, and running styles of calligraphy. It is common to contrast Tao-ch'i's approach to the orthodox tradition. Such radical statements of his as "The beards and eyebrows of the ancients cannot grow on my face nor can their lungs and bowels fit into my body; I express my own lungs and bowels and display my own beard and eyebrows"[85] create the impression of a talent nurtured without reliance on tradition, with few roots in antiquity. In fact, he continually engaged in close study and copying of past models and was as inspired by these as the orthodox masters

were. Although his paintings leave few overt traces of
borrowed mannerisms, his writings often refer to the
influence of Ni Tsan, Huang Kung-wang, and Wang Meng, among
others. His calligraphy benefited from a careful study of
Chung Yu, Ch'u Sui-liang, and Shen Chou as well. Tao-chi
shared with Tung Ch'i-ch'ang and his followers the
fundamental belief that achieving a profound spiritual and
stylistic identification with the works of antiquity was
one of the keys which unlocked the secrets of depicting
nature's vital energy. Where he differed from Wang Hui,[86]
for example, was in the eclectic freedom he exercised in
selecting his components, his daring pursuit of original,
sometimes extreme technical solutions, and the focal
emphasis he placed on realizing one's own distinct artistic
identity.

This lofty integrity was what impressed K'ung Shang-jen
most when they met in the spring of 1689. K'ung was on
inspection duty along the Han river and had been invited by
several friends in the Spring River Poetry Club to attend a
gathering at the Mi Garden.[87] Tao-chi was among the more
than thirty guests, as was the poet Cho Er-k'an.[88] Cho was
active in local poetry circles and best known for his
anthology, Poetry by Ming Survivors. K'ung had the same
high regard for him as he did for others with loyalist
sympathies and wrote a preface to one of his poetry
collections. It was probably Cho who, as master of
ceremonies at the gathering, introduced K'ung to Tao-chi,
for after the two had met K'ung wrote to Cho:

> Tao-chi possesses a spiritual manner which is lofty
> and detached. His poetry and paintings are like
> the man himself. We met briefly at the poetry
> gathering, but I was unable to express my hopes.
> When we parted, he presented me with a beautiful
> painted fan which I showed to my friends in T'ai-

chou and Hsing-hua. All said that every brush
stroke revealed an enlightened perception of
reality and the calligraphy showed an uncommon
distinction. I wanted to request an album of
paintings from him that I might look at when
composing poetry. But I feared making such a
direct request and hope you might convey it for me.
(K/515)

K'ung saw more of Cha Shih-piao and Tai Pen-hsiao.
Cha[89] was born into wealthy circumstances and was exposed
in his youth to works by Sung and Yuan masters which were
in his family collection. He had earned the Licentiate
degree under the Ming but gave up hopes of an official
career after the dynastic change in favor of a life devoted
to art. There are two sources of influence on his style.
Tung Ch'i-ch'ang's concept of form and his interpretation
of Mi Fei's calligraphy underlie Cha's "broad manner (k'uo-
pi)" which was executed freely using rich saturations of
ink and an abbreviated brush technique.[90] The other
tendency, which is prominent in his "fine manner (hsia-
pi)," has its origins in Ni Tsan via Cha's fellow Anhwei
painter, Hung-jen. In these works, the delicate yet tautly
delineated compositions are suited to smaller formats and
convey an air of spartan minimalism.[91] This combination of
careless ease and a deeper melancholy had led some to
classify him in the highest category of "i-p'in
(untrammeled)" and also reveals the duality of his
temperament. He serves as a clear example of the blending
of orthodoxy and individualism in the seventeenth century,
both in social associations and in the mixture of stylistic
affinities.

Cha's roots lay in Anhwei, where he was ranked as one
of the "Four Masters of Hsin-an," but he moved to Yangchow
after 1670 and became active in literati circles there.

Both Wang Hui and Tao-chi were close friends. As a personality, Cha possessed the kind of eccentric habits writers often expect of artists. One biographer described him as possessing a dreamy, lackadaisical nature and of being so fond of sleeping that he often would not awaken until the late afternoon. On occasion, he would flee from influential visitors and their requests, yet enjoyed riotous drinking late into the night with his friends.[92] Cha attended the gathering at the Mi Garden, his friendship with K'ung having begun in the previous year. K'ung was not one of those whom Cha avoided when he called. K'ung left a poem capturing Cha's character:

> On Visiting Cha Shih-piao
>
> The high walls and the secluded alley
>> were covered with moss.
> Braving the heat, I stopped my cart
>> and waited for the gate to swing open.
> He had loose, thinning hair
>> under a cap, carelessly worn
> Like the pots of wistful grass
>> which he planted himself.
> A monk was invited to remain
>> and was not begrudged a meal.
> Anyone requesting a painting
>> should come bringing his overnight things.
> I recognized Mi Fei topsy-turvy
>> mixed with a muddled Ni Tsan
> As we lingered in his studio,
>> loathe to part from the teacups. (K/36-7)

K'ung did not list the paintings he received from Cha in his catalog, which was limited to ancient works and those by deceased recent painters, but upon his return to Peking, Cha was one of eight artists who collaborated in an album,

"Returning to the Capital" which K'ung received in parting.[93]

Tai Pen-hsiao,[94] the son of a Ming martyr, was also active in Hsiu-ning and was best known for his scenes of Mt. Huang executed in the spartan manner of Ni Tsan and Hung-jen. He favored a dry brush which, in some of the smaller formats he preferred, builds form through soft textures rather than by individual brush strokes.[95] His larger landscapes, which are rare, reveal the same tendency to outline mountain forms as Hung-jen, while his sense of line is less stringent and the ink tones more mellow. An extant painting of his reveals a penchant for the kind of fantastic landscapes popular among such late Ming painters as Wu Pin.[96] Huge, improbable rock shapes thrust up into the sky in defiance of gravity with a disproportionate pine cantilivered out into space. Perhaps it was this style which made Tai the ideal painter to be commissioned to paint Stonegate Mountain for K'ung. In his lengthy poem celebrating the completion of the painting, K'ung writes that originally the commission had been accepted by Kung Hsien, who had died before completing it. Tai had agreed to carry on with the project and, after listening to K'ung's description of the mountain in autumn, he shut himself up in his studio for a day and painted a large scroll. K'ung's poem concludes:

> Kung Hsien valued wetness;
>> this scroll is done in sparse ink.
> Yet the faint and distant forests
>> have captured its true spirit
> The woodcutter's ax sounds "cheng-cheng"
>> everyday;
> Though the absent master's cottage
>> lies half in ruins.

An old crane stands alone and a lone gibbon

   cries in sorrow, startled:

Perhaps a courier comes bearing a letter.

Whom can I display this to,

   bursting with pride?

But since the woodcutter remains silent,

   I would feel ashamed. (K/159-60)

Of all his painter-friends, K'ung was closest to Kung Hsien.[97] Kung is often considered the leader of the Nanking School of painters,[98] a grouping of eight artists more linked by their geography and social relations than by style or even quality. Yet several, including Fan Ch'i,[99] with whom K'ung was also familiar, shared certain interests and influences. One of these was the revival of the monumental landscape of the Northern Sung in reaction to the limitations of Tung Ch'i-ch'ang's southern tradition. They sought to represent substantial volumes of landforms and experimented with realistic lighting effects in an effort to represent a convincing actuality beyond the post-Sung interest in flat surfaces and calligraphic formulas. Another characteristic of some members of this group was the new influence of Western concepts of shading and perspective which derived from contact with prints brought over by Jesuits.

Yet Kung Hsien is perhaps better understood as a leading individualist painter with roots in the orthodox tradition. In his early and middle years, he frequented the circle of Chou Liang-kung,[100] one of the most active connoisseurs, whose property was adjacent to his in Nanking. Largely through Chou's collections and tastes, he was introduced to the work of Tung Ch'i-ch'ang and spent some years studying it together with Yang Wen-ts'ung,[101] who had been a pupil of Tung's. No known paintings of his

exist from the late Ming years but his own remarks and some
of his later works reveal the debt he owed to Tung's style.

Kung was also active in literary and political circles
during the Ch'ung-chen reign and had close acquaintances in
the Fu-she.   One of these, Fang Wen,[102] had signed the
Nanking Manifesto of 1639 protesting the revival of Juan
Ta-ch'eng's influence.   Later, when Juan regained power
during the Nanking Restoration of 1644-45, the Fu-she was
purged and Kung Hsien was one of those arrested.   With the
fall of the Ming, Kung left the city and set out to wander
across the landscape, traveling as far as Mt. T'ai in
Shantung.   Upon his return, he became increasingly
reclusive and generally avoided contact with all except his
fellow survivors.   At some point, a distaste for life in
Nanking led him to move briefly to Yangchow, which he also
came to detest.   He moved back to Nanking and purchased a
small property--his "Half-Acre Garden" at the foot of Mt.
Ch'ing-liang, which he was said to have rarely left.[103]

Kung's mature style was achieved by the 1660s and it is
from the latter two decades of his life that most extant
works of his date.   In developing the distinctive
chiaroscuro and the interplay of light and shadows, Kung
progressed in attitude from the detached, minimalist manner
of Ni Tsan to a more complex and profound composition of a
personal, inner world.   The Northern Sung influence is
apparent in the somber, naturalistic tones of green, brown,
and grey and in the weighty solidity of forms, conveying a
sense of melancholy grandeur.   This is sustained by the
contrast of a finely wrought luminescence.   Dense overlays
of brush strokes leave slight patches of the underlying
paper shining through while unpainted areas are defined to
suggest mists, clouds, and water.   In avoiding the large
technical vocabulary of brush strokes employed by orthodox
masters, Kung chose a limited range which, in his hands,

was capable of great variety, especially in the inventive compositions of his album leaves. His scenes all possess a remote depth and a tactile sensitivity suggesting Western techniques of shading.   Kung himself was aware of his attainment of Tung Ch'i-ch'ang's ideal of "metamorphosis (pien)" of the tradition of Chinese painting when he once stated, "I have no predecessors nor will there be any followers after me."[104]

Yet his sketchbook,[105] which he painted as a guide for students, reflects ideas common among the literati painters of his time.   He criticizes the "northern" tradition and recommends combining Ni Tsan's method of abbreviation with Huang Kung-wang's looseness.   His categories of brushstokes, compositions, rocks, and trees and his process of study are closely related to The Mustard Seed Garden Manual compiled by his student, Wang Kai.[106]

Critics have noted that while Kung Hsien creates a compelling world which attracts the viewer, there is at the same time a forbidding remoteness which prevents genuine intimacy. He provides no human figures to identify with nor are there connecting paths along which the eye could wander.   Had Kung Hsien lived to execute K'ung Shang-jen's commission to paint Stonegate Mountain, it might have resembled the scene in his masterpiece, A Thousand Peaks and Myriad Ravines in the Drenowatz Collection, which has been described as

> a panorama of vast expanse, crowding the entire area of the composition, not even confined at the top by a horizon, and so implying infinite extension.   It is divided diagonally into nearer and more distant parts, with other firm diagonals further dividing these into geometric areas.   The expanses of water and mist provide horizontal recession.   The thrusting cliffs and peaks build

vertically. Enigmatic repetitions of shape--the turreted mass rising above the lake repeated, for instance, upside down to its right--and geological anomalies bemuse the eye. A dramatic, unnatural illumination adds to the visual excitement of the scene; mysterious areas of radiance, lighting on the undersides for forms that suggests and emanation of light from underground."[107]

K'ung Shang-jen met Kung Hsien in 1687 when his boat was moored along the Han River and Kung was on a short visit to Yangchow. His first poem to Kung celebrates their meeting and expresses gratitude for a gift of painting and calligraphy:

> Overjoyed at Meeting Kung Hsien
>
> On your own you've achieved the
>   patina of antiquity.
> Your romantic style improves with age.
> Every scroll is a scene from Tung Yuan.[108]
> Year after year, you've interpreted
>   the Mid-T'ang.
> For a short poem, you bestowed a "Homeward
>   Bound" elegy[109]
> And on a lengthy sheet of paper,
>   you brushed a Quick Achievement.[110]
> It was not by chance that we met amid
>   the water reeds
> And passed the evening moored
>   in Yangchow. (K/36)

As K'ung alludes, Kung Hsien was an accomplished poet as well and studied the masters of the middle and high T'ang. He possessed an enviable collection of little-known anthologies and once began to print a selection of these in Yangchow. Chou Liang-kung's recollection notes the strong-willed individualism behind his creative efforts:

He would write poetry when it pleased him but not
in an offhand manner. He had to spit out his heart
and gouge out his marrow in order to complete a
piece, fearful lest even one word imitate some
other writer.[111]

An extant poem of Kung's widely printed at the time
captures his characteristic attitude as a Ming survivor
during his years of wandering after the fall of Nanking:

On a Small Boat

The small boat sets out at dawn
Past empty stretches of sandy coast.
Voices sound beyond the southern mist;
Chickens cry through the sea air.
I left my fallen homeland,
   clad in commoner's clothes
And am still wind-swept,
   though white-headed now.
I never read the tale of Ching K'o[112]
So I've hesitated about becoming a hero.[113]

The two friends frequently visited each other and
exchanged paintings and poems. Despite Kung Hsien's known
dislike of socializing, he apparently found K'ung's circle
convivial and attended a number of poetry gatherings. In
one of the many letters to him, K'ung Shang-jen wrote:

I received your marvelous paintings and poems,
which now fill my table. This small craft of mine
is now pointed to by others as "Mi Fei's Yacht."
It makes all who sit by my window with a cup of tea
in their hands gaze about in an elegant attitude.
Who says one can't cure vulgar people? Is not your
influence like that of the great physicians Chi-po
and the Yellow Emperor?

I rose early today and moved my boat to the
Great Eastern Gate in order to meet some guests. I

Kung Hsien, <u>A Thousand Peaks and Myriad Ravines</u>

Cha Shih-piao, <u>Old Man Boating on a River</u>

didn't realize that it meant that we would be
farther apart, as if I were purposely avoiding you.
Now I realize that one should not allow everything
to burden one's mind, otherwise one may have many
regrets.

I looked at the lengthy hand scroll which I
gratefully received from you. Not only did it
contain many characters, but you also wrote some
poems to me. It was so terribly hot last night,
how could you ever lift a brush? It's hard for me
to imagine the efforts you took. (K/510)

In the autumn of 1687, Kung Hsien, then approaching his
70s, fell seriously ill and returned to Nanking.[114] A
little over a year later, K'ung visited him while on his
journey to the former Ming capital and wrote:

Visiting Kung Hsien's Studio by

Crouching Tiger Pass

Crouching Tiger is an ancient,
   strategic pass
Whose fierce appearance resembles
   some wild animal.
The imperial aura has dimmed
And the gate is not what it once was.
Scattered abut the gate are the
   remaining villages
Amidst tall bamboo and the flourishing forest.
Once there was a gentleman
   aloof from the world
Who built a house and garden there.
At night, he can see mist envelop the city;
In the morning, he views clouds
   surrounding the peaks.
Throughout, he experiences
   Nature's profundity,

Converging with its essential spirit.

Every painting, every poem

Reveals his learning from the

    master creator.

After a while, the world will be improved

And a pure simplicity will fill the universe.

I came by the gate to visit him

    already advanced in years.

He sat me down in the shade of an

    ancient tree

And filled me up with a bowl of porridge.

Fascinated, I listened to his tales

    of the past

And sighed that I had been born too late.

The sun set behind the western forest;

Autumn chilled the oranges and pomelos.

He drove me back in his crude carriage.

At parting, we clung to each other's sleeves.

How few of us there are,

    along this difficult route

Playing a solo on the ch'in. (K/140-1)

During this final year of Kung Hsien's life, he was under heavy pressure by someone of considerable power in Nanking who insisted on obtaining some of his writings.[115] Considering Kung's reclusive life during his later decades, it has been suggested that the matter may have stemmed from his activist days during the late Ming.[116] Whatever the cause or precise nature of this vexing affair, it led to a relapse of Kung's illness. K'ung Shang-jen became aware of the problem in a letter from his bed-ridden friend conveyed by a student begging him to intercede. Kung replied that he would help devise "a strategy to overcome the dragons and subdue the tigers."[117] However, Kung Hsien succumbed shortly thereafter, in August 1689.

K'ung Shang-jen was the only person of importance in
the vicinity to whom the family could turn, for Kung Hsien
had died in utter poverty without even leaving enough to
cover the funeral expenses. K'ung not only paid for these
out of his own pocket but arranged his other posthumous
debts. He continued to support the surviving children and
even printed Kung's collected works.   Such acts of
generosity were characteristic of K'ung but were
nevertheless considered exceptional and noted by his fellow
literati.[118]

K'ung Shang-jen bid his friend farewell in a series of
four poems, the final one stating:

> ### Mourning Kung Hsien: No. 4
> I had nothing to give you from our last visit,
> Just a round fan to blow away the dust.
> A pity that the lines of the inscription
> Are too late to even make you frown.
> Now it is displayed before you.
> Stained with a torrent of tears.
> "Playing a solo on the ch'in" --
> How prophetic these words were.
> Now there will be no more playing
> In farewell to you, my old friend.[119]   (K/153)

K'ung Shang-jen's painter-friends were not only
acquaintances of his leisure but, in a number of cases,
were living links to the late Ming and encouraged him in
his quest to understand the past by telling their stories.
Kung Hsien, in particular, cherished memories of the
Nanking of the 1640s and, as the poem "Crouching Tiger
Pass" relates, he provided K'ung with some engrossing
material for The Peach Blossom Fan. In his play, K'ung
created two characters who were painters.   Yang Wen-
ts'ung,[120] the friend of Kung Hsien's early years, is a
major character of considerable thematic and structural

significance. It may be recalled that it was the story of
Yang's creation of the peach blossom fan heard in his youth
which first inspired K'ung. Kung Hsien probably provided
new insights into Yang's personality which endowed him with
a greater depth in K'ung's imagination.

The other painter is Lan Ying,[121] an important artist
of the mid-century active in Nanking, Hangchow, and
Yangchow. He died about 1664, before K'ung could meet him,
but the character no doubt contains composite features of
the artists K'ung knew personally. K'ung admired Lan's
work and owned three paintings by him.[122] It seems that
Lan and Yang Wen-ts'ung were well-acquainted, judging from
an extant painting on which they collaborated.[123] In The
Peach Blossom Fan, the two are closely linked, although Lan
plays a minor role. He first appears in the middle of the
play as a refugee from Peking in 1644 after the city has
fallen. In the second half, he becomes a denizen of the
pleasure quarters of Ch'in-huai in Nanking under the
partonage of Yang, who has become the city's magistrate.
Lan contributes to the efforts to reunite the hero and
heroine and it is in his studio that Yang paints peach
blossoms on the fan. Towards the end, when the Restoration
collapses, Yang urges Lan to flee with him but the latter
decides to join others in entering a Taoist monastery
instead. This portrait of Lan Ying is not confirmed in the
meager historical sources on him and is certainly more a
product of K'ung's needs as a dramatist. That both Yang
and Lan were represented in the center of events indicates
the significance which K'ung felt such painters played in
the cultural and political life of the times. The longer
K'ung traveled in the south, the more he became involved
with the idea of recreating this lost world whose scenes,
legends, and surviving figures he continually encountered.

The search to recover the past increasingly preoccupied him
and was reflected both in his writings and his travels.

IN SEARCH OF THE FLOWER OF THE PAST

Perhaps K'ung's striving for identity with the meaning
of the past was best expressed at his most lavish party
when he invited over seventy guests to view the moon at the
Hortensia Temple[124] in Yangchow in early 1688.   This Taoist
monastery had been famous since the Han dynasty for a
unique bush which had produced a rare breed of hortensia.
The bush had withered in the Yuan and, in the course of the
Manchu conquest in 1645, the monastery itself was severely
damaged.   The spot was largely neglected in K'ung's time
and had taken on a decayed appearance which to Ming
loyalists symbolized the destruction of literati culture.
On visiting it one day, K'ung had been impressed by what he
described as "its quietude, though located in a noisy area
and enduring purity near the city's dust."[125]   He decided
to hold a gathering there in which he and his friends would
try to enter into the spirit of antiquity and seek to
understand the meaning of the vanished flower.   As was
customary, they drank, listened to opera, and wrote poetry
until dawn.   K'ung himself wrote:

> Yangchow's splendor absorbs the moon's light.
> Matchless is the hortensia.
> The good moon shines on the unique flower,
> Its pure light breaking through the
>   chaotic void.
> By the time I came to Yangchow
> Both flower and moon had long waned.
> Wind and rain filled Wu-ch'eng
> As I slept unsettled on my solitary boat.
> In the morning, I awoke and pawned
>   my winter clothes

Which forced me to expose my unadorned self.

The traces of immortals lie before
   the old temple

All the worthies keep on flowing in.

This elegant assembly approaches the
   Orchid Pavilion[126]

And the lofty emotions resemble
   Hsi and Juan.[127]

A cup of wine between each poem,

A crow flies by, river and sky darken.

Gazing up at the white moon gleaming,

I sadly recall the Sui Garden.[128]

When I turn to face the Hortensia Terrace,

The Dance of the Rainbow Skirt
   seems not so far away.[129]

The monks strike their bowls and
   our poems are completed.

In the frosty cold,
   the outer gates are locked.

Seated, I mull over the fine night;

Lingering feelings fill the room.

Yet I could not see the flower of the past

While the moon strolled home
   to the sound of flutes.   (K/56)

K'ung begins the poem with an ideal image which acts as a rhetorical preface. The fullness of the moon, representing the classic vision of perfection, is juxtaposed against the singular hortensia flower as a unique element symbolizing a flourishing interiority. Ironic distance between the two does not exist in this purely natural perspective enveloped by the enlightening brightness of the moon. The poem shifts abruptly to a mimetic level of human experience in which the poet's own situation in time is precisely one of an inability to overcome the disparity between a moon now imperfect and the withered flower. Unable to attain the total vision, he finds himself tormented by nature and places his hope in the lyric world of the poetry gathering as a momentary opportunity to overcome both time and space. When perception blends into an inebriated darkness, it seems possible to experience the blossoming of the great sensations of the past and relive Wang Hsi-chih's archetypal gathering at the Orchid Pavilion in 353. Such insight, however, is ephemeral and the sudden impingement of the Taoist's daily ritual shocks him back into the present. K'ung's characteristic realism, which so often leads to the tragic, is apparent in his candid admission that he could not actually realize an absolute and enduring sense of the past. He finds himself isolated from the universal vision of the full moon just as the second part of the poem remains detached from the ideality of the beginning. Ultimately, his final solution is in the spatial fade-out. As the moon rejoins the flower in another dimension and the poet's struggle withdraws from consciousness, K'ung reasserts his fundamental faith in their ultimate identity in a realm beyond imagination.

K'ung also assessed his experience at the Hortensia Temple in a prose essay. Here he searched for a more philosophical resolution in the spirit of Wang Hsi-chih's "Preface to Poems Written at the Orchid Pavilion":

> The joyous gatherings of those before us accumulate to become the object of our melancholy reflections today, while our reflections are what provoke the joyous gatherings of later worthies. On the one hand, joy, and on the other, melancholy—they follow in a cycle throughout myriad generations. The flourishing and withering of the flower is inconstant and the waxing and waning of the moon is

uncertain. Somewhere between dawn and dusk, joy
and melancholy are each distinguishable but when
one triess to calculate in human experiences what
it is that can be both joyous and melancholy it
seems impossible to record it in its totality. If
the gathering of today could by chance be
transmitted it would be no more than another trace
of joy and melancholy within this inability to
record totality. And yet, if it were not recorded,
then there would be neither joy nor melancholy.
The flower and the bright moon, however, will
forever lie outside this cycle. (K/450)

While K'ung was exploring the vestibules of the past
poetically, he also continued his scholarly inquiry into
ancient ceremonies and music. He and Fei Mi,[130] his
closest intellectual friend during these years, often met
to discuss such matters. Fei was a noted Confucian
philosopher who resided in T'ai-chou. In his earlier
years, he had organized military defenses against Chang
Hsien-chung's peasant rebels in his native Szechuan and
continued to be active in the Ming resistance through the
late 1640s. He finally chose the Yangchow area as his
residence in 1657, supporting himself by teaching and
writing. As a scholar, Fei was one of the earliest of his
generation to adopt the historical approach in reassessing
Sung and Ming philosophy. Thus he and K'ung shared a
similar interest in Empirical Studies and in the
methodology of the School of Han Learning.

In a letter to Fei, K'ung wrote:

Music theory is profound and abstruse, hardly
capable of being understood by erratic or vulgar
minds. I have long studied my family's teachings
and was fortunate to have used the official ritual
vesels which they have preserved, only a tenth of

which have survived. For the past twenty years, I
have conducted careful research on them and used it
in ceremonies in Ch'ü-fu and in the Imperial Palace
in Peking. Yet I fear that over time, error has
compounded error so that the original methods and
intentions of the ancients have been lost. Now
that it is fall, and the weather is cooler, would
you come to advise me on these subjects and put
them right? I am completing a book to guide those
in the future and your help will aid my efforts.
(K/531)

This work in progress was probably <u>Theory of Pitch in
Classical Music</u>, which was printed in his later years.[131]

K'ung had another close friend, Min I-hsing,[132] who was
an art collector and admirer. In addition to gifts of
paintings, he presented K'ung with a bronze ruler from the
Han dynasty. This latter gift, dating from A.D. 81, was
highly treasured by K'ung who named his library the "Hall
of the Han Ruler." He used it as an archaeological relic
and produced a short essay on its origins.[133] Upon his
return to Ch'ü-fu, he donated it to the Temple to be used
as a standard for casting new ritual vessels. K'ung wrote
two other essays at the same time exploring the measurement
system of the Chou dynasty in comparison to those of later
dynasties.[134] Assembling a variety of ancient and medieval
sources, K'ung sifted the evidence to summarize the
historical changes in standard lengths and concluded that
his Han ruler was identical to those of the Chou. As a
result of K'ung's interest in these matters, another
acquaintance presented him with a second bronze ruler.
This too became the subject of a study and was found to be
a measure for lengths of cloth in the Sung.[135]

TRACES OF GOLDEN POWDER

Towards the end of August 1689, official business summoned K'ung to Nanking, the city which had been the cultural capital of the Ming and, from June 1644 to June 1645, the site of the Southern Ming Restoration under the Hung-kuang Emperor. He left by boat from I-cheng and, after a week-long journey up the Yangtze, sailed past Swallow Cliff, the landmark signaling the entrance to the city. It was inevitable that K'ung's journeying through the south should lead him here as a climax to his survey of the scenes of the past. And this particular season, when the surrounding mountains begin to be transformed into a tapestry of subdued colors, also suited K'ung's poetic affinity for autumnal atmospheres as a setting for melancholy reflection.

Like Yangchow, Nanking had ancient traditions going back to the Chou dynasty. It first gained note as a capital when Sun Ch'üan of Wu recognized its strategic value and moved his court there in the early third century. Ever since the Eastern Chin (317-420), when the northern aristocracy fled south in the face of a barbarian invasion, writers have celebrated it for the wealth, sophistication, and romanticism of its inhabitants--an ethos alluded to by numerous later poets as the "golden powder (chin-fen)" of the Six Dynasties. Just as Sui Yang-ti endowed Yangchow with its myths of tragic glory, so Nanking had its own symbol in the man Yang-ti conquered--the last Emperor of Ch'en (r. 583-89).[136]

With the establishment of the Ming in 1368, the city underwent extensive rebuilding under the first two emperors. Talented officials from all over the nation gathered to create the policies and structures for a new native dynasty and the population was further enhanced, albeit unwillingly, by the enforced transportation of the gentry of neighboring areas whose loyalties were suspected by Ming T'ai-tsu. Even after the shift to Peking following Yung-lo's usurpation, a duplicate government was maintained with its own bureaucrary and Imperial Academy. These institutions, as well as the provincial examination halls, continued to attract literati from the hinterland, many of whom preferred the antique atmosphere, sensuality, and leisurely manners to the rigors of the northern capital.

Nanking reached its apogee beginning in the Wan-li era when it profited from the urban prosperity and cultural expansion occurring in the south. The Jesuit Matteo Ricci described it in 1595:

> In the judgment of the Chinese, this city surpasses all other cities in the world in beauty and grandeur, and in this respect there are probably very few others superior or equal to it. It is literally filled with palaces and temples and towers and bridges, and these are scarcely surpassed by similar structures in Europe.[137]

In general, the last seventy-five years of the Ming constituted a period of complex undercurrents whose heterogeneous nature and often contradictory directions were as characteristic of the times as any single trend. On the one hand, there was considerabale ferment arising from the events and perceptions of dynastic decline. Men of concern engaged in highly partisan debates over questions of literary style, scholarship, and Confucian ideals as they sought to advance practical solutions to the problems of the faltering Ming system. At the same time, the city's affluence encouraged new directions for artistic creativity and a pursuit of pleasure to an unprecedented degree, which obscured the urgency of the political and military situations.

The most notable evidence of the first trend was in the rise of literary societies whose members rapidly gained power at court. The progenitor of these was the Tung-lin, which grew out of an academy founded at Wu-hsi in 1604.[138] Under the intellectual leadership of men like Ku Hsien-ch'eng, it combined a philosophy of meditation and political activism designed to reinvigorate orthodox Confucian tenets. The emphasis on will, on inner strengthening and, most important, on engagement in critical situations, developed a heroicized sense of the traditional virtue of sincerity and was aimed at the furthering of certain reform programs within the bureaucracy. Through the examination success of their followers, the Tung-lin briefly gained power in the early 1620s, only to become the victims of a purge in 1626 led by the eunuch clique of Wei Chung-hsien.[139] Despite a recovery under the Ch'ung-chen Emperor, the deaths of many leading members reduced their strength, and their own bloodthirsty revenge against their opponents reduced their credibility.

A generation later another society, the Fu-she, arose, led by many of the sons of Tung-lin martyrs.[140] Founded in 1624, its ideals closely paralleled those of the Tung-lin, with reform of the examination system, political institutions, and economic and military programs being of greatest concern. Its members, more than a third of whom were from Nan-chih-li province, began to gain influence with the 1630 examinations and leading members soon rose to the highest offices. During this decade, Nanking became the center of their activities. This led to partisan conflicts with those whom they opposed, most notoriously, Juan Ta-ch'eng. Juan had been a minor official in Peking in the 1620s and had incurred the wrath of Tung-lin leaders when he allied with Wei Chung-hsien in order to gain preferment over a Tung-lin candidate in a promotion matter. When the Tung-lin returned to power, he was purged in revenge. Identified, somewhat undeservedly, as a prime enemy, Juan was hounded from official life for over a decade. In the late 1630s, as peasant rebels overran his native Anhwei, he came to Nanking and attempted to regain his influence. Despite overtures to the Fu-she, he was publicly denounced by them and in a rare act of public protest over 140 literati in Nanking signed an open letter drafted by Fu-she members to the Ch'ung-chen Emperor charging Juan with treason. The incident galvanized public opinion against Juan and reflected the control the Fu-she had in the city.

With the fall of Peking in April 1644 and the suicide of the Ch'ung-chen Emperor, leading officials and military leaders converged on Nanking, where in June a grandson of the Wan-li Emperor was enthroned as the Hung-kuang Emperor. His brief reign witnessed both the peak of the Fu-she's influence and its thorough demise amidst the fatal factionalism preceding the Manchu conquest. The very enthronement of Hung-kuang over other candidates was a victory for the anti-Fu-she faction of Ma Shih-ying, and the subsequent deployment of Shih K'o-fa away from court consolidated the former's power in the capital. Through Ma, Juan Ta-ch'eng was able to regain power and, in the final days, he instituted a purge of his Fu-she enemies which destroyed the organization.

In contrast to these tumultous events was another side of late Ming Nanking, namely the insouciant pursuit of romantic pleasures in seeming disregard of the historical situation. The continuing affluence of the elite made possible the growth of a demimonde of artists, courtesans, performers, and aesthetes who set tastes and manners which even the most politically engagé of literati aspired to

participate in. It was the heady life of this insulated
world which led many memoirists to look back and speak
nostalgically of this era as one of peace and prosperity.
The pleasure quarters of Ch'in-huai became a focus of
cultural life as the affluent flocked from the provinces to
enjoy the sensual atmosphere of the riverside houses. Our
omnipresent observer Chang Tai recalled:

> The houses along the Ch'in-huai River were
> convenient for lodging, for forming social
> acquaintances, and for carousing. The rates were
> exhorbitant yet not a day went by when there
> weren't guests. Painted boats with their sounds of
> drums and flutes went back and forth, winding in a
> circular path. Outside the houses were balconies
> with vermilion balustrades and intricate latticed
> windows, bamboo shades, and silken drapes. In
> summer, one could relax on the balcony after taking
> a bath, while from the other riverside pavillions
> along both banks a jasmine breeze wafted through,
> the men and women exuding a pungent fragrance.
> Courtesans would hold round fans of fine white silk
> as their flowing side-locks of hair and slightly
> tilting hair buns attracted men with a soft
> allure.[141]

In this neighborhood, located across from the
examination halls, a wide spectrum of colorful figures met
in a perfumed setting centered around elegant literary
gatherings, patronage of the theater, and the pursuit of
love. It was at this time that K'un-ch'ü spread to Nanking
and became a national style set by the troupes and leading
actors of the quarters. The stars of this world were the
famous courtesans, who numbered around thirty. Each was
distinguished not only for her beauty but for her aesthetic
accomplishments. Poets vied with each other to celebrate

their qualities and pay them immortalizing tributes. The
quarter maintained its own customs and festivities, among
which was the celebration of noted love affairs between the
courtesans and talented literati which soon were
mythologized into local lore.[142]

One of the tales of those years which continued to be
told in Ch'in-huai long after was about the affair between
the courtesan Li Hsiang-chün[143] and the literatus Hou Fang-
yü. K'ung first heard the story in his youth in Ch'ü-fu.
Hsiang-chün was the adopted daughter of another famous
courtesan, Li Chen-li,[144] who maintained a house in the
quarter which became a salon for some of the leading
figures of the time, many of whom were connected with the
Fu-she. K'ung's friend, the memoirist Yü Huai, recollected
that Hsiang-chün had a petite figure with a clear
complexion, and earned the name "perfumed fan-tassel" for
her intelligence and seductive wit.[145] Hou Fang-yü
likewise remembered her as a lively personality and a
strong individualist.[146] She was, in addition, a skilled
performer who at thirteen began to study the plays of T'ang
Hsien-tsu with the foremost teacher of K'un-ch'ü, Su K'un-
sheng. It was the custom in Ch'in-huai to initiate a young
courtesan into the profession by arranging a match with a
prominent literatus of wealth and talent, thereby
establishing her ranking among her sister entertainers.
The obvious choice in 1639 was the 21-year-old Hou, who had
just arrived in the city for the examinations.

Hou was the son of a president of the Board of Revenue
and had already distinguished himself in government circles
for his policy recommendations. Among his own generation,
he was recognized as an important leader of the revival of
the prose style of the T'ang and Sung masters, one of the
goals of the Fu-she, with whom he developed close ties.
This was around the time that Juan Ta-ch'eng had been

publicly denounced and was seeking a way to mend political fences with the activists. To this end, he conceived the strategy of forming a friendship with Hou in the hope that the latter would use his considerable prestige to conciliate the Fu-she leaders. Through an agent, Hou was lavishly entertained in the quarter and Juan attempted to pay the expenses for the match with Hsiang-chün. According to Hou, it was Hsiang-chün who first saw through the scheme and in a righteous speech urged Hou to break off contact with the agent. This immortalized her in the eyes of her lover and others in Ch'in-huai for possessing a degree of political insight and moral courage rarely seen in a courtesan. Later in 1639, Hou failed the examinations for writing a taboo character, and the following year prepared to return home to Honan. After their parting, Hsiang-chün sang a p'i-p'a ballad in which she again urged her lover to maintain his political purity and avoid Juan's party. The two apparently did not meet again.

In the subsequent five years, Hou valiantly tried to sustain the Ming through serving as an advisor to his father and various loyalist generals. When the Nanking Restoration was established, he was among the principal targets of Juan Ta-ch'eng's purge of the Fu-she and barely escaped to the protection of Shih K'o-fa. Meanwhile, Hsiang-chün maintained her vow of loyalty and refused to entertain Juan's followers. One of them was rejected after offering her 300 gold pieces for an evening's pleasure. In revenge, his men injured her, causing her to drip blood on a farewell fan given her by Hou. As the story goes, these bloodstains were later transformed into peach blossoms by the inspired brush of her admirer, the painter Yang Wen-ts'ung.

It is clear from the wealth of period detail in his play that K'ung took advantage of his trip to Nanking to gain a thorough acquaintance with the sites associated with this story and built up his knowledge of various members of the circles of Hou and Hsiang-chün. The titles of a number of poems indicate his retracing of their old haunts: Ch'in-huai, Peach-leaf Ferry, Misty Perch Temple, Lake Sans-Souci, Green Stream. The general mood of the poems from this visit is more somber than those written in Yangchow. There is less gaiety and frivolity, fewer celebrations of the joys of literati society, and none of the confident ambitions of the dedicated official. In a number of pieces written from monasteries in the surrounding hills, Confucian optimism has given way to the need for Buddhist contemplation. Perhaps it was because the atmosphere of Nanking in the early Ch'ing was far different than a half-century before. Under the new dynasty, the city continued to maintain its economic importance but had been stripped of its political significance as the southern capital and had been overtaken by Yangchow culturally. Divided into two districts, it was carefully administered by bond servants and others close to the Manchu emperors. Many of the great monuments of the former dynasty were in a state of deterioration through neglect and vandalism. It became almost a set theme for visitors in the early Ch'ing to write poetry lamenting the state of decay into which these places had fallen. Gone as well were the idealistic young activists, the famous courtesans, the colorful generals and politicians, and the heady sense of being in the midst of great events. As Yü Huai wrote:

> Nanking was since ancient times known for its beauties where the gentry and literary culture flourished more than anywhere else in the south; and its romantic style was the finest in the world . . . yet since the dynastic change, times

have altered, things have changed, like a Yangchow
dream.   The pleasure quarters have been overgrown
by wild weeds; the red clappers with green ribbons,
the excellent dances and ethereal arias can no
longer be heard.   The latticed windows, bamboo
shades, and embroidered curtains of the courtesan
bedchambers can no longer be seen; nor can the rare
flowers and fragrant plants, the marvelous zithers
and rhinocerous-skin ornaments be appreciated.
When I went by it once, creeping vines filled my
eyes and dilapidated houses of the beauties had
vanished like dust.   Can there by any greater
feelings of melancholy than over the rise and fall
of a dynasty?[147]

These were not just the nostalgic yearnings of an aged
playboy but sentiments echoed by others for whom the
visible decay and a vanished ethos impressed upon them the
inescapable changes of the times.

K'ung's poem, written while partying on a pleasure
barge on the Ch'in-huai, is in this mode:

Leaves whirl about the palace as
    dust rises in the market place
Yet traces of spring remain
    in Ch'in-huai.
We stop the boat, but not because
    songs reach our ears;
Whenever such sorrow strikes me
    I forget to quench it with wine.
Along the mountains, by the waterside,
    autumn grasses grow;
In pleasure houses or on the party barges,
    few of the old crowd remain.
I ask about for romantic tales
    from the past,

Wondering whether these enthralling yarns

are absolutely true. (K/140)

Here K'ung seems to have donned the garb of a survivor
as he refers to "the old crowd." As a first-time visitor
to the city, he cannot be referring to any former
acquaintances of his own but rather the heroes and heroines
of the stories he was collecting. The enveloping nostalgia
has led to his assuming the emotions of those he so admired
and sympathized with.

K'ung did not neglect to visit many of those places
most sacred to loyalists. At a temple on Mt. Chü-po in the
southern section of the city, he paid homage to the spirit
of Fang Hsiao-ju.[148] Fang, like T'ieh Hsuan, was killed in
the early Ming while defending the Chien-wen Emperor
against the Prince of Yen's usurpation. He was the most
prominent martyr among the loyal court officials, a highly
idealistic Confucian who suffered the extreme penalty of
having his entire clan wiped out. Only in the Wan-li reign
did the dynasty relent and allow a temple to be dedicated
on a site where his disciple had buried his bones. It had
taken on added significance for anti-Ch'ing loyalists who
often sacrificed there, for it had been severely damaged by
the Manchu occupation.

K'ung also visited two other sites which reflected the
faded glory of the city in his time and which were
appropriate scenes for voicing melancholy reflections over
a lost past--the old Imperial Palace and the tomb of Ming
T'ai-tsu. Both had fallen into disrepair following the
conquest. Army troops and their animals had been quartered
in these places; even the neighboring monks had cut down
the trees for wood. Some of the buildings had collapsed
while others had been denuded of their ornaments. The
loyalist poet Ch'ü Ta-chün wrote, after visiting the tomb:

There was a Manchu herdsman who was about to cut down a pillar in the pavilion--one of those with the golden dragon claws on top already half missing. I offered him some money instead and begged him to spare it.[149]

K'ung described a similar situation in his poem upon visiting the former palace:

> In a scurry, yet another game of
>   chess was done.
> I rode over to view the former
>   palace's remains.
> Ravens dotted the scene in the
>   twilight glow;
> In the autumn wind, there but lacked
>   "rows of wine-millet."[150]
> The gate led to the inner court
>   along crumbled red walls.
> A bridge faced the central avenue,
>   its jade pillars tilting.
> Most vexing of all are the pitiless neighbors
> Who steal glazed tiles for their
>   own snail-shell huts.   (K/145)

K'ung's feelings of melancholy are formulated in the genre of poems written upon viewing fallen capitals. The type has origins in the earliest expressive poetry, as indicated in the allusion in the fourth line to a poem in The Book of Poetry. There, an official laments the destruction of the former Chou capital, seeing only rows of wine-millet where once stood a city. K'ung's initial perception is one of intellectual detachment. The "chess" of the first line refers to the Ming dynastic enterprise seen from the olympian perch of time as just another game of human ambition. Yet his emotions are engaged when actually viewing the palace, a site which, despite periodic

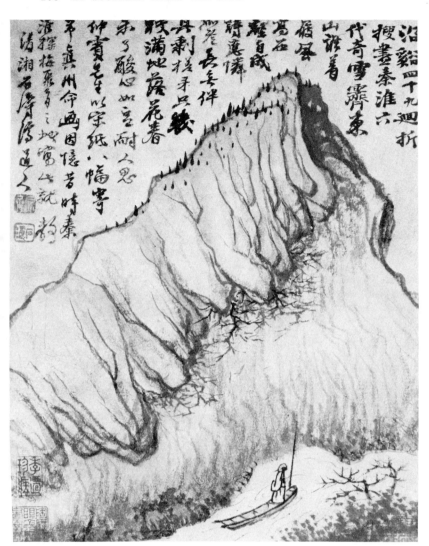

Tao-chi, <u>Reminiscences of Ch'in-huai River</u>

The Tomb of Ming T'ai-tsu

official orders to conserve, continued to have a seedy, depressing look. The irony between the once aristocratic palace and the mediocrity of the present neighbors evokes the well-known sentiment voiced by the T'ang poet Liu Yü-hsi upon visiting a quarter in Nanking once renowned during the earlier Six Dynasties:

> The swallows which once perched
> on the mansions of Wangs and Hsiehs,
> Now fly though the houses
> of very ordinary folk.[151]

In K'ung's view, the role of the common people is even more malevolent, as signaled by the presence of the unfelicitous ravens. The neighbors are not just innocently ignorant of the meaning of what came before, but unhesitatingly destroy an irreplaceable landmark for their own puny economic needs. Thus by the end of the poem, K'ung's feelings reach a height of outrage over his powerlessness to halt this inexorable process of cultural erosion.

In addition to the painter-friends already mentioned, K'ung called on various survivors and recluses, as was his custom. Towards the end of the trip, he paid a visit to Chang I,[152] who was living in seclusion on nearby Mt. She. A native of the city, Chang was the son of a martyred Ming general and had served in the Embroidered Uniform Guard at the Palace in Peking during the Ch'ung-chen reign. When Li Tzu-ch'eng's forces entered the capital in 1644, he was captured and tortured for refusing to surrender though his captors later released him and spared his family, out of respect for his loyalism, it was said. In the chaos of the Manchu conquest, Chang eventually made his way back to Nanking only to find that his wife had died; and so for the remainder of his life, he retreated to a monastic existence as a Taoist in his White Cloud Cottage on the mountain. One of his surviving poems, a five-character chueh-chü expresses the mystical yearnings of his later life:

Listening to Orioles on the Mountain

White Clouds occupy the massive ravine,
Verdant trees veil a thousand valleys.
Not knowing the way to Spirit Crag,
I keep on wandering, almost lost.[153]

Chang was one of those survivors who found the dynastic change so unbearable that he completely shut himself off from the world, refusing contact with most other literati. Unlike Mao Hsiang, he was not a socialite nor did he even aspire to posthumous fame by publishing his writings. Though Mt. She was a popular spot for excursions, few who wandered by in K'ung's time realized that he had been dwelling there for almost five decades. One rare visitor, the scholar Fang Pao,[154] was amazed to see the walls of his cottage lined with thousands of manuscripts containing commentaries on the classics and histories which had been compiled over a lifetime. Chang, however, refused to allow him to make any copies and ordered the writings buried with him.

K'ung seems to have always been welcomed by such people, despite their reputation for stubbornness and eccentricity. His poem on the visit recalled:

Visiting the Taoist Chang I
at his White Cloud Cottage

Across a cold stream which roared
"ch'uang-ch'uang,"
On a winding, rock-strewn path,
I saw white clouds, after a while,
And from their midst, a yellow dog barked.
The gate was opened when I called out;
The Master was still eating.

I entered and paid him my respects.
He seemed so glad that he slipped his
    sandals on wrong.
Manuscripts filled the room to the rafters.
I wanted to read them, but where to begin?
In a few words, he expressed their essence
And what I learned was by no means shallow.
The gentleman is pained by the state
    of the world;
His meaning is not confined
    to the classics.
He secrets his name in the depths
    of the mountains.
Though poor and hungry,
    he procrastinates to the end.
Every night, he cries wind and thunder;
Ghosts emerge, spirits appear.
He spoke to someone sympathetic
So how could his tears
    have been held back? (K/162)

In Chang I, K'ung found a clear example of the human
tragedy wrought by the conquest. The personal suffering,
the fall from aristocratic heights, dissipated talent, and
a singular commitment to self-cultivation were all
powerfully present in Chang's predicament. Through his
sacrifice for the sake of a moral ideal, he had achieved
that heroic purity K'ung admired and found so elusive in
the mundane world. Yet he also knew that the monumentality
of Chang's commitment was at the price of a lonely,
unrecognized existence of no real public consequence beyond
what a few visiting literati might later recall of his
personality in their poems or memoirs--hence the final
images of turbulence and inner conflict in the poem. The
two met but once and did not maintain a correspondence, yet

Chang impressed K'ung more deeply than would appear. In
The Peach Blossom Fan, he is recreated as one of the
"regulating" characters of the work and given a coequal
status with the dramatist's persona, the only figure in the
play (aside from the offstage Mao Hsiang) whom K'ung
actually knew from life.

RETURNING TO THE CAPITAL

There was another reason for the general sense of
melancholy which K'ung felt in Nanking, for he knew that
this was to be his final journey in the south. As early as
1688, Sun Tsai-feng's river control project had begun to
run into trouble at court over sealing the water-gates on
the Grand Canal south of Huai-an. The plan was opposed by
Chin Fu, who believed the gates were necessary to drain off
any overflows. Chin had proposed another plan for building
a secondary dike by Lake Hung-tse to divert flood water
north to Ch'ing-k'ou and south to the Yangtze, but again Yü
Ch'eng-lung argued against him. K'ang-hsi then appointed a
commission under Fo-lun[155] to investigate the matter and,
early in 1688, it recommended support for Chin's plan. But
immediately in February, Censor Kuo Hsiu,[156] following
Chin's successful attack against his patron, impeached Chin
for incompetence, for sabotaging Yü Ch'eng-lung's efforts,
and for forming a clique with the disgraced Mingju. These
charges set the stage for a conference in Peking on April 8
and 9 consisting of all the participants including Chin Fu,
Yü Ch'eng-lung, Fo-lun, Sun Tsai-feng, and Kuo Hsiu. Three
days later, it was decided to shelve Chin's plan and
dismiss him. To maintain political parity, Sun Tsai-feng,
as a member of Yü's faction, was demoted in rank and
replaced.[157]

During the entire period that K'ung was in the south,
he was affected by the confused policies and the

uncertainty emmanating from Peking. Frequent cancellations of work on the project left him feeling useless and underemployed while sudden revisions of the plan in midstream frustrated what little had been accomplished. "My official duties are always changing and my comings and goings are never predictable," he lamented.[158]   His disillusion became more vocal and in the same year at his patron's dismissal he wrote:

When I was posted to Yangchow on official business, I was quartered in the Lodge for Awaiting the Command in the eastern wing of the Temple of Heavenly Peace. Yet Yangchow is not the capital of Peking nor a Buddhist temple the walled palace of the court. Is not the name "Awaiting the Command" presumptuous? One of the managers said, "This is a lodge for visiting Salt Commissioners. Whenever a Commissioner arrives, he spends the night here in preparation and then attends to official business." Now the Emperor's majesty is forever before us; although we may be located far away, his officials and his people maintain a respectful heart and dare not slacken. Thus the name of the lodge is appropriate, even though dwelling here has given me profound regrets.

Did I not come to deal with the floods plaguing the seven districts of the Huai-nan area? In the autumn of 1686, His Imperial Majesty bid us farewell in the Palace of Pure Creativity, his celestial words urging us to exert all our energies. High officials likewise exhorted us, so that we all believed that before long we could report the completion of our task. Then we came south. The President of the Board of Works was in charge of the overall project while officials of the inner and outer courts and various staff members all cooperated with each other in the belief that, before long, we could report the completion of our task.   The governors, financial commissioners, prefects, district magistrates, and police led the elders and youths under their control, all of whom were enthusiastic about aiding in the task in the belief that before long we would report the completion of our task.

Now we are in the third year of the project. The Huai River still flows from west to east, its estuaries are still silted up.   Grain is not yet being planted in the fields; fish and turtles are still trapped in the submerged houses.   Wells, kitchens, and gardens are flooded; floating coffins and corpses have been washed away to places unknown.   Meanwhile, the heated debates continue in government offices, leading to investigations and purges.   Lesser officials hide themselves, fearful of the dangerous course.   And as for those officials who were my colleagues, some have been recalled to the capital, some retired home, others have left while still others have died.   I can't even count on my fingers the few who remain.   Only I alone moan sickly in this hall.   There is no use in my staying but I have no permission to leave. It is rather like being an eternal traveler or a banished official.   So when I see the Salt Commissioners in embroidered robes riding on spotted steeds mightily grasping their commands as they solemnly approach this place, is it not a source of profound regret for me?   (K/456)

K'ang-hsi's second Southern Tour during the first half of 1689 did not salvage the project, for one of its primary aims was to inspect key river control works and gain a firsthand view of the issues debated at court. "Although we have sent officials to investigate matters many times, they never agree on a common policy towards the construction projects," the Emperor complained.[159] Among the experts he ordered to accompany him were Yü Ch'eng-lung, Chin Fu, Wang Hsi, who had replaced Chin Fu, and K'ai-yin-pu, a Manchu Sub-Chancellor, who had replaced Sun Tsai-feng. The entourage of about 300 persons set out on January 28, pausing at Te-chou in Shantung, where they were again greeted by the Duke and other K'ungs, then proceeded down the Grand Canal. Along the route southwards, stops were made at such important points as Ssu-ch'ien and Ch'ing-ho-hsien and the town of Ch'ing-k'ou.

The official record of the journey records K'ang-hsi as an astute investigator who asked pointed questions about specific problems. "The river system is vital to the transport of grain and the people's welfare. If sudden changes in the geography and nature of the water flow are not carefully observed, and opinions are only formed on the basis of what is on paper, then one may well follow a certain policy only to find that the construction projects will end up being destroyed," he advised.[160] At several points, he ordered his advisers to present recommendations and, after viewing poorly maintained sites in the Kao-yu area, ordered immediate repair of the stone embankments. Apparently, the Emperor's sharp eye was discomforting to some of his officials. When he reached K'uei-chi in Chekiang and wished to proceed further, Yü Ch'eng-lung and Hsu T'ing-hsi persuaded him to return, saying that the water level would not accommodate the imperial barges and that the projects there were only half completed.[161] K'ang-hsi reluctantly turned back to Hangchow and went on to Nanking. As in his earlier tour, he once again courted

local sympathies by sacrificing at the tomb of Ming T'ai-
tsu.

K'ung Shang-jen was ordered to greet the entourage at
Chin-shan Temple in Chen-chiang on March 21.   Despite the
growing reservations K'ang-hsi was having about the project
K'ung was involved in, their meeting gave the Emperor an
opportunity to once again express his personal esteem.
When the barge moored at Chen-chiang, K'ung was invited to
attend a waterside sacrifice and banquet.   Two days later,
he met the Emperor further down the river and was invited
on board the barge for another banquet, after which he was
presented with a gift box of delicacies.   His response,
couched in the hyperbole of court poetry, went:

> I humbly welcomed the Emperor
>> by the banks of the Yangtze River
> Then, an attendant beckoned me
>> aboard the dragon boat.
> One can pity my haggard look
>> after inspecting the lakes and seas
> Yet I must appear at ease
>> when worshipping the pearly crown.
> When the imperial feast was spread
>> the crowds onshore were startled
> And the golden bowl which I grasped
>> dazzled both my eyes.
> For three years my stomach has accustomed
>> itself to being filled with coarse grain.
> Now surfeited with delicacies
>> my tears flow out in billows.   (K/121)

More gifts of fruit cakes followed as K'ung escorted
the entourage back to Yangchow and finally bid it farewell
at Huai-an on the 24th.[162]   His friend, Teng Han-i,
impressed by the display of imperial favor, commented,

K'ang-hsi Inspects a River Control Project

the Emperor showed his personal concern for him a number of times, and when the people saw this they were elated and spread word of it. Soon, everyone in the Huai-yang area knew he was a virtuous official much favored by the Emperor who had received the greatest of honors. He himself, though, was serene and humble, without the slightest appearance of pride. One would never have known about it by looking at him.[163]

K'ang-hsi reached Peking on April 7. As a result of what he witnessed on the tour, he once again placed his confidence in Chin Fu's policies and restored his rank. Shortly thereafter, K'ung's entire dredging project was canceled and he along with the remaining staff were ordered recalled to the capital.

By October of 1689, K'ung had already returned to Yangchow from Nanking and put up at a merchant guild as he prepared to return north. One of the last of his group left, he had already seen off most of his colleagues and spent the few months before the end of the year bidding his friends farewell. There were a few more gatherings at famous spots in Yangchow and a round of dinners on his boat along the route back. As a parting gift, eight of his painter-friends presented him with an album titled "Returning to the Capital."[164] Althoughf he would not miss the heat of the southern summers or the mosquitoes which plagued him, he was leaving behind the true scene of his imagination—events, places, and figures whom he composed into a personal myth in which K'ung was a literatus hero and survivor from the time warp of the late Ming. In later years, he would look back at this period as the most artistically inspiring, for it provided him with all the elements for a full-scale recreation of that era. However reluctant he was to leave, the return to Peking was to have

the benefit of providing him with the distance and the
disciplined routine he needed to set about writing The
Peach Bossom Fan.

One of his final poems to those he knew in Yangchow:

I came to these scenic places
chanting lofty sentiments
And recall it all now,
these past three years.
I sat on the autumnal plains with all of you.
We followed each other
before the evening willows.
Clouds and rose-tinted mist
were gathered in my hands.
Jade and pearled expressions
all became poems.
As for any talk of me as an innovator,
I merely walked behind ancient masters
with a humble heart. (K/179)

Commented Huang Yun: "our feelings upon parting could
be compared to the River's flow, for like the thoughts one
has after someone has left, they extend far beyond the
sky."[165]

Chapter Four
BELOW THE PALANQUIN

Anybody can make history.
Only a great man can write it.--Oscar Wilde

K'ung returned to his old position in the Imperial
Academy with mixed emotions. He regretted leaving his
friends in the south, knowing that many of them were in
their final years. Yet he welcomed the greater stability
of life in the capital; and he hoped that once back in the
center of the official world his career might overcome the
failure of the river-control project. After arriving in
Peking, he moved into a modest house on Wavecrest Lane
where he was later joined by his mother, two sons, and
nephew, Yen-shih. Located near Hsuan-wu Gate just outside
the Forbidden City, the neighborhood boasted such literary
luminaries as Chu I-tsun and, earlier, Kung Ting-tzu. Up
the street was a quiet temple, and an open field stood
opposite. It was about five miles to the Academy where he
was required to hold lectures six times a month. K'ung
purchased the necessary carriage and other accoutrements,
then began to lament the expenses he incurred as he
equipped himself to reenter political life.

At first, the change in scene was not conducive to his
poetic efforts. As before, he grew restless with the

leisurely routines of an Erudite and yearned for more stimulation. "Few of my southern friends can come by, my scrolls of poetry are clogged up with dust, my emotions are awry."[1] His poems, less prolific than during the southern years, reflect official life--farewells to acquaintances setting out to take up office in the provinces, celebrations of the imperial ethos, and gatherings with men of high rank. Peking was not without its pleasures, though. K'ung the collector enjoyed strolling along nearby Tile Factory Lane, a decorative street lined with the finest curio shops, and he often foraged for old editions through the bookseller stalls at the Temple of Charity. Among the antiques he obtained was a painting attributed to Wang Wei[2] and several ancient musical instruments.

During these years, K'ung reached a turning point in his physical life when he began to visibly age and feel the loss of his youth. He often refers to his whitened hair, the slackening of his drives, and the abandonment of some of his earlier ambitions. The perception that he had fully matured and was entering his last vigorous period must have spurred him on to attempt the great work which he had been envisioning through the years. A miraculous invention came to his aid as he joyfully wrote:

<u>Trying on Glasses</u>

I am now more than forty
And feel both eyes growing dim.
Addicted while young to reading,
I dissipated all my energies
   burning the midnight oil,
Facing the dawn still clothed in fur robes.
I've ground on like this, even now,
Well aware, yet still in the same rut.
But white glass from across the
   Western Seas

Is imported through Macao.

Fashioned into lenses big as coins,

They encompass the eyes in a double frame.

I put them on--it suddenly becomes clear;

I can see the very tips of things!

And read fine print by the dim-lit window

Just like in my youth.

So my eyes magnify from the brightness

   of the lens

As the lens magnifies the candle light.

Each depends on the other, never ceasing.

The principle of this is hard

   to grasp indeed.

I just haven't learned enough about things.

But why worry over children's taunts?

If Heaven grants me a few more years,

I'll make use of these

   to study the Tao.[3]   (K/190-1)

Soon after his return, K'ung joined the entourage which centered around a figure he had long admired, Wang Shih-chen. Wang was at the peak of his influence during this decade of the 1690s, holding a succession of the highest positions in the Censorate and on several boards. As a poet, he presided over a coterie of disciples and fellow writers, making him the leading literary figure in the capital, if not the empire.

A recent study of K'ung's poetry has correctly emphasized the social and political nature of his relationship with Wang.[4]   In Chinese politics, where similar geographical origins constitute a strong bond, Wang's home town of Hsin-ch'eng was close enough to Ch'ü-fu for K'ung to naturally look to Wang as a patron. Both had had similar career experiences--the benefit of imperial favor, service in the Imperial Academy and in Yangchow--and they shared a number of friends, such as Mao Hsiang, Yü Huai, and Wang Hui. K'ung was as anxious as ever to move from the cloistered life of the Academy into government and it was probably Wang, as a Vice-President of the Board of Revenue, who facilitated his appointment there as a Secretary in 1694.

From their first meeting, the two shared interests in connoisseurship and bibliophily, as K'ung reveals in his rather formal poem:

On Wang Shih-chen's Visit to My Home

Accumulated rain has turned the earth green
And wisteria vines hang about my double-gate.
Though at leisure the whole morning through,
Few friends have wandered by.
Then the President's arrival was announced.
My humble surroundings didn't bother
   him at all.
When I parted the curtains and
   drew forth some books,
Our feelings took flight as we read.
When I unrolled some painted scrolls,
   his discernment recognized their worth.
The Magistrate maintains an
   impressive dignity
While I need a staff to prop myself up.
One condescends to visit,
   the other dwells in solitude.
Our lives make us seem like
   two different species.
But are recluses really different,
   in or out of court?
How many nowadays
   can understand this? (K/204)

It was Wang, incidentally, who named this residence "The Waterside Studio" because of its location on Wavecrest Lane. K'ung valued his contact with the private side of Wang and, in another poem, jokingly complained that while he sometimes had difficulty gaining access to Wang the official, he could always find him poking around the bookstalls of the Temple of Charity.[5] Wang, for his part, seems to have had a high regard for K'ung as a scholar and antiquarian. Yet, he made no references to K'ung's literary work, indicating that in the theory and practice of poetry they adopted different, though not incompatible, approaches.

Wang's theory was primarily metaphysical and centered around the critical concept of "spiritual resonance (shen-yun)." A recent study has interpreted this as containing three ideas: "shen" refers to the poet's intuitive cognition of the universal Tao and also to his intuitive control of poetic technique; "yun" refers to an individual tone or manner.[6] To this interpretation of "yun" has been added another possibility, that it may also indicate a resonant consonance between the poet's spirit and that of the object of his cognition.[7]

For Wang, the function of poetry was to lead both poet and reader to a state of spiritual enlightenment. In this, he was greatly influenced by Ch'an ideals and the poetic theories of Yen Yü, in which language is ultimately a bridge to a higher reality, to be abandoned like a raft after the journey. K'ung was also concerned with evincing the Tao in poetry but more as a part of the poet's cultivation and with a highly ethical focus. The communicative drive for K'ung placed a primacy on a direct encounter between poet and reader resulting in a shared understanding of individual sensibilities. The role which individuality plays in Wang's poetry, however, depends in part on how one reads the term "yun." As "personal tone," it does refer to an aspect of the poet's self; yet this is to be expressed in an oblique and distant manner. While discrete elements in the formation of scene--chosen symbols and their specific relations--reveal something about the poet, his unique specificity is mediated by the evocation of the essence of reality. If "yun" is read as "resonant consonance" then personality is even less forefronted in an ethereal atmosphere of universals.

A comparison of one of their respective practices highlights another difference. Among Wang's four axioms was "allusiveness (tien)."[8] One can hardly ignore pages of scholarly exegesis in reading his most famous set of poems, "Autumn Willows," often interpreted as concealing pro-Ming sentiments.[9] This wealth of learning required to decipher esoteric dimensions of meaning creates a kind of paradox in his style. Whereas his transcendental ideals theoretically relegate language to the status of an evanescent function, his allusiveness reifies it on the level of a complex intellectual game which often competes with the spiritual impulse for the reader's attention. K'ung, on the other hand, maintains a close control on any tendencies to display excessive erudition, and his allusions are either fairly accessible or related concretely to the subject.

If one were to categorize their essential diversion, it would be to see Wang as an idealist in his belief that poetry could be a vehicle to a higher reality, while K'ung's realism employs poetry as a means of expressing such themes as the poet's tragic confinement within time and consciousness from which he felt there were few escapes. Wang did not particularly care for poetry which dealt with social issues and generally avoided the use of history to comment on the present. Such distinctions should not obscure the actual bonds which existed between

the two. As an established literary figure who had easily
won acceptance in his youth, Wang found it possible to
display a generous attitude toward other artistic
positions. In his writings, he often adopts a policy of
benign tolerance and was comparatively restrained as a
polemicist. Wang and K'ung attended gatherings, wrote
poems to each other, and together visited other
independently minded poets. K'ung, as we have seen
possessed transcendental yearnings and shared with Wang an
affinity for the Wang Wei style of nature poetry. A most
important link, as K'ung reveals in the last lines of his
poem on Wang's visit, was a covert loyalism and the common
predicament they shared of being highly rewarded servants
of an alien dynasty.

Another poet with whom K'ung shared political interests
and who was somewhat closer to him theoretically was T'ien
Wen. The two had met earlier in Yangchow when T'ien, then
Governor of Nanking, was inspecting the Yellow River.
Their quick friendship was interrupted by T'ien's service
as Governor of Kweichow but they reencountered each other
in Peking when he returned to serve as Vice-President of
the Boards of Justice and Revenue. Like Wang Shih-chen,
with whom he had studied poetry, T'ien was also from
Shantung and in the late 1690s, when he moved over to the
Board of Revenue, he became K'ung's superior. From Wang,
T'ien developed a love of erudition and allusion which
surpassed that of his teacher. T'ien's poems were noted
for their idiosyncratic use of language, giving rise to the
story that he only took medicines which bore unusual names.
Yet it was his earlier teacher, Shen Han-kuang, who gave
him the pragmatist leanings with which K'ung felt an
increasing affinity.

T'ien began to study with Shen at the age of 35 and,
despite his later penchant for uniqueness in diction,

maintained allegiance to the ethical influence of poetry. K'ung had earlier given him a copy of Poems from the Lakes and Seas, which he referred to as the "sounds of my anguished chanting."[10] T'ien was apparently a close adviser of K'ung's and was one of those who encouraged him to try his hand at drama. K'ung considered T'ien's collection, Poems of "Mountain Ginger," as influential as Wang's work. In a cycle of epigrams on the Peking scene, he wrote admiringly:

> The Grand Secretary once more stands
>> close to the imperial presence
> But whitened is the moustache of this Governor
>> returned to court.
> Weariness of life on the miasmic
>> frontier,
> Can be gathered from the sapient poems
>> of "Mountain Ginger." (K/368)

A poet whom K'ung often visited along with Wang Shih-chen was Chiang Ching-ch'i.[11] Chiang had held the post of district magistrate but declined high office by refusing to sit for the Po-hsueh-hung-tz'u examination. His Library by the Old Wisteria stood across from K'ung's house and was once the mansion of a grand tutor. K'ung flatteringly wrote:

> A grand tutor once chanted poems in his hall.
> Now Chiang has cut his own path through
>> the thicket.
> The wisteria is not a wu-t'ung tree
> Yet phoenixes have continued
>> to perch on it. (K/371)

Chiang collected a volume of poems from each of thirteen writers of the day into an anthology entitled, Harmonizing Below the Palanquin, published in 1692.[12] Forty-three pieces by K'ung composed after his return to

Peking were included under the title, Poems from the Waterside Studio.[13]

The range of this collection reflects a certain narrowing of focus when compared to his writings from the southern years. Composed largely of social poems and miniaturist observations of his daily life, the pieces lack the tragic emotions or the concern with wider philosophical, moral, or historical issues. No doubt, the decorum of capital society was a constraining influence. In Yangchow, his mobile existence brought him into contact with a variety of stimulating environments and he could give free rein to his sentiments in the company of recluse scholars. In Peking, poetry assumed a greater political significance among a readership composed primarily of fellow officials. As an informal indication of character in a government based on Confucian ethics, it was prudent for an ambitious bureaucrat to sacrifice the exposure of any perceptions of cosmic irony to the artful voicing of noncontroversial, orthodox sentiments. It is this altered social context which explains, in part, K'ung's renewed pragmatist leanings and also suggests why he began to feel the need for a new mode of expression in which he could communicate those feelings about the past which he never really abandoned. As the decade progressed, drama increasingly appealed to him. Not only were arias a new avenue for his displaced poetic impulses, but the monumental structure of the ch'uan-ch'i genre was capable of encompassing the multiple aspects of his summary vision.

THE EARLY PLAYS: "LITTLE THUNDERCLAP" AND
"GREAT THUNDERCLAP"

In 1691, K'ung purchased an extraordinary musical instrument from a provincial graduate which he later described:

Hu-ch'in were originally played by northern soldiers and were called "two-stringed p'i-p'a." So it probably evolved from the p'i-p'a. The New Accounts from Southern Regions recorded that during the T'ang, Han Huang, Duke of Chin, obtained some rare wood on a visit to Shu (modern Szechuan) which was hard and solid like flourspar. An artisan said, "Nothing could be better for making a hu-ch'in—other woods cannot compare." So two were carved out of it, named "Great Thunderclap" and "Little Thunderclap." These were presented to the Emperor Te-tsung (r. 780-805).[14] The Miscellany of Music records that during the reign of Wen-tsung (r. 827-41), the two "Thunderclaps" were still in the palace treasury and the courtesan, "Councillor" Cheng, was adept at playing them. During the Kan-lu Rebellion (835), they disappeared.[15] In 1691, I purchased the smaller one in Peking. It is like fine jade in the flawlessness of its materials, while the ingeniousness of its carving could only be the work of some demonic spirit. Over eight centuries have passed since it was made. It survived all kinds of misfortune in vain, for no one nowadays can play it nor recall the popular entertainment of that era. How sad for those who long to hear the music of Shao.[16]

The instrument was about a foot long and made of an exotic wood dark purple in color. According to one view, its Chinese name, "hu-lei," referred to the crocodile whose teeth and skeleton were once used as musical instruments.[17] Han Huang was a noted painter of dragons and the instrument resembles such a form, with its gourd-shaped box covered with snakeskin and its neck carved into a dragon's head through whose mouth two strings passed. In another

description, however, K'ung Shang-jen interpreted the name
"hu-lei" literally, meaning "thunderclap" because of the
sudden, sharp tone emitted when the strings are plucked.[18]
K'ung had "Little Thunderclap" carefully restored to its
original condition. To Han Huang's inscription of 781,
inlaid on the back of the neck, were added two chueh-chü by
K'ung in his own hand, engraved on the rollers:

Spring's breezes waft far from

the ancient frontier.

High above an empty camp, the moon glows.

How many are the general's regrets?

Ask this piece of wood what it knows.

The "Councillor," an imperial courtesan

of T'ang,

From this pair of strings plucked melodies.

Since the partying ceased in the palace

It's been desolate for

nine centuries.[19] (K/196)

K'ung's purchase of this instrument reflects a new
direction in his musical interests. Hitherto, he had been
mainly concerned with the theory of Confucian ritual music
and its performance in temple ceremonies. Although he
continued his researches in this area, he began to develop
a fascination for more secular, popular music. He became
an enthusiastic patron of Fan Hua-po,[20] a celebrated p'i-
p'a player who had come to Peking. Fan was from K'ung's
own area of Shantung and a descendent of several high
ministers during the Ming. A professional musician who
depended on the support of wealthy literati, he had, in
K'ung's eyes, a martial appearance combined with a delicacy
of expression. This suited him for performing the kind of
tragic ballads expressing heroic sentiments over great
military battles or the fall of dynasties. It would appear
that parallel to his other aesthetic interests, K'ung's

approach to such music was strongly historical and he derived great pleasure from the revival of early forms played on the kinds of original instruments he collected. On one occasion, he showed Fan "Little Thunderclap," which the musician readily took to, spontaneously adapting several ancient tunes which he played on it.[21]

K'ung also turned to the theater. He seems to have regularly attended the Garden of Peace, where the official opera troupes performed and celebrated such famous actors as Li Hsiu-lang.[22] He became familiar with the standard repertory including T'ang Hsien-tsu's The Peony Pavilion. Among the other plays whose performance attracted his attention during this decade were The Hortensia Flower and Yangchow Dream,[23] both based on tales associated with Yangchow's romantic past.

Despite these activities, it is remarkable that K'ung should have produced all together three dramas of high quality with as little experience as he had. Perhaps no other major Chinese dramatist had less of a foundation in theatrical art. He did not maintain a private acting troupe or belong to an amateur opera circle; his interest as a spectator came rather late in life. Nor did he enter via the other common route, as a writer of arias. The poetic forms he preferred were the conventional ones of shih poetry and his few attempts at tz'u and ch'ü remain occasional experiments. Few among his acquaintances were dramatists.[24] In short, he possessed little of the usual background and this accounts in part for the innovative nature of his plays as well as his dependence on a collaborator in technical matters.

Around this time he met Ku Ts'ai,[25] the figure who aided his emergence as a dramatist. A literatus from Wu-hsi who lived on the same street as K'ung in Peking, Ku was an amateur playwright well-versed in the K'un-ch'ü style.

He wrote five plays before they met though only one, Songs of the South, about the poets Ch'ü Yuan and Sung Yü, enjoyed brief exposure when it was performed by the Nan-ya troupe.[26] Ku became one of K'ung's closest friends during the latter part of his life. In Peking, they were fellow members of a poetry society, frequent visitors to each other's homes and guests together at literati gatherings. Later, perhaps through K'ung's influence, Ku was employed in the establishment of the Duke in Ch'ü-fu and was a traveling companion on excursions to Stonegate. According to Ku:

> I recall that in 1694, Mr. K'ung pointed to a T'ang dynasty instrument called "Little Thunderclap" which was hanging in his studio and asked me to help score a play about it. We marked a fixed time on the candle and collaborated, blending like resounding drums and flutes. We felt a spontaneous outflowing like writing linked verse at midnight as our natural feelings sprouted forth. The next day, the actors had their clappers ready anticipating the rhymes, and the day after that red banners of celebration hung throughout the town.[27] (P/268)

It is by no means easy to ascertain the precise contributions of each. In a preface, K'ung states that he first approached writing the drama by drafting a short narrative out of the material he read in T'ang sources and histories about the instrument and the figures associated with it during the reign of Wen-tsung.[28] Elsewhere, he quotes a few lines of poetry by Ku Ts'ai in praise of K'ung's ability to write a tight story, and he responds with a few lines of his own giving Ku credit for the arias.[29] "Although I know something about music," K'ung confessed, "I cannot write for the voice."[30] In the printed edition, Ku is similarly given credit for the arias while K'ung takes the title of general editor. Some critics thus believe that K'ung drafted the plot and wrote the dialogue while Wu singlehandedly wrote the arias.[31] Yet this may be giving Ku too much credit. As he indicated above, the two collaborated together; moreover, many arias contain diction entirely familiar to a reader of K'ung's poetry while those which Ku wrote by himself in the prologue act are more florid than K'ung's style.[32]

The writing of arias involves two stages, which one critic has termed "composition (<u>tso-ch'ü</u>)" and "scoring (<u>p'u-ch'ü</u>)."[33] In the first stage, the writer chooses the mode (<u>kung-tiao</u>) and the set of aria forms (<u>t'ao-shu</u>) appropriate to the mood of the scene, each set being a sequence of individual aria forms. In <u>ch'uan-ch'i</u> drama, where the conventions are less strict than in the <u>tsa-chü</u> form, a scene may include sets from several musical modes and the arias in the sets themselves may be subject to variation in arrangement and structure. Each aria is comprised of patterns of various numbers of lines and line lengths; in addition, there are fixed tonal and rhyme schemes based on linguistic categories standardized from the Soochow dialect. The writing of such forms is, initially, not unlike writing <u>shih</u> or <u>tz'u</u> poetry and is largely an act of verbal art. "Scoring," on the other hand, assimilates the verbal text to the more complex metrical, tonal, and melodic requirements of <u>K'un-ch'ü</u> music, which is represented by the <u>kung-ch'e</u> notational system. It is possible, therefore, for an acceptably written text to need further revision if it is to be sung by a performer. Ku's contribution was mainly in the latter area and ranged beyond the musical scoring to advising K'ung as to the choice and compositions of particular forms. He probably recast K'ung's arias in various ways, changing diction, rearranging syntax, or even substituting one form for another. Nevertheless, their collaboration

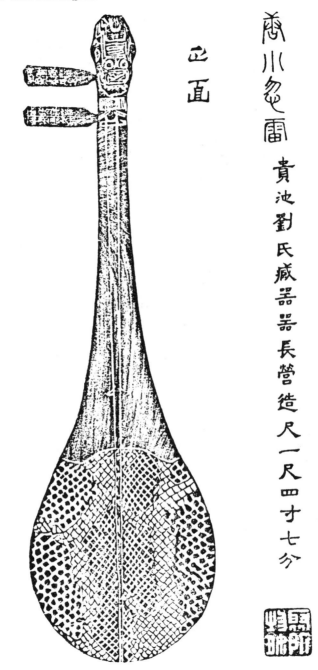

慶川忽雷

正面

貴池劉氏藏器器長營造尺一尺四寸七分

The T'ang Dynasty Instrument, "Little Thunderclap"

was a close one and K'ung played more of a role in the
shaping of the arias than is generally thought. The plot
of "Little Thunderclap", in 40 scenes, has been summarized
as follows:

Liang Hou-pen, courtesy name Tao-sheng, is the
nephew of the Privy Councillor Liang Shou-ch'ien,
and the younger brother of Liang Cheng-yen. In the
seventh year of the Yuan-ho era (812), Hou-pen is
enjoying some wine at the Pavilion of the Winding
Stream when he comes across a poem by Po Chü-i. He
writes his own response on the wall, which is
admired by Po and Tu-ku Yü when they suddenly
arrive. Hou-pen is invited to join them. Yü later
mentions Hou-pen to his father-in-law, Prime
Minister Ch'üan Te-yü, who invites him to study
together with Yu.

Cheng Chu, a physician who often visits the
Ch'uan household, arrives and is invited to stay
for entertainment. He later returns home and,
after discussing the matter with his wife, nee Li,
decides to betroth his younger sister, Ying-ying,
to Liang Hou-pen. She is none other than the
future palace entertainer, "Councillor" Cheng.

"Little Thunderclap," created out of teak by
the Military Governor of Hsi-ch'uan, Han Huang, was
obtained by the Emperor Te-tsung for the palace
collection but disappeared during the Chu Tz'u
Rebellion. It fell into the hands of Chao Er, who
puts it on sale in his antique shop, where it is
purchased by Liang Hou-pen. A palace eunuch, Ch'iu
Shih-liang, arrives and steals it from him,
claiming that it is official property. Hou-pen
insults him. Ch'iu learns that Liang Cheng-yen is
a member of Ch'üan Te-yü's party and is trying to

arrange for Yü T'i to become a Military Governor. He decides to use this affair to implicate Hou-pen.

Cheng-yen meets Yü T'i's son, Min. Having bribed Cheng-yen on behalf of his father without success, Min demands that he return the money but the latter refuses. Yü Min then has Cheng-yen killed. Cheng Chu earlier met Cheng-yen on the road. He is arrested with the others involved and is arraigned before the Ch'ang-an Justice, Kuo Tuan. Also presiding is the Censor, Cheng Kuang-yeh. Kuang-yeh wants to impeach Ch'üan Te-yü and Liang Shou-ch'ien and forwards a draft of the charges to Kuo. By mistake, he sends a poem he has written to a courtesan, Glistening Maiden. Kuo keeps it until it is agreed that they will visit her together. There is a feast at which another courtesan, Autumn Maiden, performs a ballad. Kuo takes Glistening Maiden as a concubine. One day, Kuo meets Cheng Kuang-yeh on the road and when Glistening Maiden speaks with him, Kuo whips her. Cheng then passes by the Kuo mansion and she throws a poem to him, to which he responds. She subsequently leaves the Kuo household and is remarried to a tea-dealer in Chiang-chou. Meanwhile, Po Chü-i has been demoted to Chiang-chou and is drinking on his boat on his way there when he hears someone singing a p'i-p'a ballad.

Prior to this, Cheng Kuang-yeh, on orders from Ch'iu Shih-liang, impeached Ch'üan Te-yü and Liang Shou-ch'ien over the Liang Cheng-yen affair. Both were dismissed from office. Tu-ku Yü and Liang Hou-pen moved to the western part of the Chao-ying quarters of the capital where they met Po Chü-i. Po has been demoted to Magistrate of Chiang-chou

for protesting the assassination of the Prime
Minister, Wu Yuan-heng, and takes Liang Hou-pen
along with him. Liu Yü-hsi was also banished to
Lien-chou, Liu Tsung-yuan was banished to Liu-chou,
and Yuan Chen was demoted from Supervisor of
Chiang-ling to Magistrate of T'ung-chou. They all
meet to bid each other farewell. At the same time,
Po Chü-i recommends Liang Hou-pen to P'ei Tu as a
Military Adjutant to help quell the rebellion in
the Huai-tsai area. Cheng Chu, because of Ch'iu
Shih-liang's recommendation based on Cheng's
expertise in concocting immortality drugs, is
falsely given credit for military achievements and
is rewarded with an official position. He regrets
that he has betrothed Ying-ying to Hou-pen and
urges Ch'iu Shih-liang to present her to the
palace. Because of her talent in playing "Little
Thunderclap," she is favored by the Emperor, who
gives her the title of "Councillor." Po Chü-i is
promoted to Governor of Hangchow and Hou-pen
arrives there. Glistening Maiden has also found
refuge in the city. Cheng Kuang-yeh, now Vice-
Minister of Rites, is ordered to recruit official
entertainers and visits Glistening Maiden in
Hangchow. He appoints her to train entertainers in
the Springtime Pavilion, where the "Councillor" is
one of her pupils. Before long, Cheng Chu and Li
Hsun instigate the Kan-lu Rebellion. Chu is
assassinated by Ch'iu Shih-liang, who also orders
the strangulation of Ying-ying. Liang Hou-pen, who
has failed the examinations, is living next door to
Glistening Maiden and rescues Ying-ying from the
Imperial Canal. This is discovered at court, where
Po Chü-i has been promoted to Minister of Justice

and, after consulting with Cheng Kuang-yeh, orders
Hou-pen and Ying-ying to be married. Po also
arranges the wedding of Glistening Maiden with
Cheng Kuang-yeh.[34]

The reader is immediately made aware of K'ung's focus
on the historical basis of the plot. One preface,
"Chronology," presents a table of incidents which engage
four major characters during the course of the play from
the years 812 to 837.[35] According to K'ung, his sources
included both official and unofficial accounts of the reign
of Wen-tsung and he emphasizes his use of facts, reason,
and naturalness in developing the story.[36] Not only did he
appropriate the authority of textual evidence developed by
the Empirical Studies Movement, but he also relied on what
has been termed the "historical imagination"[37] to
interpolate contemporary incidents and fictional material.
There is little precedent in Chinese drama for supplying
such a wealth of information abut authorial intentions.
While earlier dramatists may have briefly mentioned the
origins of their stories, few claimed such a degree of
fidelity to sources other than their own inventiveness. It
is possible that the chart was composed prior to the play
itself as a working outline indicating a shaping of the
plot based more on a linear conception of chronological
history than the circular form of romantic comedy. This
inclusion of background material recalls K'ung's approach
as editor of the Genealogy of the K'ung Clan, where he also
provided much data about the process of compilation. From
a purely literary angle, it indicates a hitherto unseen
degree of self-consciousness about dramatic form and
reveals the innovative approach which the neophyte
dramatist was attempting to bring to the genre.[38]

The factual tone is designed less to present the play
as an act of scholarship than to add credibility to one of

K'ung's prime motivations as mythologizer of the literary civilization.   In China, where history replaced religious legends at an early point as the most authoritative narratives of collective truths, records of verifiable figures and events contributed the archetypes of existence which writers of drama and fiction felt free to interpret. In doing so, they sought to incorporate two modes: the reexperiencing of a past actuality and the representation of timeless patterns of human action.   Thus, behind the accumulation of fact is K'ung's desire to convincingly dramatize the perennial dilemma of the literatus-official set in the heightened context of a great age.

In the conventions of Chinese romantic comedy, the dualism of inner and outer self is presented in terms of the hero's love affair with the heroine and his involvement in the public events of the dynasty.   Through respective cycles of separation and union, and rise and fall, the competing demands of each world creates a curve of tension which finds its resolution in the reunion act.   In K'ung's play, this is viewed more in Confucian than romantic terms, as the classical tension between the inner concerns of "personal cultivation (hsiu-shen)" and the outer activities of "ruling the nation (chih-kuo)" and "pacifying the world (p'ing-t'ien-hsia)."   Of all the characters in the play, Po Chu-i stands out as the perfect embodiment of the literati ideal, reflecting K'ung's lifelong admiration of his poetry.   He shares, with other positive figures, the kind of natural sensibility expressed through art which entitles him to rule the Confucian state.   Although subject to slander at court and exile, he regains his prestige to become the primary force aiding the reunion of the lovers. Initially, it is through discovery of some of Po's immortal lines on the wall of a pleasure pavilion that the hero, Liang Hou-pen, makes his acquaintance and gains patronage.

Scene from "Little Thunderclap"

Throughout, such friendships based on literary ability are contrasted to those based on expediency, lust, and unprincipled ambition. This ethos is further evoked through key scenes in the play which present well-known events of literary history. Po's famous poem, "The Lute Song,"[39] describes à performance by an aging courtesan which he heard while traveling into exile on his boat. The original contains few details as to the identity of the performer, allowing K'ung to recreate the incident by having the character Glistening Maiden sing as Po reencounters her in Scene 15. Later, in Scene 24, Glistening Maiden performs Po's poem in its entirety when they meet again years later in Hangchow. The attendance at this gathering is another example of the use of familiar bits of literary lore. Present are Liu Tsung-yuan, Yuan Chen, and Liu Yü-hsi, each on his way to exile. Although the actual dates of their banishments did not coincide, K'ung brings them together in celebration of the genius of the age. Such scenes are among the longest in the play and they constitute high points, both as ritual actions balancing those of conflict and transition, and as nostalgic panoramas.

The majority of scenes, however, unfold an intricate saga of the ups and downs of court politics during Wen-tsung's reign, in which K'ung explores the interface of human nature and power. Several key figures are given the conventional moral coloring of good and evil while a range of others appear in neutral tints shading their ambiguous qualities. K'ung is as fascinated by the behavioral permutations of this latter group as he is in delineating clear aggression and victimization. Such characters as Cheng Kuang-yeh, Liang Shou-ch'ien, Ch'üan Te-yü, Li Hsun and, ultimately, Ch'iu Shih-liang occupy indeterminate positions in the moral framework or receive a final

judgement which is ambivalent. Such an honest depiction of
the complex aspects of human motivations is one of K'ung's
most identifiable qualities as a dramatist and endows his
vision with a detached realism which makes him seem so
modern. Yet it is not unfair to point out that in this
early play, his allegiance to historical fact and realism
on the one hand, and the conventions of romantic comedy on
the other, are not fully integrated, leading to several
flaws in the work.

On one level, the predominant attention to the events
of the political world has resulted in the neglect of the
love theme. Liang Hou-pen and Cheng Ying-ying are first
brought together not through passion, karma, or chance, but
through the ambition of Ying-ying's brother, Cheng Chu, who
sees a profitable alliance in their betrothal. Ying-ying
is only 5 years old at the time and Hou-pen is 15, thus
insuring a delay in the consummation of their love and
limiting the possibilities of developing their sensual
attraction for one another. In fact, they meet only once
again before the reunion in Scene 14, and then do not even
recognize each other at first. When they do, their
reactions are based on the ethical bond of their betrothal
rather than on individual feeling. Although Liang
frequently avows great devotion to Ying-ying in the course
of the play, this appears to result more from a reaction to
the efforts of his enemies to separate them than from any
passionate involvement. Thus the reader finds it difficult
to identify with his expressions of tragic emotions during
their separation.

Aware of this vacuum, K'ung attempts to create interest
in Glistening Maiden as a figure of sensual beauty during
the early part of the play. Though an attractive
courtesan, her love life is doomed to disappointment, for
her social status renders her vulnerable to exploitation

and betrayal by her lovers. As the play advances through
the years, she becomes less suitable as a substitute for
the heroine as age robs her of her allure. In the end, she
is reunited with an early paramour but more as a mechanical
requirement of the reunion act rather than as the
consummation of an interrupted affair.

In part, the problem stems from a lack of a balanced
sequence of scenes. There are far too many which
concentrate on the events of the public world and an
insufficient exposure of private desires. K'ung seems so
concerned to weave as many historical elements together as
possible that the plot threatens to run away with its
excessive concatenation of subplots, villains, and
rebellions. Such complexity reflects an inheritance from
certain mid-century playwrights, such as Juan Ta-ch'eng, Li
Yü, and Wu Wei-yeh, for whom the staging of embroglios was
an essential part of their vision of a confused, disordered
world. The absence of the strong lyric focus of these
precursors, however, is a serious impediment to
representing the conflicts of the emotional self and
creates an imbalance of internal proportions.

The conventional moral framework requiring a clear
disposition of villains and the comic celebration of the
new society centered about the lovers is another area of
weakness. In the case of Cheng Kuang-yeh, for example,
K'ung is obliged to include him within the reunion act
although his actions have been both beneficial and harmful
to the lovers. Cheng was an early lover of Glistening
Maiden who abandoned her due to blackmail from his
political colleague, Kuo Tuan; but since she has become the
principal attendent of the heroine, it is fitting that she
too be married at the end and Cheng is resuscitated in the
latter part of the play as a sympathetic figure rescuing
her from oblivion and aiding the lovers. Nevertheless, in

the first part, he was responsible, under pressure from Ch'iu Shih-liang, for employing a pretext to purge the Liang-Ch'üan party, thus depriving the hero of his patron and commencing his separation from Cheng Ying-ying.

The amorality of politics is more clearly apparent in K'ung's final treatment of Ch'iu Shih-liang, who has been one of the principal villains throughout the course of the play. Ch'iu denies Liang his rewards for military achievement, arranges for Ying-ying to become palace courtesan, and prevents Liang from passing the examinations. That he is a palace eunuch further appeals to the early Ch'ing antipathy toward these imperial favorites, recalling such powerful figures as Wei Chung-hsien during the late Ming. In tracing the source of the Kan-lu Rebellion to resentment over eunuch control of the Emperor, K'ung propounds a contemporary historical view which saw the fall of the Ming as due, to a large degree, to such factional struggles as that between Wei and the Tung-lin activists. It would therefore seem proper to expel Ch'iu at some point as an anticomic force impeding the reunion. Yet there is a sudden reversal of attitude towards him in the final act. He appears, after a hiatus, as pitiable and old, his influence over the Emperor diminished. When the lovers have been reunited and Liang Hou-pen attains power as a successful examination candidate, Ch'iu decides to swallow his pride and congratulate them, hoping to profit by an alliance. There follows an agon scene in which both Liang and Ying-ying confront him with each of his crimes against them, including his attempted strangulation of Ying-ying. To each, he replies with devious and incredulous explanations hardly convincing to the reader. Yet instead of receiving punishment he is forgiven at the end and integrated into the new social order, a resolution which strikes the reader

as highly unsatisfactory. Was it due, perhaps, to K'ung's
fidelity to the historical record, showing that Ch'iu not
only survived the Kan-lu Rebellion but gained even greater
power, enabling him to name Wen-tsung's successor? The
mechanical nature of Ch'iu's final disposition highlights
the outer limits of the generic conventions. Although the
play reaches a new height in its honest depiction of
political man, it remains suspended within the traditional
form, neither able to dialectically advance nor achieve a
complete compromise with the old.

Critical appraisal of the play runs the spectrum of
opinion. Wu Mei believed that Ku Ts'ai wrote the arias and
commented, "The diction is ordinary and there are only a
few sets worth reading. The writer is rather
overconfident."[40] Aoki Masaru concurred, stating that it
indicated Ku's talents were limited to performing arias,
rather than writing them.[41] But Liang Ch'i-ch'ao rates the
arias of the play even higher than those of The Peach
Blossom Fan: "Their superiority lies in their avoidance of
decorative elegance, in their simplicity and naturalness.
Not one line is for mere display or a single rhyme
forced."[42]

After completion of the play, friends of K'ung
attempted to submit it to the official opera troupe for
performance, but without success. Such exposure would have
instantly made his reputation as a playwright among the
capital elite and would have brought the work to the
attention of the palace. Nevertheless, "Little
Thunderclap" was staged privately by the Ching-yun troupe
in 1696. Within a month, it had caught on and earned the
praise of seasoned connoisseurs. A printed edition was
published in 1698, for which K'ung prepared the various
prefaces.[43]

"Great Thunderclap" was of similar shape but about twice as large as "Little Thunderclap," with a pair of phoenixes engraved on the back, inlaid with red lacquer and gold.[44] K'ung never acquired the larger instrument but unified the two, at least on the literary level, by writing another play. Ku Ts'ai also collaborated with him and the result was two short scenes, "Purchasing the Instrument" and "Destroying the Instrument."[45]

In the first scene, the young literatus Ch'en Tzu-ang arrives in Changan determined to make his mark on the literary world. On his way to the Imperial Academy, he encounters two other students. Without revealing his identity, the three of them proceed until they meet a peddler selling "Great Thunderclap." Ch'en appears mesmerized by the instrument and immediately dispenses almost all his remaining silver to purchase it. His new-found friends, amazed by his grand gesture, are asked to invite all the eminent literati in the capital to a gathering to hear Ch'en perform on it. Yet Ch'en has no particular musical ability and upon being questioned by his nervous servant admits that the entire scheme is but a cleaver way to gain recognition.

In the second scene, over a hundred guests have arrived at Ch'en's residence and eagerly await his performance. Instead of giving a concert, Ch'en shocks them by castigating the instrument and smashing it before them. Just as the party is about to disperse in confusion, he brings out his collected works and distributes them to each of the guests. The group recognizes him as Ch'en Tzu-ang, already known to them by reputation, and welcomes him as they praise his statesmanlike writings.

The textual background and date of these scenes is unknown, for neither K'ung nor contemporary critics referred to it. It may well have been his initial attempt

at writing drama, preceding "Little Thunderclap." That
K'ung chose the early T'ang poet Ch'en Tzu-ang as the hero
and mentions other famous literati of the time is
consistent with his penchant for historical settings. The
rather slight premise of the scenes makes it unlikely that
they were intended for serious public performance, however.
They may be no more than a playful statement of his own
desire to be more accepted by Peking society as a
literatus-official rather than as antiquarian or aesthete
or even as a dramatist.

THE PEACH BLOSSOM FAN

The success of "Little Thunderclap" was an
encouragement to K'ung's literary efforts. His poetic
output revived as he continued to attend official banquets
and meetings of poetry clubs, and continued to host
gatherings at the Waterside Studio. Many of these
activities were related to his ambitions in government in
that, given his political limitations, he relied instead on
the influence of his writings to enhance his reputation.
In 1698, after four years as a Secretary, he was promoted
to Assistant Department Director of the Kwangtung Bureau in
the Board of Revenue. In addition to his mundane duties,
he compiled on his own A Record of Senior Citizens which
was a statistical listing of citizens over seventy,
arranged by province.[46]

The following year after his promotion, The Peach
Blossom Fan was completed after a long gestation which
K'ung described in a preface:

   Before I began to serve in office, I had intended
   to write this play but feared my experience was
   insufficient and that what I might write would be
   unhistorical. Though it was always on my mind, I
   only drafted its general outlines and did not

attempt to embellish it with any literary style. Still, I enjoyed boasting to my close friends, "I have a play, <u>The Peach Blossom Fan</u>, which I keep hidden away inside my pillow." After arriving in the capital, I would always bring it up when banqueting with my official colleagues. After ten or so years, though, my interest in it began to wane. Then, Vice-President T'ien Wen came to Peking and, whenever we met, he would grasp my hands in hope of obtaining a copy. So the only thing to do was to keep the lantern light burning until I finished the arias and could satisfy his request. It was finished in July 1699, after three drafts. (T/5)

In this same preface as well as another one, K'ung traces his inspiration back to his youth in Ch'ü-fu when he began to collect reminiscences from his relatives.[47] However, the serious writing must have taken place in the several years after completion of the first two plays. By that time, Ku Ts'ai had left the capital and K'ung turned to another specialist, Wang Shou-hsi,[48] for guidance. Like Ku, Wang was a southerner with a native familiarity with K'un-ch'ü. He had been a friend of Ting Chi-chih,[49] one of the great actors of mid-century Nanking whom K'ung incorporated into the play as a character. Wang was more of a professional than Ku, however, and had been brought to the capital by the Manchu aristocrat, Yueh-tuan,[50] who became his patron. K'ung was acquainted with Yueh-tuan. He had attended a performance of his play and admired his poetry and painting. Probably through this talented though ill-fated aesthete, K'ung was introduced to Wang and they worked together day and night while collaborating. Chief among the things he credits Wang for teaching him was that arias should be treated as a unified set instead of as a series of individual poetic forms. There was yet a third collaborator, an unnamed actor who performed the arias as soon as they were written, noting the <u>kung-ch'e</u> score as he sung it. Thus, K'ung confidently stated that any words in the text which might prove an obstruction in singing <u>K'un-ch'ü</u> were remedied in the original version. K'ung did not have the close personal relationship with Wang that he had with Ku, and it might be expected that by the time he wrote this play he had attained a surer grasp of the technical problems. Consequently, except for acknowledging him in a preface, K'ung did not give him credit in the authorship of the work. The plot, with its 44 scenes, has been summarized as follows:

Hou Fang-yü from Honan, the son of the President of the Board of Revenue, has come to Nanking for the examinations but has failed. He is staying beside Lake Sans-Souci and, when spring arrives, arranges with Ch'en Chen-hui and Wu Ying-chi of the Fu-she to visit Fair City Monastery to view the plum blossoms. However, they learn that Master Hsu of the Wei Palace is entertaining guests there. Since all the space is occupied, they go over to Liu Ching-t'ing's house and listen to him recite ballads. Although Liu is a mere performer, he is actually a man of moral vision. The story shifts to the Ch'in-huai quarters, where a famous courtesan, Li Chen-li, has an adopted daughter named Fragrant Lady (Hsiang-chün), who is a matchless beauty at the age of 16. An impeached magistrate, Yang Wen-ts'ung, is an old friend of Li Chen-li and comes by to visit. He meets the <u>K'un-ch'ü</u> master Su K'un-sheng, who has come to teach Fragrant Lady arias from <u>The Peony Pavilion</u>. Yang notices that she is both beautiful and clever.

Since Hou Fang-yü is seeking a lover, he wants to introduce Fragrant Lady to him and discusses this with Li Chen-li, who happpily agrees.

Juan Ta-ch'eng, formerly connected with the clique of the traitorous eunuch Wei Chung-hsien, has been living in Nanking after the defeat of the clique and is trying to return to public life. He has been ostracized by the activists in the Fu-she and other famous literati. When he tried to attend a Confucian sacrifice at the Temple of Literature, Wu Ying-chi, Yang Wei-tou, and other Fu-she members refused to let him participate and humiliatingly beat him. Juan's household troupe is able to perform his play, The Swallow Note, and is famous throughout Nanking. Ch'en Chen-hui borrows it for a banquet and Juan happily orders them to go, hoping that he can conciliate the opposition. When Ch'en happens to discuss politics at the banquet, he heaps scorn on Juan Ta-ch'eng. Juan has sent spies along who report back and he becomes even more embittered. Yang Wen-ts'ung is a sworn brother of Juan's and suggests a plan: since Ch'en, Wu, and Hou are close friends and Hou is looking for a lover in Ch'in-huai, why not gain Hou's good will by contributing the expenses and then use Hou to overcome Ch'en and Wu's criticism. Juan agrees and gives Yang three hundred taels in gold.

Hou Fang-yü, having heard of Fragrant Lady's beauty from Yang, wishes to deflower her but is prevented from accomplishing this by a shortage of funds. On the Festival of Pure Brightness he is alone and bored so he goes out to stroll and comes upon Liu Ching-t'ing. The two walk over to Ch'in-huai and visit Li Chen-li's house but find that she

and Fragrant Lady have gone to the Halcyon Lodge
for a hamper party, so they proceed there. Yang
and Su have already arrived and welcome them
downstairs. Hou sees Fragrant Lady and tosses a
fan-tassel to her upstairs; she throws down a
kerchief full of cherries as a symbol of her
willingness. Li Chen-li accompanies Fragrant Lady
downstairs and serves tea to everyone, followed by
a wine feast where games are played until all
disperse. Following Yang's arrangement of the
expenses, he accompanies Hou to Li Chen-li's house,
where the match is set. Hou writes a poem on a fan
which he gives to Fragrant Lady. The morning
after, Yang arrives again and conveys Juan Ta-
ch'eng's intentions. Hou is inclined to forgive
him but Fragrant Lady hears this and angrily
refuses to accept tainted money. She immediately
takes off her jewelry and finery, moving Hou by her
impassioned denunciation to decline.

On the Double Fifth Festival, Ch'en Chen-hui,
Wu Ying-chi, and other Fu-she members are partying
at a waterside pavilion on the Ch'in-huai River
when they see a barge approach, which contains Hou
and Fragrant Lady. They are invited to attend but
as the evening ends Juan Ta-ch'eng's boat
approaches. When he sees a sign stating that it is
a meeting of the Fu-she, he dims his lights and
escapes in the dark. Around this time, General Tso
Liang-yü, whose army is stationed in Wuchang, is
having difficulty controlling his troops because of
low supplies, and announces that he will march on
Nanking to obtain food. When this news is heard in
Nanking, the President of the Board of War, Hsiung
Ming-yü, has no recourse. Since Tso was a protégé

of Hou Fang-yü's father, Hsiung asks Yang Wen-
ts'ung to enlist Hou's aid by having Hou write a
letter on behalf of his father urging Tso to
abandon his march. Liu Ching-t'ing volunteers to
carry the message. Liu brings it to Tso's
headquarters and also jestingly criticizes him.
Tso replies that he has no intention of marching on
Nanking. But Juan Ta-ch'eng takes advantage of the
situation to slander Hou and orders him arrested,
claiming that Hou and Tso are secret allies. When
Yang hears this, he quickly warns Hou and urges him
to seek refuge with his father's protégé, Gov. Shih
K'o-fa.

Previously, when news of Li Tzu-ch'eng's
capture of Peking and the Ch'ung-chen Emperor's
suicide reached Nanking, Ma Shih-ying and Juan Ta-
ch'eng decided to enthrone Prince Fu. Only Shih
K'o-fa opposed them but Ma and Juan prevailed and
Prince Fu was enthroned in Nanking as the Hung-
kuang Emperor. Ma was appointed President of the
Board of War, Juan was made Director of the
Banqueting Court, Yang Wen-ts'ung became a
Secretary in the Board of Ceremony, while Juan's
fellow local, T'ien Yang, became a Governor. The
latter, before taking up his post, wants to
purchase a concubine and has spoken about it to
Yang Wen-ts'ung, who wants to marry Fragrant Lady
to him. She adamantly refuses. Ma Shih-ying then
sends his servants to coerce her. Yang accompanies
them and, recognizing that the matter is serious,
urges Fragrant Lady to accept, attempting to force
her downstairs. She resists, striking her
kidnappers with the fan Hou gave her, until she
faints and injures her head on the floor. Since

Yang realizes that she will never agree, he persuades Li Chen-li to act as a substitute.

Later, Yang and Su K'un-sheng visit Fragrant Lady when she is alone upstairs asleep. The fan in front of her is covered with spots of blood which resulted from her injury during the struggle. Yang is a talented painter and paints a picture of a sprig of peach blossoms by squeezing sap from a plant to use as color. "It is an authentic peach blossom fan!" he exclaims. When Fragrant Lady awakes, she sees it and sighs, for she wishes to send it to Hou Fang-yü as a sign of her suffering for her vow of chastity. Su K'un-sheng volunteers to convey it and rides off on a mule in search of Hou, who is at a military camp in Honan. But upon reaching the Yellow River, he encounters stray troops who steal his mule and push him into the river. Fortunately, he is saved by a boat which is carrying Li Chen-li, and they meet again. After Li married T'ien Yang, she fell victim to the jealousy of his principal wife, was remarried to an old soldier, and wound up in her present state. They then encounter Hou Fang-yü, who has resigned his position and is on a boat headed south. The fan is presented to him.

Following Su K'un-sheng's departure, Fragrant Lady was conscripted into Prince Fu's palace, leaving her house, the Tower of Enchanted Fragrance, empty. The painter, Lan Ying, who has fled from Peking, moves in due to his old friend Yang Wen-ts'ung, who has helped him settle in Nanking. Hou Fang-yü is unaware of this and comes to visit Fragrant Lady. He is surprised to see the change of occupants and learns that Fragrant Lady

has entered the palace from Yang, who comes to
visit.   Hou complies with Lan's request for a
colophon on a painting he has just completed, The
Peach Blossom Spring.   Later, Hou and Su K'un-sheng
go to Three Mountain Street, where they know Ch'en
Chen-hui and Wu Ying-chi are staying with a
bookseller, Ts'ai I-so.   Juan Ta-ch'eng passes by
and discovers them, whereupon he orders Ch'en, Wu,
and Hou arrested.   This is witnessed by Su, who
seeks aid from Tso Liang-yü.   He meets Liu Ching-
t'ing there and is received by Tso, who, angered
over Ma and Juan's misuse of power, issues a
manifesto denouncing them, which Liu brings to
Nanking.   Liu is caught and arrested.   But the
prisoners are released as Manchu troops conquer
Nanking and Prince Fu flees.   Hou Fang-yü and Liu
Ching-t'ing seek refuge on Cloud's Roost Mountain.
Fragrant Lady, having met Su K'un-sheng after
escaping the palace, has also sought refuge there.
They meet Chang Wei, a former member of the
Embroidered Uniform Guard, who became a Taoist and
lives in the White Cloud Cottage, as well as the
painter Lan Ying and the bookseller Ts'ai I-so, who
have become Chang's disciples.   On the fifteenth
day of the seventh lunar month, a grand sacrifice
is held for the Ch'ung-chen Emperor and all the
loyal officials who died for the Ming.   Hou and
Fragrant Lady unexpectedly meet again and are
overjoyed as he produces the peach blossom fan, a
sign of his enduring love.   When Taoist Chang sees
this he descends from the altar and destroys the
fan, shouting "The world's turned upside down and
you still think of love . . . !   Where is your
country?   Where are your families . . . ?   You've

nothing left but the roots of romantic passion. Can't you sever them once and for all?" Both of them thereupon experience enlightenment and become his disciples.

Later, Su K'un-sheng becomes a woodcutter and Liu Ching-t'ing becomes a fisherman. They retire outside Nanking, where they often meet. One day, the two of them are conversing by a stream when the Old Master of Ceremonies arrives with wine. They all sit down and drink together. The Old Master sings a "spirit's song," Liu recites a ballad, and Su sings arias in the I-yang style as each expresses his tragic sentiments over the dynastic change. Suddenly, a bailiff from the district office appears searching for recluses. He wishes to summon the three but they escape to unknown parts.[51]

This final scene, unique in the ch'uan-ch'i genre, symbolically unifies the dualities of the play. Liu, as a mentor of the hero, has been principally active in the political world; Su, the heroine's drama teacher, served as the intermediary of the lovers. Mediated by the dramatist's persona, a master of Confucian ceromony, the concert of narrative, lyric, and ritual visions is K'ung's summary solution to the tragic conflict between history and romance which is at the heart of the work. For, unlike his predecessors, K'ung was not merely presenting a set of conflicts within a holistic dramatic tradition but exploring that tradition's conventions and philosophical underpinnings in the light of the events of his own time. More than a stylized replay of an inherited form, The Peach Blossom Fan daringly charts the fall of late Ming romanticism which romantic comedy had epitomized. After his two initial attempts, K'ung had now attained a fully

Scene from The Peach Blossom Fan

matured grasp of the meaning and methods of historical
drama and was able to innovatively employ the ch'uan-ch'i
form to resolve the aesthetic problems he had faced in
"Little Thunderclap". As in the case of his earlier play,
K'ung provided several prefaces.[52] One of them, written
just after the play's completion, reveals his choice of the
form for its encyclopedic breadth, which was capable of
representing the complexities of an entire period:

> Ch'uan-ch'i may be considered a lesser vehicle of
> the Tao yet it contains every other literary form,
> such as shih, fu, tz'u, ch'ü, parallel prose, and
> fiction. It depicts character and evokes a scene
> just like a painting. It follows the principles of
> The Book of Poetry and contains the moral judgement
> of the Spring and Autumn Annals. Its style is that
> of the Tso Commentary, the Conversations of the
> States, and the work of the Grand Historian. In
> awakening the world and uplifting its habits, it is
> most immediate and effective, fostering the sagely
> Tao so as to achieve kingly transformation. Is
> there any doubt that our performing arts today are
> like those of antiquity? This play, The Peach
> Blossom Fan, is all about the recent incidents of
> the Nanking Restoration, from which there are still
> survivors. Dancing and singing onstage refers to
> that which occurred offstage in order to know about
> a 300-year-old enterprise. What men destroyed it?
> Through which incidents was it ruined? In what
> year was it extinguished? In what place did it
> cease? Not only can it make the reader lament and
> weep but it can also reform men's minds and be the
> salvation for these latter days. (T/1)

Elsewhere, K'ung asserted that the dates and places for
each event of the Nanking Restoration were based on fact

and that while he may have interpolated or enhanced incidents in the love story, in no case were they purely a creation of his imagination.[53]

Underlying the dramatist's choice of characters and events was his usual scholarly attitude, which combined textual research and personal experience. As he himself had mentioned, his study of the period began in his youth and continued throughout his life; but in addition to the people and places he encountered, he also read widely in a variety of sources. Another one of his prefaces is a bibliography listing thirteen works.[54] They represent a selective group of materials which he casually jotted down as an indication of his formal preparation. Among them were unofficial histories, eyewitness accounts, biographies, personal letters, poems, and public memorials as well as dramas. It may well be an impossible task to recreate the complex process by which an artistic product emerges, but from this cursory list we can at least suggest the kinds of factual materials available to K'ung and some of the ways he developed them.

The first work on his list is an anonymous, little-known account entitled A Woodcutter's History. It provided K'ung with a basic pattern of events from which he was able to date each scene by month and year. Listed in chronological order are 25 events. Of these, he chose to include 17, either as the basis for entire scenes, as elements in more imaginatively constructed scenes, or as tangential facts briefly mentioned in passing. An example of his use of factual information is a series of events marking the establishment of the Nanking Restoration which he condensed into a sequence of three scenes. The debate over the enthronement of Prince Fu as the Hung-kuang Emperor, which climaxed on May 18, 1644, is dramatized in Scenes 14 and 15 and is used by K'ung to present the political conflict within the court. Historically, a group of high officials in Nanking with ties to the Tung-lin and Fu-she supported the enthronement of Prince Lu, unaware that the Commander of Feng-yang, Ma Shih-ying, was supporting another candidate, Prince Fu. The Nanking group opposed the latter because of his checkered past. Fearful that he would revive the partisan struggles of the 1620s, they drafted a manifesto against him. Shih K'o-fa, as Minister of War, was but a peripheral supporter although, in a reply to a letter from Ma, he stood with his fellow officials and reiterated the points of the manifesto.[55]

In Scene 14, however, Shih K'o-fa is cast as the leader of the officials against Prince Fu and is advised by Hou Fang-yü, who historically was not involved in the incident. The scene shows Shih despondent over the Ch'ung-chen Emperor's suicide and initially amenable to Ma's letter. As such, K'ung uses him to typify the vacillation of the Nanking group, which was unable to reach a decision and thus allowed Ma to name the successor by default. It is Hou, rather than Shih, who presents the case against Ma's choice and urges him to reject Ma's appeal, enunciating the principles of the manifesto as if he were the author. This is designed to demonstrate Hou's attainment of the political wisdom and moral judgement which enables him to become an advisor to the loyal elements within the Restoration. K'ung further introduces Juan Ta-ch'eng into the scene as Ma's agent, who comes to Shih's residence for a reply. Two patterns of action essential to his character are thereby developed: his growing association with Ma Shih-ying which leads to his political resurrection; and yet another rejection by loyal elements as Shih refuses to meet him when he arrives.

In Scene 15, the setting shifts to Ma and Juan, who are shown gathering the military support to force the Nanking officials to accept their candidate. This agrees with the historical record, according to which an alliance with a group of loyalist generals known as the "Four Commanders"[56] enabled Ma to emerge as the dominant factor. K'ung employs the scene to show the cementing of the relationship between the two traitors, and to signal Juan's return to public life as both go off to welcome the new Emperor. K'ung skips over the actual ceremony along the banks of the Yangtze on June 3 as well as the new Emperor's sacrifice at Ming T'ai-tsu's tomb on June 5, and in Scene 16 goes directly to the establishment of the court which followed the sacrifice. Given Hung-kuang's advance publicity as a vindictive intriguer, the public ceremony in which he proclaims noble aims of national recovery appears a sham, a brief moment of unanimity before the concealed tensions erupt. In contrast to the loyalist fervor is the reality of the proclamation issued, which demonstrates Ma's control as Shih is demoted and banished to coordinating military affairs in Yangchow. A final touch of the irony which pervades the scene is Shih's expression of gratitude over his new duties. In these few scenes, K'ung is able to deftly sketch the fatal lines of antagonism within the court. Without misrepresenting the basic course of history, it can be seen that he exercised considerable imaginative freedom in choosing which facets of events to emphasize and which figures to forefront as the representative protagonists.

The only event which K'ung dramatized from this source, which is notably at odds with the historical version, is the death of Shih K'o-fa on May 19, 1645. The sacrifice of the last defender of the Restoration occurred in Yangchow after a futile resistance. When all was lost, Shih attempted suicide but failed and was being escorted from the city by his aides when the Manchus captured him. Brought before the commander, Dodo, he refused to surrender and was ignominiously executed by the conquerors, his body never identified.[57]   K'ung, however, preferred the popular legend that Shih drowned himself in the Yangtze.   In Scene 38, he is shown escaping from Yangchow after the city has fallen, on his way to Nanking to mount further resistance.   When he encounters a refugee on the road and learns that Hung-kuang has already fled the capital, he takes off his official robes and heroically jumps in the river.   This enabled K'ung to satisfy the audience's emotional need to dignify Shih's end as well as avoid arousing anti-Manchu sentiment. Moreover, it gives legitimacy to the uniform, which was later interred in the tomb dedicated to Shih on Plum Blossom Hill in Yangchow.

The remainder of K'ung's sources provide background information of a more general kind, which he interpreted with a similar mixture of fidelity to fact and artistic license.   The biography of Hou Fang-yü by Chia K'ai-tsung mentions important incidents in the hero's life and offers impressions of his personality.   Hou was welcomed by fellow literati in Nanking in the 1640s, rejected Juan Ta-ch'eng's patronage, and served the loyalist general Kao Chieh--these elements K'ung selected for his characterization.   However, Chia pictured Hou as a heoric figure of great vision and forcefulness whose talents found no outlet in the chaotic times and who finally succumbed to a life of hedonism and despair.   K'ung alters this somewhat, for he wished to portray Hou as a symbol of the tragic fall of the romantic "genius."   He renders him as a talented, well-intentioned, though vacillating literatus who is overwhelmed by historical forces and ultimately finds release in religious cultivation.   Wu Wei-yeh's sympathetic biography of Liu Ching-t'ing[58] presents the close friendship which grew between the storyteller and the loyalist general Tso Liang-

yü.[59] His clever wit filled the peasant general's need for
a common-sense advisor and resulted in Liu's gaining an
unheard of degree of influence in Nanking by serving as
Tso's emissary to the court. K'ung saw the possibilities
in this unique situation and expanded the performer's role
to that of a major spokeman for the dramatist's moral point
of view. In order that Liu serve as Hou Fang-yü's mentor,
however, K'ung created an antagonism between Liu and Juan
Ta-ch'eng which did not historically exist; in fact, it was
because of their good relationship that Tso sent Liu to the
capital to act as a mediator between himself and Juan.

The majority of K'ung's sources are literary works,
particularly poems, and these largely serve to document the
social relationships of the period. The works of such
active figures as Wu Wei-yeh, Ch'ien Ch'ien-i, and Kung
Ting-tzu establish the basis for the complex world of
Ch'in-huai, closely linking performers with their literati
admirers and patrons. Poems on the waterside pavilion of
Ting Chi-chih, a K'un-ch'ü actor who became wealthy and
entertained the leading lights of the day, are mentioned in
several collections. From this K'ung created Scene 8, in
which a gathering of the Fu-she is held there.

Two plays by Juan Ta-ch'eng, Recognition of Ten Errors
and The Swallow Note,[60] are important for understanding
both the character of the man whom K'ung portrayed as the
villain of the play, and the aesthetics of the period. The
former work was a comedy of errors whose final arias were
generally interpreted as Juan's apology for his political
association with the eunuch Wei Chung-hsien. The latter
play was the most popular work of the period, which earned
Juan the reputation of being the leading interpreter of the
T'ang Hsien-tsu style. Moreover, it was a favorite of the
Hung-kuang Emperor, who sponsored performances of it at
court. The Swallow Note occupies a conspicuous role in

K'ung's own play, symbolizing the misalliance of art and politics. The character Juan Ta-ch'eng uses it to gain the Emperor's favor and then to summon the denizens of Ch'in-huai into the palace troope.

As extensive as these sources are, it seems surprising that several important works which were accessible to K'ung and no doubt consulted by him were not specifically mentioned. Hou Fang-yü's biography of Fragrant Lady is the primary source detailing their relationship, revealing that it was she who influenced him to reject Juan's patronage. Nor did K'ung give credit to his boyhood acquaintance Chia Fu-hsi for the ballads he borrowed and put into the mouths of Liu Ching-t'ing and Su K'un-sheng. It seems fair to regard the bibliography as a fairly specific but by no means exhaustive list of works which he used to gain a factual basis for his broad sense of the period.

Facts, however, are but the keystones of historical drama. They are placed at focal points in the work in order to provide a necessary degree of veracity to support the entire conception of the period. K'ung viewed the fall of the Ming as due not to Manchu invasion or even peasant rebellions, but to a fundamental tension within the civilization, which he represented as two worlds in collision--the romantic and the political.

The romantic world is K'ung's interpretation of the generic theme of love. In recreating the Ch'in-huai quarters of Nanking, however, he goes beyond the conventional lyric capsule of the "genius and beauty" to evoke a complex envionment unique in its manners and highly social in nature. A sense of place is convincingly defined by the frequent references to well-known landmarks which give it its self-contained boundaries. Lining one bank of the Ch'in-huai river, this playground of the late Ming stands just across from the examination halls and the

Confucian Temple, prime symbols of the political world to
which it is linked by the celebrated Planked Bridge.
Peopled by actors, courtesans, and their patrons, its
denizens share an aesthetic approach to life as an
expression of their authentic selves. K'ung recaptures its
glamor by recreating a "hamper party (ho-tzu-hui)," one of
the noted customs of the quarter whereby the leading
courtesans gather and entertain each other as they feast on
boxes of delicacies.[61] In Scene 5 they are joined by the
regular patrons, including the hero, who is introduced to
the heroine. Each participant then defines himself by what
he performs in the course of a drinking game. Hou Fang-yü
produces a spontaneous love poem about Fragrant Lady while
Yang Wen-ts'ung parodies his official identity by
improvising an examinaion essay on the subject of her
handkerchief. But the most significant contribution is
that of Liu Ching-t'ing, who tells a tale which winds up
punning Juan Ta-ch'eng's name. Although designed to
celebrate the prior expulsion of the villain from the
Confucian Temple, it forebodes, in the midst of the gaiety,
the destructive effect Juan will have. Liu thus conveys
the fundamental irony of K'ung's romantic world. Just as
the lovers will unknowingly consummate their passion with a
trousseau donated by Juan, so Ch'in-huai is shown to
insouciantly pursue its eternal pleasures, unaware of the
fatal truth that it is inextricably bound up with the
political world and subject to the latter's vicissitudes.

Of all the figures in the play, Liu is the one who most
clearly represents the dramatist's historical perspective.
At several points in the plot, he seems to be most aware of
the meaning of situations, employing the insights of the
popular literary tradition to urge a morally realistic
comprehension of the course of events. That K'ung should
have chosen an illiterate performer and placed his vision

higher than those of the elite literati around him
indicates the new social consciousness of many early Ch'ing
dramatists. Played by the traditionally lowly "ch'ou
(clown)" role, Liu reflects a kind of social primitivism in
which pure voices of the people become the vehicles for
reaffirming the civilization's most fundamental values in a
time of crisis and change.[62] K'ung's portrait of him is one
of the most successful recreations of the play, vividly
capturing his rapid wit and earthy honesty, as a recent
translation conveys:

> LIU: Whom do you gentlemen think I resemble? I
> think I resemble Yama, God of the Underworld, who
> keeps such a bulky account-book. The names of
> innumerable ghosts are recorded in it. Perhaps I
> also resemble the Laughing Buddha. All the
> vanities of this world have been digested in this
> belly of mine. When I beat my drum and clappers, I
> seem to sway wind and thunder, rain and dew. Days,
> months, and seasons are bodied forth when I move my
> lips and tongue. I avenge the wrong of filial sons
> and loyal ministers who suffered death unjustly,
> and make their spirits rejoice. To villains who
> led happy lives on earth I mete out the punishment
> their crimes deserve. My power, however limited,
> is genuine, and serves good causes well. (P/75)

In the romantic world, the highest activity is true
love and its society is harmoniously organized around the
beautiful and the talented. The political world, whose
intrusion Liu often warns against, is the state of
contention for dominance set at the court in Nanking and at
the military camps of the Restoration's supporters. It
suffers from an inherent instability caused by competing
hierarchies--the moral order, composed of those loyal to
the Ming, versus the power order of those who possess force.

K'ung concatenates several axes of conflict which
ultimately cause the front-line defenses to implode,
leaving the court easy prey to the Manchu invaders. One is
the antagonism between the Ma-Juan faction and the
activists in Nanking, another, Tso Liang-yü's quarrel with
the court, and thirdly, the contentions among the "Four
Commanders" guarding the capital. The central struggle
within the court is a clear antithesis of good and evil,
but K'ung was also interested in characters in which
loyalty and a moral will were admixed. Kao Chieh,[63] for
example, is historically regarded as an avaricious peasant
rebel whom the Ming was forced to rely on. A former ally
of Li Tzu-ch'eng, he had switched loyalties and became one
of the "Four Commanders" but ultimately contributed to the
Restoration's demise. K'ung found a redeeming quality in
Kao's close relationship with Shih K'o-fa and Hou Fang-yü,
and portrays him as stubbornly impulsive, with a curiously
childish mentality, someone easily affronted yet vulnerable
and overconfident. After provoking the combined attack of
the other commanders with his arbitrary occupation of
Yangchow, Kao can only humble himself before Shih and beg
for protection when outnumbered. The relationship between
Shih and Kao recalls that between Liu Pei and Chang Fei in
the classic Chinese novel, The Romance of the Three
Kingdoms, where one, representing legitimate Confucian
authority, seeks to restrain and direct the martial
exuberance of the other:

> SHIH: General Kao, you are responsible for
>   this mischief.
> Why be so blinded with false pride
> By grabbing the seat of honour,
> You have drawn jealous swords against you.
> No tongue, however eloquent,
>   can restrain them;

Till my throat were dry,

   I could not shout them down.

The future is ominous

Our mission is endangered.

KAO: Never mind, Commander-in-Chief.   I
shall settle accounts with them tomorrow.
Then all the cavalry under this command
will be brought under mine.   United, I
shall lead them to victory.   The recovery
of the central plain will then be an easy
matter.   (P/132-33)

But Kao is less remorseful over his excesses than Chang and
in the tragic scheme of the play, he comes to personify the
flaw of _hubris_.   A latter-day knight-errant whose fate is
to be betrayed by his own false pride, he later refuses the
diplomatic advice of Hou and provokes the enmity of an
allied general who has him murdered at a feast.

While K'ung's worlds of romance and politics may seem
antithetical in nature, their collision stems, to a large
extent, from shared values as the end-products of late Ming
romanticism.   Energized by the unleashed potential of
individual will and guided by illusions of autonomy and
power, the key protagonists, Fragrant Lady and Juan Ta-
ch'eng, both seek to realize visions of their authentic
selves.   One sacrifices everything to demonstrate the
purity of her emotions; the other uses the brilliance of
his literary works to dominate the dynasty.

In Fragrant Lady's progress from discovery of love
through suffering to religious renunciation, K'ung charts
the tragic fate of the great tradition of the "beauty."
She initially appears with her drama teacher, Su K'un-
sheng, who is training her to sing the role of Tu Li-niang
in T'ang Hsien-tsu's play, The Peony Pavilion.   With that
heroine as alter ego, she proceeds to play out Li-niang's

key quality of will which uncompromisingly struggles for the realization of her love against the array of anticomic forces.   But the triumph of T'ang's heroine was gained primarily in psychological and fantastic realms; the same strategies used by Fragrant Lady in the social dimension are shown to be doomed to failure as her inner genuineness of feeling is insufficient to overcome the vicissitudes of historical events.   She uncomprehendingly provokes her own separation from her lover when she persuades Hou to reject Juan Ta-ch'eng's gift.   Though on firm ground in the romantic tradition of expelling the villain, she sets into motion the vendetta which results in Juan's slandering Hou at court, forcing the hero to flee Nanking.   Unwittingly the agent of her emotional destruction, she not only lacks the universal insight into the mechanism of events but possesses no alternative patterns of action by which to protect herself.   Fragrant Lady's experience is one of the finest delineations of the Chinese sense of tragedy in that its essence is a progressive isolation from one's society. Hers shares with Western tragedy a compulsive purpose, the sudden fall and the passion of suffering, yet it differs in that the Chinese heroine does not experience what the Greeks called "mathema (perception)" along the way. Whereas a typical western character gains progressive insight into human fate and his own flawed nature, she remains bound up until the very end in the karmic repetition of her primary illusion--the inviolable autonomy of the inner self.   In her most famous aria, she sings of her utter despair after resisting the attempted kidnapping by Juan's agents:

> FRAGRANT LADY (sings):
> The cold wind pierces my thin gown,
> I am too weary to burn incense.

A streak of bright blood still glistens on
   my eyebrow.
My languid soul floats over my lone shadow;
My life is spring gossamer in this frosty
   moonlit tower.
The night seems endless:
When dawn appears, the same grief
   lingers on.

(Speaks):   In a moment of despair, I tore
my flesh to defend my virtue.   Alone, I
peek and pine in my empty room.   I have
lost my sole companion.   (Sings):

Long Bridge is wrapped in cloud and
   frozen snow,
My tower is closed and visitors are few.
Beyond the balustrade,
   a line of wild geese;
Outside the curtain,
   icicles are dripping.
The brazier is burnt out,
   all perfume faded--
I shrink and shiver in the biting wind.   (P/168)

This exquisite mixture of eroticism and moral purity
which are the poles of Fragrant Lady's character were
captured by K'ung in the symbolism of the peach blossom
fan, about which he wrote:

"ch'uan-ch'i" means "transmitting (ch'uan)" that
which is "unique (ch'i)" in an incident.   If the
incident lacks uniqueness, then it doesn't deserve
to be transmitted.   What is so unique about a peach
blossom fan?   The fan of a courtesan, the colophon
of a playboy, the painting of a patron are all
common things . . . the common and yet unique thing

about it is the peach blossoms which are the
bloodstains of a beauty. These came from
preserving her chastity while waiting for her
lover, from injuring her head until it dripped with
blood, refusing to be shamed by traitorous
politicians . . . who ruined the foundations of a
three-century-old dynasty. With the dynasty no
longer surviving, where were the traitors then?
Only the bloodstains of a beauty--those peach
blossoms on the face of the fan continue to exist,
drawing praises from the mouth and regaling the
eyes. This is the unique element in this ordinary
event, what can be transmitted out of what need not
be transmitted. (T/3)

Although Juan's motivations would seem far removed from
Fragrant Lady's, his actions also proceed from the period's
faith in the primacy of the inner sanction. K'ung was
clearly more fascinated by him than the hero, for Juan
defied both his fellow literati and public opinion to
orchestrate a surprising reversal in his fortunes and
briefly reemerge at the center of national life. As one of
the great literary talents of the age who trained the most
accomplished acting troupe in Nanking, Juan has roots in
the world of Ch'in-huai as much as its other denizens. His
identification with the ideals of the authentic self
reflect K'ung's ironized view that the anticomic force,
hitherto a figure of external aggression, is actually to be
found within.

Juan's villainy comes to focus on his use of his most
famous work, The Swallow Note, for political purposes. A
romantic comedy noted for its ingenious plot and the grace
of its arias in the T'ang Hsien-tsu style, it is
essentially a comedy of errors in which the hero, a
brilliant literatus during the T'ang dynasty, falls in love

with two heroines.   One is a beautiful courtesan and the other, the equally alluring daughter of the prime minister. Juan represents the anticomic forces as the vicissitudes of time and man's natural ambition for success, ultimately uniting the hero with these figures of sensuality and power in traditional fashion.   K'ung shows the pleasure-loving Hung-kuang Emperor delighted with the work, which he proclaims is representative of the spirit of his reign. Juan thus gains entrée to the inner circle of the court and is empowered to invade Ch'in-huai and conscript its denizens for the palace troupe.   Juan's revenge over Fragrant Lady for her many rejections of him involves not only imprisoning her within the palace but degrading her to the role of clown within the troupe.   What then follows is a bizarre mirror-image of the romantic world as Hung-kuang himself takes a fancy to her, giving her a peach blossom fan of his own and promoting her back to heroine.   Perhaps Juan's basic sin as villain is that of literalness.   In acting out the imaginative fantasies of his dramas, he adopts a gamesman's view of reality devoid of any concern for the transcending moral consequences of action.   As he states upon his return to office:

> I can see the black and white
>
>   of events as on a chessboard;
>
> Brushing my eyebrows and beard again,
>
>   I shall play a role in the drama.   (P/89)

Juan's use of The Swallow Note symbolizes the attempt to totally subject life to art and is K'ung's most profound critique of unrestrained aestheticism.

Although K'ung maintains a predominantly critical view of the politicalization of Juan's play, as a dramatist heir to the great tradition of ch'uan-ch'i he reveals an ambivalent attitude towards Juan as a precursor.   In Scene 4, Yang Wen-ts'ung visits Juan in his mansion and through his sympathetic eyes Juan is seen as a sensitive man of taste schooled in the best traditions of the civilization.[65] The activists of the Fu-she are holding a banquet and ask to borrow his troupe to perform his new work. Juan happily lends them out in hope of convincing them of his true qualities and effect a reconciliation. As Juan and Yang sit awaiting the reactions, they first learn of the activist's praise of the play's artistic merits, then hear of their public reviling of the author's career. This is another instance in which Juan's attitude is hardened by the callous rejection of the young scholars. It is K'ung's critique of the Fu-she's inflexible dogmatism. Thus Juan is viewed from an alternate perspective. As a fallen "genius," his untimely ambition has enmeshed him in a lifelong vendetta which has made him cynical and vengeful in return.

This ambivalence of K'ung's runs deeper than just his dual attitudes towards the villain. It is rooted in his divided loyalties to the aesthetic ideals of late Ming romanticism and to his historical objectivity, which recognizes the period's inherent flaws. This is nowhere more evident than in the character of Yang Wen-ts'ung. As the primary catalyst of events who both provokes and seeks to remedy the conflicts, his access to all worlds and characters places him in the center of the drama's action. Yang is one of the great painters of the time and a welcome patron of Ch'in-huai who is the first to discover Fragrant Lady. He is the principle intermediary of her bethothal to Hou and intervenes at points to protect the hero and heroine as well as bring about the reunion of the lovers. But he is also the brother-in-law of Ma Shih-ying and a close friend of Juan Ta-ch'eng, who becomes a high official in the Restoration. Thus he serves as the broker for Juan's offer of the trousseau, and attempts to betroth

Fragrant Lady to one of Juan's followers. As the ultimate player of life, his amicable though fumbling attempt to balance all the complex forces around him is the most realistic presentation of the play's human dilemma, in which the sagely goal of "universality (t'ung)" can only be accomplished in society through amoral politics. Although modern Marxist critics have criticized Yang's "watery nature (shui-hsing),"[66] K'ung himself is unable to either praise or blame him. In the end, when all the major characters face judgement, he alone is allowed to escape offstage.

The major aesthetic problem for K'ung remained the reconciliation of his tragic vision with the philosophical ideal of an integrated cosmos so central to the Chinese dramatic experience. For, having abandoned the reunion formula, he sacrificed the primary vehicle of the festive celebration of universal harmony.[67] Unlike his modern western counterparts, K'ung was no more willing than any other traditional Chinese to create an imitation of life in which the fragmentation of man's emotional and social selves are posited as a permanent state of the Tao. In searching for a pattern of action to resolve the tragic rhythm, K'ung turned back to his own origins in Confucian ritual to create an archetypal superstructure based on the classical polarity of yin-yang.

In The Organizing Principles Behind The Peach Blossom Fan,[68] K'ung organizes the 30 major characters into categories based on moral hierarchy, complementarity, and a division between human and universal vision. Sixteen characters are classified in the romantic world of "Beauty (se)" headed by Hou Fang-yü on the left and Fragrant Lady on the right. They are allegorically termed the "Principal Beauties (cheng-se)" and are followed by the denizens of Ch'in-huai arranged according to their function in the action of separation and union: "Intermediaries (chien-se)," "Unifiers (ho-se)," and "Supplements (jun-se)." The 12 characters of the political world, termed that of "Power (ch'i)," are presided over by those most loyal to the dynasty. Shih K'o-fa in the odd column, and Tso Liang-yü together with Huang Te-kung in the even column, head the list as the "Central Powers (chung-ch'i)." Below them are the "Evil Powers (lei-ch'i)" of Hung-kuang, Ma Shih-ying, and Juan Ta-ch'eng, followed by various generals as "Excess Powers (yü-ch'i)" and "Destructive Powers (sha-ch'i)," all of whom are involved in the action of rise and fall.

K'ung did not represent the parallelistic implications of this allegorical chart within the play in its entirety, for to do so would have overburdened his work with a static, mechanical design. Rather, he focuses on a number of key pairs of characters such as Hou and Fragrant Lady, Liu and Su, Ma and Juan, Shih and Tso, as well as two who fall into his third category of "Regulators (ching-pu)." These latter figures are distinguished from those above in that they also exist in dimensions beyond the historical and thus possess a wider insight into the true operation of the Tao.

Taoist Chang as the "Warp Star (ching-hsing)" is K'ung's recreation of Chang I, whom he had met in Nanking. In his early appearances in the drama, there is a similarity to the prototype in that the character Chang is also a member of the Imperial Bodyguard in Peking who flees south following the suicide of the Ch'ung-chen Emperor. Chang relates to his fellow companions on the road that it was he who found the bodies of his martyred sovereigns and performed a simple funeral ceremony for them. He continues to enact a daily sacrifice to their spirits as expiation for all who failed the dynasty in its hour of need. The trauma of his experience gives Chang nightmares in which he

sees the disembodied spirits of Ch'ung-chen and his court
floating aimlessly, unable to find lasting peace. Thus,
Chang's practice of ritual becomes a means of exorcising
his personal ghosts and it becomes his mission to make his
way to Nanking and hold a grand sacrifice which will
finally pacify all spirits.

Before Chang can bring about a general absolution,
K'ung has him experience the vanity of human contention and
the struggle against history. Upon arriving in Nanking,
Chang joins the Restoration as a magistrate, only to find
himself becoming a pawn of the Ma-Juan faction. The
inevitable moral corruption sets in and Chang defends
himself by retiring to his studio, from the detached
vantage point of which he views the impending debacle.
Prior to the final collapse, he prefigures the general
solution for the positive figures by undergoing religious
enlightenment and being reborn as a Taoist monastic. In
what would normally have been the reunion scene, Chang
emerges to hold his grand sacrifice at a temple outside the
city. At a climactic moment, he induces the collective
recognition of the fundamental interdependence of inner and
outer selves, which leads the hero and heroine to renounce
passion and transcend the illusions of both romantic and
political worlds.[69]

If Taoist Chang represents the religious view of ritual
as spiritual liberation, The Old Master as the "Woof Star
(wei-hsing)" is the dramatist's personal spokesman for the
Confucian view of it as the ideal pattern of social
action.[70] Cast in the archetype of the Sage, The Old
Master transcends time to exist in three dimensions, yet
his pattern of action remains constant as he urges the
continual practice of li. In the prologues to each half of
the play, set some 40 years after the main action, he
appears onstage at the Garden of Peace, a theater which

K'ung often attended, and presents himself as an aged
"survivor" who views the play with nostalgic emotions. As
he describes himself:

> In bygone years, reality was the play;
> The play becomes reality today.
> Twice have I watched its progress:
> Heaven preserves
> This passive gazer with his
> cold clear eyes. (P/153)

The character is played by the <u>fu-mo</u> role, which
conventionally appears only in the prologue act to greet
the audience and sing an aria summarizing the plot. K'ung
has not only endowed the hitherto anonymous role with an
autobiographical personality but extends his function
within the play itself.

In the historical world, The Old Master's actions
principally involve officiating at ritual ceremonies. In
accordance with classical ideals, he attempts to create a
balanced society by unifying individual energies and
directing them towards the creation of a collective order.
But in the context of time, these are shown to be but a
momentary achievement of harmony; indeed, the rituals serve
another function, that of highlighting the conflicts and
foreshadowing the fragmentation of the polity. In Scene 3,
"The Disrupted Ceremonies," he presides over the spring
sacrifice to Confucius. Attending are the leading literati
of the Imperial Academy including members of the Fu-she.
K'ung creates this scene to present the moral idealism of
the activists as well as isolate the villain, for when Juan
Ta-ch'eng attempts to participate, he is publicly reviled
by the others. Unable to defend his past, he is beaten by
them and by The Old Master as well, who denounces him as a
traitor. Here, ritual is used to express the dramatist's
highest point of view towards his characters and serves a

structural function, overriding the alternative prespectives expressed elsewhere in the course of the play. Likewise, in Scene 32, "The Imperial Mourning," a court sacrifice on the first anniversary of the Ch'ung-chen Emperor's death serves as the final meeting of the key political figures before the collapse of the Restoration. It is The Old Master himself who forebodes the end as he appears before the ceremony to voice his fears over the general state of affairs. Attending are Ma Shih-ying, Juan Ta-ch'eng, Yang Wen-ts'ung, and Shih K'o-fa. Again, it is Juan who disrupts things as he denounces the activists at the altar, causing Shih to leave in protest. In these complementary scenes, The Old Master's attempt to sustain the ritual pattern are shown to be doomed by the forces of history. Yet he continues to maintain a Confucian faith in the necessity of striving for positive action. As one of the activists states:

Heaven may loosen Chaos; 'tis for Man
To conjure order wheresoever he can. (P/30)

After completion, the play remained in manuscript form for several years, but this did not prevent it from gaining instant popularity in Peking literary circles. Not only was it read by K'ung's own friends but admirers sent gifts requesting copies for their household troupes.[71] By autumn of 1699, news of the play had reached the Imperial Palace, which sent a eunuch to K'ung's house requesting a copy. Having lent out his own, he had to scurry around to borrow one and hurriedly delivered it to the proper office at midnight.[72] Copies of the play were making their way to the provinces as well. Ku Ts'ai, who was traveling in the Hukuang area at the time, reported that he had attended performances staged by the household troupe of a member of the local gentry.[73] One of the more lavish presentations was recalled by K'ung:

Hardly a day seemed to go by without a performance of The Peach Blossom Fan somewhere in Peking, but that held in the Sojourn Garden[74] was the most magnificent.   Famous aristocrats, high officials, and talented literati gathered in such a crowd that it was impossible to find space for one's legs. The furnishings formed an embroidered universe, and the banquet a landscape of jeweled delicacies.   The performers were divided into two groups—the pretty ones played the central characters while the slow-witted ones were given the supporting roles.   The props were readily available.   Encouraged by their generous wages, the performers strived for the finest artistry.   Their singing and acting were marvelous.   No doubt, this was because the host was a grandson of the noble lord from Kao-yang,[75] a man who leads a fashionable life rivaling the aristocratic Wangs and Hsiehs.[76]   Nothing was spared for this glorious occasion.   Yet, in the midst of this dazzling theater, there were a few who sat quietly weeping behind their sleeves— former officials and "survivors."   When the lanterns had flickered out and the drinking was over, they uttered sighs and went their ways. (T/6)

In the spring of 1700, K'ung suddenly resigned from office.   Because this reversal followed closely after the completion of The Peach Blossom Fan, a number of scholars have attempted to link the content of the play with his political fortunes.   It has been assumed, despite the absence of definite evidence, that the supposedly anti-Ch'ing content of the play rendered K'ung's loyalties to the dynasty suspect and that he was the victim of a "literary inquisition."[77]   As a recent study has pointed

out, however, not only are there few facts supporting this
view but it is also based on a misreading of the
nationalist sentiments in the play.[78]

K'ung himself was tight-lipped about the affair and
merely offered hints as to the cause. Commenting on a poem
to a departing friend, Ts'ai Wang-nan, he stated, "Wang-nan
knows all about the circumstances surrounding my punishment
and sent over a gift of money to console me."[79] He was
more revealing in another poem written when a number of his
friends came by to show their support:

> Some "hero" with a fine-toothed comb
> Found an error of mine and sent in a
>   report.
> I was just a white-haired keeper of
>   acccounts
> Who was slandered and failed to protect himself
>   like someone deaf and dumb. (K/236-37)

Clearly it involved some document written by K'ung in which
an error of language or figures was blown out of proportion
and used to build a case against him. This is further
hinted at in Li Kung's poem to K'ung in which K'ung is
compared to the Ming official, Chang Ch'un, who was
unfairly besmirched before his superiors. Chang chose to
fight the accusations, only to become embroiled in a series
of lengthy investigations before finally proving his
innocence. In the light of the costliness and the dangers
of such a course, Li urged K'ung to retire quickly back to
Stonegate.[80]

The circimstances directly following his resignation
cast further doubt on the view that it was related to his
drama. In May 1700, barely a month later, Li Mu-an, the
Senior Censor who had earlier staged a performance of The
Peach Blossom Fan, put on yet another performance attended
by a number of high officials. "I was given the seat of

honor," K'ung recalled, "and was asked to rank the actors who took turns toasting me. The audience reacted with discerning praise and I felt like I was floating on a cloud."[81] This would have been a grossly insensitive act on the part of the host had the play been the cause of K'ung's leaving office; and it is questionable whether K'ung would have been in such an ebullient mood upon viewing it.

There is little reason to believe that K'ang-hsi personally disapproved of the play. An unconfirmed tradition has it that the Emperor was actually quite fond of seeing it performed and sympathized with the plight of Hung-kuang surrounded by duplicitous officials. He was said to have particularly enjoyed Scene 15, "The Coronation," and Scene 25, "The Cast Selected." Upon being moved by the desperate situation of the Nanking Restoration, he reportedly sighed in consternation, "Oh Hung-kuang, although you did not want things to fail, how could you have prevented it?" And then he would down a cup of wine.[82] As for the ideological content of the play, not only did K'ung go to considerable lengths to voice loyal sentiments in the prologues, but he omitted dramatizing well-known incidents which might be interpreted as provoking anti-Ch'ing sentiment. As a recent study has found, the historical view of the fall of the Ming and the Manchu invasion is in accord with that propounded by the Ch'ing dynasty itself and with K'ang-hsi's own views.[83]

The abrupt end of K'ung's public career seems to have been a minor, though not uncharacteristic incident in Peking politics. Then, as now, the official stage was a scene of constant maneuvering where it was rare for anyone to remain in a particular office for any great length of time. Even Wang Shih-chen, possessing far greater power than K'ung, would eventually run afoul after half a century

of public service in the highest positions. That K'ung
lasted as long as he did is perhaps a testament to his
caution and lack of aggressiveness. If his play was at all
related to his departure, it may well have been that its
sudden success so increased his prestige that his
competitors felt obliged to move against him and prevent
the growth of his influence.

K'ung became rather philosophical about it all and
wrote:

> It's good to retire.
> Today's guests have gone,
>   leaving no trace.
> The wisteria which I have been growing
>   has not yet sprouted buds
> And the books and lute in my room
>   are all strewn about.
> Old friends grasped me by the hand
>   and with worried brows
> Urged me to retire
>   and protect myself.
> I was born amidst mountains and marshes—
>   and eater of "turtle-foot" roots,
> Just someone who's thought of himself
>   as a wizened recluse.
> I'll pack up my plain socks
>   and don my black shoes,
> Draw water from a stream and at night
>   bathe away the red dust,
> Relying on old colleagues
>   to give me some money for wine.
> The mountains east and west
>   await my exploration.
> It's good to retire. (K/235)

K'ung lingered in the capital for two more years hoping for a change in the situation which would return him to office. Once again a gentleman of leisure, he continued to pursue his favorite pastimes of socializing, attending poetry gatherings, and collecting art. In his poems, he began to accept the role of retired scholar and nurtured thoughts of returning home. Eventually, it became clear that his position would not be restored to him and that his career was finished. Towards the end of 1702, he set about bidding farewell to his friends as he prepared for the journey back to Ch'ü-fu. He was beseiged by callers and estimated that he had complied with over a hundred requests for colophons.[84] To Wang Shih-chen, he dedicated a lengthy poem recollecting the high points of their friendship and portraying himself, in the end, as a Ch'ü Yuan misunderstood by those above: "I fear the fragrant plant has been sullied, / And have come to doubt the Fair One's beauty. /My regrets will cling to the Tuan-wu Festival. /The laments of the cuckoo urge me to return . . . "[85] The philosopher, Wang Yuan, [86] summed up the feelings of K'ung's friends on his departure:

> Mr. K'ung served as Secretary and Assistant Department Director in the Board of Revenue but resigned and returned home. Aristocrats, men of rank, and ordinary literati all felt regret over his leaving, but he said, "There is no need for regret. My mother is old and I cannot look after her properly. So I am going home to support her. I will repair the Studio of the Solitary Cloud and spend the rest of my days there engaged in writing. I feel fortunate, so why have any regrets?" . . . Alas, when it comes to seeking worthy associates, how many consider their friends to be as important as themselves? Mr. K'ung was

highly regarded at court for his writings, his elegance, and his erudition--a model for others. Yet he never tired of meeting literati. Regardless of status, anyone possessing the slightest merit would be courteously received; and those individualists who could not find their place in the world all looked to him as a friend. He exhausted his resources and pawned his clothes to be able to provide simple food and wine. Chanting poetry and chatting, he would drink and happily console them. But now he has returned. I gazed off sadly towards the Golden Terrace as I walk back and forth about the market place wondering who it was singing that tragic song in a drunken manner? When I gaze about and think of now and then, how can I help but weep?[87]

A LINGERING STAY

It is sometimes the case in the biography of a great artist whose fame rests largely on a single masterpiece that the life appears to diminish in intensity after the opus is delivered to the world. It is as if everything up to that point is a period of gestation: early experiences nurture the development of the vision; utterances sound like preliminary gropings toward the ultimate formulation. The unique complex of diverse activities are assumed to find compensation or fulfillment in the birth of the artistic product which, once accomplished, permits the subject to drift offstage and finish his days in relative obscurity. K'ung returned to Ch'ü-fu in time to celebrate the Chinese New Year of 1703. He was welcomed back by the K'ung clan, with pride and commiseration, as a distinguished son who had achieved fame in the capital. Now 55, K'ung would live 15 years more. He never wrote another drama, nor was he impelled in these final years by that particular combination of Confucian ambition and personal imagination which brought forth The Peach Blossom Fan. Yet it is fair to say that this period, despite the burden of failing eyesight, was perhaps his most contented. Freed from his earlier creative tensions, he traveled and continued to write poetry and collect art, gradually assuming the image of the "old survivor" which he had so admired throughout his younger years. By this time, almost all of the late Ming figures he had known had departed the scene. Now it was K'ung and his generation who were the last ones to have had some personal contact with the bygone romanticism of that era. In the growing nostalgia of the times, K'ung assumed the venerable patina of his dramatic persona, The Old Master of Ceremonies, as he ritualistically engaged in interests which he had cultivated over the course of a lifetime.

Public interest in The Peach Blossom Fan continued through these years and K'ung found himself honored in the provinces for his play:

> In 1706, while traveling around Mt. Heng (Shansi), I met an old superior of mine, Liu Ch'i,[88] who had become a prefect. He and his fellow officials invited me to a grand banquet during which The Peach Blossom Fan was staged for two whole days. The performance was rich in feeling and brought out the nuances. The other colleagues knew that it had come from my hand and toasted me. I noticed a few minor points needing correction so I called over the director and offered some guidance on the spot. (T/7)

In 1708, the play was finally published due to the generosity of an admirer. K'ung penned several prefaces for the edition,[89] in one of which he stated:

My manuscript of <u>The Peach Blossom Fan</u> was becoming
worn to the point where I could hardly read it.
T'ung Che-ts'un from Tientsin, a poet, had been a
friend of Ch'ü Ta-chun. He had raised Ch'ü's
orphan and arranged his marriage as if he had been
his own child, an act of charity which all
acclaimed. He came by to visit me when he was
traveling in Shantung and I gave him the manuscript
copy to read. After only a few lines, he started
beating out the rhythm and exclaiming his
appreciation. He spent fifty gold pieces out of
his own pocket to engage an engraver whose efforts
were scarcely less difficult than a thirty-mile
journey; surely there is nothing easy about having
something printed. (T/7)

There was also much traveling during these years. Liu
Ch'i, the Prefect of P'ing-yang, Shansi, who staged K'ung's
play, had long had an interest in Confucian ritual.
Following a severe earthquake in his district, he sponsored
the restoration of the local temple, replacing the
ceremonial vessels that had been destroyed. K'ung had
known Liu as a fellow provincial in Peking and was invited
to visit P'ing-yang in 1706. He stayed there and
contributed his expertise for two years, during which he
also served as general editor of the local gazetteer.[90] The
year 1709 found him passing through Kaifeng, Honan, and
later in Wuchang, Hukuang (modern Hupei), where he
sojourned through the following year before returning to
Ch'ü-fu. Scattered poetic references indicate more
journeys to such places as Tsinan and Tung-lai in Shantung.

His last trip was a sentimental return to the south
beginning in January 1715. Almost all his associates from
thirty years earlier were gone but he found a new friend in
Liu T'ing-chi.[91] K'ung had heard of Liu during his first

trip in the south and later came across a copy of Liu's poetic works in a bookstall at the Temple of Charity in Peking. The two finally met in January, when K'ung stopped at Yuan-p'u in Kiangsu and sought an interview. Liu had been recently demoted to Intendent of the Huai-yang Circuit and, finding himself with much free time, responded warmly to K'ung's request. Their mutual admiration quickly flourished into a solid friendship which encouraged K'ung to remain in the vicinity for several months.

Liu's poetry was seen by a fellow critic as based on a synthesis of the styles of Po Chü-yi and Lu Yu,[92] and assessment which he himself concurred in.[93] This may refer to the combination of Lu's formally intricate couplets and Po's simple diction, as well as agreement with the latter's concern with a moral view-point. Such values were always congenial to K'ung, who further praised Liu for his ability to achieve freshness and individuality within the tradition, something he ascribed to Liu's independent spirit.[94] During his visit, he contributed a preface and an essay to Liu's miscellany, Random Notes by the Garden Denizen and, with the latter's aid, put in order his own poems of the previous two decades. This resulted in the publication of a final collection, Poems from a Lingering Stay, containing 630 pieces in 12 chüan.[95] K'ung's preface reiterates his progressive attitude towards stylistic innovation and pays allegiance to Liu's theoretical influence, especially the orthodox position exalting the poetry of the Book of Songs as "mild, tender, sincere and profound (wen-jou tun-hou),"[96] proceeding out of the cultivation of the poet's character:

A guest once stated, "to be 'mild, tender, sincere and profound' are the guiding ideals of a poet. Although poetry is based on expression, it values understatement more. Since the High T'ang,

however, these have been lost sight of, yet poets
should still seek to attain them." I replied,
"Poetry derives from a person. My concern is that
the person might not be refined for if he is, then
he will be mild and tender; or I worry that he
might not possess substance, for if he does, then
he will be sincere and profound. It is a daily
renewal of sensibility and an inexhaustible source
of meaning, for whenever emotions respond to a
scene where words can capture it all—that is
expression. And when emotions and scene are so
bound up in each other that words cannot fully
describe it—that is understatement. This does not
mean that words which are lukewarm and muddled,
purloined and hackneyed, which neither provoke nor
even stimulate, deluding others by their self-
delusion, can be called "understatement." If the
High T'ang is used to demean contemporary art, then
anyone can hold up the Airs and Odes to demean the
poetry of the Han and Wei dynasties. In short,
ever since the first stroke of the trigrams was
made, civilization has gradually unfolded through a
natural process. Even the Sages would not dare to
demean the clarity of the Six Classics by invoking
the primacy of the first written line. The changes
which have occurred since the Airs and Odes are of
similar value. (K/493)

Of the very end of K'ung's life, little is known save
that shortly before his death he was visited by an old
friend, Chin Chih, with whom he spent much time in
antiquarian pursuits.[97] Together they spent many
pleasurable hours reading The Peach Blossom Fan, searching
the environs for the site of a Han palace, and examining
K'ung's collection of antique paper. Chin was still a

guest in Ch'ü-fu when K'ung Shang-jen died on February 14, 1718 at the age of 69.

A few years before his death, K'ung made one of his last visits to Stonegate where he had continued to maintain his retreat through the years. In a narrative poem, he celebrated the renewing pleasures of the landscape and the primary role which the natural scene had played throughout his life:

A Journey to Stonegate in Late Spring, 1714,
   Along with Some Friends
Depressed by this passage through Spring's
   remains,
I was frittering away the interminable days.
So I journeyed, gladdened by companions,
Setting out on an impulse requiring no omen.
Folks can be stingy--they begrudged us
   their horses.
But quickly we packed for the distant road.
As we walked along, the servants turned
   merry;
Friendship deepened when we shared a carriage.
After crossing the Ssu River,
   the reins were drawn in,
The horses were halted to view the pines.
We scanned forested peaks, coolly detached
And cast off the city like and old,
   worn sandal.
Each path through the wilderness was a
   familiar way,
The country dwellers, all old acquaintances.
The killed some chickens and
   we agreed to delay
For who needs prompting to empty a winecup?

Then, departing through the gate
  past tree shadows tilting,
We crossed over hills with cloud vapors
  moist.
We avoided tumbling about the sharp cliffs
Yet the walking was difficult,
  forcing us to crawl.
With a clamor we halted the horses and
  carriage
And strung along, portering umbrellas
  and packs.
There was a covey of monks who had long
  been isolated.
Only now did they straighten up Buddha's
  abode.
They boiled congee, lit lanterns and we
  dined;
Assigned rooms, couches, and we slept.
Awakened from our dreams to the warbling of
  birds,
Our earthly thoughts vanished in the echoes
  of prayers.
Who could wait for the morning meal?
Each went off along with a companion.
I rubbed off the moss to read all the
  tablets
And grasped onto vines to descend
  precarious steps.
A winding stream pierced the mountain
  depths;
Sharp peaks soared further into the
  Ultimate.
The shifting sands wore down my sandals.

Tai Pen-hsiao, <u>Landscape</u>

Clothes ripped at the seams in the bramble
patches.

Though concerned that the wind would blow
open our sleeves,

We still drank from our winecups along the
road.

Advancing, I leaned on a servant's
shoulders;

Resting, I massaged my aged thighs.

We wound sinuously from east to west;

Having traveled but a hundredth part of the
road's length.

Households remain beside ancient ruins;

Scenes are still connected with honored
names.

I point them out, a bit off-hand.

Some are restored, others, not yet.

Grasping a staff, I leaned beside Cinnabar
Terrace.

Then together we entered the Ch'an chamber.

We gulped down tea, and our throats spouted
steam;

We wrung out our clothers and sweat
trickled down.

We found coolness beneath the weft of
wisteria,

Picked a clean rock and dusted it off.

Seating ourselves on round bamboo mats,

We raised the teapot and poured in turn.

Paired banners stood for archery targets;

Two games of chess were played.

We countered with strategies like Sun and
P'ang;[98]

Our   friendship   was   bonded   like   lacquer   and
   varnish.
Suddenly came rain in the midst of the   drought.
We drank to it, but the wine ran out.
Dripping wet, we lazily took our leave
Beneath the crashing patter on our bamboo   hats.
Though drunk, we managed the slippery steps
By my old studio whose roof still leaks.
How lucky to have come across an ambrosial   rain,
To have spent a night savoring sweet   dreams!
That evening we bathed in perfumed waters
And in the morning, dined on fine grains.
We returned with wine bottles emptied
But the horses, well-filled, were full of   power.
Each of us sang verses in turn
And   we   discussed   the   merits   of   the   passing
   scenes.
Time and again, we set a date for a reunion;
Over and over, we kept glancing back.
Excitedly, we consider building dikes
And urgently plan to conserve the forest.
Yet I am but a recluse, not a modern-day   worthy.
Let the magistrate by praised as an ancient   sage.
I have   already   surrendered   to the   decline   of my
flesh
But   how   can   I   cease   longing   to   dwell   on   the
   mountain?   (K/224-25)

EPILOGUE

Nearly three hundred years after the K'ang-hsi
Emperor's visit, Ch'ü-fu appears surprisingly well-
preserved to the modern pilgrim. As in the past, one
arrives first at Yen-chou, now but ten hours by rail from
Peking. Gone are the "gentleman's oxen," replaced by
1950s-style autos which ferry the visitor along a tree-
lined road to Ch'ü-fu. From the sight of the broad green
fields along the way, it is evident that the traditional
economic sufferings of the locality have been largely
overcome. The rivers are now controlled through modern
technology. Corn has replaced <u>kao-liang</u> as the major crop
and bumper harvests have been registered in the past few
years, making Ch'ü-fu an exporter of foodstuffs. The town,
though still mostly composed of old grey farmhouses, shows
signs of growth as new brick quarters rise amongst the
crumbling mud and thatch residences.

There are now over 100,000 K'ungs in Ch'ü-fu,
constituting about one fifth of the entire population of
the county. The descendents now run into the 80th
generation. Most are still named according to their
genealogical order and may be buried in the Confucian Grove

according to their branch. But many younger descendents
have been named outside the order and are barely aware of
their lineage. Unlike under the emperors, when
registration in the genealogy exempted one from corvée
labor, there remain few outward advantages to being a
K'ung. Yet they seem as secure today in their locality as
ever. Despite being deprived of their ideological function
by the Revolution, they have weathered, by their sheer
numbers, the upheavals of the past few decades. Today,
clan members staff the local branch of the China Travel
Service and the Cultural Properties Bureau, and are
prominent in local government. K'ung Shang-jen's own
descendants number in the thousands, most of them farmers
and workers. Their ancestor is remembered for his literary
accomplishments, but also as a member of the gentry who
owned several houses in town, a farm outside and the studio
on Stonegate, now disappeared.

The once-sacred sites in Ch'ü-fu are now considered
important cultural monuments and are directly administered
by the Ch'ü-fu Bureau of Cultural Properties, which is
under the Ministry of Culture. The 120 or so employees are
charged with maintaining the Confucian Temple and Grove as
well as curatorship of the archives of documents and
artifacts. Some 40 artisans are constantly involved in
restoration work, and there is a staff of scholars, many of
whom are K'ungs.

Like almost every other historical place in China,
these sites suffered considerable damage from the barbarism
of the Culture Revolution. Gone are the statues of
Confucius and the Attendant Sages from the Hall of
Accomplishment. Missing as well are the parasols which
K'ang-hsi donated after his visit. In the Confucian Grove
many prominent headstones, including that of K'ung Shang-
jen, were toppled.

Today, there is an active restoration project being carried out funded by Peking. The Hall of Accomplishment has been repaired and repainted. Its shiny vermilion pillars and green and gold rafters are perhaps a bit too striking for an ancient temple. However, it should not be long before the gentle decay which overtakes all new things in China tones it down to an appropriately antique patina. The Hall of the Literary Constellation, locked and empty, broods over its courtyard of ancient steles. It is genuinely delapidated and, for that reason, a far better vehicle for the pilgrim's melancholy reflections. Unfortunately, it too is slated for a facelift.

The Ducal Mansion, whose scale recalls the fictional Jung mansion of The Dream of the Red Chamber, is well-maintained. The eastern courtyard where the Dukes were tutored in their Confucian studies now serves as a quaint hotel for visiting foreigners. The extensive official and domestic quarters, with their furniture, dishes, and clothing, are kept frozen in time, as if the last inhabitants had just left. The inharmonious blend of late Ch'ing articles accented by art deco gadgets imported during the 1920s and 30s evokes the decadence of the Great Tradition in its final hours.

Local inhabitants still speak with nsotalgic respect of the present Duke, K'ung Te-ch'eng of the 76th generation, who has been living in exile in Taiwan for more than thirty years. There, he dwells with his immediate family in circumstances which are a far cry from the aristocratic splendor of Ch'ü-fu. He is, however, accorded a high degree of dignity in the society as befitting his title, which the Nationalist Government still recognizes. Every year, he appears in his official robes to preside over sacrifices at the Confucian Temple in Taipei and also serves as a faculty member of Taiwan University and a

Presidential Advisor.   Like the treasures of the Palace Museum, he is a link with a mythologized past and an important symbol of Taipei's claim to political legitimacy. His departure from Ch'ü-fu has left a void amongst the K'ungs which has not been filled although what kind of role the Dukes of the Sagely Posterity can play in the new society is far from clear.   It is certainly not the first time that the clan has been divided due to the vicissitudes of history.   When and under what circumstances the K'ungs will be reunited remains a mystery at present, known only, perhaps, to the diviner of hexagrams.

R.E.S.

Ducal Mansion
Ch'ü-fu
Summer 1981

PREFACE

1. Leon Edel, "The Figure Under the Carpet," in M. Pacter, ed., <u>Telling Lives: The Biographer's Art</u> (Wash., D.C.: New Republic Books, 1979); 20.

CHAPTER ONE

CH'Ü-FU, THE SACRED PRECINCT

1. The name "Ch'ü-fu" or "winding plain" describes its geographical form in contrast to the surrounding hills and mountains. Ying, <u>Feng-su</u>, 10/5b-6a; <u>Shih-chi</u> 4/128.

2. For a description of Stonegate (Shih-men-shan) which was the site of K'ung Shang-jen's retreat, see pp. 49-70. Mt. Ni, also known as Mt. Ni-ch'iu, stands some 15 miles from the city. It is composed of five peaks, the middle one rising through the clouds, and was the site of several shrines and an academy. It was here that Confucius was reportedly conceived after his mother prayed to the mountain spirit for a son, hence his courtesy name, "Chung-ni." <u>Shih-chi</u> 47/1905; <u>Ch'ueh-li kuang-chih</u> 5/1b; P'an <u>Ch'ü-fu</u> 36/1077. A woodblock illustration appears in K'ung, <u>tsu-t'ing</u>/plate 4.

3. For an ancient description of the Ssu and other rivers in Ch'ü-fu, see Li, <u>Shui-ching-chu</u> 25; a more recent description can be found in P'an. <u>Ch'ü-fu</u> 36/1079-85.

4. P'an, <u>Ch'ü-fu</u> 31/941-32/979.   <u>Shan-tung</u>/843-46. For a vivid narration of such disasters in nearby T'an-ch'eng, see Spence, <u>Woman Wang</u>/1-8.

5. P'an, Ch'ü-fu 29/889-90.

6. Yuan, Ch'ü-fu/35b-36a.

7. Shen Nung, second of the Three Sovereigns (San-huang), moved his capital from Ch'en to Ch'ü-fu.   His treasury building is mentioned in Tso-chuan: Chao 18/2 and was still standing in the eighth century, when it was visited by Li Po, who wrote a poem on it.   Cheng, T'ung-chih 1/32b.

8. The Yellow Emperor (Huang-ti), third of the Three Sovereigns, was reputedly born in nearby Shou-ch'iu.   He made his capital in Ch'iung-sang and later moved to Ch'ü-fu.   Huang-fu, Ti-wang/7.

9. Shao-hao, the first of the Five Emperors (Wu-ti), is traditionally believed to have reigned for 84 years in the middle of the third millenium B.C.   He died at the age of 100 and is buried on Mt. Yun-yang, 2 ½ miles northeast of Ch'ü-fu.   Huang-fu, Ti-wang/7; Shih-chi 1/9-10; a woodblock print and description of the tomb appears in P'an, Ch'ü-fu 4/135-43; also photographed in Chang, K'ung-meng/14.

10. The Duke of Chou (Chou-kung) (d. 1105 B.C.) was enfeoffed in 1110 B.C., the first of 34 dukes of Lu. According to Meng-tzu 49/6b,, the area measured 100 li or a little over 30 miles in circumference.   He did not reside in his fief, however, preferring to remain in the Chou capital.   His son, Po-ch'in (d. 1063 B.C.), succeeded to the title and was responsible for building the ancient wall.   After the Duke of Chou's death, a temple was built outside the city but was destroyed with the fall of Lu. Another was not rebuilt until the Sung after Chen-tsung's (r. 998-1023) pilgrimage in 1009.   His collateral descendents continued to live in the area and were finally enfeoffed by K'ang-hsi in 1684.   Shih-chi 4/127; a

woodblock of the temple and description appears in P'an, Ch'ü-fu 4/144-52.

11. For maps of Ch'ü-fu city, the Confucian Temple (K'ung-miao), the Confucian Grove (K'ung-lin), and the surrounding area, see Ch'ueh-li kuang-chih 1/6a-12b; more maps as well as discussions can be found in Pan, Ch'ü-fu, 3-8/127-272. A modern description with maps is presented in Nagel's China/740-71.

12. The text of this stele, officially known as "The Stele of the Han Chancellor of Lu, I Ying, Requesting the Establishment of an Officer with an Emolument of a Hundred Bushels (Han lu-hsiang i ying ch'ing-chih pai-shih tsu-shih-pei)," is recorded in K'ung, wen-hsien-k'ao 33/1a-2a.

13. Photographed in Chang, K'ung-meng/45.

14. Woodblock prints of these appear in Ch'ueh-li kuang-chih 1/21a-23b.

15. See Lun-yü 34/16/13: "Tzu-ch'in asked Po-yü, 'Have you learned anything different from your father than we have?' He replied, 'No.' Once, when he was standing by himself, I hurried past him in the courtyard and he asked me, 'Have you studied poetry yet?' and I replied 'Not yet.' 'If you do not study poetry, you will not be able to express yourself.' So I withdrew and studied poetry. On another day he was also standing alone while I was hurrying across the courtyard and he asked me, 'Have you studied ritual yet?' and I replied, 'Not yet.' 'If you don't study ritual, you will find yourself without a place.' So I withdrew and studied ritual. After hearing this, Tzu-ch'in left and happily exclaimed, 'I asked one question but learned about three things: about poetry, about ritual and how the gentleman keeps his son at a distance."

16. In 213 B.C., the head of the clan, K'ung Fu (q.v. note 40), secreted copies of the Shu-ching (Book of History), Li-chi (Book of Ritual), Hsiao-ching (Book of

Filial   Piety),   and   Lun-yü   (Analects)   in   a   wall   of
Confucius' mansion to avoid the Ch'in bookburning.   These
were accidentally recovered in the Han by Prince Kung of Lu
(enfeoffed 159 B.C.).   While demolishing the mansion to
expand his nearby palace, he heard the sounds of musical
instruments issue forth, halted construction, and found the
works.   These were later reedited and propagated by K'ung
An-kuo (see note 50).   Han-shu 53/2414; P'an, Ch'ü-fu
49/1390. The wall is photographed in Chang, K'ung-meng/54.

17. The name "Ch'ueh-li," often used as a literary
appellation for Ch'ü-fu,, derives from the site of two
towered gates of the Duke of Lu's palace.   See the
commentary to Tso-chuan: Ting 2/2 (Shih-san-ching 6/943).
It is also associated with Confucius' mansion, which stood
nearby. See Ch'ueh-li kuang-chih 6/1b.

18. See Chuang-tzu 86/31/1; a photograph appears in
Chang, K'ung-meng 1/29.   The site actually dates from the
Ch'ien-hsing period (1022-23) renovation when the main hall
of the Temple was moved further north and the old
foundations were rebuilt.   The area was landscaped and
K'ung Tao-fu, head of the clan in the 45th generation,
designated it as the "Apricot Terrace."   Photographed in
Chang K'ung-meng/31.

19. For a woodblock print see K'ung, tsu-t'ing/plate
11; photographed in Li, Ch'ü-fu/36.

20. The hall is photographed in Chang, K'ung-meng/28.
A woodblock print of the statue of Confucius appears in
Ch'ueh-li kuang-chih 1/3a.

21. These and other vessels are illustrated in Ch'ueh-
li kuang-chih 1/17a-20b; illustrations and descriptions
also appear in P'an, Ch'ü-fu 10,11.

22. Chang Tai (1597-c.1684), courtesy name Tsung-tzu,
also Shih-kung, artistic name T'ao-an, also Tieh-an, was
born in Shaohsing, Chekiang, into a wealthy family.

Several generations earlier, his forebears had been metropolitan graduates and held high positions, but in his grandfather's time, during the Wan-li (1573-1620) era, the family turned to extravagance. Chang Tai himself was noted for his luxurious manner of living, particularly during the 1630s and 40s in Nanking. Prior to that, he often visited his father in Yen-chou, Shantung, where the latter was a secretary to the Prince of Lu from 1627 to 1631. These reminiscences of Ch'ü-fu must have originated from this period. In Nanking, he was noted for his acting troupes, of which he owned five altogether, and for his many aesthetic interests. After the fall of Nanking in 1645, Chang retired to Shaohsing where his house was pillaged by renegade loyalist forces and his fortune destroyed. The final four decades of his life were spent in poverty as a hermit in the nearby hills, where he refused to shave his head in submission to the Manchus. Most of his writings date from this period. Chang was regarded as a fine prose stylist, producing essays and writings on Ming history. His chief surviving work, a collection of reminiscences entitled T'ao-an meng-i (Dreamlike Memories from the Studio of Relaxation), is one of the most widely read sources of the cultural life of the South during the first half of the seventeenth century. Hummel, Emminent Chinese/53-54; T'ai, "Preface," in Chang, T'ao-an/1-7.

23. Ch'iao Chou (199-270), courtesy name Yun-nan, artistic name Fu-yü-tzu, was from Szechuan and was noted for his literary talents as well as his knowledge of astronomy. He served under Chu-ko Liang (181-234) in the Kingdom of Shu and was made Marquis of Yang-ch'eng-t'ing. Upon the Chin victory over Shu, he refused to serve the new dynasty. Among his writings are Fa-hsun (Legal Codes), Wu-ching-lun (Discussions on the Five Classics), and Ku-shih k'ao-shu (Research on Ancient Historical Treatises).

24. K'ung-ts'ung-tzu (The Discourses of the Confucian School) was compiled by K'ung Fu (see note 40), head of the K'ung clan in the 9th generation, in 21 chüan. It contains the remarks of Confucius and his disciples. See Chi, ssu-k'u ch'üan-shu/1876-77.

25. T'ai-p'ing yü-lan 560/2531, popularly known as the Huang-lan (Imperial Encyclopedia), contains a similar entry, though not in the exact words quoted by Chang.

26. Chang, T'ao-an/16-7.

27. K'ung's courtesy names were P'in-chih and Chi-chung, and his artistic names were Tung-t'ang (Eastern Pond), An-t'ang (the Waterside Studio) and Yun-t'ing shan-jen (Hermit of the Pavilion of the Solitary Cloud).

28. See K'ung, shih-chia-p'u/1300.

29. Yen-chou fu-chih hsu-pien 16 (1719 ed.). Quoted in Jung, nien-p'u/3.

30. Ni Shih-ch'ing, Shih-tsui. Quoted in Ch'en, nien-p'u/18.

31. See Ch'un-ch'iu 366: Chao 7/6; Legge, The Chinese Classics 5/618-19. The account in Shih-chi 47/1905-47, long accepted as the authoritative version, was based in part on information which Ssu-ma Ch'ien gathered from his own journey to Ch'ü-fu. It contains a number of inconsistencies though, and much legendary information leading some to claim that the author had Taoist sympathies. See Creel, Confucius/246. More factual genealogies exist in K'ung, tsu-t'ing 1; Ch'ueh-li kuang-chih 2/8a-47b. The most reliable traditional account is that which K'ung Shang-jen himself compiled in K'ung-tzu shih-chia-p'u.

32. Ho, courtesy name Fu-fu, was the rightful heir but was usurped by his uncle who was subsequently murdered by Fu-fu's younger brother. Fu-fu refused to reoccupy the

position, which then passed to the line of this younger brother who became Duke Li. See K'ung, shih-chia-p'u/159.

33. For a biography of Chia, courtesy name K'ung-fu, see K'ung, shih-chia-p'u/160.

34. The K'ungs accept the Kung-yang and Ku-liang traditions over the Tso-chuan. According to the latter, Hua-fu Tu killed K'ung-fu in order to steal his wife and then murdered Duke Shang for fear of reprisal. See Legge, The Chinese Classics 5/37-38. However, the two former commentaries explain that Hua-fu Tu's object ws to usurp the state and K'ung-fu, as the major supporter of the Duke, was killed first. Ch'un-ch'iu 24: Heng 2/1, 2; K'ung, shih-chia-p'u/162-63.

35. The K'ung genealogy places the emigration with K'ung-fu's son Mu, courtesy name Chin-fu, while the K'ung-tzu chia-yü records this as occurring two generations later, with Fang-shu. K'ung, shih-chia-p'u/160, 163.

36. For additional biographies of Confucius, named Ch'iu, courtesy name Chung-ni, see K'ung, shih-chia-p'u/166-211; Ch'ueh-li kuang-chih 2; P'an, Ch'ü-fu 57. A more recent Chinese study is Ts'ui, Shu-ssu k'ao-hsin-lu. A major study in English remains Creel, Confucius and the Chinese Way. There are also scattered anecdotes ranging from the factual to the mythical in such early works as K'ung-tzu chia-yü, K'ung-ts'ung-tzu, Meng-tzu, Lun-yü, Chuang-tzu, Mo-tzu, Yen-tzu, Ch'un-chiu, Kuo-yü, Hsun-tzu, as well as the Li-chi. As regards the date of Confucius' birth, some sources give 552 B.C. but most accept 551 B.C. For a summary of the scholarly debate on this point, see Creel, Confucius/296-97.

37. K'ung Ko, courtesy name Shu-liang, had nine daughters by his first wife and a crippled son, Meng-p'i, by his first concubine. The graves of Confucius' father and his mother, who survived until he was 25, are located

on nearby Mt. Fang, later the site of several temples to their memories. K'ung, shih-chia-p'u/161; Ch'ueh-li kuang-chih 5/2b.

38. See Shih-chi 47/1945.

39. Among the more notable was K'ung Chi, courtesy name Tzu-ssu. A grandson of Confucius, he is ranked as his successor inasmuch as Confucius' son, Li (531–485 B.C.), courtesy name Po-yü, predeceased him. Tzu-ssu was a disciple of the master in his youth and subsequently was active politically in Lu, Wei, and Sung. He is credited with writing Chung-yung (The Doctrine of the Mean) and is also said to have met Mencius. K'ung, shih-chia-p'u/215-18.

40. For a biography of K'ung Fu, also named Fu-chia, courtesy name Tzu-yü, also Tzu-fu, also known as K'ung Chia, see K'ung, shih-chia-p'u/224-26.

41. Ch'in Shih-huang visited Mt. Tsou just south of Ch'ü-fu where he assembled Confucian scholars to draft a text for a stone engraving. Shih-chi 6/242.

42. Shih-chi 7/304.

43. Shih-chi 8/379; P'an, Ch'ü-fu 18/499. Han Kao-tsu allowed Hsiang Yü to be buried with the honors accorded a Duke of Lu.

44. For a short biography of K'ung Chü (222–170 B.C.), courtesy name Tzu-yen, see K'ung, shih-chia-p'u/226. Chang Shou-ch'ieh's commentary to Shih-chi 8/379 identifies the general as K'ung Hsi, but according to P'an, Ch'ü-fu 70/1791, this is the same person.

45. A similar situation arose during the Wang Mang Interregnum (A.D. 9-23). K'ung Chun, courtesy name Ch'ang-p'ing, of the 16th generation, was deprived of his rank as marquis for refusing to serve Wang Mang as Grand Commandant. His cousins, Fen, courtesy name Chün-yü, and Ch'i, courtesy name Tzu-i, both fled Ch'ü-fu to Ho-hsi, the

former actively joining the military resistance of Tou Jung. Such loyalism later earned the clan the gratitude of Emperor Kuang-wu (r. 25-58) after the Han restoration. However, K'ung Jung of the 15th generation, grandson of the influential clan head in the 13th, served Wang Mang as Grand Minister of Mount and was enfeoffed as a Marquis, a fact not clearly stated in K'ung's genealogy. K'ung, shih-chia-p'u/234-36; P'an, Ch'ü-fu 18/524.

46. The K'ungs may have been able to demonstrate their usefulness on one occasion when Kao-tsu, appalled at the boisterousness and vulgarity of his court, heeded the advice of the Confucian Shu-sun T'ung. The latter proposed the creation of a new system of court etiquette and brought some thirty scholars from Lu to train the newly minted nobility. The system was formally inaugurated in 200 B.C., much to the Emperor's satisfaction. Shih-chi 99/2722-23; Han-shu 43/2126-28.

47. P'an, Ch'ü-fu 18/501.

48. K'ung T'eng, courtesy name Tzu-jang, was a noted specialist in the classics and was later promoted to Erudite and Provincial Governor of Ch'ang-sha under Emperor Hui (r. 194-87 B.C.). K'ung, shih-chia-p'u/226.

49. The dual loyalties of Han Wu-ti were not atypical of the K'ungs' imperial patrons. While publicly promoting Confucianism, he put his faith in oracles and alchemists and seems to have had little personal use for its moral and philosophical aspects. See Hu, "The Establishment of Confucianism"/31-33.

50. K'ung An-kuo (c.156-74 B.C.), courtesy name Tzu-kuo, was an 11th-generation descendant, the second son of the clan head, K'ung Sui. In his youth, he specialized in the study of the Shih-ching (Book of Poetry) and the Shu-ching. One of the most influential figures of his time, he later rose to Grandee Remonstrant and Provincial Governor

of Lin-huai.   It was K'ung An-kuo who became custodian of
the "ancient text" classics of K'ung Fu found in the wall
of Confucius' mansion.   As few people could read the early
form of script, he transcribed and reedited them, appending
new commentaries to the Shu-ching, Hsiao-ching, and the
Lun-yü. These were submitted to the court where he was an
energetic proponent of the authenticity of the "ancient"
over the "recent texts".   K'ung, shih-chia-p'u/227-28; Han-
shu 58/3607.

K'ung Yen-nien was a nephew of K'ung An-kuo and the
head of the clan in the 12th generation. He subsequently
served as Junior Guardian and later, Grand General. K'ung,
shih-chia-p'u/229.

51. For a short discussion of the "ancient" vs.
"recent text" debate in the Han, see Hou, Chung-kuo ssu-
hsiang 2/313-30.   In Hou's opinion, the factors leading to
the triumph of the former over the latter were primarily
pragmatic and political.

52. K'ung Jung (153-208), courtesy name Wen-chü,
artistic name Pei-hai, was a 20th-generation descendent
whose prolific writings earned him inclusion as one of the
"Seven Talents of the Chien-an Period (196-220)." He held
a variety of civil and military posts, rising to Palace
Grandee. Until his treacherous murder by Ts'ao Ts'ao (155-
220), he was a key supporter of the Emperor Hsien (r. 189-
220).   Among his 25 chuan of writings were works on
classics, and poetry and essays. He also gained note for
energetically establishing Confucian schools in districts
under his authority. K'ung, shih-chia-p'u/245; P'an, Ch'ü-
fu 76/1837-43; Hou-han-shu 70/2261-80.   A fictional
treatment of him is in Lo, San-kuo yen-i 11, translated in
Brewitt-Taylor, Romance of the Three Kingdoms/100-13.

53. K'ung Ying-ta (574-648), courtesy name Chung-ta,
was a 32nd-generation descendent who rose to prominence in

his youth under Sui Yang-ti (r. 605-17). Yang-ti gathered Confucian scholars to glorify his court and made the brilliant Ying-ta preeminent among them. Surviving an assassination attempt by his jealous colleagues, Ying-ta went on to serve the first two T'ang Emperors, Kao-tsu (r. 618-27) and T'ai-tsung (r. 627-50), who were even more lavish patrons. Under the latter, he was selected as one of the eighteen scholars given national honors and helped compile the Sui-shih (Sui History). Highly honored throughout his life, he was enfeoffed as a Viscount and is best remembered for his standard compilation of the classics with commentaries, the Wu-ching cheng-i (Orthodox Commentaries on the Five Classics) in 280 chüan. K'ung, shih-chia-p'u/263-65; P'an, Ch'ü-fu 78/1857-77.

54. For lists of these benefits, see P'an, Ch'ü-fu 39-43, 47-48; Ch'ueh-li kuang-chin 7, 9.

55. Ch'ueh-li kuang-chih 7/8a.

56. P'an, Ch'ü-fu 47/1339.

57. P'an, Ch'ü-fu 47/1336.

58. See p. 110. The request was granted in 1685, a year after K'ang-hsi's visit to Ch'ü-fu.

59. The Meng, Yen, and Tseng clans were often grouped together with the K'ungs and collectively referred to as the "Four Clans (Ssu-shih)." The other three received imperial benefits as well, though to a lesser extent than the K'ungs. Sometimes the Chung clan descended from Chung Tzu-yu was also included and the group referred to as the "Five Clans (Wu-shih)." In addition, more peripheral clans such as the Tung-yeh, descendents of the Duke of Chou, were recognized and supported. See P'an Ch'ü-fu 6, 58, 61 for woodblock illustrations and discussions of the Four clans and their historical sites.

60. This was the second year of the Huang-ch'u reign of Wei Wen-ti (r. 220-27) and was accepted as the founding of

the first clan school by K'ung Hsien, clan head in the 21st generation. Ch'ueh-li kuang-chih 9/15.

61. For woodblock prints and discussions of these country academies, see P'an, Ch'ü-fu 7.

62. P'an, Ch'ü-fu 42/1173.

63. For a description of the examination system in Ch'ü-fu, see P'an, Ch'ü-fu 42. There were also quotas for military students and students of music and ceremony.

64. Originally the office corresponding to the District Magistrate in the Ch'ing was concurrently occupied by the head of the clan and was made a hereditary privilege under Emperor Chang-tsung (r. 1190-1209) of the Chin. It was not until the end of the Yuan that it began to be held by another clan member upon the recommendation of the head. This was made hereditary in 1375. For a description of official ranks and titles, see Ch'ueh-li kuang-chih 9; P'an, Ch'ü-fu 40.

65. The rank of Erudite of the Five Classics in the Han-lin Academy was made hereditary in 1503. One of the ceremonial responsibilities was presiding over the spring and autumn sacrifices at the Chung-yung Academy in Tsou-hsien. The Erudite at the Court of Imperial Sacrifices was established the same year and was likewise responsible for ceremonies at the Sheng-tzu Academy in Wen-shang-hsien. There were altogether fifteen Erudites of the Five Classics, including the two K'ungs mentioned above and a third representing the southern branch (see note 71) as well as others representing descendants of Confucius' disciples in Ch'ü-fu. All were nominated by the head of the K'ung clan upon reaching the age of 16. Ch'ueh-li kuang-chih 9/10a-12b; P'an, Ch'ü-fu 40/1135-36.

66. The appointment of a K'ung as Registrar of the Academy of the Four Clans was begun in 1426. The Sub-Registrars of the Ni-shan and Shu-ssu Academies were

established in 1437. All of these were nominally within the Imperial Academy, where another office held by a K'ung, Director of Studies, was begun in 1535. Since 1368, the Director of the Academy of the Four Clans was deliberately chosen from outside the clan but only upon recommendation of the clan head. Ch'ueh-li kuang-chih 9/15a-25b; P'an Ch'ü-fu 39/1124-26; 40/1137-40.

67. In addition to the above titles and offices, the Duke recommended candidates for the following positions: Controller of Estates, Archivist of the Hall of the Literary Constellation, Music Director, Clan Administrator, and Shrine Administrator, the latter two held by K'ungs. These were offices supported by the state; there were numerous other ones which the Duke dispensed personally from clan resources without the need for government approval. Ch'ueh-li kuang-chih 9/26a-31b; P'an, Ch'ü-fu 40/1145-54.

68. For a biography of K'ung Kuang-ssu (869-912), see Kung, shih-chia-p'u/281. Kuang-ssu began his career as a Libationer at the end of the T'ang and became Magistrate of the Ch'ü-fu area and Shrine Administrator in 906. With the fall of the T'ang, he lost these positions and it seems that K'ung Mo was able to usurp power due to the unstable conditions following the dynastic collapse. For the story of K'ung Mo's usurpation, see K'ung, shih-chia-p'u/284-85. Understandably, he is not recognized as a legitimate descendant in the genealogy. His ancestor back in 452 had been exempted from corvée labor and became a maintenance tenant. Over the centuries, the power of this branch had grown to where K'ung Mo was able to ally with local bandits, take over Ch'ü-fu, and execute K'ung Kuang-ssu. After the Restoration, K'ung Mo's descendents were banished from the Ducal Mansion, declared "false K'ungs," and

recorded along with the common population of Ch'ü-fu. K'ung, shih-chia-p'u/147-51.

69. K'ung Jen-yü (912-56), courtesy name Wen-ju, is recorded as being tall and distinguished in appearance and an expert in the Ch'un-ch'iu. At the age of nineteen, he was restored as head of the clan holding at the time the title of "Duke of Literary Annunciation," as well as the various magistracies of the district. He held these under the Latter T'ang, Chin, Han, and Chou dynasties and hosted Emperor T'ai-tsu (r. 951-54) of the Latter Chou upon his visit to Ch'ü-fu in 952. Subsequently he was appointed Censor. K'ung Jen-yü's mother, née Chang, was posthumously honored with regular sacrifices and an endowed temple. K'ung, shih-chia-p'u/284-85.

70. Jen-yü had four sons, of whom two, I and Tsui, produced the twenty branches. I's line produced branches 1-6 (sub-branches 1-25) and Tsui's 7-20 (sub-branches 26-60). According to the general genealogy, there were major shifts in the successions in the 9th, 17th, 40th, 43rd, and 53rd generations. Lesser shifts could occur due to the lack of an heir, or if the head were disestablished for political reasons. It was also common to rotate among the descendants of several sons of an earlier head, i.e., K'ung Ch'ien in the 8th generation had three sons--Fu, T'eng, and Shu--whose lines alternately held the office until Fu's died out after seven generations and Shu's after thirty. For charts and discussion of this, see K'ung, shih-chia-p'u/129-37. Theoretically, then, the more than 10,000 living K'ungs listed in K'ung Shang-jen's genealogy were all descended from Jen-yü. This means, at the very least, that most clan members in the seventeenth century could only trace their roots back to the tenth century, and it leaves open the question of what happened to the descendents of the other K'ungs in Jen-yü's time.

71. K'ung Tuan-yu, courtesy name Tzu-chiao, was appointed Master of the Odes in 1105 and succeeded to the dukedom upon the death of his uncle. Together with other clan members, he fled south and established a domicile in Hsi-an-hsien, San-ch'ü-chou in Chekiang. This was recognized by the Southern Sung court, which confirmed his title of Duke and appointed him Magistrate of Pin-chou, Shansi, where he died. His nephew, Chieh, succeeded to the title in 1132 becoming Director of Education in San-ch'ü in 1136. There, he founded a Confucian temple and endowed it with five ch'ing of land. Five generations after Tuan-yu's self-imposed exile, his descendant Shu, courtesy name Ssu-lu, refused to return north under the Yuan and relinquished all claims to the title; he and his heirs were appointed Libationers and were no longer recorded in the clan genealogy. During the Ming, the Prefect of Ch'ü-chou-fu memoralized the throne to upgrade the status of the southern K'ungs, and in 1506 Tuan-yu's descendants were appointed Erudites by hereditary right, responsible for maintaining sacrifices at the southern shrine. K'ung, shih-chia-p'u/299; Ch'üeh-li kuang-chih 2/41b, 9/13a-14b.

72. For a biography of Tuan-yu's nephew, Chieh, courtesy name Hsi-lao, see K'ung, shih-chia-p'u/303. Chieh was the third son of K'ung Tuan-ts'ao, Tuan-yu's brother who had remained in the north.

73. For a biography of K'ung Tuan-ts'ao, see K'ung, shih-chia-p'u/299-300; Ch'üeh-li kuang-chih 2/41b. He was succeeded in the north by his eldest son, Fan, courtesy name Wen-lao. Thus, in the second generation after the split, the reigning northern and southern Dukes were brothers.

74. The 51st Duke in the north, K'ung Yuan-ts'o, had moved to Pien-liang (modern Kaifeng) in 1215 to support the endangered Chin, leaving his cousin Yuan-yung in charge of

affairs in Ch'ü-fu.   While he was away, Southern Sung
armies briefly recaptured the area in 1219 and made Yuan-
yung Duke in 1225.   The same year, Mongol armies conquered
Ch'ü-fu and Yuan-yung surrendered to them.   They
reconfirmed his title and he joined their military
campaign, leaving his own son, Chih-ch'üan, in charge.
Chih-ch'üan succeeded to the title; but then he had to
relinquish it in 1233 when Yuan-ts'o, who had been in Pien-
liang all along, was ordered by the Yuan to return to Ch'ü-
fu as Duke.   Yuan-ts'o later died childless but was able to
secure the succession for his great-nephew, Chen, in 1251.
Chen is recorded as a dour, ascetic loner.   Others in the
clan, perhaps led by Chih-ch'üan, accused him of neglecting
official duties and spending his time hunting.   Even more
serious was the charge that he was not really a K'ung,
being the son of a concubine and later adopted by the Lis
who were originally registered as prisoners-of-war.   Chen
was removed in 1258, and for the next four decades no one
occupied the troublesome position at all.   It was not until
the succession of Ch'eng-tsung (r. 1295-1308) that K'ung
Chih, a son of Chih-ch'üan, was enfeoffed in the 53rd
generation, thus representing the triumph of the faction
which sought to gain control in the north ever since Yuan-
ts'o had left for Pien-liang.   The final irony was that
K'ung Chih's heir, Ssu-ch'eng, was also removed on the
grounds that he was the son of a concubine.   The title then
passed to a cousin, Ssu-hui, in 1316.   The clearest single
narrative of these events is in P'an, Ch'ü-fu 60/1660-3.
The apologetic accounts sponsored by the K'ung clan in
various biographical entries of Ch'ueh-li kuang-chih and by
K'ung Shang-jen himself in shih-chia-pu/308-22 are less
reliable, propounding different versions of the succession
in order to minimize the actual degree of internal
dissension.

75. For a concise statement of the view of ritual traditionally ascribed to Confucius, see the Li-yun chapter of the Li-chi, a text generally thought to date from early Han.

76. See Lun-yü 12/1: "Yen Yuan asked about humanity (jen). Confucius replied, 'Mastering the self through ritual is the path of humanity. If the ruler accomplished this for but one day, the world would become humane. For humanity proceeds from the self--how could it be derived from others?' Yen Yuan asked for more details. Confucius replied, 'Neither look, listen, speak, nor act in any way contrary to ritual.' Yen Yuan said, 'Although I am not quick in understanding, I will try to practice what you have said.'"

77. Lun-yü 11/24: "ritual is the means of statecraft."

78. Lun-yü 2/23: "Tzu-chang asked whether the situation ten generations from now could be known. Confucius replied, 'The Shang based their rituals on the Hsia and how they modified them can be known, the Chou based theirs on the Shang and how they modified them can be known. So we can predict the ways of the successors to the Chou, even if they do not appear for a hundred generations."

79. See chapter 2, p. 76.

80. These sacrifices are described in considerable detail in P'an, Ch'ü-fu 45-46; Ch'ueh-li kuang-chih 3.

81. Ch'ueh-li kuang-chih 7/13a-14a.

82. Lun-yü 9/15: "Confucius said, 'Only after I returned to Lu from Wei was the music corrected. The ya and sung odes were each given their proper place.'"

83. Lun-yü 3/9: "Confucius said, 'I can discuss the Hsia rituals but the state of Ch'i supplies no evidence. I can discuss the Shang rituals but the state of Sung supplies no evidence. This is because texts and experts

are lacking. If they were not, then these rituals could be confirmed.'"

84. See Sung Lien (1310-81), "On the Confucian Temple (K'ung-tzu miao-t'ang-i)"; Ch'ü Chiu-ssu (c. 1580), "On the Music of the Confucian Temple (K'ung-miao yueh-i)." Both rpt. in Ch'ueh-li kuang-chih 17/37a-42b.

85. For a biography of K'ung Ch'eng-tz'u, courtesy name Yung-fu, see K'ung, shih-chia-p'u/1272.

86. For biographies of K'ung Hung-chieh, courtesy name I-ch'i, see K'ung, shih-chia-p'u/1279; K'ung, wen-hsien-k'ao 94/10a.

87. For a biography of K'ung Ch'eng-t'i (Senior Licentiate, 1568), courtesy name Yung-kuan, see K'ung, shih-chia-p'u/1272-73.

88. For biographies of K'ung Wen-na, courtesy name Chih-min, see K'ung, shih-chia-p'u/1286; K'ung, wen-hsien-k'ao 94/10a.

89. For a biography of K'ung Chen-fan (1585-1653), courtesy name Yung-p'u, see K'ung, shih-chia-p'u/1294; Ch'ueh-li kuang-chih 93/2a.

90. Again, an uncle seems to have presented a complementary pole. K'ung Chen-yü, courtesy name Yung-hsin, the younger brother of Chen-fan, was a successful official in the south during the late Ming but was more noted for his romantic personality and his devotion to the arts of lute-playing and chess. A literary stylist as well, he was compared to the enthusiasts of "pure-conversation (ch'ing-t'an)" in the Chin due to his pursuit of elegance and a cultivated individualism. K'ung, wen-hsien-k'ao 92/2a.

91. K'ung's mother was born on February 6, 1623. The poem, dated February 16, 1703, is reprinted in K/328.

92. See note 29.

93. K/620.

94. K/585.

95. K'ung eventually catalogued his collection in Hsiang-chin-pu (Catalogue of Antiques I Take Pleasure In), which the bibliophile Teng Shih obtained in 1941 in Shanghai and reprinted in Huang and Teng, Mei-shu ts'ung-shu: ch'u-chi 7; the catalogue is also reprinted in K/573-625.

96. For source material on local resistance to the Ch'ing in Shantung, see Hsieh, Ch'ing-ch'u nung-min/74-116; esp. pp. 78-90.

97. "Tao-hu (Rebels)." In P'u, Liao-chai chih-i/1086-87. A translation appears in Giles, Strange Stories/373.

98. K'ung Shang-tse, courtesy name I-chih, also Chun-chih, artistic name Fang-shun, earned his Provincial Graduate degree in 1627 and served, in addition to the offices mentioned, as Secretary of the Shantung Bureau and as Vice-Director of the Kwangsi Bureau, both in the Board of Justice. Later he was given the honorary title of Great Officer with Direct Access to the Throne (Feng-chih ta-fu), probably in the Nanking Restoration. He retired to Ch'ü-fu where he engaged in philosophical studies and taught prose style. It is not known whether K'ung Shang-jen ever met him directly or heard of him through Ch'in Kuang-i. K'ung, shih-chia-p'u/765; K'ung, wen-hsien-k'ao 90/5a.

99. K'ung, "T'ao-hua-shan pen-mo (All About The Peach Blossom Fan)". In T/5.

100. Chia Fu-hsi (1589-c.1670), named Ying-ch'ung, courtesy name Ssu-t'ui, also Ching-fan, also Fu-hsi, artistic name Tan-p'u, also Mu-p'i san-k'o, has only recently been discovered after almost 250 years in oblivion. After his death, his ballads continued to circulate locally through handwritten copies and were only publicly printed in the late Ch'ing by such bibliophiles as Wu Wo-yao (1867-1910), Yeh Te-hui (1864-1927), and Wang I-

jung (1845-1900). However, none identified "The 'Wood-and-Leather' Wanderer" as Chia. Eaven K'ung Shang-jen, in his biography of Chia, is careful to conceal his real name. Positive identification occurred in 1931 when the Shantung Provincial Museum obtained a fan signed by Chia bearing a seal with this artistic name. For biographical information and the textual history of his writings, see Liu, Mu-p'i/1-56.

101. Reprinted in Liu, Mu-p'i/57-107.

102. Reprinted in Liu, Mu-p'i/108-16. The aria set also appears in T/259-60; translated in P/307-9. For a study supporting Chia Fu-hsi's authorship, see Tseng, "T'ao-hua-shan." A poem by Chia to K'ung Shang-tse is reprinted in Liu, Mu-p'i/48.

103. Reprinted in Liu, Ch'ing-ch'u ku-tz'u/105-12.

104. Reprinted in Liu, Ch'ing-ch'u ku-tz'u/23-44. Another ballad, Ch'i-ching-kung tai k'ung-tzu wu-chang (Duke Ching of Ch'i Receives Confucius (in five parts), is attributed to either Chia or his friend Ting Yeh-ho (see note 109). See Liu, Ch'ing-ch'u ku-tz'u/10-11; 113-36.

105. King Wen, also known as the Western Earl (Hsi-po), was slandered by enemies and imprisoned for seven years by King Chou (r.c.1154-22 B.C.), the tyrannical last ruler of the Shang. By offering him a beautiful woman and rare gifts, King Wen was able to gain his release and later assisted in the founding of the Chou dynasty. Shih-chi 4/116.

106. Lun-yü 17:11: "The 'carping villager' is a despoiler of virtue."

107. Tan-p'u heng-yen (Enduring Words from Placidity Patch) was not printed and does not seem to have survived although it is mentioned under Chia's name in several local gazetteers. Liu, Mu-p'i/47.

108. Li Chih (1527-1602), originally named Tsai-chih, courtesy name Hung-chai, Ssu-chai, artistic name Cho-wu, also Wen-ling chü-shih, was born in Chin-chiang, Fukien. One of the most original and iconoclastic thinkers of the late Ming, Li spent the first half of his life pursuing a conventional bureaucratic career, but by 1581 he decided to retire. In the remaining decades of his life, he wandered about, dwelling in temples or with friends and writing the works which established him as the leading opponent of orthodox Neo-Confucianism. Seven years later, he took the tonsure and became a Buddhist priest. Fen-shu (A Book to be Burned) appeared in 1590 and contained his ideas on the unity of Buddhism, Taoism, and Confucianism, the spontaneity of the authentic self, intellectual tolerence, and antitraditionalism. He returned to dwell in Ma-ch'eng in 1593, and six years later his second major work, Ts'ang-shu (A Book to be Hidden), appeared containing his revisionist critiques of historical figures. Li's growing notoriety brought him difficulties with local Confucian activists and officials; on one occasion, his house was destroyed by a mob. In 1602, while visiting T'ung-chou near Peking, he was charged by Censor Chang Wen-ta (d.1625) and jailed. He committed suicide in prison that same year. In addition to his philosophical thought, Li was active in promoting popular literature and produced commentaries to such dramas as Hsi-hsiang-chi (The Western Chamber), P'i-p'a-chi (The Lute), and the novels San-kuo yen-i (Romance of the Three Kingdoms) and Shui-hu-chuan (Water Margin). Goodrich and Fang, Ming Biography/807-18; Ming-shih 221/5817; DeBary, Self and Society/188-225.

Hsu Wei (1521-93), courtesy name Wen-chang, artistic name T'ien-ch'ih, also T'ien-shui-yueh, also Ch'ing-t'eng, also Shan-yin pu-i, was born in Shan-yin, Chekiang, the son of a magistrate who died soon after he was born. A brilliant eccentric who lived a tortured life, he was one of the most symbolic figures of late Ming romanticism, creating a unique style in prose, poetry, painting, and drama. Despite early poverty, Hsu pursued a classical education and earned his Licentiate degree in 1540; however he was unable to pass succeeding examinations for higher degrees. The following year, he married a magistrate's daughter and went to live in Canton, where she died in 1545. Two years later, he returned to Chekiang as a teacher in Shaohsing where he was exposed to Wang Yang-ming's (1472-1529) interpretation of Neo-Confucianism as well as Buddhism, philosophical Taoism, and Chinese medicine. A 1550 lawsuit reduced him to poverty again and he withdrew to a monastery, living off friends and a district stipend. He then turned to professional writing, the theater, and the study of military strategy. He married again in 1557 and was divorced two years later. Then, when his patron Hu Tsung-hsien (1511-62) fell from power and was imprisoned, Hsu became temporarily insane, beating his third wife to death and castrating himself. He was imprisoned in 1566 and saved from execution only by the intercession of influential friends who gained his release after seven years of confinement. Hsu returned to writing, teaching, and serving again as a military advisor until his retirement in 1577. In addition to his essays and poems, he is noted for his calligraphy, painting, four tsa-chu plays titled Ssu-sheng-yuan (Four Cries of the Gibbon), a work on contemporary theater, Nan-tz'u hsu-lu (Discussions on Southern Drama), a commentary on Hsi-hsiang-chi, short stories, and works on the occult. Goodrich and Fang, Ming Biography/609-12; Ming-shih 288/7387-88; Yuan, Hsu Wen-chang-chuan (Biography of Hsu Wei) in Yuan, ch'üan-chi/1-2.

Yuan Hung-tao (1568-1610), courtesy name Chung-lang, also Wu-hsueh, also Liu-hsiu, artistic name Shih-kung, also

Shih-t'ou chü-shih, was one of the leading literary figures
in the late Ming whose advocacy of an authentic style in
prose and poetry helped define what has been called the
"Kung-an School." Born in Kung-an, Hukuang (modern Hupei),
into a family with a long line of civil and military
officials, he was the second of three brothers, all of whom
were close artistic influences on each other, achieving
great fame in their lifetimes. At 15, Hung-tao organized a
literary society and quickly gained the higher degrees,
becoming a Provincial Graduate in 1588 and a Metropolitan
Graduate in 1592; however, he was uninterested in a
bureaucratic career, a result perhaps of Li Chih's
influence, for he had met the latter in Canton. In 1595,
he was made Magistrate of Soochow but resigned after a
year, preferring to journey to the famous sights in the
area and spread his theories of a natural, personal prose
style unhampered by traditionalism. He joined his brothers
in the capital in 1598 as an Instructor in the National
University and, while in Peking, the three of them
organized the Grape Society (P'u-t'ao-she) to further their
literary views. By 1600, Hung-tao was a Secretary in the
Bureau of Ceremonies in the Board of Rites but resigned to
return home due to ill health. Soon after the death of his
brother Tsung-tao (1560-1600), Hung-tao began a period of
religious retreat near Kung-an. He returned to the Board
of Rites in 1606 and held various offices, ultimately
directing the provincial examinations in Shensi in 1609.
He returned home to die the following year at the age of
42. In addition to his prose and poetry, Hung-tao also
wrote on Ch'an and Pure Land Buddhism, as well as a
historical romance, Tung-hsi-han yen-i (Romance of the
Han). Goodrich and Fang, Ming Biography/1635-38; Ming-shih
288/7397-98; Kuo, p'i-p'ing-shih/264-382.

109. Yen Ku-ku (1603-79), named Er-mei, courtesy name Yung-ch'ing, also Tiao-ting, artistic name Pai-er shan-jen, also Ta-er shan-jen, was born in P'ei-hsien, Kiangsu. A noted Ming loyalist, he fled from Kaifeng back to his native place upon Li Tzu-ch'eng's (d.1645) conquest and fasted for several days in sorrow over the fall of Ming. After the Manchu conquest, he dispersed his family property and went underground, swearing to resist the Ch'ing. In 1663, while traveling in the Hopei-Honan area, he was forced to flee to escape a vendetta and made his way to Shantung where he spent several years in hiding. Though some of his writings survive, his anti-Manchu works were expurgated. Liu, Mu-p'i/21-22; 26-28.

Ting Yeh-ho (1607-78), named Yao-k'ang, courtesy name Hsi-sheng, artistic name Ho-yeh-hang, also Mu-chi tao-jen, also Tz'u-yang tao-jen, was born in Chu-ch'eng, Shantung, the son of a censor during the Ming. An exuberant personality, he was orphaned while young but read widely and quickly gained the Licentiate degree. Then he went south to study with Tung Ch'i-ch'ang (1555-1636) becoming active in literary societies. Upon returning to Chu-ch'eng, he organized his own society, which emphasized "practical studies" designed to save the faltering Ming system; well aware of the dynastic decline, he wrote T'ien-shih (History as Decreed by Heaven), examining the causes for similar periods in the past. When peasant rebellion spread to Shantung, he decided to remain in the area despite threats to his safety. He raised several thousand troops in alliance with the loyalist general Liu Tse-ch'ing, (d.1648) and was able to rescue the town of An-ch'iu. With the collapse of the Nanking Restoration in 1645, however, he made his way to Peking where, by 1649, he received a teaching diploma and taught in the Bordered White Banner. While in the capital, he was able to meet such luminaries as Wang To (1592-1652), Fu Shan (1607-84), and Kung Ting-tzu (1616-73). Subsequently, he rose to Instructor in Jung-ch'eng and Magistrate of Huai-an but retired from the latter position. In 1664, he became involved in a lawsuit over his writings which ruined him financially; it was at this time that he found it convenient to go into hiding and visited his friend of over twenty years, Chia Fu-hsi. He later continued his literary activities, despite suffering from increasing blindness in the last twelve years of his life. A prolific writer, his poetic works were gathered in Yeh-ho shih-ch'ao (The Collected Poems of Ting Yeh-ho); he also wrote five dramas including the loyalist play Piao-chung-chi (A Display of Loyalty) and a novel, Hsu-chin-p'ing-mei (A Continuation of Chin-P'ing-Mei), later redacted as Ko-lien hua-ying (Flowers behind the Curtains). Shan-tung t'ung-chih 175/5042.

110. Lun-yü 5:22: "When the Master was in Ch'en, he said, 'Let me return! Let me return! My followers are a hasty lot. Though elegant and accomplished, they know not how to trim their passions.'"

111. Lun-yü 13:21: "Confucius said, 'If unable to join those along the middle path, I would prefer the headstrong and the cautious; for the headstrong, at least, are assertive while the cautious do not attempt to do everything.'"

112. "Kuang-ling-chün hsueh-hui chiang-hsu, wu-ch'en (Remarks Delivered at the Yangchow Educational Assembly in 1689)." In K/458.

113. A local gazette merely records that "at twenty, he served to transmit the correct Confucian teachings but did not abandon the examinations, still hoping to carry out the Way in office." See Yen-chou fu-chih hsu-pien 16. Quoted in Ch'en, nien-p'u/19.

114. Upon visiting T'ai-chou in 1687, K'ung made a pilgrimage to the shrine honoring a local son, Wang Ken (1483-1541). Wang Ken was one of Wang Yang-ming's most prominent and controversial followers in the late Ming who began a popular movement which swept through the area. He has been aptly described as displaying a "new heroism" in his determination to bring Confucianism to the masses in a simplified, essential form. By emphasizing the needs of the self, the challenges of daily affairs, and the search for a spontaneous spirit of joy, he reached a wide cross section of people and vividly demonstrated the effect that Confucianism could have as a grass-roots motivator of the people. In his homage to Wang's memory, K'ung wrote:

Reading your recorded sayings inspires, guides and attracts one to learning. So clear and immediate is it that it shows how the true Way is manifest even in the daily affairs of life--this is far from the impractical and complicated concerns of the philologists. Rather, the focus of your discussions has helped inform the world. (K/439)

For a discussion of Wang Ken's thought, see De Bary, "Individualism and Humanitarianism"/162-78.

115. For bibliographical information on Sheng-men li-yueh-chih (Ceremonial Music of the Confucian Shrine) and Lü-lü kuan-chien (Theory of Pitch in Classical Music), see Ch'en, nien-p'u/111-12.

116. K'ung Yü-ch'i (1657-1723), courtesy name Chung-tsai, also I-ch'en, artistic name Lan-t'ang, was hereditary head of the K'ung clan in the 67th generation, succeeding to the title of Duke of the Sagely Posterity on the death of his father in 1667. In his first audience with the young K'ang-hsi Emperor, K'ung Yü-ch'i attracted his attention with his precociousness and was granted an interview with the Empress Dowager as well as various

ceremonial honors during his stay in Peking.   In 1675, he was appointed Junior Preceptor of the Heir Apparent.   He was the formal host to the Emperor in 1684 during the latter's visit to Ch'ü-fu and is usually credited with obtaining new privileges for the clan on that occasion. The following year, he submitted Hsing-lu sheng-tien (The Imperial Visit to Ch'ü-fu) to the court as an official record of the visit.   It has been suggested that this work was actually written for the Duke by K'ung Shang-jen (see Ch'en, yen-chiu/116).   Throughout his life, K'ung Yü-ch'i continued to be an effective representative of the clan and died in Peking in 1723, attended by the imperial physician. In addition, he was noted as an accomplished calligrapher and painter of orchids, hence his artistic name meaning "Hall of Orchids."   K'ung, wen-hsien-k'ao 10/3b-5b.

117.   This group of five poems was published in 1689 by K'ung's friend, Teng Han-i (see chapter 3, note 50) in Shih-kuan san-chi (Poetic Perspectives: third series).   Two more poems from this visit were published in T'ao Hsuan, Kuo-ch'ao shih-ti: Shan-tung (Best Poems of the Ch'ing Dynasty: Shantung) and in Ni K'uang-shih, Shih-tsui (Collected Poems) (1688).   Though of lesser interest, they are reprinted along with the first five in K/4.

118. Chu Ti (1360-1424), Prince of Yen, temple name T'ai-tsung, also Ch'eng-tsu, posthumous name Wen-huang, reigned as the Yung-lo Emperor from 1403 to 1424.   The fourth son of Ming T'ai-tsu, he usurped the throne from his nephew, the Chien-wen Emperor (r. 1399-1403) in a military campaign noted for its cruelty.   In one of the major batles, he beseiged Tsinan on June 5, 1400, but eventually was forced to lift the seige in September due to the clever defense of T'ieh Hsuan.   Goodrich and Fang, Ming Biography/355-64.

119. T'ieh Hsuan (1366-1402), courtesy name Ting-shih, was born of a Se-mu family in Teng-chou, Honan. He graduated from the Imperial Academy and served Ming T'ai-tsu with distinction as a judicial official. Upon the accession of the Chien-wen Emperor, he became Vice-Commissioner in Shantung and was involved in military defenses against Chu Ti. T'ieh is credited with luring Chu's forces into a trap and temporarily saving the situation around Tsinan; however, he was later captured in November 1402, and when he denounced Chu to his face as a usurper he was given the unusually cruel punishment of being sliced to death and then boiled in oil. A temple to T'ieh's memory was built on the northwest bank of Lake Ming and regular sacrifices were held. Goodrich and Fang, Ming Biography/1284-86; Wang, Chi-nan/99, 1551; a late Ch'ing description of the temple and area appears in Liu, Lao-ts'an/7-8; translated by H. Shadick in Liu, The Travels of Lao Ts'an/13-14.

120. For a plot summary of Mang-shu-sheng (The Rude Scholar) (anon.), see Huang, Ch'ü-hai/1985; T'ieh-shih-nu (The Daughters of T'ieh Hsuan), also known as Hsia-nu hsin-sheng (A New Tale of Heroines), was a tsa-chu by Lai Chi-chih (Metroplitan Graduate, 1640). Summarized in Huang, Ch'ü-hai/435-36.

121. For the legend of Mt. Nü-lang, named after three drowned daughters of an ancient official, see Wang, Chi-nan/532-33.

122. See Tung Pi, "Lun k'ung shang-jen" for a discussion of K'ung as a "pragmatic" and materialist poet.

123. Shan-tung t'ung-chih/844.

124. Tse-hua Bridge is one of seven bridges across Lake Ming. It is located on the southern bank and references to it go back as early as the Sung. Wang, Chi-nan/887.

125. Mt. Li is located about three miles south of the city wall and is reputedly where the Sage-king Shun farmed. Southwards, it joins the Mt. T'ai range and eastwards is connected to Lang-yeh. Wang, Chi-nan/507; photographed in Liu, The Travels of Lao Ts'an/18.

126. See Trevor, The Ox and His Herdsmen/15-16. This contains copies of ten pictures traditionally ascribed to the Chinese Zen monk Kuo-an who lived during the twelfth century. It also contains translations of poems by him and other monks. The Chinese text appears in Ōbayashi, Togyūzo kunchu/41-46.

127. For a study and translation of Hsu Hsia-k'o's (1586-1641) travel diaries, see Li, Hsu Hsia-k'o.

128. For a study of Liu Tsung-yuan's landscape essays, see Nienhauser et al., Liu Tsung-yuan/66-79.

129. For a map of Stonegate Mountain including the site of K'ung Shang-jen's studio, see Li, Ch'ü-fu/map 4.

130. The Five Alps (Wu-yueh) are the most celebrated mountains in China, well known for their awesome scenery and sacrificed to by emperors as cornerstones of the universe. They are arranged corresponding to the five directions as follows: Mt. T'ai (East) in Shantung, Mt. Hua (West) in Shensi; Mt. Heng (South) in Hunan; Mt. Heng (North) in Hopei; Mt. Sung (Center) in Honan.

131. An allusion to T'ao Yuan-ming's (365-427) utopian fable, T'ao-hua-yuan-chi (The Peach Blossom Spring), in which a fisherman loses his way along a stream only to come across an ideal village where people dwell in perfect harmony, isolated from the centuries of war which have plagued the outside world. Upon his return, the fisherman related the existence of the place to others but few attempts were made to rediscover it and it was later forgotten. A Chinese text appears in Ting, T'ao Yuan-

ming/175-78; an English translation appears in Birch, Anthology/167-68.

132. Mei-yuan and Ching-ssu remain unidentified, no mention being made of their surnames, although their personal names, Cho and K'o respectively, appear elsewhere (K/423). A letter to Mei-yuan also exists, written later during K'ung's stay in the south in 1685-89, in which K'ung asks his friend back in Ch'ü-fu to look after his family affairs for him (K/502).

133. Han-chu-t'ai (The Terrace of the Chinned Pearl) derives its name from the scene where the moon appears to be a pearl held by a dragon between its chin and throat. For an early version of this symbol, see Chuang-tzu 32:42-45, where the pearl held by a black dragon asleep in the deepest abyss represents official rank and wealth.

134. Yang Hu (221-78) from T'ai-shan, Shantung, held the titles of Marquis of Nan-ch'eng and Generalissimo of the Southern Campaigns and was instrumental in conquering the Wu area for the Chin dynasty. He often enjoyed the scenery on Mt. Hsien near his headquarters in Hsiang-yang, Hupei. After his death, the local people mourned him and built a temple there, erecting a stele to his memory which his successor, Tu Yu (735-812) sorrowfully titled, "The Stele of Fallen Tears." Chin-shu 34/1022.

135. K'ung Yen-shih, courtesy name Mao-fa, artistic name Shih-ts'un, was a nephew of K'ung Shang-jen, although they were about the same age. He served as Sub-Director of Schools in nearby Chi-ning-fu but resigned after becoming a Provincial Graduate and resisted all other attempts to honor him. He was noted for his paintings and his widely read theoretical treatise, Hua-chueh (Secrets of Painting). K'ung Shang-jen introduced him to Yangchow and Peking society and, in a colophon to one of his landscapes, affectionately recorded Yen-shih as a shy eccentric,

talented in both essay writing and in art, who refused to publicize himself. K'ung, wen-hsien-k'ao 94/11a; K/95-96, 363.

136. Hsi Shih, who lived in the early fifth century B.C., was one of the most renowned of Chinese beauties. A native of Yueh, she is celebrated for her love affair with the official Fan Li and for her patriotic use of her feminine wiles which aided Yueh in undermining the enemy King of Wu in 473 B.C. A fable relates that once, when Hsi Shih fell ill, she knitted her brows in discomfort, which only added to her charm. An ugly woman in the neighboring village to the east sought to imitate her but only made herself look more repulsive. See Chuang-tzu 14:42-4.

137. "Liu chiu fa-ts'ao cheng hsia-ch'iu shih-men yen-chi (A Poem to Judge Liu Chiu and Mr. Cheng who Serves in Hsia-ch'iu on the Occasion of a Banquet on Stonegate Mountain)" (CTS 224/2393) was probably written shortly after 736 when Tu Fu (712-770) journeyed to Shantung. Hsia-ch'iu was an administrative district next to Stonegate.

138. Yang Chu, courtesy name Tzu-chü, was from Wei and lived sometime around the fourth century B.C. His ideas represent an early phase of Taoism and focus primarily on the preservation of self, escapism from an injurious society, and the avoidance of the temptations of power and profit. His ideas survive in scattered form in such works as Lieh-tzu, Meng-tzu, and Lu-shih ch'un-ch'iu. Mo Ti, who was either from Sung or Lu, lived c.479 to c.381 B.C. and was the founder of a major philosophical school. His ideas, which appear in the work Mo-tzu, emphasized a universalist ethic of "all-embraciang love (chien-ai)," a pragmatic, ascetic activism, and a belief in spirits. See Fung, A Short History/49-59, 60-67.

139. There is not much evidence from Confucius himself on his relationship to the I-ching (Book of Changes) except the questionable passage in Lun-yü 7:17 which may be read: "Confucius said, 'If I were to be granted more years to my life, I would spend fifty of them studying the Book of Changes.'" Ssu-ma Ch'ien, in the K'ung-tzu shih-chia (Biography of Confucius and His Descendents) (Shih-chi 17/1937) mentions that Confucius began studying the hexagrams at a late age and edited the various strata of interpretations then current. This view is also propounded in K'ung-tzu chia-yü and expanded on in greater detail in K'ung Ying-ta's Chou-i cheng-i-shu ("Preface to the Orthodox Commentary on the Book of Changes") where Confucius is credited with editing the classic and arranging the "Ten Wings (Shih-i)" of commentaries. For further study of this question, see Dubs, "Did Confucius Study The Book of Changes?" In Ch'ü-fu, local legend identified Stonegate as the place where this occurred. See Li, Ch'ü-fu/map 4.

140. The Ting Sacrifices were held for Confucius and the sage-kings on the first occurance of the day denoted as "ting" in the horary cycle in the second month of each of the four seasons. The ceremonies were often limited to the most important ones in spring and autumn.

141. K'ung Sheng-yu was hereditary head of the K'ung clan in the 46th generation, acceding to the title of Duke of Literary Annunciation in 1021. He held numerous honorary posts, rising to Undersecretary of the Heir Apparent in the Right Secretariat before dying sonless at the age of 35. See K'ung, shih-chia-p'u/293.

142. Huang Kung-wang (1269-1354), one of the four great masters of Yuan literati painting, was noted for his compositions of terraced mountains and his sparing use of

ink.   For   a   general   discussion   of   Huang's   style,   see Cahill, Hills/85-113.

143. The   Huang   Ch'ao   Rebellion   led   by   Huang   Ch'ao (d.884),   the   sixth   son   of   a   wealthy   salt   manufacturer, lasted for ten years during the reign of T'ang Hsi-tsung (r.   874-89).   He   succeeded   in   gaining   control   of   the widespread   uprising   already   underway   and   eventually captured   the   capital,   proclaiming   himself   emperor   and forcing Hsi-tsung to flee to Szechuan.   The rebellion was finally defeated by Li K'o-yung (856-908) in 885.   See Chiu-t'ang-shu 150c/5391-98; Hsin-t'ang-shu 225c/6451-64.

144. Goose   Creek   silk   was   a   local   product   from   T'ung-ch'üan-chou, Yen-t'ing, Szechuan which was submitted as tribute to the T'ang court.   Its shiny white surface was in great demand for calligraphy, particularly among such Sung literati as Su Shih (1037-1101).

145. Meng-tzu 7A:24: "Mencius said, 'Confucius ascended East Mountain from which Lu appeared dwarfed; and when he ascended Mt. T'ai, the entire world appeared dwarfed.   So it   is   difficult   to   be   impressed   with   mere   water   after having gazed at the sea and words alone hardly impress those who have studied with a sage.'"

146. The River Wei originates near Lan-chou, Kansu, and flows down into the Yellow river at T'ung-kuan, Shansi.   It was recorded in the earliest geographical works due to its proximity to ancient capitals including Ch'ang-an.   The archetypal scene by the River Wei was evoked by the T'ang poet Wang Wei (669-759) in his "Wei-ch'uan t'ien-chia (Farm Houses by the River Wei)":   "The sunset rays shine on the hamlet/   As   water-buffaloes   return   through   the   vacant alley./   An old villager ponders the herd-boy,/ Leaning on his   staff   beside   a   bramble   gate./   Roosters   crow,   the millet sprouts are slender;/ Silkworms sleep, few mulberry leaves remain./ The farmers arrive bearing their hoes,/meet

and talk, loathe to part./ At this point, yearning for the
simple life,/ I sing the ode 'How Few of Us are Left.'"
(CTS 125/1248).

147. The Jade Emperor (Yü-huang) is the highest god of
the Taoist pantheon, said to occupy the central throne in
the Heavenly Palace of the Jade Pure Realm of the Three
Epochs.   A popular deity who, over the centuries,
accumulated many Buddhist and Confucian legends as well, he
was further legitimized in the Sung when the Chen-tsung
Emperor (r. 998-1023) claimed to have had personal guidance
from him; and later the Hui-tsung Emperor (r. 1101-26)
equated him with the popular Confucian god Shang-ti.

148. The Spirit of the Earth (Hou-t'u) has a bewildering
number of forms including the patron deity of the soil,
various imperial ancestors, and an earth-mother figure.   It
was first sacrificed to formally by the Han Emperor Wu-ti
in 113 B.C. with ceremonies appropriate to various kings of
Heaven.

149. The Green Ruler (Ch'ing-ti) is one of the five
rulers of the universe.   According to the five elements
theory, his color is green, his domain the east, and his
season spring.   He also appears astronomically as the Wood
Star (Mu-hsing), corresponding to Jupiter.

150. There is a Kao-shih-chuan (Biographies of Eremite
Scholars) listed in Chi, ssu-k'u ch'üan-shu/1265-66 as
being by Huang-fu Mi of the Chin.   This, however, is an
expanded edition containing ninety-six biographies while an
earlier version printed in T'ai-p'ing yü-lan 507-9 contains
seventy-one,   approximating   another   bibliographical
reference to the work in the Southern Sung as containing
seventy-two biographies.   Perhaps it is related to Liu
Hsiang's (77-76 B.C.) Lieh-hsien-chuan (Biographies of
Various Immortals), which does date from the Han.   The
T'ai-ping yü-lan version contains a short biography of the

Morning Gatekeeper as follows: "There is someone called the Morning Gatekeeper of Stonegate, a man of Lu, who withdrew from the world.   He refused to hold office and dwelled in seclusion, also going by the name of 'Master of the Stone Gate of Lu' whereby he oversaw its opening and closing, day and night.   When Tzu-lu was a disciple of Confucius, he passed through Stonegate and spent the night there.   The Morning Gatekeeper asked him, 'From whom do you come?' Tzu-lu replied, 'From Confucius!' and he ridiculed Confucius by saying, 'Ah, he is the one who realizes the impossibility of things yet continues to attempt them.' People of that time considered him a worthy."   See T'ai-p'ing yü-lan 507/2311.   The incident involving Tzu-lu is taken from Lun-yü 14:38.

151. Tzu-lu's carrying rice to sustain his parents is a well-known incident appearing in such sources as Shuo-yuan (A Garden of Tales), Meng-ch'iu (Lessons for the Budding Student), and Er-shih-ssu-hsiao (Twenty-four Examples of Filial Piety).   In one version," formerly, when Tzu-lu was serving his parents, he would often eat pulse himself while he would carry rice for his parents from villages more than thirty miles away.   After his parents died, he served as advisor in Ch'u, had an entourage of a hundred carts and stored up ten thousand bushels of maize.   He sat on layers of cushions and ate from an array of bronze vessels.   Yet he yearned for pulse and for the time when he was serving his parents; it could never be recaptured."   Ch'en ed., K'ung-tzu chia-yü/48.

152. Hsuan-wu (Indigo Carapace) is shaped like a tortoise with the tail of a snake.   Astronomically, he is a seven-star constellation located in the northern sector and is historically personified by Hsu K'un, a minister of King Chou of the Shang.   One of the Four Guardian Spirits in

Buddhism, his domain is the north, his element water, and his color black.

153. See I-ching: 10/2:2 hsiang (under Hexagram 10, Lü: Treading): "Nine in the second place: He travels a level road; the secluded person perseveres and gains good fortune." Wilhelm comments: "The situation of a lonely sage is indicated here. He remains withdrawn from the bustle of life, seeks nothing, asks nothing of anyone, and is not dazzled by enticing goals. He is true to himself and travels through life unassailed, on a level road. Since he is content and does not challenge fate, he remains free of entanglements." Wilhelm, The I Ching/46.

154. Tu Fu's "Yu-jen (The Secluded Person)" was written while residing in Hunan: "The solitary cloud also travels with others/ For spiritual beings have such inclinations./How could a phoenix in the vermilion mist/Emerge splendiferously all alone?/ I went to join my friend Hui Hsun,/ To meet him, middle-aged, in the Province of Reclusion./ But the sky was lofty and contained no movement./ Cast off, I was, ignored like a leftover./ I fear I am unfit to course with the Way/ The Secluded Person perceives my flaws./ Billowy waves conceal his laughter/As he poles across P'eng-lai Lake./ The sun over Fu-sang's rocky summits/ Illuminates the coral branches./ His sailboat heaves close to the emerald umbrage/ While at sunset he fetches the Eastern Emperor's robe./ But to wash my mouth from the Stream of Harmony/ And contemplate how impalpable is the smoky mist./ I know my name scarcely deserves mention/ Confined as I am at the foot of Mt. Shang./ Yet, the five lakes still flow on/ As my sadness overflows at year's end." CTS 218/2287.

155. K'ung quotes lines 1-10 of a 16-line poem, no. 4 in a group collectively titled "Ni-ku chiu-shou (Nine Poems in the Ancient Manner)." The remaining lines are "The pines

and cypresses have been felled by others/ But the grave-mounds still eye each other up and down./ No longer a caretaker for the crumbled groundwork;/ Whither their wandering spirits now?/ Though glory indeed had brought them rank,/ Still, they evoke a heartfelt pity." The theme varies in each poem of the group. Here, the poet conveys his reflections on the evanescence of worldly power and the vanity of human contention, suggesting in the sixth line that an even placidity is the attitude which ultimately meets the least resistance. For a Chinese text, see Ting, T'ao Yuan-ming/137-38; and English translation and brief commentary appears in Hightower, T'ao Ch'ien/175.

156. See I-ching: 24/39: Chien: Obstruction: "It profits one to travel southeast but not northeast. It profits one to visit the Great Man. Perseverance brings good fortune." Wilhelm comments: "The hexagram pictures a dangerous abyss lying before us and a steep, inaccessible mountain rising behind us. We are surrounded by obstacles; at the same time, since the mountain has the attribute of keeping still, there is implicit a hint as to how we can extricate ourselves . . . the southwest is the region of retreat, the northeast that of advance. Here an individual is confronted by obstacles that cannot be overcome directly. In such a situation it is wise to pause in view of the danger and to retreat. However, this is merely a preparation for overcoming the obstructions. One must join forces with friends of like mind and put himself under the leadership of a man equal to the situation; then one will succeed in removing the obstacles. This requires the will to persevere just when one apparently must do something that leads away from his goal. This unswerving inner purpose brings good fortune in the end." Wilhelm, The I Ching/151.

157. An allusion to the inhabitants of Peach Blossom Spring. See note 131.

158. Wang Wei wrote a number of poems celebrating his villa at Wang River, the most famous being a cycle of twenty entitled "Wang-ch'uan-chi (Poems on Wang River)" CTS 128/1299-1303. It contains one on a spring there named "Chin-hsiao (Golden Powder)," doubtless the source for the one K'ung so named on Stonegate. Wang Wei also did a landscape painting of his villa which had quite an influence on later literati painters; however, it has not survived and is only represented by rubbings from stone engravings and copies. Cheng P'u, courtesy name Tzu-chen, was an eremite in the Han who lived in a place called "Ku-k'ou (Mouth of the Vale)," where he practiced Taoist self-cultivation. Legend has it that he sang highly transcendental songs without words which had a positive moral influence on the official world at the time. He is briefly mentioned in Han-shu 72/4056.

159. See Lun-yü 7:10, where Tzu-lu is criticized by Confucius for being one of his more impetuous disciples. Somewhat jealous over the Master's preference for Yen Yuan, "Tzu-lu asked, 'If you were to command an entire army, whom would you have along with you?' Confucius said, 'I would not have one who would beat a tiger with his bare hands or ford a river without a boat, not caring whether he died or not. But I would certainly need one who approached matters with caution, who would plan strategies and carry them out.'" Later, however, Tzu-lu became popularly known for his filial piety. See note 151.

160. Blue Dragon (Ch'ing-lung) is an auspicious animal dwelling in the deep. He is also characterized as one of the Four Guardian Spirits who is astronomically a star in the east, and historically the Shang general Teng Chiu-kung.

161. Lines 11 and 12 from Li Po's (699-762) poem. "Sung han chun, p'ei cheng, k'ung ch'ao-fu huan-shan (Escorting Han Chun, P'ei Cheng, and K'ung Ch'ao-fu Back to the Mountain)": "The hunter pulls tight his rabbit-snare/ But fails to catch either dragon or tiger./ So those who dwell amongst the blue clouds/ Loftily sing from their craggy abodes./ Scholar Han believes in worthy heroism;/ Master P'ei cultivates purity and truth;/ And Marquis K'ung is likewise distinguished;/ All are close to the clouds and mist./ Their fortitude transcends the distant pines;/ They sleep under one cover on the stone plateau;/ They axe the ice to gargle the frigid stream;/ Three gentlemen matched like a pair of clogs./ At times they may follow a sudden impulse/ For clouds are always spontaneous./ They left the mountain to greet the Governor/ But loudly hooted in their simple clothes./ Last night, I dreamt that they had returned/ Saying it was to sport with the moon by Bamboo Brook./ This morning at the eastern gate to Lu,/ I toasted you farewell beneath a banqueting tent./ The snowy cliffs are slippery for departing horses;/ The tangled path, confusing for returning men./ Our thoughts of each other are like the grass in the mist--/ Scattered and blurred for all time." CTS 175/1791.

162. Duke Lu, courtesy name Shu-p'ing, was the father of Empress Lu, consort of Han Kao-tsu. Skilled in the art of physiognomy, he recognized the imperial qualities of Kao-tsu when the latter was living in relative obscurity and had the foresight to betroth his daughter to him. Although he was popularly known as a Duke, he was actually enfeoffed as Marquis of Lin-ssu. See Han-shu 97a/3937.

163. The Pavilion for Cleansing Ears (Hsi-er-t'ing) is named after the incident where the Sage-King Yao offered to yield the empire to the eremite Hsu Yu. Hsu felt so defiled by the mention of such worldly ambition that he

cleansed his ears. See Huang-fu, Kao-shih-chuan (T'ai-p'ing yü-lan 506/2310).

164. Wang Chih of the Chin went into the mountains to gather wood and came across two youths playing chess who gave him dates to soothe his hunger. When the game was over, one of the youths pointed out that Wang's ax-handle had rotted away; and when Wang returned to his village, he found that a century had elapsed. See Chien-su-tzu, Tung-hsien-chuan 1/33.

165. Shao-t'ung-chün (The Shao-t'ung Divinity) is a Taoist demigod who lived during the time of the Yellow Emperor and is associated with herbal medicine, serving on the committee of Learned Men in the Celestial Ministry of Medicine. Tzu-t'ung-chün was historically Chang Ya who lived in Tzu-t'ung, Szechuan, during the T'ang and rose to high office. He was later canonized in the Yuan as the God of Literature associated with the stars that form the oblong part of the Big Dipper. Botanically, Shao-t'ung may also refer to the sterculia plantanifolia tree, and Tzu-t'ung to the lindera.

166. Chang Shu-ming is mentioned in Tu Fu's Tsa-shu (Random Notes) as a lifelong friend of great intellectual brilliance. His name also appears in the "Li po-chuan (Biography of Li Po)," where he is included in a group of hedonistic scholars known as the "Six Eremites of Bamboo Brook," with whom the young Li Po spent a period of retreat on Mt. Ts'u-lai. Chiu-t'ang-shu 190c/5053.

167. "T'i chang-shih yin-chü er-shou (Two Poems Written to Mr. Chang Who Dwells in Seclusion)" (CTS 224/2391) were probably written around the same time as his poem to Judge Liu Chiu and Mr. Cheng.

168. The Queen Mother of the West (Hsi-wang-mu) sprang from spiritual forces in the continent of Shen-chou and dwells in celestial style on Mt. K'un-lun. She has a human

form, panther's tail, tiger's teeth, and disheveled hair.
She is noted for her birthday celebrations by the Jasper
Pool, at which immortals would gather to feast on the
peaches of immortality.

169. Yu shih-men-shan chi (Wandering on Stonegate
Mountain) is included in the manuscript copy of Shih-men-
shan-chi (Collected Works on Stonegate Mountain) recently
discovered in Ch'ü-fu. For bibliographical information see
K/630, 639.

CHAPTER TWO

DOWN FROM THE MOUNTAIN

1. For bibliographical information on the Genealogy,
see Ch'en, yen-chiu/113-5.

2. K'ung, T'ao-hua-shan chu (Liang ed.)/3.

3. Copies of K'ung's Ch'ueh-li hsin-chih (A New
Gazetteer of Ch'ü-fu) have apparently not survived, though
it was reputedly reprinted in 1929. For bibliographical
information, see Ch'en, yen-chiu/124-26; Ch'en, nien-
p'u/111.

4. For biographies of K'ung Yen-p'u, courtesy name Yü-
ts'un, also Hsiao-an, and K'ung Yen-chih, artistic name Po-
ts'un, see K'ung, wen-hsien-k'ao 89/76, P'an, Ch'ü-fu/8-9.

5. For a discussion of the Shih-ts'ai (Oblation of
Legumes) see K'ung, wen-hsien-k'ao 15, P'an, Ch'ü-fu 45.

6. For a discussion of the Shih-tien (Grand Oblation),
see K'ung, wen-hsien-k'ao, 14, 21, P'an, Ch'ü-fu 45.

7. Ch'u-shan i-shu-chi (The Extraordinary Events
Whereby I Came Down from the Mountain) is dated by K'ung as
having been completed on May 1, 1685. Several excerpts
have previously been translated in Spence, Emperor of

China/69-70,71. The text translated here is that found in
Chang, Chao-tai 81/1a-27a, printed in 1700, and is complete
except for the first 13 lines which repeat information
already presented. A reprint also appears in K/425-37
although this version contains some textual errors. An
earlier version of the translation appeared in Ch'ing-shih
wen-t'i 3:9 1978)/31-75. The writer is indebted to the
editors for permission to reprint a revised version.

8. For a discussion of K'ang-hsi's Imperial
Progresses, see Spence, Ts'ao Yin and the K'ang-hsi
Emperor/124-51; ceremonies proper to receiving an Emperor
in Ch'ü-fu are described in K'ung, wen-hsien-k'ao 16, 20.

9. Chang P'eng (d.1689), courtesy name Fu-wan,
artistic name Nan-ming, was from Tan-t'u, Kiangsu. He
became a Metropolitan Graduate in 1661 and began his
official career as a Secretary in the Grand Secretariat.
In 1672, he was a Vice-Examiner at the Shantung Provincial
Examinations and was later involved in the Ming History
Project. By 1684, he had risen to Junior Vice-President of
the Censorate and Governor of Shantung. Chang was a
valuable advisor to K'ang-hsi on this tour, particularly on
local matters in Shantung, and he was primarily responsible
for lowering taxes on the lands belonging to the K'ung and
Yen clans. His later career was distinguished in the areas
of famine relief, bandit suppression, and river control.
Although he was domoted to Governor-General of Yunnan and
Kweichow in 1687, he was pardoned and ended his career as
Vice-President of the Board of Personnel. Li, Kuo-ch'ao
52/14a-18b.

10. An allusion to the story about the poet Ts'ao Chih
(192-232) who was mistreated by his jealous brother Ts'ao
P'i (187-226), Emperor Wen of the Wei dynasty. On one
occasion, the latter ordered him to compose a poem in the
time it took to walk seven paces, on pain of death. The
poet's genius was such that he not only fulfilled the task

but wrote a poem so expressive of his plight that his brother was moved and subsequently honored him. See Liu, Shih-shuo 1/28b-29a.

11. For a woodblock print and discussion of the Temporary Palace of Ch'ü-fu, see P'an, Ch'ü-fu 3/127-34.

12. Sun Tsai-feng (1644-89), courtesy name Ni-chan, was from Te-ch'ing, Chekiang. He placed second on the first list of the Metropolitan Graduate examinations of 1670 and became a Compiler of the Second Class in the Han-lin Academy, attached to the Office for Keeping a Diary of the Emperor's Movements. He rose steadily in the Han-lin Academy, from Expositor to Reader and was Editor-in-Chief of the Ming History Project in 1682. The following year, he became a Grand Secretary and concurrently Vice-President of the Board of Rites and Chancellor of the Han-lin Academy. Subsequently, Sun was to serve as Vice-President of the Board of Works and, in 1687, had major responsibility for the River Control Project in the Huai-yang area. He was soon to become K'ung Shang-jen's principal political patron in the early part of the latter's career, bringing him to Yangchow to serve in his establishment. In 1688, he was implicated in the ongoing court debate over river control policy, removed from office, demoted five ranks, and reassigned back to the Han-lin Academy, where he continued to serve until his death the following year. Ch'ing-shih-kao lieh-chuan 66/1099; Li, Kuo-ch'ao 56/1a-8b.

13. K'ung Shang-li, courtesy name Li-chih, was the son of K'ung Chen-k'an, who held the title of Hereditary Magistrate. Shang-li became a Provincial Graduate in 1672 and later held the position of Secretary of the Second Class in the Board of Revenue. Li, Kuo-ch'ao 142/Addenda 1b; K'ung, wen-hsien-k'ao 77/11b.

14. An allusion to a poem by Tu Fu, "Chueh-chü ssu-shou-chih-san (Four chueh-chü: No. 3)," written in 764 in

Ch'eng-tu: "Two yellow orioles sing amongst emerald willows;/ A line of white egrets ascends to the blue heavens./ Windows frame the eternal snow on the western hills;/ The gate moors boats on the endless journey to eastern Wu." CTS 77/11.

15. For a woodblock print and description of the Temple of the Perfect Sage, see Pan, Ch'ü-fu 5/170-208; Li, Ch'ü-fu/29.

16. Silda (d. 1709) was a member of the Bordered Red Banner and was descended from a line of military officers. He entered government service in 1673 and was named a Captain in his banner. Silda's success was due to his linguistic abilities in Chinese and Manchu and his knowledge of ritual and military affairs. In 1677, he became a Director of the Court of Sacrificial Worship and in 1684 was made Vice-President of the Censorate, and Grand Secretary and Vice-President of the Board of Rites. Later he was involved in the initial investigation of Galdan's (1644-97) activities and accompanied K'ang-hsi on the ensuing campaign to crush him in 1696. In his final years, he held such posts as President of the Boards of Civil Personnel, War, and Rites, and was Governor-General of Szechuan and Shensi. Ch'ien, Pei-chuan-chi 19/16a-20b.

17. Mingju (1635-1708), courtesy name Tuan-fan, was a member of the Plain Yellow Banner and was descended from rulers of the Yehe Nation, which had been conquered by Nurhaci (1559-1626) in 1619. His forbears consequently became high officials in the Ch'ing related by marriage to the imperial clan. He rose from an officer in the Imperial Bodyguard to President of the Board of Justice in 1668, President of the Censorate a year later, and President of the Board of War in 1671. He was one of the most influential advisors to the K'ang-hsi Emperor during the Wu San-kuei Rebellion and became a Grand Secretary in 1677. By the time of the Emperor's Southern Tour of 1684, Mingju

was one of the most powerful officials in the empire. However, he was soon undermined by the informal criticism of Kao Shih-ch'i (see note 23) and others and was impeached by Censor Kuo Hsiu (see chapter 3, note 156) for corruption. Although deprived of his titles and offices, his huge fortune remained intact and he was made a Senior Assistant Chamberlain in the Imperial Bodyguard. Later he was employed as Commissioner of Grain Transport for the expedition against Galdan. Mingju's eldest son, Singde (1655-85) was a successful scholar and official, gaining fame as one of the greatest tz'u poets of the Ch'ing period. Ch'ing-shih-kao lieh-chuan 57/1082-83; Ch'ing-shih lieh-chuan 8/12b-16; Hummel, Eminent Chinese/557-58.

18. Wang Hsi (1628-1703), courtesy name Tzu-yung, also Hsu-t'ing, artistic name Mu-chai, was born in Peking, the son of Wang Ch'ung-chien (1602-78), a noted Ming official who surrendered to the Ch'ing and was made a Sub-Chancellor in the State Historiographer's Office. Wang Hsi became a Metropolitan Graduate in 1647 and also joined the State Historiographer's Office as a Bachelor. In 1658, he became the first Chancellor of the reorganized Imperial Academy and was an intimate confidant of the Shun-chih Emperor, reputedly drafting his last will, which was later destroyed. He became President of the Censorate in 1666, President of the Board of Works in 1668, and President of the Board of War in 1673. He served as an advisor in the early part of the Wu San-kuei rebellion. After a period of mourning, he returned to become a Grand Secretary in 1682 and was one of the most powerful officials after Mingju was purged in 1688. A man of great prudence and popularity, his career was unblemished and he retired with honors as a Junior Tutor of the Heir Apparent. Ch'ing-shih-kao lieh-chuan 37/1046; Ch'ing-shih lieh-chuan 8/1a-3b; Hummel, Eminent Chinese/819.

19. Isangga (1638-1703) belonged to the Plain Yellow Banner and became a Metropolitan Graduate in 1652. By 1676, he had risen to be Junior Vice-President of the Board of Rites. During the Wu San-kuei Rebellion, he was attached to the Board of Works and charged with building a fleet to intercept Wu's supply line in the Lake Tung-t'ing area. In 1682, he was sent to the Huai-yang area to inspect the river control project there and subsequently became involved in mediating the court controversy surrounding Chin Fu's (see chapter 3, note 6) program of dike construction. It was because of his expertise in this area that he accompanied K'ang-hsi on his 1684 Southern Tour and later advocated dredging the river deltas. His later career was, on the whole, distinguished and he served as President of the Board of Civil Personnel and Grand Secretary of the Wen-hua Palace, the latter office involving him in a number of editing projects. In 1697, he was demoted three ranks because of negligence but continued to serve in the government, accompanying K'kang-hsi on the expedition against Galdan the following year. Ch'ing-shih-kao lieh-chuan 37/1047; Ch'ing-shih lieh-chuan 9/24b-25b.

20. Chieh-shan (1622-95) was the son of a Manchu officer who had assisted in the conquest of the Ming. He began his career as a Clerk in the Board of Revenue, moving up to Director. In 1649, he joined Dorgon (1612-50) in quelling the rebellion at Ta-t'ung, Shansi. Subsequently, he held such posts as Junior Vice-President of the Board of Works in 1660 and Junior Vice-President of the Board of War in 1661. In the latter capacity, he was sent to Kwangtung to police restrictions against foreign trade, returning to Peking in 1663. Fired in 1669 for inefficiency, he was pardoned and demoted one rank instead, going on to become Director of the Court of the Imperial Stud in 1670, Captain of a banner company in 1674, and Junior Vice-President of the Censorate a year later. In 1676, he was sent to help

quell the rebellion of Keng Ching-chung (d. 1682) in Fukien. His last office was that of President of the Board of Rites, to which he was appointed in 1683. Li, Kuo-ch'ao 8/6a-7b.

21. Samha (d. 1704) belonged to the Plain Yellow Banner and became a Metropolitan Graduate in 1654. He began as a Secretary of the Second Class at the Board of Revenue and was promoted in 1658 to Assistant Department Director. In 1673, he was sent to Kweichow to construct a fleet to guard against the rebellious tendencies of Wu San-kuei (1612-78). Despite obstacles created by officials friendly to Wu, he was able to return to Peking and was one of the first to warn the Emperor of the seriousness of the situation. He held numerous offices afterwards, such as Department Director in the Board of Justice in 1674, Director of the Court of the Imperial Stud in 1676, and Sub-Chancellor of the Han-lin Academy in 1677. In 1681 he was appointed President of the Board of Works. He was active in earthquake relief in Shansi and was sent to the Huai-yang area in 1685 to inspect the river control project. Samha was critical of both Yü Ch'eng-lung's and Chin Fu's policies but later supported the former and Sun Tsai-feng in widening the lower reaches of the Yellow River. He was among those demoted in the court debate over the project in 1688. Although he later returned to power as President of the Board of Works in 1693, his final years after 1700 were marred by investigations, demotions, and imprisonment resulting from renewed charges of corruption in connection with the earlier river control project. Ch'ing-shih lieh-chuan 10/40b-42b.

22. Hsu T'ing-hsi held the office of Vice-Governor of Peking and was later to be involved in river control when he was appointed in 1692 to assist the ailing Chin Fu, Director-General of Yellow River Conservancy. He was dismissed by Chang P'eng-ko (see note 27) in 1700 when the

latter assumed control and attempted to reorganize personnel for more efficiency. Hummel, Eminent Chinese/50.

23. Kao Shih-ch'i (1645-1703), courtesy name Tan-jen, artistic name P'ing-lu, also Chiang-ts'un, also Chu-ch'uang, was from Hangchow, Chekiang. A talented poet and calligrapher, he became the favorite literatus of the K'ang-hsi Emperor and achieved high position despite the lack of an advanced degree. Beginning as a poor student at the Imperial Academy, he entered the Han-lin Academy and in 1675 was made a Clerk in the Supervisorate of Imperial Instruction. After attracting the attention of the young Emperor, he was ordered to serve in the Imperial Study and frequently helped K'ang-hsi with his calligraphy and poetry. In addition, he accompanied him on many of his Southern Tours as a court poet and private confidant. Kao was said to have been one of those responsible for the downfall of Mingju by being the first to bring accusations of corruption to K'ang-hsi's attention. Kao himself, however, was later likewise impeached for corruption by the same Censor, Kuo Hsiu. He was ordered to retire in 1689, just after having accompanied the Emperor on his second Southern Tour, during which he hosted him at his lavish Hangchow villa. He was recalled to Peking in 1694 and accompanied the Emperor on his expeditions against Galdan in 1696 and 1697. In his later years, he was a personal secretary in the Imperial Study and died highly honored. In the text, K'ung mistakenly identifies him here as a Chancellor, when his rank, as later mentioned, was actually that of Expositor. Ch'ing-shih-kao lieh-chuan 58/1085-86; Ch'ing-shih lieh-chuan 10/11a-13a; Hummel, Eminent Chinese/413-14.

24. Fiyanggū (1645-1701) belonged to the Plain White Banner and was related by marriage to the Shun-chih Emperor. He thus inherited the rank of Earl, Third Class, in 1658 and went on to win distinction in the field against

the army of Wu San-kuei in 1674.   He became a Chamberlain
in the Imperial Bodyguard in 1680 as a reward but his
greatest achievements took place during the following
decade.   Fiyanggū began to confront Galdan in the early
1690s and was made Military Governor of Kweihua charged
with border defense.   He took a major part in the
expedition against Galdan in 1696, commanding the Western
Army, which inflicted the critical defeat on the rebel.   He
was subsequently raised to the rank of Duke, First Class,
and returned to the duties of Chamberlain.   A successful
diplomat in border affairs, he won the confidence of the
Mongols as well as the people of Kweihua, who honored him
posthumously.   Ch'ing-shih lieh-chuan 11/1a-8b;   Hummel,
Eminent Chinese/248-49.

25. K'ung Yü-t'ing, courtesy name Chung-yü, was the
younger brother of K'ung Yü-ch'i and succeeded to the title
of Hereditary Erudite of the Classics in 1679.   A widely
versed scholar, he was noted for his collections of prose
and poetry which won the praise of the K'ang-hsi Emperor.
K'ung, wen-hsien-k'ao 73/1b.

26. K'ung Chen-cho, courtesy name Chien-hsing, was a
member of the 63rd generation noted for his loyalism during
the fall of Ming.   For a period, he retired to the
countryside where his prestige was such as to deter peasant
rebels from harming his household.   Li, Kuo-ch'ao 467/18a;
K'ung, wen-hsien-k'ao 96/3a.

27. Chang P'eng-ko (1649-1725), courtesy name Yun-
ch'ing, artistic name K'uan-yü, also Hsin-yang-tzu, was
from Sui-ning, Szechuan, and became a Metropolitan Graduate
in 1670.   He began as a Secretary of the Second Class in
the Board of Justice, moving up to Department Director in
the Board of Rites.   In 1680, he became Prefect of Soochow,
retired to observe a period of family mourning, and
returned in 1683 as Prefect of Yen-chou, which administered
Ch'ü-fu.   Chang's career was long and distinguished,

particularly in the areas of river control, border
disputes, and investigations of bureaucratic corruption.
He was a member of the 1688 Embassy to Russia which was,
however, intercepted by Galden. From 1689 to 1694, he was
Governor of Chekiang and in 1699 was sent to investigate
corruption in Shensi. He gained praise in the latter role
from the K'ang-hsi Emperor for his impartiality. In 1700,
he succeeded Yü Ch'eng-lung as Director-General of River
Conservancy and for the following eight years reorganized
the administration, in general following Yü's policies. At
his death, he held the position of President of the Board
of Civil Personnel and the title of Grand Tutor of the Heir
Apparent. Ch'ing-shih-kao lieh-chuan 66/1099-1100; Ch'ing-
shih lieh-chuan 11/16a-25b; Li, Kuo-ch'ao 11/Addenda 1a;
Hummel, Eminent Chinese/49-51.

28. Ta-hsueh (Li-chi 42/1).

29. I-ching 7:1.

30. The Four Attendant Spirits (Ssu-pao-shen) are Yen
Hui, Tseng Shen, Mencius, and Tzu-ssu. For a description
of the typical arrangement of spirits in a Confucian
temple, see Watters, A Guide; also K'ung, wen-hsien-k'ao
42-72 for those in Ch'ü-fu.

31. For a photograph of one such tsun vessel see Chang,
K'ung-meng/32.

32. Photographed in Chang, K'ung-meng/1. For woodblock
prints of this painting, see K'ung, tsu-t'ing kuang-
chi/plate 1; also Ch'en, Ch'ueh-li-chih 1/2a.

33. The authenticity of this painting as explained by
K'ung is doubtful since hardly any original works seem to
have been preserved from the painter Ku K'ai-chih (c.345-
c.406), let alone anything traceable to the disciple Tzu-
kung. There is a discussion of this picture in Ch'en,
Ch'ueh-li-chih 1/5b-6a.

34. This inscription was later carved in wood and hung inside the Hall of Accomplishment. For a photograph, see Chang, K'ung-meng/30.

35. Woodblock prints of these can be found in K'ung, Sheng-men/35a-b; also P'an, Ch'ü-fu 9/275-77.

36. Mi Fei (1051-1107) courtesy name Yuan-chang, was from Hsiang-yang in modern Hupei. Although he served in a number of high official positions, he is best remembered for his versatile calligraphy and distinct style of landscape painting.

37. For a woodblock print see K'ung, tsung-t'ing kuang-chi/plate 11; also photographed in Li, Ch'ü-fu/36.

38. The Yung-lo reign spanned 1403-24 and Hung-chih, 1488-1506.

39. For a photograph of the Gate of Unified Script, see Li, Ch'ü-fu/36.

40. See chapter 1, note 12.

41. These offices are discussed in K'ung, wen-hsien-k'ao 18/10b; P'an, Ch'ü-fu 40/1145-54.

42. The text of this stele, officially known as "The Stele Commemorating the Restoration by Imperial Command of the Labor Force for the Yen and Ch'i-shih Clans and the Recasting of the Ritual Vessels Under Prime Minister Han Ch'ih of Lu (Han lu-hsiang han ch'ih fu yen-shih ch'i-kuan-shih yao-fa chi-hsin li-ch'i-pei)" is recorded in K'ung, wen-hsien-k'ao 33/2a-3a; also recorded and discussed in P'an, Ch'ü-fu 51/1452-56.

43. This stele, officially known as "The Memorial to the Provincial Inspector during the Han Dynasty, K'ung Ch'ien (Han chün-chu-ts'ao-shih k'ung ch'ien mu-chieh)" is discussed in P'an, Ch'ü-fu 51/1451-52.

44. The text of this stele, officially known as "The Wei Dynasty Stele of the Confucian Temple in Lu (Wei lu k'ung-tzu miao-pei)" is recorded in K'ung, wen-hsien-k'ao

33/4a-6a; also recorded and discussed in P'an, <u>Ch'ü-fu</u> 51/1471-74.

45. The text of this stele, officially known as "The Stele Comemorating the Sacrifice at the Confucian Temple of the Prime Minister of Lu, Shih Ch'en (<u>Han lu shih ch'en ssu-k'ung-tzu miao-pei</u>)" is recorded in K'ung, <u>wen-hsien-k'ao</u> 33/3a-3b; also recorded and discussed in P'an, <u>Ch'ü-fu</u> 51/1459-61.

46. The text of "The Stele of the Commandant of Mt. T'ai, K'ung Miao (<u>Han t'ai-shan tu-wei k'ung miao-pei</u>)" is recorded in P'an, <u>Ch'ü-fu</u> 51/1456-59; photographed in Chang, <u>K'ung-meng</u>/36.

47. The text of "The Stele of the Prefect of Po-ling, K'ung P'iao (<u>Han po-ling t'ai-shou k'ung p'iao-pei</u>)" is recorded in P'an, <u>Ch'ü-fu</u> 51/1464-68.

48. The Hung-wu reign spanned 1368-99 and Ch'eng-hua, 1465-87. The latter stele may be the one photographed in Chang, <u>K'ung-meng</u>/37 erected in 1468 upon the restoration of the Confucian Temple.

49. Photographed in Chang, <u>K'ung-meng</u>/54.

50. See chapter 1, note 15.

51. Photographed in Chang, <u>K'ung-meng</u>/53.

52. See chapter 1, note 40.

53. Hsuan-tsung (reigned 713-56) wrote: "What else could Confucius do/ But perch here and there in his time?/Yet the land still contains the villages of Tsou/ And the dwelling became the Prince of Lu's palace./   He lamented that a phoenix did not appear, that he would never succeed;/ He was pained that there was no magic unicorn, weeping to the point of exhaustion./ As I look at the sacrifices by the Twin Pillars,/ It all seems just like a dream." K'ung, <u>wen-hsien-k'ao</u> 41/la.

54. A woodblock print appears in K'ung, <u>tsu-t'ing</u>/plate 7; another along with a description appears in P'an, <u>Ch'ü-fu</u> 5/160-69; Chang, <u>K'ung-meng</u>/46 contains a map and also

photographs on pp. 47-50; a photograph of the road to the tomb appears in Li, Ch'ü-fu/42.

55. See K'ung An-kuo's commentary to Lun-yü 18:10: "The Duke of Lu was the Duke of Chou's son, Po-ch'in, who was enfeoffed in Lu." In K'ung Ying-ta's commentary to Tso-chuan: Ting-kung 5 (Shih-san-ching 6/958) Tung-yeh is identified as the place where the Chi clan was enfeoffed. P'ei-jan's later reply to the Emperor reveals that the clan has hitherto been sacrificing to the Duke of Chou's son and that his request is to upgrade the temple by rededicating it to the Duke of Chou, thereby enhancing the position of his clan. For a photograph of the temple, see Li, Ch'ü-fu/28. For a discussion of the genealogy of the Tung-yeh clan see P'an, Ch'ü-fu 61/1685-89.

56. Photographed in Chang, K'ung-meng/47.

57. Photographed in Chang, K'ung-meng/17.

58. Photographed in Chang, K'ung-meng/50.

59. The Pistacia chinensis Bunge (anacardiaceae) (Chinese: k'ai-mu) is a relative of the pistachio nut tree. It grows to 60 feet or more and has leaves which are evenpinnate, turning to crimson in autumn. for a discussion of these famous trees in Ch'ü-fu, see Bretschneider, "Botanicum Sinicum"/399.

60. I-ching: Hsi-tz'u A:8.

61. Photographed in Li, Ch'ü-fu/24.

62. Photographed in Ni, Ch'ü-fu/63.

63. Photographed in Chang, K'ung-meng/68.

64. Photographed in Chang, K'ung-meng/49.

65. Photographed in Li, Ch'ü-fu/42.

66. The poem by Pi Mao-k'ang (1573-1619) is recorded as follows: "The Shu and Ssu Rivers wind around, split, like two schools;/ Dragonish Mt. T'ai protects the tomb of the Throneless King./ He transmitted the classics and taught three thousand disciples/ While those who offered gifts were seventy rare gentlemen./ On the buildings and in the

courtyards, vines and grass grow;/ Trees entangle carved
pillars thrusting to the cool clouds./ The tall mountain
commands respect and I hasten to pay it reverence,/ Humbly
facing the spring breeze of learning which advanced the
talents of Lu." K'ung, wen-hsien-k'ao 41/10a-b.

67. Prince Kung, named Ch'ang-ning (1657-1703), was the
fifth son of the Shun-chih Emperor and thus the younger
brother of K'ang-hsi. The latter elevated him to the
position of Prince in 1671. He was later active in the
expeditions against Galden and was appointed Field Marshall
for Pacifying the North. Although he helped to defeat
Galden militarily, he was demoted and fined for not
capturing him. He joined the subsequent expedition in 1696
along with Fiyanggū which resulted in Galdan's death. In
the text, K'ung Shang-jen gives his name as "Yung-ning."
T'ieh, Pa-ch'i t'ung-chih 133/14a-b; Hummel, Eminent
Chinese/69-70.

68. Weng Shu-yuan (1633-1701) originally named Chan,
courtesy name Pao-lin, artistic name T'ieh-an, was from
Ch'ang-shu, Kiangsu. He won third place in the Palace
Examination of 1676 and entered the Han-lin Academy.
Subsequently, he was in charge of the Shantung provincial
examinations and in 1679 became a compiler of the Ming
History Project.   His career was distinguished and
uninterrupted although he was briefly criticized for having
associated in 1687 with the faction of Mingju. However, he
became President of the Board of Works in 1688 and
President of the Board of Justice in 1692. Ch'ing-shih-kao
lieh-chuan 48/1084-85; Hummel, Eminent Chinese/859-60.

69. Chang Shih-chen (1624-93) courtesy name Hsiu-tz'u,
artistic name T'ieh-chih, was from T'ung-chou, Chihli
(modern Hopei), and became a Metropolitan Graduate in 1649.
He started out as a Bachelor in the Department of Study in
the Han-lin Academy and rose to Compiler of the Second
class.   In 1659, he entered the Imperial Academy as

Libationer, becoming an Expositor a year later. Upon the accession of the K'ang-hsi Emperor in 1662, he was made a Chancellor of the Grand Secretariat and accompanied the Emperor on his journey to Soochow. Subsequently he served as Vice-President of the Board of Rites and Vice-President of the Board of Civil Personnel. He became highly valued by the Emperor because of his literary talents and in 1685 served as President of the Board of Justice. In 1687 he was appointed President of the Board of Rites, retiring five years later. Hsu, Ta-ch'ing chi-fu 3/13a-14a.

CHAPTER THREE
BY SOUTHERN LAKES AND SEAS

1. See chapter 2, note 12.

2. The most outstanding example of intentional destruction occurred in October 1642. The Ming Provincial Governor, Kao Ming-heng, ordered the dikes at Chu-chia-chai breached in order to flood the armies of Li Tzu-ch'eng camped on the plain outside of Kaifeng. Li's armies avoided the onrush, however, which only innundated the city and set off a series of other catastrophes for miles around. this caused the death of several hundred thousand inhabitants and though the breach was closed the following year, the dislocation eventually resulted in the shifting of the mouth of the Yellow River in Kiangsu. Of equal concern to Ch'ing engineers were the numerous smaller breachings in the south by Ming loyalists resisting the Manchu invasion.

The last great Ming effort at river control was under Vice-Minister of the Grand Court of Revision, P'an Chi-hsun

(1521-95) who was appointed in 1565 as Imperial Commissioner for the Yellow River. Over the next three years, P'an championed the policy of using the clear current of the Huai to cleanse the silt of the Yellow River and concentrated on building dikes at Kao-chia-yen along Lake Hung-tse to allow the Huai to retain its full power. He also recommended use of a second line of dikes as a back-up to the main ones as well as safety valves and retention basins. Cheng, shui-li-shih/49-59, 64; Goodrich and Fang, Ming Biography/1107-11. for a discussion of the scientific aspect of Chinese hydraulic engineering, see Needham, Science and Civilization 4/211-378.

3. Among the other approaches of Ch'ing experts was the search for the source of the Yellow River in the hope of controlling its flow at the origin. However, technological limitations prevented this strategy from having any real effect on river control. There were two distinct differences between early Ch'ing policy and that of P'an Chi-hsun: (1) emphasis on controlling the middle reaches of the Yellow River as well as the lower reaches; (2) dredging the deltas and constructing dikes, especially at Yun-t'i-kuan, Kiangsu, to facilitate the speedy flow of the silt out to sea. Ch'ing-shih-kao 101/462; Tsen, Huang-ho/609-13.

4. Spence, Emperor of China/148.

5. See chapter 2, note 19.

6. Chin Fu (1633-92), courtesy name Tz'u-yuan, was born in Liao-yang into the Chinese Bordered Yellow Banner. He began as a Compiler in the State Historiographer's Office and rose rapidly to become Governor of Anhwei by 1671.   He was active in suppressing the Wu San-kuei Rebellion in his area and became Director-General of the Conservation of the Yellow River in 1677. He served in this position for the next eleven years although his plans

were frequently attacked by opponents and he suffered dismissals on several occasions. Nevertheless, the K'ang-hsi Emperor, through his personal inspections on the Southern Tours of 1684 and 1689, finally became convinced of his accomplishments and restored him to his position in his later years. He died in office and was given numerous posthumous honors. Ch'ing-shih-kao lieh-chuan 66/1097-98; Hummel, Eminent Chinese/161-63.

7. These policies were: (1) dredging and construction of dikes along the lower reaches from Ch'ing-chiang; (2) widening the Yellow River at Ch'ing-k'ou so as to allow the Huai to flush out the silt deposits; (3) strengthening the embankments along Lake Hung-tse at Kao-chia-yen; (4) repairing 34 breaches in the dikes from Chou-ch'iao to Ti-chia; (5) dredging the Grand Canal from Ch'ing-k'ou to Ch'ing-shui-t'an; (6) taxing the fields and shipping in the Huai-yang area to pay for the projects; (7) consolidating personnel and appointing officials on the basis of expertise; (8) strengthening security by stationing military forces at key points in the dike system. Ch'ing-shih-kao 101/463; Cheng, shui-li-shih/68-72.

8. Ts'ui Wei-ya (Metropolitan Graduate, 1646), courtesy name Ta-ch'un, was born in Ta-ming, Chihli (modern Hopei) and began as District Director of Schools in Hsun-hsien, Honan, becoming District Magistrate of I-feng in the same province. While serving in this area, he became acquainted with the problems of river control and achieved distinction for his construction after the 1657 flooding of the Yellow River. During the K'ang-hsi reign, his predictions about the efficacy of various construction projects proved correct. Subsequently, he served in the south as Prefect of Ningpo, Chekiang, Assistant River Taotai for Honan and Lieutenant-Governor of Hunan and Kwangsi. While in the latter capacity, he opposed Chin

Fu's plans in a 24-point program generally advocating dike construction and dredging of waterways to direct the flow of the river. However, the court did not approve it. At his death, he held the position of director of the court of Judicature and Revision. Ch'ing-shih-kao lieh-chuan 66/1097.

9. Yü Ch'eng-lung (1638-1700), courtesy name Chenchia, artistic name Ju-shan, was born in K'ai-p'ing, Liaotung, into the Chinese Bordered Red Banner. He was appointed Magistrate of Lo-t'ing, Chihli, due to the meritorious service of his adopted father and distinguished himself as a popular official. His reputation grew and in 1681 he was made Prefect of Nanking. The K'ang-hsi Emperor, upon visiting Nanking in 1684, wass unusually impressed with Yü's administration of what had been the center of Ming loyalism. Upon his return to the capital, he chose Yü to supervise dredging the Yellow River delta. However, Chin Fu's objections eventually led to the cancellation of the project. Yü served as Governor of Chihli, President of the Censorate, and in 1693 Director-General of the Conservation of the Yellow River after Chin Fu died. In later years, he served on the expedition against Galdan, again as Governor of Chili and as Director-General. Ch'ing-shih-kao lieh-chuan 66/1099.

10. See chapter 2, note 21.

11. T'ang Pin (1627-87), courtesy name K'ung-po, artistic name Ching-hsien, also Ch'ien-an, was born in Suichou, Honan, and became a Metropolitan Graduate in 1652. He became a Corrector in the State Historiographer's Office and later distinguished himself as Intendant of the T'ung-kuan Circuit, Shensi. In 1659, he was transferred to the Ling-pei Circuit, Kiangsi, where he helped suppress allies of Cheng Ch'eng-kung (1624-62). T'ang passed the special Po-hsueh-hung-tz'u examination of 1679 and entered the Han-

lin Academy as a Sub-Expositor, becoming involved in the Ming History Project. Eventually, he rose to Governor of Kiangsu in 1684, from which position he memorialized the emperor on river control policy. T'ang's support of Yü Ch'eng-lung's plan in 1686 provoked the antagonism of Chin Fu and Chin's ally, Mingju. He was removed from several posts and wound up serving in the Board of Works when he died in 1687. The following year both Chin and Mingju were impeached by Censor Kuo Hsiu who had been recommended to his position by T'ang. Ch'ing-shih-kao lieh-chuan 52/1075.

12. There were more than a score of separate construction works in this plan, such as the widening of Kang-men-hsieh, Pai-chu-p'ien, and Ting-hsi, and the dredging of Ts'ao-yen. In addition, Sun sponsored relief efforts for flood victims. Ch'ing-shih-kao lieh-chuan 66/1099.

13. Shih K'o-fa (d. 1645), courtesy name Hsien-chih, artistic name Tao-lin, was born in Hsiang-fu, Honan, and became a Metropolitan Graduate in 1628. For distinguishing himself as a police magistrate in Sian, Shensi, he was given command of troops against the peasant rebel Chang Hsien-chung (1605-47) in 1635. He subsequently became Governor of the western Kiangsu region and later Vice President of the Board of Revenue. He also served as Director of Grain Transport and Governor-General of Feng-yang, Huai-an, and Yangchow prefectures. He became President of the Board of War in Nanking in 1643, and the following year planned to march against Li Tzu-ch'eng when Peking fell. Shih returned to Nanking and helped establish the Southern Court; however, he was outmaneuvered by the faction of Ma Shih-ying (see note 52) and Juan Ta-ch'eng (see note 52) whose candidate, Prince Fu, was made the Hung-kuang Emperor. His influence diminished, Shih was compelled to leave the court and accept the position of

Grand Secretary, headquartered in Yangchow. There, he tried to encourage a counterattack against the north while at the same time keep peace among the various quarreling generals defending Nanking. The Manchu attack on Yangchow in May 1645 found the city short of supplies and Shih, after an unsuccessful suicide attempt, was killed as he fled the city. His corpse was never found, leading to the popular rumor that he had drowned himself in the Yangtze. Later, his clothes were buried at Plum Blossom Hill just north of the city. Ming-shih 274/7015-24; Hummel, Eminent Chinese/651-52.

14. Wang Hsiu-ch'u, an eyewitness to the holocaust, recorded a typically gruesome moment when "suddenly, fire erupted on all sides. In front and in back of the Ho family graves stood thatched houses which were immediately consumed. Only a few slivers of acreage escaped the net of flames. Everyone who had hidden under the houses to escape the fire was forced to come out by the heat and when they did, nine out of ten were killed. There were also those who locked themselves up inside and wound up burned to death—from several to as many as a hundred in each room—who could tell how many died from the piles of charred bones. Unquestionably, at this critical point, there was nowhere to hide nor could one remain undiscovered even if one tried. Those with money and those without both perished. The only escape was to lie down among the bodies strewn along the roadside, not knowing whether they were dead or alive. My wife and son went to crouch behind the gravemound. So covered with mud were we from head to foot that we scarcely seemed human. The fire continued to spread and soon, the tall trees about the grave were fiercely burning, giving off a glow like lightning, crackling like an earthquake. The wind fanned the flames with ferocious might, rendering the sun pale and dim by

comparison. Before us, it seemed that innumerable demons were driving hundreds and thousands of souls into Hell to meet their end. We fainted from fright a number of times and were so numb and dazed that we no longer knew whether or not we were in the realm of living men." Wang, Yang-chou. In Ch'en, Yang-chou/501-2; another translation appears in Mao, "A Memoir"/531-32.

15. The construction of the canal is recorded in Tso-chuan 480: Ai 9:fu 2. For historical information on early Yangchow, see Chiao, Han-chi. Both the waterway and King Fu-ch'ai were later worshipped in a temple near the site. See Li, Yang-chou 1/15-16.

16. For a discussion of Yangchow under Yang Kuang, see Wright, The Sui Dynasty/158-61.

17. The fictional image of Yang-ti is discussed in Hegel, Novel/84-111; also in Wright, "Sui Yang-ti."

18. For a short biography of Tu Mu (803-52) in Yangchow, see Miao, Tu mu-chuan/37-43.

19. An allusion to the poem by Tu Mu containing the lines, "Who knows the road by the western bamboo, where all Yangchow gathers to make music and song?" Here he comments on the scene unchanged from the days of Sui Yang-ti. The Pavilion of the Western Bamboo stood beside the Temple of Ch'an Awareness, north of Mandarin River; it was also known as the "Music and Song Pavilion." Li, Yang-chou 1/15; Wu, Yang-chou/416.

20. The Hall Level with the Peaks stands on Szechuan Hill about two miles to the northwest of the city and was built by Ou-yang Hsiu (1007-72) in 1048 while he served as Governor. It is noted for poetry gatherings through the ages and famous for its custom of having courtesans fetch lotus flowers for guests. Li, Yang-chou 16/377-79; Wu, Yang-chou/414.

21. The Pavilion of Kuan-yin was located on Szechuan Hill on the ruins of the Tower of Mazes. The latter had been an exquisite pleasure dome built by Sui Yang-ti to house his favorite beauties. The layout was so intricate that Yang-ti boasted that only immortals could venture in without getting lost in its mazes. It was destroyed by T'ang soldiers and became a symbol of Yang-ti's extravagance. Wu, Yang-chou/410. A poem by K'ung upon visiting the site can be found in K/9. In Tu Mu's aria, the "idle blossoms and rustic grass" refer to the courtesans who frequented the area.

22. The Pool of Nine Turns was located about 2 1/2 miles north of the city and was fed by two pure streams. It later became part of the Chang Family Garden, noted for its many pavilions as well as its greenery, which was allowed to grow freely. Li, Yang-chou 14/338-39.

23. Little Gold Mountain was located on the southeast bank of Slender West Lake, on whose northern bank stands the Hall Level with the Peaks. The mountain is surrounded on all four sides by water and is said to resemble an upturned cauldron because of its round shape. Wu, Yang-chou/413-14; Li, Yang-chou 1/23.

24. The Temple of Heavenly Peace is chief among the eight major temples of Yangchow, dating back to the Chin dynasty when the site was originally the residence of the Governor Hsieh An (320-85). It was especially connected with recitals of the Hua-yen-ching (Lankavatara Sutra) and in later dynasties became a center for performing dramas. Li, Yang-chou 4/82-83. For a map of the temple in the eighteenth century, see Mackerras, Peking Opera/69.

25. Ch'iao, Yang-chou-meng/795.

26. For a discussion of this economic transformation and the class of salt-merchants which evolved, see Ho, "The

Salt Merchants of Yang-chou"/143ff; also Spence, Ts'ao Yin/166-212.

27. Li, Yang-chou 6/149-50.

28. For a well-known satirization of the salt-merchant, see Wu Ching-tzu's Ju-lin wai-shih (The Scholars), especially the characters Wan Hsueh-chai (chapters 22, 23) and Fang Cho (chapter 48).

29. The Rainbow Bridge Garden also known as Red Bridge Garden belonged to the Hung family, which began its salt business in the late Ming. By the early Ch'ing, the Garden had become a noted gathering spot due to the elegance of its design which skillfully incorporated bodies of water into 24 famous scenes. Both Wang Shih-chen and K'ung Shang-jen hosted gatherings here. Li, Yang-chou/217-67.

30. For a description of the theatre in Yangchow during the eighteenth century, see Mackerras, Peking Opera/49-80. In discussing the general theater situation, he distinguishes a quasireligious theater maintained by powerful clans, a secular theater of the literati, and a popular theater of ordinary people; the latter category includes commercial, religious and folk forms (pp. 20-40). Mackerras' execellent study is largely based on Li Tou's Yang-chou hua-fang-lu (1794); however, Li's information on the theater is mostly from the late eighteenth century, and there are some difficulties in applying it to K'ung Shang-jen's time a hundred years earlier. For one thing, imperial patronage was not yet a factor in the seventeenth century, having arisen largely through Ch'ien-lung's (r. 1736-96) southern tours. Secondly, local opera was only beginning to rival the K'un-ch'ü style in elite circles and the later distinction between ya-pu ("elegant" companies, i.e., those specializing in K'un-ch'ü) and hua-pu ("flowery" companies, i.e., those performing local opera) was not yet widespread. Nor had the various forms of local

opera undergone the consolidation into what later developed into Peking Opera. It is more accurate to see the Yangchow theater in K'ung's time as being in a transitional phase, that is, a continuation of the late Ming situation with the dislocating effects of the conquest taken into consideration.

31. For poems recording K'ung's attendance at performances of Yü Chin-ch'üan's troupe, see K/39, 40, 51, 103, 171. At K'ung's gathering at Chao-yang in the autumn of 1688, to which Yü brought his troupe, was K'ung's friend Mao Hsiang (see note 50), another great patron of the theater. Although K'ung must have gained considerable knowledge about drama during these years, there is surprisingly little evidence about his interest in the theater and he does not seem to have become involved with it until after his return to Peking.

32. Li, Yang-chou/107 records that the Liang-huai Guild traditionally organized troupes for grand performances at the Temple of Heavenly Peace. In the early Ch'ing, the government maintained official courtesan houses in the city at Ch'ung-ch'eng, which K'ung's friend Wu Ch'i (see note 71) records as a continuous scene of nighttime revelry. These courtesans were simply known as "yueh-hu (musicians)" and performed dances and dramas at public festivals such as the welcoming of spring, but their primary function was to entertain at banquets given by high officials. According to Li Tou, yueh-hu were abolished later in the K'ang-hsi reign. Wu, Yang-chou/406; Li, Yang-chou/197-98.

33. These were: the Pao-feng, Ch'ung-ning, Kao-min, and T'ien-ning. Mackerras, Peking Opera/69-70.

34. Government proscriptions against the mixing of the sexes on stage go back as early as the T'ang yet the practice subsequently became widespread. Sporadic edicts on morality issued by the authorities over the century

rarely affected the prostitution and homosexuality which remained a part of the Chinese theater in traditional China. Similarly, the actual effect of laws controlling the length and organization of performances, as well as the prohibition against actors and their descendents sitting for the examinations, remains to be determined. For a history of courtesan performers see Wang, ch'ang-chi-shih.

35. One of the most notable examples of mobility among performers at this time was the Ch'ang-chou performer Ch'en Ming-chih, who was able to escape the life of an actor in a traveling troupe to become a palace performer under K'ang-hsi. He was later given official privileges and retired to a luxurious life in Soochow. Such success was extremely rare, however. Chiao, Chü-shuo/199-201.

36. Wei Liang-fu (born c.1522), artistic name Shang-ch'üan, was born in K'un-shan, Kiangsu, a town north of Soochow, and later dwelled in neighboring T'ai-ts'ang. He originally studied the northern style of music but abandoned this in favor of various local styles such as Hai-yen and I-yang. After a decade of study, he evolved K'un-chü or "melodies from K'un-shan" as a synthesis of the best elements of these styles, teaching a number of musicians who became active in the Soochow area. The style spread further through the influence of the work of Liang Ch'en-yü (c.1510-82), particularly his ch'uan-ch'i drama Wan-sha-chi (The Rinsed Silk). Ch'ü-lu, an early treatise, has been traditionally attributed to Wei. A discussion of Wei and the rise of K'un-ch'ü appears in Aoki, hsi-ch'ü-shih/165-78; for a discussion and translation of a modern treatise on performance, see Strassberg, "The Singing Techniques of K'un-ch'ü."

37. K'u Ch'i-yuan (1565-1628), a contemporary observer, recorded: "In Nanking before the Wan-li period, nobles, gentry, and wealthy families would entertain by having

arias performed by several actors or perhaps many actors, singing in the northern style. For instruments, they used the zither, the lute, the banjo and wooden clappers. . . . But later there was a change and they began to use southern arias. Singers employed only one small set of clappers or a fan as a substitute, perhaps adding a drum or other clappers. Now, people from the Soochow area have added the flute and moon guitar. . . . Southern dramas are performed at large feasts. Originally, there were only two main styles--I-yang and Hai-yen. I-yang uses colloquial language and literati from the provinces enjoyed watching it. In Hai-yen, there was a lot of the official dialect and it was popular in Nanking and Peking. And now there is also the K'un-shan style. It is clearer and more mellifluous than Hai-yen yet combines both harmony and sudden changes in melody, exending one word for several breaths. The literati have endowed it with their spirit and greatly enjoy it. As for Hai-yen and the other styles, they seem to make one want to fall asleep in the daytime; and as for northern drama, it is like blowing on flutes and beating clay pots--people are bored with it and even scoff at it." Ku, K'o-tso ch'ü-yü. In Hsin-ch'ü-yuan/166-67. For discussions on the rise of K'un-ch'ü drama, see Chou, hsi-ch'ü-shih chiang-tso/144-49; Aoki, hsi-ch'ü-shih/165-73.

38. See Chou, hsi-ch'ü-shih chiang-tso/195-210 for a discussion of the decline of K'un-ch'ü in the early decades of the Ch'ing and the role of The Peach Blossom Fan in its revival. Aoki likewise considers the mid-K'ang-hsi to late Ch'ien-lung period to be the aftermath of K'un-ch'ü's period of ascendency. Aoki, hsi-ch'ü-shih/376-436.

39. An early mention of the I-yang style occurs in Hsu Wei, Nan-tz'u hsu-lu (1559), where he mentions it as being popular in Kiangsi, Nanking, Peking, Hunan, Fukien, and

Kwangtung; at the time, it appears to have been more widespread than K'un-ch'ü, which was still limited to the Soochow area. Hsu, Nan-tz'u hsu-lu/242. For discussions of I-yang, see Chou hsi-ch'ü-shih/475-99; hsi-ch'ü-shih chiang-tso/163-74; 195-206.

40. Chou, hsi-ch'ü-shih/469-70.

41. The following story of an elite gathering attended by Wang Shih-chen (see note 45) where I-yang was performed is often cited to indicate the change in taste in early Ch'ing: when Wang Shih-chen was sent to sacrifice in Chiang-tu, Hsiung Fang-po gave a farewell banquet to entertain him and the I-yang play Pai-hua ssu-chieh (Chang Ssu-chieh, the Flower Arranger) was performed. Hsiung asked Wang what the origin of the story was and Wang was unable to reply. Hsiung later told others, "Who said Wang shih-chen was erudite? Today I have bested him." Chiao, Chü-shuo/154. This story seems to have been misunderstood by Mackerras, who translates it so as to make it appear that Wang is being criticized for performing I-yang instead of K'un-ch'ü. However, as Chou I-pai mentions, the point is that Wang's fame for erudition is being questioned because he did not know the origin of a popular play, a somewhat unfair aspersion since Wang's reputation was based on his allusive poetry rather than drama. In any event, it shows that I-yang could be performed on the highest levels of literati society. Mackerras, Peking Opera/31; Chou, his-ch'ü-shih/476.

42. For a discussion of Little Ch'in-huai, see Li, Yang-chou/215.

43. Twenty-four Bridges was located on the avenue leading to the West Gate in the old city. In K'ung's time, the name denoted a single bridge but the origin of the name was not clear. According to Wu Ch'i, the name derived from twenty-four courtesans who used to gather there to sing

arias. However, Li Tou disagrees and records several other explanations. One, by Shen Kua (1030-94) in his Pu-pi-t'an (Additional Comments), states that there were originally twenty-four famous bridges in the city. The notion of courtesans was a later association deriving, perhaps, from the poems of Tu Mu. This explanation is supported by a tz'u by Chiang K'uei (c.1155-1235) which contributed the additional names of "Pondering Bridge" and "Red Peony Bridge." Wu, Yang-chou/408; Li Yang-chou/341; Liang, Lang-chi/781.

44. Chang, T'ao-an/52-53.

45. Wang Shih-chen (1634-1711), posthumously renamed Shih-cheng, courtesy name Tzu-chen, also I-shan, artistic name Juan-t'ing, also Yü-yang shan-jen, posthumous name Wen-chien, was born into an affluent family of officials from Hsin-ch'eng, Shantung. Regarded as one of the great poets of his time, he was a leading force in the literary world from his youth. He became a Metropolitan Graduate in 1658 and then served as a police magistrate in Yangchow from 1660 to 1665. The numerous poetry gatherings he held in the city were well-remembered decades afterwards and his poems on these occasions continued to have local influence. With the encouragement of such arbiters of taste as Ch'ien Ch'ien-i (1582-1664) and Mao Hsiang (see note 50), as well as the recommendation of his superiors, Wang commenced a public career which eventually led to the presidencies of the Board of War, the Board of Punishments, and the Censorate by the end of the century. Along the way, he also served in the Han-lin Academy and in the State Historiographer's Office, largely through the recommendation of the K'ang-hsi Emperor. It was not until the 1690s, when K'ung Shang-jen had returned to Peking, that he met Wang and joined his circle. Wang wrote over twenty collections of poetry and about eighty other works

including anthologies and poetry criticism. His final years were marred by controversy over an earlier judicial decision of his and he was deprived of his ranks after forty-five years of public service. These were restored, however, a year before he died. Ch'ing-shih-kao lieh-chuan 53/1078; Hummel, Eminent Chinese/831-32. For studies of Wang's poetry, see Lynn, "Orthodoxy and Enlightenment;" Wang Shih-chen; Hashimoto, Ō Gyoyō.

46. There was a famous Hall of Thirteen Chambers (Shih-san-lou) in Hangchow during the Sung. It was associated with Su Tung-p'o who often stayed there while Governor. The poem may be referring to a place in Yangchow of a similar name.

47. Wu-ch'eng, literally the "Overgrown Fortress," was the citadel of Prince Pi of Wu during the Han and was located on top of Szechuan Hill in the northern part of Yangchow. It has long fallen into disrepair and even in the time of Pao Chao (c.421-65), who wrote "Wu-ch'eng-fu (A Fu on Wu-ch'eng)," it symbolized the decay of empire. Wu, Yang-chou/408; the fu is reprinted in Chao-ming t'ai-tzu, ed., Wen-hsuan 11/149-50.

48. An allusion to the poem by Li Po, "Huang-ho-lou sung-pieh meng hao-jan chih yang-chou (seeing off Meng Hao-jan at Yellow Crane Tower on his journey to Yangchow)," CTS/1785.

49. For poems and an essay written at Rainbow Bridge, also known as Red Bridge, see K/10, 67, 70, 71, 123, 170, 455. The Garden was also the meeting place of the "Seductive Spring" Poetry Society which K'ung participated in.

50. The following figures at this gathering have been recorded: Mao Hsiang (1611-93), courtesy name Pi-chiang, artistic name Ch'ao-min, also P'u-an, was born in Ju-kao, Kiangsu, into a wealthy family which had produced a number of officials under the Ming. Active in Fu-she politics at

the end of the dynasty, he retired in the early Ch'ing and became known as one of the most prominent "survivors." The writings of his later years appeared in Ch'ao-min shih-wen-chi (Collected Works of Mao Hsiang); a broad selection of his works and those by other members of his family appeared in Mao-shih ts'ung-shu (Collected Works of the Mao Family) (pub. 1911-17). Ch'ing-shih-kao lieh-chuan 288/1557-58, Ch'ing-shih lieh-chuan 70/7a-b; Hummel, Eminent Chinese/ 566-67.

Mao Tan-shu (b. 1639), courtesy name Ch'ing-jo, artistic name Mao-chün, was the son of Mao Hsiang. Unlike his father, he became a Senior Licentiate under the Ch'ing and Sub-prefect of the First Class. He gained fame as a filial son for his defense of his father against armed bandits in 1680, during which he was wounded. Mao Tan-shu was known as a poet in his own right, producing such collections as Chen-yen-t'ang-chi (Collected Works from the Hall of Slumbering on Mist) and Hsi-t'ang-chi (Collected Works from the Western Hall). He frequently attended K'ung's gatherings and there is a poem written as a colophon to a portrait of Mao in which K'ung praises his poetry for its similarities to Hsieh T'iao (464-99) and Li Po (K/51). Ch'ing-shih lieh-chuan 70/7b.

Huang Yun, courtesy name Hsien-shang, also Chiu-chiao, lived in T'ai-chou, Kiangsu, and was the father of two sons, T'ai-lai, courtesy name Chao-san and Yueh-fang. His writings were published in Yu-jan-t'ang-chi (Collected Works from the Distant Hall) and T'ung-yin-lou-chi (Collected Works from the Hall of the Inviting Wu-t'ung Tree). Chang, Kuo-ch'ao shih-jen 5/15:260; Yang-chou fu-chih 32/23b. Quoted in Ch'en, nien-p'u/35; Shen, Ch'ing-shih 8/141.

Teng Han-i (d. 1689), courtesy name Hsiao-wei, was from T'ai-chou, Kiangsu. In his youth he was known as a child prodigy and in his mature years as a social poet and man of versatile talents. Ch'ing-shih-kao lieh-chuan 271/1495; Ch'ing-shih lieh-chuan 71/73a; Chang, Kuo-ch'ao shih-jen 12/16:438-39; Shen, Ch'ing-shih 12/219.

Ho Shu-shan, courtesy name O-t'ing (d. 1688) was friendly with K'ung for over a decade, both in Peking and in Yangchow. He had failed the examinations, subsequently lost a minor official position, and was reduced to dwelling in a Buddhist temple in poverty. He was a talented if unrecognized poet, and K'ung praised the quickness and quality of his writing. He died shortly after this gathering, while attending another poetry gathering with K'ung. K/69, 519-20.

Wu Ch'iang, courtesy name Wen-wei, also Yü-ch'uan, was from Wu-chiang, Kiangsu. He is recorded as a lifelong traveler who enjoyed writing poetry and attending literati gatherings, where he was remembered for his sharp intellect. Chin-shih-shuo 6. Quoted in Ch'en, nien-p'u/38.

Hsu Ping-wen was an anthologist who, according to a letter to him by K'ung, was a guest at the latter's official residence in early 1687 while collecting literary works. K/503.

Ni K'uang-shih, courtesy name Yung-ch'ing, was an anthologist as well as a poet of local note. He frequented K'ung's gatherings and is recorded as an outspoken personality who saw military service, perhaps with loyalist forces. In a farewell letter to him, K'ung praises his heroism and urges him to accept the quieter life of a civilian. Ni edited the anthology Shih-tsui (Gathered Poems), published in the spring of 1688. This included some of K'ung's earliest poems predating the Yangchow years as well as a short biography of him. Ni's mother, wife, and sister were also noted poets in their own right. K/548, 630-31; Shih, <u>Ch'ing-tai kuei-ko</u> 3/19:168.

Chang Ch'ao, courtesy name Shan-lai, also Hsin-chai, was from She-hsien, Anhwei. A Senior Licentiate of the Second Class, he rose to Junior Archivist in the Han-lin Academy. Although he was a talented <u>tz'u</u> poet, he is best known as an anthologizer, particularly for his <u>Chao-tai ts'ung-shu</u> (<u>A Collection of Literature of Our Age</u>) in three series containing a wide range of works of early Ch'ing authors. In addition, his anthology of biographies of performers and other personalities, <u>Yü ch'u hsin-chih</u> (<u>New Tales After Yü Ch'u</u>), and another anthology, <u>T'an-chi ts'ung-shu</u> (<u>Collectanea from the Sandalwood Table</u>), were also widely read. Chang and K'ung were close friends in Yangchow and Chang presided over this first of K'ung's gatherings. Two of K'ung's works, <u>Ch'u-shan i-shu-chi</u> and <u>Jen-jui-lu</u> (<u>A Record of Senior Citizens</u>), were included in the second series of <u>Chao-tai ts'ung-shu</u>; Chang also presented K'ung with copies of his works for the Ch'ü-fu library when they were published. K/49, 507; <u>She-hsien-chih</u> 12/15b. Quoted in Ch'en, <u>nien-p'u</u>/38.

Chang Hsieh-shih and K'ung were friends through poetry and maintained a correspondence during the Yangchow years. K/519, 26, 39, 56, 69.

Yao Lun-ju was a successful businessman and the author of a collection of anecdotes about Yangchow personalities and events, <u>Kuang-ling tsa-kan</u> (<u>Random Reflections about Yang-chow</u>), which K'ung praised. K/534.

Li Jo-ku was an occasional guest at K'ung's official residence and the husband of a noted woman poet, Wang Cheng. K/513; Shih, <u>Ch'ing-tai kuei-ko</u> 3/13a.

51. Hou Fang-yü (1618-55), courtesy name Ch'ao-tsung, was born in Shang-ch'iu, Honan. His father, Hou Hsun (Metropolitan Graduate, 1616), was one of the Tung-lin

members persecuted by Wei Chung-hsien (1568-1627) (see note
139). Hou Fang-yü studied under the eminent official Ni
Yuan-lu (1594-1644) and entered politics in 1633, when his
father was made President of the Board of Revenue. He came
to Nanking but failed the 1639 examination because he used
a taboo character. Upon returning home in 1640, he
organized the Hsueh-yuan-she, a local branch of the Fu-she.
In 1642, his father was in charge of the defense of his
native area in Honan. Hou urged him to rescue Kaifeng,
which was under seige, by using bandit armies which had
turned loyal. He also advocated the execution of Hsu Ting-
kuo (1576-1646) as a show of strength. Hou Hsun could then
join up with Tso Liang-yü (1598-1645) (see chapter 4, note
59) at Hsiang-yang and defend the area. His advice was not
taken, however, and Hou Hsun lost the territory to Li Tzu-
Ch'eng's forces. Hou went south to Nanking where he soon
had to flee due to Juan Ta-ch'eng's (see note 52) purge of
the Fu-she. He first sought refuge in I-hsing with the
loyalist-general Kao Chieh (d. 1645) (see chapter 4, note
3). When Kao was murdered by Hsu Ting-kuo, Hou moved to
Shih K'o-fa's camp, where he served as an unofficial
advisor. Hou was said to have been the author of Shih's
famous reply to the Manchu Prince Dorgon in which he
refused to surrender. In 1645, Hou retired to Shang-ch'iu
after the fall of Nanking. He took the examinations again
under the Ch'ing in 1651 but failed once more. Hou was
respected for his solitary nature, his humility, and his
distance from political manipulations. He was also famous
for his poetry and prose and for his troupe of actors from
Soochow, which he trained himself. Hou was considered one
of the great talents of his age who was unable to find his
proper place in the chaos of dynastic collapse. Ch'ing-
shih-kao lieh-chuan 271/1494; Hummel, Eminent Chinese/291-

92; Chia, "Pen-chuan;" T'ien, "Hou Ch'ao-tsung;" Hu, "Hou Ch'ao-tsung."

Ch'en Chen-hui (1605-57), courtesy name Ting-sheng, was from I-hsing, Kiangsu. His father was a censor during the Ming who had been a member of the Tung-lin party and a victim of the purge by Wei Chung-hsien. Despite failing the provincial examinations, Ch'en gained wide influence in the Fu-she. Along with his close friend Wu Ying-chi (1594-1645), he sponsored the Nanking Manifesto of 1639 which denounced Juan Ta-ch'eng's attempts to gain power. Ch'en was imprisoned in 1644 when the latter's faction gained control of the Nanking Restoration; however, he was freed and later returned home, where he spent the rest of his life in seclusion. One of his sons, Ch'en Wei-sung (1626-82) was raised by his fellow "Esquire" Mao Hsiang after Ch'en's death. Wei-sung later became one of the most famous prose writers of the early Ching. Ch'ing-shih-kao lieh-chuan 288/1558; Hummel, Eminent Chinese/82-83.

Fang I-chih (d. 1671), courtesy name Mi-chih, artistic name Man-kung, also Lu-ch'i, Buddhist name Hung-chih, courtesy name Wu-k'o, artistic name Fou-shan yü-che, also Yao-ti ho-shang, also Wu-lao, also Mu-li, was from T'ung-ch'eng, in modern Anhwei. His family had produced a number of high officials under the Ming. Fang passed the provincial examinations in 1640 and entered the Han-lin Academy, where he became tutor to a son of the Ch'ung-chen Emperor. When the military situation deteriorated due to Li Tzu-ch'eng's rebellion, Fang unsuccessfully tried to obtain a military appointment. He was captured and tortured when Peking fell but refused to surrender, later achieving release through ransom. Then he went south to join loyalist forces in Nanking but was opposed by the faction of Ma Shih-ying (see note 52) and Juan Ta-ch'eng for his activities in the Fu-she. He escaped from Nanking

after the Manchu conquest and made his way south to other
loyalist regimes. In 1646, he served in the government of
Prince Kuei in Kwangtung but left due to internal
dissention. He was then captured by the Manchus.
Released, he spent the rest of his years in peripatetic
wandering as a Buddhist monk. Fang was considered one of
the great scholars of the early Ch'ing, with wide interests
in science, linguistics, history, and literature. Ch'ing-
shih-kao lieh-chuan 287/1555; Hummel, Eminent Chinese/232-
33. For a recent study of Fang in English, see Peterson,
Bitter Gourd.

52. Juan Ta-ch'eng (c.1587-1646), courtesy name Chi-
chih, artistic name Yuan-hai, also Shih-ch'iao, also Po-tzu
shan-chiao, was born in Huai-ning, Anhwei, into a family of
poets and high officials. He became a provincial graduate
in 1616 and served in Peking. Although Juan had some
connections with Tung-lin activists, he found them opposing
him when promotion to an import post came up in favor of
their own member, Wei Ta-chung (1575-1625). Juan then
allied with the faction of Wei Chung-hsien. However, fear
of Tung-lin reprisals caused him to resign his new post
and, when Wei Chung-hsien fell in 1627, Juan sent in two
memorials criticizing both Wei and the activists. Although
not an important official himself, he became a particular
object of the Tung-lin's wrath when they gained power under
the new Ch'ung-chen Emperor. Juan was demoted and returned
home. While in retirement, he wrote nine ch'uan-ch'i
dramas, of which four--Yen-tzu-chien (The Swallow Note),
Mou-ni-ho (The Buddha Jewels), Ch'un-teng-mi (Riddles on
Spring Lanterns), and Shuang-chin-pang (The Two
Graduates)--are extant. During the 1630s and 40s when Juan
moved to Nanking, he returned to public life through an
alliance with Ma Shih-ying, this despite activist attempts
to discredit him through the Nanking Manifesto of 1639.
With the fall of Peking, loyalist elements gathered in

Nanking to support the Restoration Court under Prince Fu. Both Juan and Ma gained control of the court and proceeded to purge their opponents. With the fall of Nanking in 1645, Juan surrendered to the Manchus and became a military advisor, aiding them in their Fukien campaign where he died. Ming-shih 308/7937-45; Hummel, Eminent Chinese/398-99; Crawford, "Juan Ta-ch'eng."

Ma Shih-ying (1591-1646), courtesy name Yao-ts'ao, was born in Kweiyang, Kweichow, in 1591. He earned his Licentiate degree in 1616 and his Metropolitan degree in 1619. He was made Governor of Hsuan-fu but was impeached one month later and exiled. Juan Ta-ch'eng's influence enabled him to be recalled and he later rose to Governor-General of Feng-yang, Anhwei. Together with Juan, he engineered the enthronement of Prince Fu as the Hung-kuang Emperor in the Nanking Restoration. Ma quickly became the most powerful official in the Southern Court as Grand Preceptor of the Heir Apparent and as Grand Tutor; however, historians have held him responsible for the factionalism which led to the Restoration's demise. It was he who ordered Shih K'o-fa stationed in Yangchow, supported the purge of the Fu-she, and made the fatal error of weakening the Yangtze defense by shifting troops to block the loyalist general Tso Liang-yü. With the subsequent fall of Nanking to Manchu troops, he fled to Hangchow to organize resistance but was defeated. Ma attempted to go to Fukien where the loyalist court under Prince T'ang rejected him. He is supposed to have then become a monk and was discovered by the Manchus, who executed him. Ming-shih 308/7937-45; Hummel, Eminent Chinese/558.

53. Ying-mei-an i-yü (Reminiscences of the Studio of Shadowy Plum-blossoms) narrates Mao's love affair with the courtesan Tung Po (d. 1651), courtesy name Hsiao-wan. For an English translation see Pan, Reminiscences.

54. The painting and collophon is recorded in K'ung's catalog and reprinted in K/596.

55. K/516.

56. The incident is mentioned in Ch'ing-shih-kao lieh-chuan 288/1557-58. Mao gave a party at Peach Leaf Crossing in Nanking for six friends who were sons of Tung-lin figures. Juan Ta-ch'eng, their old enemy, wanted to conciliate their opposition and lent them his famous opera troupe for entertainment; however, this only caused Mao and the others to further revile him as they watched the performance. Juan subsequently hardened his attitude towards them and, upon regaining power, instituted a purge against these and other Fu-she members in 1644. For a translation of this act as dramatized in K'ung's play, see K'ung, The Peach Blossom Fan, Scene 4 (Strassberg, trans.).

57. K/505.

58. Liang-ch'i is located in Wu-hsi, Kiangsu.

59. "Wu Songs" were rhythmical folk songs indigenous to the mountains of the Wu area, which comprises Kiangsu, Anhwei, and Chekiang. (The poem appears in Shen, Ch'ing-shih 8/141.)

60. For K'ung's poem on this visit, see K/18.

61. Tsung Yuan-ting, (c.1688) courtesy name Ting-chiu, artistic name Mei-ts'en, also Hsiao-hsiang chü-shih, was a native of Hsing-hua District, Yangchow, Kiangsu. Both his grandfather and father were officials who had achieved literary note. He first attracted attention as a child prodigy for poems written about plum blossoms at the age of seven. He felt a lifelong affinity for this poetic subject, and in his late years he retired to a residence in I-ling which contained an old plum-blossom tree; this led his friends to give him the nickname, "Plum-blossom Tsung." His straightforward personality derived from years of struggle with poverty, for the meager land he inherited was

poorly situated and barely provided a living. Still, it
contained attractive willows in front, which led his
friend, the poet Kung Ting-tzu (1616-73), to give it the
name, "The Hall of Young Willows." Tsung later moved some
twenty miles northeast of Yangchow to another house of the
same name; in addition, he also acquired the Hibiscus Villa
said to have once belonged to Hsieh An (320-85). Although
Tsung dwelled in obscurity, he was highly regarded by such
luminaries as Chou Liang-kung (see note 100), Ts'ao Jung
(1613-85), and Wang Shih-lu (1633-81), who often made the
journey to visit him. In 1679, he entered the Imperial
Academy as a Licentiate and placed first in his group of
examinees. Though slated for a prefectural position, he
declined to serve. He was especially known for his seven-
character quatrains, his tz'u, prose, and chanting of
poems. His poetic style tended towards orthodoxy and the
traditionalism of the former and later "Seven Masters" of
the Ming. In his youth, he modeled his poetry after the
late T'ang, and in his maturity changed to the early and
high-T'ang. Wang Shih-chen, with whom he was close when
Wang was in Yangchow, wrote highly of the "feng-tiao
(personal tone)" of his writings. Tsung was also an
accomplished painter in the archaic style of Ch'ien Hsuan
(c.1235-c.1301) and had a fascination for flowers. He
would weave flowers out of grass and sell them daily by
Rainbow Bridge to earn money for wine. His principal
writings appeared in Hsin-liu-t'ang shih-chi (Poetry from
the Hall of Young Willows); Fu-jung-chi (Collected Works
from the Hibiscus Villa), and Hsiao-hsiang-tz'u (Tz'u by
Hsiao-hsiang). Several poems were printed in Shen, Ch'ing-
shih 8/141-42. Ch'ing-shih lieh-chuan 70/20a-b; Li, Yang-
chou 10/226-27.

   62. See K'ung's letter to his friend Cho Er-k'an (see
note 88) in which he speaks of the uncertainty of his life

as an inspector and refers to "mornings on the lakes and evenings by the seas." K/518-19.

63. K'ung, Hu-hai-chi/1. Ts'ung's preface is dated April 1688; Huang's in July of that year.

64. A selection of Ch'ing poetry criticism can be found in Wang, Ch'ing-shih-hua.

65. For a description of a poetry club meeting in eighteenth century Yangchow, see Li, Yang-chou/180-81. According to Li, performance of dramatic arias were frequently part of the occasion.

66. See Liu, Wen-hsin 7/1a-4a; 6/8a-13b. The terms 'hsing-ch'ing" and 'ch'ing-hsing" are generally used interchangeably. Translations of the two chapters appear in Liu, The Literary Mind (Shih, trans.) /245-51; 222-26.

67. For a discussion of the theories of Yuan Hung-tao and others in the Kung-an School, see Kuo, p'i-p'ing-shih/242-82.

68. For a discussion of "pragmatic" literary theories in China, see Liu, Chinese Theories/106-16. The T'ung-ch'eng School is discussed in Kuo, p'i-p'ing-shih/337-441; Aoki, Ch'ing-tai wen-hsueh/151-79.

69. Shen Han-kuang (1620-1677), courtesy name Fu-meng, also Ho-meng, artistic names Fu-meng, Ts'ung-shan, Wo-ch'u lao-jen, was born in Yung-nien, Chihli (modern Hopei), the son of a martyr to the Ming cause. From his youth, he took Tu Fu for his model, largely because of the latter's patriotism. Together with Yin Yueh (1603-70) and Chang Kai, Shen formed the Ho-su School in the north, which maintained close connections to such philosophers as Sun Ch'i-feng (1585-1675) and Yen Yuan (1635-1704). Shen's advocacy of Tao in poetry, which he considered distinct from Wang Shih-chen's metaphysical approach, can be summed up in the following quote: "There was always something underlying the poetry of the ancients and that is the Tao.

The Tao is the basis of self-establishment and what all affairs flow forth from--it is poetry that visibly records it. In general, the poetry of the ancients grasped hold of pure, firm virtue and possessed a bright, direct conception. It was based on loyalty and filial piety which was expanded so as to create harmony. The three hundred selections of the Book of Poetry are all poems as well as examples of the Tao." (Quoted in Tung, "Lun k'ung shang-jen"/149.) Ch'ing-shih lieh-chuan 271/1494; Hummel, Eminent Chinese/642.

T'ien Wen (1635-1704), courtesy name Tzu-lun, also Lun-hsia, artistic name Shan-chiang, also Meng-chai, was born in Te-chou, Shantung, the son of a prefect under the Ch'ing. He became a Metropolitan Graduate in 1664 and began his career in the Grand Secretariat. In 1669, he studied poetry with Shen Han-kuang and two years late with Wang Shih-chen. From Shen he derived his pragmatist leanings and from Wang a love of erudition and allusion. In contrast to Wang's emphasis on "feng-yun (personal tone)," T'ien cultivated a distinctive style based on elegant diction and intellectual complexity. Despite failing the 1679 Po-hsueh hung-tz'u examination, he had a long and successful career both at court and in the provinces. While K'ung was serving in Yangchow, T'ien was Governor of Nanking and in 1687 made an inspection tour of the lower reaches of the Yellow River together with Chin Fu. K'ung and T'ien first crossed paths when both were traveling. During the formal interview on T'ien's boat, the two chatted amiably about a variety of subjects. In a subsequent letter, K'ung requested T'ien to serve as a sponsor for a fund-raising effort K'ung was leading to huild a Confucian school in Yangchow in memory of his ancestor, K'ung Jung, who died while supporting the last Han Emperor against Ts'ao Ts'ao. He also forwarded T'ien a

copy of Hu-hai-chi which he described as "the sounds of my
anguished chanting" (K/521). Their growing friendship was
interrupted by T'ien's sudden transfer to the governorship
of Kweichow. Later, when K'ung had returned to Peking,
T'ien was Junior Vice-President of the Boards of Punishment
and then of Personnel. It was T'ien whom K'ung credited
with encouraging him to finish writing The Peach Blossom
Fan (T/5). T'ien retired in 1701 and returned to Shantung.
His works are collected in Ku-huan-t'ang-chi (Collected
Works from the Hall of Antiquarian Pleasures). Ch'ing-shih
lieh-chuan 271/1495; Hummel, Eminent Chinese/719.

70. For a discussion of K'ung as "pragmatist," see
Tung, "Lun k'ung shang-jen." Tung's argument is largely
based on K'ung's relationship with T'ien Wen, his alleged
distance from Wang Shih-chen (disputed in Ch'en, nien-
p'u/23), and the historical nature of his drama. The
several poems of social concern which he cites, though
worthy of critical note, are rather singular examples in
the larger context of his oeuvre.

71. Wu Ch'i (1619-94), courtesy name Yuan-tz'u,
artistic name T'ing-weng, also Hung-tou tz'u-jen, was born
in Yangchow. He began his career as a Senior Licentiate of
the First Class and served in the Imperial Patent Office,
later rising to Secretary, Second Class, and then
Department Director in the Board of War. His reputation as
an honest administrator derived from a brief term as
Magistrate of Hu-chou, Chekiang. Upon retirement, he
purchased a small garden estate named the "Garden of
Cultivated Letters," where K'ung Shang-jen gathered with
friends in 1688 to reminisce about his period of retreat on
Stonegate (K/113). Wu was often ranked together with Ch'en
Wei-sung for his parallel prose as well as for his tz'u,
examples of which K'ung had read during his youth in Ch'ü-
fu. He was an easygoing, gregarious person and K'ung

became close friends with him and his sons in Yangchow. They attended gatherings together and exchanged a number of poems, including one from K'ung to Wu on his seventieth birthday (K/100). According to Ch'en, nien-p'u/59, these 24 poems on Yangchow appeared with critical comments by K'ung's friends Tsung Yuan-ting, Huang Yun, Teng Han-i, and Wu Ch'i. Wu's works were collected in Lin-hui-t'ang ch'üan-chi (Collected Works of the Hall of the Wild Orchid). Ch'ing-shih lieh-chuan 271/1497.

72. For a discussion of Ho Hsun (d.c.434) and the critical tradition which later arose, see Frankel, "The Plum Tree"/97-98.

73. See Tung, "Lun k'ung shang-jen."

74. For a discussion of the "dual-allegiance" of the Chinese storyteller, see Hsia, "Society and Self."

75. For a discussion of the philosophical relationship of painting and poetry, see Chang, Creativity/169-241; a comparative approach is presented in Frankel, "Poetry and Painting"; also Chaves, "Poetry and Painting" and Bush, The Chinese Literati/22-28.

76. See K'ung's essay on a gathering he hosted on April 20, 1687, at a private garden in T'ai-hsien, Kiangsu: "Altogether there were twenty-two poems chanted, two paintings executed, two selections performed on the ch'in zither, three on the p'i-p'a lute and seven Wu chants." (K/440). Among the guests were Teng Han-i, Huang Yun, Mao Tan-shu, and the painters Cha Shih-piao (see note 89) and Li T'ai (fl. 1688).

77. Fu, Connoisseurship/1-13.

78. For studies of Tung Ch'i-ch'ang's (1555-1636) orthodoxy, see Fong, "Tung Ch'i-ch'ang"; Wu, "Tung Ch'i-ch'ang"; Ho, "Tung Ch'i-ch'ang"; Sirén, Chinese Painting 5/1-10.

79. Fu, Connoisseurship/11.   For a discussion of the Yangchow school, which reached its height with the "Eight Eccentrics (pa-kuai)" of the eighteenth century, see Siren, Chinese Painting 5/235-50.

80. For information on 23 of K'ung's artist friends, see Ch'en, yen-chiu/46-78.

81. Wang Hui (1632-1717), courtesy name Shih-ku, artistic name Keng-yen san-jen, also Ch'ing-hui chu-jen, also Wu-mu shan-jen, was born in Ch'ang-shu, Kiangsu, into a family of painters of only moderate resources.   He did not study for a literary degree but decided in his youth to become a painter.   His opportunity to gain expert training and exposure to the works of great masters first came at the age of twenty through Wang Chien (1598-1677), one of the great seventeenth-century painters who, together with Wang Hui, Wang Shih-min (1592-1680), and Wang Yuan-ch'i (1642-1715), were termed the "Four Wangs (Ssu-wang)" of early Ch'ing painting.   His education was furthered by the patronage of Wang Shih-min, a great collector and connoisseur as well who sponsored Wang Hui at his T'aits'ang villa for over twenty years.   The two often traveled together to visit nearby collections and view great models from the past.   Through this relationship, Wang Hui was exposed to the orthodox tradition of literati painting which Wang Shih-min had learned from Tung Ch'i-ch'ang. Stylistically, Wang Hui began with a study of the idioms of Huang Kung-wang, Wang Meng (1308-85) and Chü Jan (active c.960), rendering their sense of landscape form with a firmer grasp of the calligraphic basis of brushstroke. This was accomplished particularly through the "dragon vein (lung-mo)" technique, which indicated the "fundamental momentum (shih)" of mountain formations.   In this period, Wang also studied the manners of Li Ch'eng (active c.940-67), Kuan T'ung (c.907-50), and Fan Kuan (990-1030), which

differed from the orthodox tradition in their descriptive rather than calligraphic use of brushstroke. By the 1670s, Wang had achieved his "great synthesis" of these two schools, which he further refined during the following two decades. In 1691, Wang Hui was summoned to Peking to oversee the composition of a series of scrolls commemorating the K'ang-hsi Emperor's Southern Tour of 1689. Thus he was in the capital at the same time as K'ung Shang-jen and the two were able to meet again. Wang retired after the completion of the project in 1698 with imperial honors. Ch'ing-shih lieh-chuan 291/1564; Hummel, Eminent Chinese/823-24; Whitfield, Antiquity/19-47, 177-79; Fong, "The Orthodox Master."

82. K/587. Interestingly, K'ung considered Wang a poet who achieved fame as a painter. They met again in Peking in the 1690s when Wang was executing the imperial commission for a series of scrolls of the second Southern Tour. The work was still not completed after three years and K'ung wrote a teasing poem about him (K/368).

83. Tao-chi (1641-c.1710), original name Chu, named Jo-chi, courtesy name Shih-t'ao, artistic names K'u-kua ho-shang, Ch'ing-hsiang lao-jen, Hsia-tsun-che, Ta-t'i-tzu, Hsiu-jen, Buddhist names Tao-chi, Yuan-chi, Ch'ao-chi, was born in Kweilin, Kwangsi, a descendent in the eleventh generation of Chu Shou-ch'ien, a grand-nephew of Ming T'ai-tsu. In 1645, his father, Prince of Ching-chiang Chu Heng-chia, was defeated in his attempt to establish a restoration court. An agent of his rival, Prince T'ang (1602-46), captured and sent him to Foochow, Fukien, where he was executed. Tao-chi escaped with the help of a servant to Ch'üan-chou, Fukien, and was placed in a Buddhist monastery. There, he was brought up in the charge of another monk, Ho-t'ao. From Tao-chi's later statements, his education seems to have been based on the Ch'an

tradition. Beginning in the 1660s, Tao-chi's movements are recorded. He settled in several monasteries at Mt. Ching-t'ing near Hsuan-ch'eng, Anhwei, and traveled to Mt. Huang. He also met painters in the locality such as Mei Ch'ing (1623-97) and became familiar with the works of other masters such as Hung-jen (1610-63) and Cha Shih-piao. In the early 1680s, he moved with Ho-t'ao to the Pao-en Temple in Nanking where he spent the next six years. It was while residing at this temple that he met the visiting K'ang-hsi Emperor in 1684. He further expanded his painting acquaintances by forming friendships with K'un-ts'an (1612-86), Tai Pen-hsiao (see note 94), and Wang Kai (see note 106). Tao-chi moved to Yangchow, which he had visited earlier, in the spring of 1687. In addition to meeting Cha Shih-piao and Kung Hsien (see note 97), he gained the patronage of an important Manchu, Bordu (d. 1701), who was a grandson of the Ch'ing founder, Nurhaci. Bordu, himself a painter and collector, had accompanied K'ang-hsi on his second Southern Tour in 1689 and met Tao-chi at the Hall Level with the Peaks. Through his sponsorship, Tao-chi traveled to Peking, where he resided from 1689 to 1692. He found wider opportunities for executing commissions from the capital elite and viewed many of the private collections. His exposure to this public solidified his reputation as a painter and the influences he received deepened his understanding of his spiritual and artistic aims. His return to Yangchow in 1693 marked the final phase of his life, during which he underwent several major transformations. Around 1696, he renounced his Buddhist vows and became a Taoist. It has been suggested, first, that this represented a release from the fears of persecution which led him to adopt monkhood in his youth and, second, that he came to accept the permanence of Ch'ing rule, giving up hopes for a Ming restoration (Fu,

Connoisseurship/37-38). Having left the priesthood, Tao-chi turned to professional painting as an economic necessity, and produced a large number of works, despite the difficulties of satisfying a clientele. The actual date of his death is not known but has been approximated at c.1710. His influential theories on the philosophy and technique of painting appeared in the treatise, Hua-yü-lu (Remarks on Painting) (printed 1728). Fu, Connoisseurship/36-70; Ch'ing-shih lieh-chuan 291/1564; Fu, Shih-t'ao; Cheng, Shih-t'ao/3-46, Sirén, Chinese Painting 5/156-72.

84. Among Tao-chi's more unusual commissions while in Yangchow was the designing of a garden for the Yü family, the Wan-shih-yuan (Garden of Ten Thousand Stones). Li, Yang-chou 2/41.

85. Huang, hua-yü-lu/21.

86. For reproductions of two interesting bamboo and rock compositions which Tao-chi executed in the 1690s in Peking in conjunction with Wang Hui and Wang Yuan-ch'i, see Fu, Connoisseurship/50. None of the three was apparently present when the other contributed his part and the link may have been Bordu. It is worth noting, as a further indication of the close relationship between orthodox and individualist artists, that Wang Yuan-ch'i had great praise for Tao-chi and considered him one of the finest southern painters (ibid./49).

87. For K'ung's poem celebrating the gathering, see K/38.

88. Cho Er-k'an (c.1650-c.1700), courtesy name Tzu-li, also Tzu-jen, was descended from an official who remained loyal to the early Ming emperor, Chien-wen (r. 1399-1403) during the Yung-lo usurpation. His education was interrupted in his youth and he mastered the art of poetry while serving in the Ch'ing army. K'ung met him in Yangchow and they became close friends, as his 1689 preface

to Cho's collected works indicates: "For three years I have known Cho Er-k'an and we have never failed to meet, despite wind and rain, in summer or in winter. When we do, we discuss poetry and always wind up agreeing. After I finish a poem, I feel like a starving man awaiting food if I can't show it to him. Whenever he writes one, he never fails to show it to me; not to do so would be as unbearable as a boil on one's back" (K/474-75). Cho was a popular figure in Yangchow poetry circles and was considered one of the local talents. Later, despite his loyalist sympathies, he served with heroic distinction in the Right Vanguard Division of the Chinese Banner on a pacification campaign in Fukien in 1700. Li, Kuo-ch'ao 327/27b.

89. Cha Shih-piao (1615-98), courtesy name Er-chan, artistic name Mei-ho san-jen, was from Hai-yang (Hsiu-ning), Anhwei, an area which rose to cultural distinction through the wealth of its merchants, particularly those involved in the Yangchow salt trade. Cha developed his connoisseurship from his family collection, which also included bronzes and other art objects. In painting, he specialized in the Yuan masters, beginning with the study of Ni Tsan and then Wu Chen (1280-1354). He was considered one of the "Four Masters of Hsin-an" together with Sun I, Wang Chih-jui, and Hung-jen. A 1670 painting records his residency in Chen-chiang, Kiangsu, and he subsequently moved to Yangchow. In 1673, Wang Hui was his guest there and produced an album containing landscapes in the style of various Yuan masters. Shih-t'ao was also acquainted with him and several of his paintings reveal the influence of Cha's casual, fluent articulation of form. Cha was held in high esteem by the intellectuals of his time for his quality of "pure elusiveness (ch'ing-i)," in Shih-t'ao's words, as well as for his natural humility. He died in Yangchow at the age of 84. Ch'ing-shih-kao lieh-chuan

291/1564; Goodrich and Fang, Ming Biography/34-35; Síren, Chinese Painting 5/117-19; Chang, hua-cheng-lu 1/15b-16a; Fu, Connoisseurship/152-57.

90. See Fu, Connoisseurship/153,157.

91. See Fu, Connoisseurship/154.

92. Chang, hua-cheng-lu 1/15b-16a.

93. For K'ung's poem on the album, see K/175.

94. Tai Pen-hsiao (1629-91), courtesy name Wu-chan, artistic name Ying-ah shan-chiao, was born in Hsiu-ning, Anhwei. His father, Tai Chung, had placed first in the 1625 palace examinations and served as magistrate of Hu-chou, Chekiang. After the fall of the Ming, he starved himself to death in loyalty to the Ch'ung-chen Emperor. Tai Pen-hsiao, his eldest son, swore never to serve the Ch'ing as an official and refused to sit for the examinations. He also followed his father's tastes in poetry, studying such T'ang poets as Tu Fu. In Anhwei, he built a retreat on Ying-ah mountain. He spent a period of residency in Peking dwelling in the Studio of the Treasured Inkstone and selling paintings for a living. An anecdote relates that one day he heard a friend describe the scenery of Mt. Hua. He was so enthralled by what he heard that the next day, he packed and set out to see it for himself. Among the friends who saw him off was Wang Shih-chen. His brushmanship was often likened to his fellow local, Ch'eng Sui (fl. 1650-91), but Tai preferred a dry brush technique in contrast to the latter's preference for wet ink. Kuo-ch'ao-shih pieh-ts'ai pen-chuan. Quoted in Ch'en, yen-chiu/58-59; Cahill, Fantastics/50-53; Fu, Ming-mo/175-76.

95. For a reproduction of a small-scale work, see Cahill, Fantastics/50-51.

96. For a reproduction of this painting, Lien-hua-feng (Lotus Peak), see Cahill, Fantastics/49. Similar fantastic

landscapes by Wu Pin (c.1568-1626) are reproduced on pp. 29, 30.

97. Kung Hsien (c.1617-89), also named Ch'i-hsien, courtesy name Pan-ch'ien, also Yeh-i, artistic name Ch'ai-chang-jen, also Pan-mou, was born in K'un-shan, Kiangsu, but spent most of his life in Nanking. Considered one of the greatest individualist painters of the seventeenth century, he evolved a style which recaptured the monumentality of such tenth-century painters as Tung Yuan (see note 108) and Fan K'uan of the Northern Sung. There is a range of critical opinion regarding Kung. He was well-known in his later years and much-appreciated by the finest connoisseurs. In the eighteenth century, however, some critics found his works ponderous and faulted his lack of light-hearted charm. His reputation revived in the modern era through Japanese collectors, and in the West he is now ranked among the foremost artists of his age. His painting theories were edited in Hua-chueh (Secrets of Painting), and a sketchbook intended as a guide for students survives. Sirén, Chinese Painting 5/131-35; Chung-kuo ming-hua-chia 2/1095-1146; Chang, hua-cheng-lu 1/11a-b; Chou, Tu-hua-lu 2/23; Cahill, "Kung Hsien"; Lippe, "Kung Hsien I, II." Wilson, Kung Hsien.

98. In addition to Kung Hsien, the Nanking School includes Fan Ch'i (see note 99), Kao Ts'en (fl. c.1670), Tsou Che (see note 99), Wu Hung (fl. c.1655), Hu Tsao, Yeh Hsin, and Hsieh Sun. This designation, however, was not contemporary with these painters and seems to have been first applied by Chang Keng (1685-1760), whose Kuo-ch'ao hua-cheng-lu was published in 1739. See Sirén, Chinese Painting 5/128-37; Lippe, "Kung Hsien, II"/168-69.

99. Fan Ch'i (1616-c.1694), courtesy name Hui-kung, also Ch'ia-kung, was from Nanking; his brothers and son both became painters and were strongly influenced by his

style. Fan shared Kung Hsien's interest in Northern Sung
masters, but his style is more delicate and less
spontaneous. His brushstrokes are precise and tightly
controlled, often employing repetitive rhythms created by
stippling effects. He also explored lighting effects and
is one of the Chinese painters who most clearly reveals the
influence of Western ideas of perspective. Skilled in
flower and figure painting as well, he was highly praised
by both Chou Liang-kung (see note 100) and the calligrapher
Wang To (1592-1652), the latter noting his affinities with
such Yuan painters as Chao Meng-fu (1254-1322) and Chao
Meng-chien (1199 to c.1256). In his later years, Fan Ch'i
lived with his brother Fan I in a wooden hut on the grounds
of the Hui-kuang Temple. K'ung Shang-jen met him on his
trip to Nanking in 1688 and wrote a polite poem in praise:
"The fork-ends' spreading comes out of ancient clouds and
mist; in a chaos, you joined the current of our time and
beg for painting money. You will always remain among those
collected in the Palace where half the labels will be from
the T'ien-ch'i and Ch'ung-chen years" (K/152). Translated
in Lippe, "Kung Hsien II" 163-64. Siren, Chinese Painting
5/129; Chou, Tu-hua-lu 3/35; Fu, Connoisseurship/158-63.

100. Chou Liang-kung (1612-72), courtesy name Yuan-
liang, artistic name Chien-chai, also Li-chai, also Li-hsia
lao-jen, was born in Nanking. A provincial graduate in
1640, he served as a magistrate under the Ming and defended
his area against the Manchu invasion. With the fall of
Peking, he fled back to Nanking but did not join the
restoration of Prince Fu. After the establishment of the
Ch'ing, he served the new dynasty in a number of high
positions and suppressed the loyalist forces of Cheng
Ch'eng-kung in Fukien. His career, however, was beset by
periods of imprisonment and several death sentences which
were later rescinded. Despite involvement with the Ch'ing,

the majority of painters and writers who formed a circle about him were staunch Ming loyalists. These included Ch'en Hung-shou (1598-1652), Hung-jen, K'un-ts'an, and Yang Wen-tsung (see note 120). A great collector and admirer of Tung Ch'i-ch'ang, his influential opinions on contemporary painters were published in Tu-hua-lu (A Record of Paintings Seen) (postscript 1673). Chou's Tu-hua-lou (Hall of Paintings Seen) was adjacent to Kung's Pan-mou-yuan (Half-acre Garden) at the foot of Mt. Ch'ing-liang. For a translation of a colophon of Kung's describing Chou's collection there, see Lippe, "Kung Hsien II"/159-60. Hummel, Eminent Chinese/173-74.

101. See Kung's remark in a 1670 colophon: "If . . . this looks like Yang Wen-ts'ung, it is because during my youth I and Yang studied Tung Ch'i-ch'ang together." Quoted in Cahill, "Kung Hsien"/55.

102. Fang Wen (1612-69), courtesy name Er-chih, also Er-tzu, artistic name Yü-shan, also Ming-nung, was from T'ung-ch'eng, Anhwei. An uncle of Fang I-chih, he had been active in late Ming politics but refused to serve the Ch'ing. He cultivated an unadorned style in his prose and poetry and was influenced by the theory of "innate sensibility (hsing-ling)." Li, Kuo-ch'ao 473/14042, 14065.

103. Kung Hsien once asked Wang Hui to paint the garden, a further example of the interaction between orthodox and individualist painters during this period. In his letter to Wang, Kung described the Pan-mou-yuan as follows: "My house stands south of the Grass Hall. The remaining land is half an acre, with a few flowers and bamboo. That's why I call it like this; it is not fit to be called a garden. On Mount Ch'ing-liang there is a terrace; it is also called 'Ch'ing-liang' terrace. When you climb the terrace you can see the Great River. Across the way, in front of you, there is the Bell Hill; right behind it, to the left, you

see the ladle of Lake Sans-Souci, whose water is like a mirror. To the right, in the Lion-Range, the earth is shoveled together like eyebrows. My house is below this terrace. When I turn towards the North East to call my guest and show it to him, the barking dogs at the gate make believe they see him coming." Translated in Lippe, "Kung Hsien I"/26.

104. Chou, Tu-hua-lu 2/23.

105. For a study of this sketchbook reproduced in 1935 by Shang-wu yin-shu-kuan, Shanghai, see Wu, "Kung Hsien's Style." Although Lippe, "Kung Hsien I"/28, speaks of the sketchbook as influencing the Chieh-tzu-yuan hua-chuan (The Mustard Seed Garden Manual), it is difficult to date the former as earlier than the latter, which contains a 1667 preface by Chou Liang-kung. According to Wu, "Kung Hsien's Style"/78, the sketchbook belongs to Kung's third period (late 1670s-1689) and closely resembles an album from 1688.

106. Wang Kai (fl. c.1670), courtesy name An-chieh, artistic name Tung-k'uo, also Lu-chai, was born in Nanking into a family of painters from Chia-hsing, Chekiang. He was a student of Kung Hsien and one of the most socially active painters of his era. Though highly regarded during his lifetime, Wang is best remembered as the editor of Chieh-tzu-yuan hua-chuan, the most influential textbook for aspiring artists. K'ung Shang-jen was good friends with Wang and his two brothers. He frequently corresponded with them and they readily fulfilled his requests for paintings. On his 1688 trip to Nanking, K'ung visited Wang Kai and received a painting of Mo-ch'ou Lake (Lake Sans-Souci) from him (K/550). Ch'en, yen-chiu/60-63.

107. Cahill, "Kung Hsien"/69; see also Li, A Thousand Peaks 1/206-11.

108. Tung Yuan (died c.960) inaugurated a tradition of landscape painting called the Tung-Chü manner, after him

and his student Chü-jan. It was centered in the Chiang-nan region south of the Yangtze and, though overshadowed by Northern Sung developments, was revived in the Yuan. His major contribution was to replace the color washes used to fill in landscape forms with textured ts'un brushstrokes and tien dots, a style which particularly influenced the Yuan master Wu Chen (1280-1354). Tung Yuan was one of Kung Hsien's lifelong models, as he revealed in colophons and comments in his sketchbook. He admired Tung's use of rich ink tones, which he considered the highest attainment of "spiritual tone (ch'i-yun)," as well as Tung's absence of figures in his landscapes. Cahill, Hills/36ff; Wu, "Kung Hsien"/79.

109. "Chiang-kuei-ts'ao (Homeward Bound)" was a song performed on the ch'in zither. It is identified with the "Tsou-ts'an (Tsou Elegy)," written by Confucius, who heard of the execution of two loyal officials in Chao and returned home to Tsou rather than serve in that state. Shih-chi 47/1926.

110. Chi-chiu-chang (Quick Achievement) was a catalog of phenomena and surnames compiled by Shih Yu (c. late first century B.C.) of the Han as a textbook for young students. The original text became a model of cursive-style calligraphy and the title came to mean anything written spontaneously at great speed. Chi, ssu-k'u ch'üan-shu/847-48.

111. Chou, Tu-hua-lu 2/23.

112. "Ching k'o-chuan (Biography of Ching K'o)" sympathetically narrates the attempt of a loyal retainer to assassinate Ch'in Shih-huang. Shih-chi 86/2526-38; translated in Watson, Records/55-67.

113. The poem was printed in Shen, Ming-shih 11/189, as well as in other contemporary anthologies.

114. For K'ung's farewell poem to Kung, see K/49.

115. See the third of K'ung's four poems written after Kung's death as well as Tsung Yuan-ting's commentary. In K'ung, Hu-hai-chi/151; rpt. without the commentary in K/152-53.

116. Chung-kuo ming-hua-chia 2/1110.

117. K/558.

118. See Tsung Yuan-ting's commentary to the first of K'ung's poems on Kung Hsien's death. In K'ung, Hu-hai-chi/150. K'ung's acts of generosity have been mentioned by later biographers of Kung Hsien, such as Chang Keng in hua-cheng-lu 11/11b.

119. According to Tsung's commentary, the poem, "Hu-chü-kuan fang kung yeh-i ts'ao-t'ang (Visiting Kung Hsien's Studio by Crouching Tiger Pass)," was written on a fan, but at the last minute K'ung had second thoughts about the final line, "Playing solos on the ch'in," and was about to alter it when news came of Kung Hsien's death. He decided to offer the poem on the fan as the funeral elegy and burned it before the coffin. K'ung, Hu-hai-chi/150.

120. Yang Wen-ts'ung (1597-1646), courtesy name Lung-yu, also Tzu-shan, was born in Kweiyang, Kweichow. He became a provincial graduate in 1618 and rose to Director of Studies in Hua-t'ing (Sung-chiang), Kiangsu, where he studied painting with Tung Ch'i-ch'ang. He gained fame as an individualist painter while in his thirties and was praised by Wu Wei-yeh (1609-72) as one of the "nine friends of painting." At the end of the Ch'ung-chen reign, he was made Magistrate of Nanking but was impeached in 1644 for corruption. A year later he returned to office in the Nanking Restoration through the influence of his brother-in-law, Ma Shih-ying, becoming a Secretary in the Board of War with responsibility for the Yangtze River defense. After the fall of Nanking, he joined Prince T'ang in Foochow as Vice-President of the Board of War, was captured

by the Manchus, and died a martyr to the Ming cause. Ming-shih 277/7102-4; Hummel, Eminent Chinese/895-96; Sirén, Chinese Painting 5/53-54.

121. Lan Ying (1585-c.1664), courtesy name T'ien-shu, artistic name Hsi-hu wai-shih, also Shih-tou-t'o, also T'ieh-sou, was a native of Hangchow. He is sometimes considered the last great painter of the Che School, a misleading designation. Although he was neither an official nor a member of the scholar gentry, his style was more influenced by Shen Chou (1427-1509) of the Wu School and Tung Ch'i-ch'ang. Lan was a professional and an extremely popular painter in his time. Though later overshadowed by the orthodox school of the Four Wangs, his expert command of the manners of ancient masters, use of vibrant color, and experimentation with new formats reveal a creative spirit which has been underrated by many Chinese and Western critics. His reputation in Japan, however, has remained solid since the eighteenth century, when many of his works began to be exported there. Lan was also the teacher of Ch'en Hung-shou, and his influence on him and another major individualist, Chu Ta (1626-c.1705) can be seen in their paintings of birds. Goodrich and Fang, Ming Biography/786-87; Fu, Connoisseurship/106-17. Sirén, Chinese Painting 5/36-38.

122. See K/600-1 for the catalog entries of the three paintings by Lan Ying: "Yü-lo (The Pleasures of Fishing)"; "Ch'iu-shan fang-yu (Visiting a Friend in the Autumn Mountains)"; "Chü-chu ch'iu-lan (Chrysanthemums, Bamboo and Autumn Orchids)."

123. For a reproduction and discussion of the painting, "Bird, Rock and Camellias," which Yang and Lan collaborated on together with Chang Hung (1577-1663), see Fu, Connoisseurship/117.

124. Ch'iung-hua Temple (The Hortensia Temple), also known as Fan-li Temple (Temple of Prosperity), was located inside the East Gate and originally was dedicated to the Earth God, Hou-t'u. The hortensia tree actually dated from the Sung and sent forth pale yellow blossoms. When Ou-yang Hsiu served in Yangchow during the Sung, he had a pavilion named "Wu-shuang (Matchless Beauty)" built over it and changed the temple name to Hortensia Temple. During the Ch'un-hsi period of the Sung (1174-90), legend has it that the tree was moved south of its site and began to wither; it flourished again when replanted in its original place. It was cut down by Chin invaders in 1161. During the Yuan, it ceased to send up any new branches and there was no longer any trace of life in it by the seventeenth century. In K'ung's poems on the flowers, he uses poetic license in linking them with the fate of the Sui. Wu, Yang-chou/403-4.

125. K/449.

126. An allusion to the most famous gathering of literati held at the Lan-t'ing (Orchid Pavilion) at Mt. K'uei-chi, near Shaohsing in Chekiang in 353.

127. Hsi K'ang (223-62) and Juan Chi (210-63) were the two most prominent members of the so-called "Chu-lin ch'i-hsien (Seven Worthies of the Bamboo Grove)," a group of literati during the late Han-Wei period noted for their hedonism and avoidance of political involvement. In their celebration of self and sensuality, they were regarded as archetypal romantics by later literati. See Holzman, La Vie; also Holzman, Poetry and Politics.

128. The Sui-yuan (Sui Garden) was built in the northwest of Yangchow by Yang-ti as a pleasure estate. Among its attractions were the Yueh-kuan (Moon Terrace) where Yang-ti and his consort enjoyed theatrical

entertainments in the final days of the dynasty. Wu, Yang-chou/410-11.

129. "Ni-shang yü-i-ch'ü (The Dance of the Rainbow Skirt and Feather Gown)" was a tune which came to symbolize the taste and sensuality of the court of T'ang Hsuan-tsung. It was originally a melody from a Brahman prayer which was imported from Hsi-liang (modern Kansu). The official historical version credits the military Governor of Ho-hsi (modern Shensi, Kansu, Inner Mongolia), Yang Ching-shu, with presenting twelve verses of it to the T'ang court where the Emperor himself revised it. Several legends, however, record that Hsuan-tsung discovered it while on a mystical journey to the moon, where it was performed by several hundred costumed maidens. The dance was particularly associated with his favorite concubine, Yang Yü-huan (d. 756) who performed it in the Hua-ch'ing-kung (Palace of the Pure Flower) near Ch'ang-an. Hsin-t'ang-shu 22/476; Kuo, Yueh-fu 56/8a-b.

130. Fei Mi (1625-1701), courtesy name Tz'u-tu, artistic name Yen-feng, was born in Hsin-fan, Szechuan, into a scholarly family of Ming officials. While in his early twenties, he helped build defenses near Chengtu against Chang Hsien-chung's army but was captured by aborigines. He joined the anti-Manchu resistance effort under Lu Ta-ch'i (Provincial Graduate, 1628) but finally abandoned his military opposition to the Ch'ing, although he later refused to attend the 1679 Po-hsueh hung-tz'u examination. He spent some time in Shensi before moving to Yangchow, where he continued his activist approach to Confucianism in his teachings and writings, publishing over fifty works. His local fame was such that the magistrate exempted him from corvée labor because of lameness in one leg. Fei, together with Sun Ch'i-feng (1585-1675), with whom he briefly studied, and Li Yung (1627-1705), have been grouped

together as early advocates of Han Learning although the latter two were actually moderates who also found value in Wang Yang-ming's teachings. Fei was also a published poet whose works were praised by Wang Shih-chen. <u>Ch'ing-shih-kao lieh-chuan</u> 288/1558; Hummel, <u>Eminent Chinese</u>/240.

131. See chapter 1, note 115.

132. Little is known of Min I-hsing but he was evidently a close companion, judging from K'ung's letters to him. Min attended a number of K'ung's gatherings and was acquainted with some of his painter-friends such as Cha Shih-piao. He himself also painted and presented K'ung with a set of eight landscape scrolls. See K/503, 523, 527-28, 554.

133. The essay, "<u>Han t'ung-ch'ih-chi</u> (On a Bronze Ruler from the Han)," dated 1688, is reprinted in K/444.

134. "<u>Chou-ch'ih-k'ao</u> (Research on the Length of a <u>Ch'ih</u> during the Chou Dynasty)" and "<u>Chou-ch'ih-pien</u> (A Discussion of the Chou Dynasty <u>Ch'ih</u>)" are both dated 1688 and reprinted in K/445-48.

135. See "<u>Sung t'ung-ch'ih-chi</u> (On a Sung Bronze Ruler)" K/480-81. K'ung received the ruler from a Mr. Ju Tz'u-t'ing in the autumn of 1689, while in Nanking.

136. Ch'en Shu-pao (d. 589), courtesy name Yuan-hsiu, also Huang-nu, posthumous name Yang, was the last ruler of the Ch'en dynasty (557-89). In official history and popular myth, his reign was noted for its pursuit of pleasure and neglect of government. Later referred to as "Ch'en Hou-chu (The Last Emperor of Ch'en)," he built several extravagant palaces and entertained himself with wine and concubines. He was also a talented poet known for his pieces "<u>Yü-shu hou-t'ing-hua</u> (The Jade Tree and the Flowers in the Back Garden)." When the conquering Sui army arrived in Nanking, he was killed in the midst of feasting; two loyal courtesans, Chang and K'ung, jumped into what was

later named the "Yen-chih-ching (Rouge Well)," Ch'en-shu
6/105-23.

137. Quoted in Mote, "The Transformation of
Nanking"/152.

138. For studies of the Tung-lin, see Busch, "The Tung-
lin"; Hucker, "The Tung-lin Movement"; Wakeman, "The Price
of Autonomy"/35-55; Hsieh, Ming-ch'ing/46-71.

139. Wei Chung-hsien (1568-1627) was originally named Li
Chin-chung and was born in Su-ning, Hopei. He became a
eunuch to extricate himself from gambling debts and entered
palace service, where he was able to achieve great
influence over the Hsi-tsung Emperor (r. 1621-27) while the
latter was still a child, largely through an alliance with
Mme. K'o, the emperor's wet-nurse. Together, Wei and Mme.
K'o virtually ruled the country during Hsi-tsung's reign
and purged many of their opponents, notably the Tung-lin
party. The San-ch'ao yao-tien (Important Cases of Three
Reigns) and the death of the "Six Martyrs" dealt serious
blows to Wei's enemies in the bureaucracy; but with the
death of the Emperor, Wei quickly lost the basis of his
power. He was soon deprived of rank and ordered arrested,
but committed suicide. Ming-shih 305/7816-25; Hummel,
Eminent Chinese/846-47; Chuan, "Wei Chung-hsien."

140. For studies of the Fu-she, see Atwell, "The Fu-
she"; Hsieh, Ming-ch'ing/145-86.

141. Chang, T'ao-an/46.

142. For records of life in Ch'in-huai, see Yü, Pan-
ch'iao; Chang, T'ao-an; Wang, ch'ang-chi-shih/198-225.

143. For biographical information on Li Hsiang-chün, see
Hou, "Li Wa-chuan." In Hou, Chuang-hui-t'ang 5/11b-12b;
Yü, Pan-ch'iao/13; Hummel, Eminent Chinese/292, 435.

144. Li Chen-li, courtesy name Tan-ju, was a successful
courtesan who ran her own establishment in Ch'in-huai. She
was a capable poet and among her admirers was Ch'en Chen-

hui, one of the "Four Esquires," and a Fu-she activist who sponsored the "Nanking Manifesto" of 1639 against Juan Ta-ch'enag. Yü Huai (see note 145), another frequenter of her salon, remembered her as a heroic character who gambled for high stakes. Yü, Pan-ch'iao/20.

145. Yü, Pan-ch'iao/13. Yü Huai (1616-96), courtesy name Tan-hsiu, also Wu-huai, artistic name Man-ch'ih, also Man-weng, also Kuang-hsia, was born in P'u-t'ien, Fukien, but spent most of his life in Nanking and Yangchow. He is best remembered as an aesthete who spent his life in literary pursuits, writing poetry and treatises on a variety of cultural subjects. Yü was a student at the Imperial Academy in Nanking during the last years of the Ming and served on the staff of a high official as a secretary. He was also a denizen of the Ch'in-huai quarters and a frequent guest at Li Hsiang-chün's house. He claimed to have been among the first to promote her reputation by writing a flattering poem on the wall, beside which Yang Wen-ts'ung and another painter added rocks and orchids. His memoirs of Ch'in-huai, Pan-ch'iao tsa-chi (Random Notes form the Planked Bridge) contains intimate accounts of the personalities and manners of the quarters. It was printed by Chang Ch'ao in the first series of Chao-tai ts'ung-shu in 1697. K'ung first made Yü's acquaintance in Yangchow in 1688. In his letter to him (K/521), K'ung expressed admiration of Yü's writings and was anxious to obtain some of the 72-year-old survivor's recollections. They entered into a literary friendship and Yü attended several of K'ung's gatherings. Hummel, Eminent Chinese/942; Ch'ing-shih lieh-chuan 70/16a; Li, Kuo-ch'ao 429/14a.

146. Hou, Chuang-hui-t'ang 5/11b.

147. Yü, Pan-ch'iao/1.

148. Fang Hsiao-ju (1357-1402), courtesy name Hsi-chih, also Hsi-ku, artistic name Hsun-chih, also Hou-ch'eng-sheng, also Cheng-hsueh, was born in Ninghai, Chekiang, into a family prominent in government since the Sung. His father had served as a prefect under Ming T'ai-tsu but was implicated in a corruption case and imprisoned, where he died. In his early years, Fang studied with the noted Neo-Confucian scholar Sung Lien, who also became a victim of the suspicious first emperor. As an official and intellectual, Fang attempted to modify T'ai-tsu's despotic governing style towards the humanistic values of Neo-Confucianism but his idealism met with little success. He served as an education official in a remote part of Shensi and returned to Nanking on several occasions to oversee the national examinations. With the accession of the Chien-wen Emperor, Fang, along with other leading statesmen, was summoned to serve at court and he became an influential advisor, advocating the revival of classical models in government policy. As the civil war begun by the Prince of Yen grew increasingly serious, Fang became more important at court in military affairs, though he may have contributed to the mistaken recommendations which enabled the Prince to cross the Yangtze and capture Nanking. Chien-wen is assumed to have died in a palace fire and Fang was arrested. His caustic refusal to surrender and his public berating of the Prince's disloyalty led to torture and the vindictive execution of about 1,000 persons connected with him. Possession of his literary works carried the death penalty. It wasn't until the Wan-li era that the dynasty relented and he was enshrined in a temple in the city. In 1645, the Ming court honored him posthumously. Ming-shih 414/4017-21; Goodrich and Fang, Ming Biography/426-33; Crawford, "Fang Hsiao-ju." The

temple of Fang is mentioned in <u>Ch'ung-k'an chiang-ning</u> 13/9a.

149. Ch'ü, <u>Kung-yeh hsiao-ling-chi</u>. Quoted in Chu, <u>ku-chi t'u-k'ao</u>/197. Ch'ü Ta-chün (1630-96), courtesy name Weng-shan, also Leng-shen, also Chieh-tzu, artistic name Hua-fu, also Lo-fou shan-jen, Buddhist name Chin-chung, courtesy name I-ling, artistic name Sao-yü, was from Canton and was known as a poet and loyalist. After the Manchu conquest, he abandoned thoughts of an official career and in 1649 joined the court of the Ming pretender, Prince Kuei (1623-62) in Kwangtung. With the failure of this cause, he became a Buddhist priest and traveled widely during the 1650s, including Nanking. He later left Buddhism but retained loyalist contacts with people sympathetic to Cheng Ch'eng-kung. Later, he briefly joined the San-fan Rebellion of Wu San-kuei in 1673. Although he had to go into hiding several times because of his anti-Ch'ing activities, he escaped punishment through friendly connections with Ch'ing officials. Li, <u>Kuo-ch'ao</u> 429/12884-85; Hummel, <u>Eminent Chinese</u>/20.

150. See <u>Shih-ching</u> 65:1, 2, 3. Translated in Waley, <u>Book of Songs</u>/306. According to the Mao tradition, the poem is the lament of a Chou official who passed through Hao-ching, the capital of the Western Chou (c.1066-771 B.C.), which was in ruins with wine-millet growing in the Imperial Palace and tombs. See <u>Shih-san-ching</u> 2/146-47.

151. See CTS 365/4117.

152. Chang I (1608-95), original name Lu-wei, courtesy name Yao-hsing, artistic name Pai-yun, was born in Nanking. His father, K'o-ta, was Regional Commander of Teng-lai, Shantung, at the end of the Ming and active in anti-Manchu defenses in the northeast. Chang I inherited the rank of Battalion Commander of the Embroidered Uniform Guard upon becoming a Licentiate and was apparently involved in

protecting the Ch'ung-chen Emperor when Peking fell. After his retirement to Mt. She, he was said to have never reentered Nanking and lived as a Taoist, supporting himself on the mountain by woodcutting. Local neighbors gave him the nickname "Pai-yun hsien-sheng (Mr. White Clouds)." Although Chang refused to publish his works, some twenty titles survived. Fang, "Pai-yun;" Ch'ung-k'an chiang-ning 34/4a-b.

153. Quoted in K'ung, T'ao-hua-shan chu (Liang ed.) 2/245. "Ling-yen (Spirit Crag)" may refer to a mountain in Liu-ho district just outside the city of Nanking.

154. Fang Pao (1668-1749), courtesy name Feng-chiu, artistic names Ling-kao, also Wang-hsi, was born in the Nanking area although his family originated in T'ung-ch'eng, Anhwei. Known primarily as a scholar and prose writer, he had a long distinguished official career, though not without dramatic upsets. He attracted attention while still young, as a student in the Imperial Academy, an outstanding provincial graduate of 1699, and as a successful candidate in the metropolitan examinations of 1706. In 1711, however, he was implicated in the literary inquisition of his disciple Tai Ming-shih (1653-1713). Tai was executed, but Fang avoided being forced into servitude due to his literary talents. He was attached to the Imperial Study, from which he eventually rose to become a Sub-Chancellor of the Grand Secretariat, though he was once again deprived of his ranks by Ch'ien-lung in 1739. Under the latter Emperor, he was in charge of several literary projects including the San-li i-shu (Collected Commentaries on the Three Books of Ritual) (printed in 1748) for which he tried to obtain a copy of Chang I's manuscript, San-li ho-tsuan (Combined Commentaries on the Three Books of Ritual). It was never forwarded but was later collected for the Ssu-k'u ch'üan-shu (Four Libraries) project. Fang

apparently visited Chang in his youth in the company of his father, though his biography of Chang was written towards the end of his own life. Fang is probably best known to posterity as a founder of the T'ung-cheng School of prose, a canonical status bestowed upon him by his fellow local, Yao Nai (1732-1815), the actual leader of the movement. Ch'ing-shih-k'ao lieh-chuan 77/1117; Hummel, Eminent Chinese/235-37.

155. Fo-lun (d. 1701) was born into the Regular White Banner and, though he began as a Clerk, rose eventually to Grand Secretary. He was ordered to take charge of food supplies in Szechuan and the area occupied by the rebel Wu Shih-fan (d. 1681). Subsequently, he held a number of high positions in the Boards of Works, Justice, and Revenue. He was asked to adjudicate the dispute between Chin Fu and Yü Ch'eng-lung and, on the advice of Mingju, supported Chin. He was subsequently impeached several times for partiality to Chin, and later by Kuo Hsiu for his relationship to Mingju. A conference ordered him dismissed, but K'ang-hsi merely reduced his rank and later appointed him Governor of Shantung. Although he continued to be embroiled in repercussions from this earlier controversy, he rose to Grand Secretary of the Wen-yuan Pavilion and ended his career as an honored official. Ch'ing-shih-kao lieh-chuan 57/1083.

156. Kuo Hsiu (1638-1715), courtesy name Tuan-fu, artistic name Hua-yeh, was from Chi-mo, Shantung. He became a provincial graduate in 1670 and, later, District Magistrate of Wu-chiang, Kiangsu, where he gained a reputation for his administration. Through the patronage of the Governor, T'ang Pin, he was appointed to the Censorate and was one of the most energetic prosecutors of corruption. In 1688, he impeached Chin Fu as well as Mingju, both at the height of their influence. The

following year, he became President of the Censorate. He further impeached Kao Shih-ch'i, then K'ang-hsi's favorite literatus. The tables were turned that year, however, when Kuo himself was accused of factionalism and then corruption. He was tried in 1690 by officials friendly to Mingju and Kao Shih-ch'i and sentenced to banishment, a punishment commuted to retirement by the Emperor. For eight years, he was out of power until he met the Emperor on the Southern Tour of 1699. Kuo was then appointed Governor of Hukuang (modern Hunan and Hupei) and was dismissed in 1703 over a revolt of the Miao tribesmen in his area. Ch'ing-shih-kao lieh-chuan 57/1084; Hu;mmel, Eminent Chinese/436-37.

157. For a summary of these events, see Ch'ing-shih-kao 101/463.

158. K/449.

159. Ta-ch'ing sheng-tsu 139/1871. The entire tour, which lasted about seventy days, is recorded in ibid., 139/1868-140/1890. See also Spence, Ts'ao Yin/128-30.

160. Ta-ch'ing sheng-tsu 139/1871.

161. Among the other difficulties Yü and Hsi cited were the obstacles of the land route and the lack of accommodations. Ta-ch'ing sheng-tsu, 139/1876-77.

162. For K'ung's four other poems celebrating the tour see K/121-22.

163. K'ung, Hu-hai-chi 6/118.

164. For the poem describing the album, see K/175. The various leaves depicted a literatus-official journeying north with only his books and lute through the autumn landscape. The contributing painters were as follows: Sang Chih (fl. c.1686); Chu Chueh (fl. c.1689); Cha Shih-piao; Kao Ts'en; Hsiao Ch'en (fl. c.1674-89); Wang Yun (fl. c.1689); Juan Yueh-chiao (fl. c.1689); P'an Ping-hu (fl. c.1689). See Ch'en, yen-chiu/64-67.

165. Quoted in Ch'en, nien-p'u/61.

CHAPTER FOUR
BELOW THE PALANQUIN

1. K/188.

2. One of the works acquired at this time was a T'ang painting, Chiang-shan hsueh-chi-t'u (Landscape after a Snowfall), signed "Wang Wei." K'ung obtained it from a monk from Sung-chiang, Kiangsu, and in a humorous poem claimed to have dodged the rent collector and sold his bedding in order to purchase it (K/191). In his catalog entry, he records the seals of Sung Hui-tsung, Chao Meng-fu, Wen Cheng-ming (1470-1559), and Wu K'uan (1435-1504), among others and, although admitting the existence of many copies, believed in its authenticity (K/576-80). For reproductions of two other versions, see Ishikawa, Bunjinga/6-7, 104-5.

3. An allusion to Lun-yü 7:17: "Confucius said, 'If I am granted some more years, I would use them to study the Changes and avoid great error.'"

4. See Tung, "Lun k'ung shang-jen"/144-46.

5. K/368.

6. See Lynn, Wang Shih-chen/110-56; Lynn, "Orthodoxy and Enlightenment"; Kuo, p'i-p'ing-shih/538-60; Aoki, Ch'ing-tai wen-hsueh/47-54.

7. See Liu, Chinese Theories/43-45.

8. The others were "yuan (implication)," "hsieh-yin-lü (rhythm and rhyme)," and "li-i-tse (aesthetic beauty)." Hummel, Eminent Chinese/832-33.

9. Hui, Yü-yang shan-jen 5/6a-8b; Hashimoto, Ō Gyoyō/77-87

10. K/521.

11. Chiang Ching-ch'i, courtesy name Ching-shao, was from I-hsing, Kiangsu. His writings were published in Tung-she-chi (Collected Works from the Eastern Cottage). Ch'en, nien-p'u/65.

12. The other contributors were Wu Wen (1644-1704), Bordu, Yuan Ch'i-hsu, Yueh-tuan (see note 50), Shen Chi-yu, Ch'en Tseng-ik, So Fen, Pi Ta-sheng, Wang Shih-hung, Chu Hsiang, Ko Yu, and Lo Ching.

13. Reprinted in K/183-202.

14. See Ch'ien, Nan-pu 9/99.

15. See Tuan, Yueh-fu/26.

16. The text, dated summer 1698, was intended as a preface to his play, Hsiao-hu-lei (Little Thunderclap). One version appears in K/196 with the last line missing; a fuller version, titled "T'i hsiao-hu-lei (Preface to Little Thunderclap)" is included in K'ung, Hsiao-hu-lei/8a-b. The music of Shao was a dance traditionally believed to have been composed by the Sage-king Shun on the occasion of his succession. It is praised several times by Confucius as a perfect model of aesthetic and moral form. See Lun-yü: 3:25, 7:14, 15:11.

17. Kuei Fu, a native of Ch'ü-fu during the eighteenth century, was a friend of K'ung Ssu-yuan, who later owned the instrument. He viewed it and wrote the following explanation: "'Hu-lei' means 'crocodile.' Its teeth and bones can be made into a musical instrument which gives forth a strange sound. A classic states: 'There is a strange fish which lives in rivers called "o (crocodile)." When its body decays, there are three teeth left.' The name 'hu-lei' must be based on this." Kuei, "Hsiao-hu-lei-chi."/91b-92a.

18. This other description of the instrument was K'ung's entry for Hsiao-hu-lei in the catalog of his collection of antiques. See K/622.

19. For rubbings of Han Huang's inscription and K'ung's poems, see K/illus. 3.

20. For poems concerning Fan Hua-po, named Ling, who was from Yun-ch'eng, Shantung, see K/208, 233, 305, 377, 380, 386-87.

21. See K'ung, Hsiao-hu-lei/18b. K'ung's friend, the poet T'ien Wen, also recorded an occasion in May 1697 when he heard Fan perform on the instrument. See K'ung, Hsiao-hu-lei/3b-5a.

22. The T'ai-p'ing-yuan (Garden of Peace) is mentioned in the prologues of both halves of T'ao-hua-shan (The Peach Blossom Fan) as the theater in which the play is being performed. See T/1,133. For a short poem on it, see K/369. Li Hsiu-lang was a noted actor who for years was inaccessible to the public while he lived under the patronage of a noble. Upon being cast out, he returned to the professional stage, an event which K'ung celebrated in a poem in K/381.

23. See K/380. Ch'iung-hua-meng (The Hortensia Flower) by Lung Shih-lou is recorded in Yao, Chin-yuch 9/266; among the other enthusiasts was Wang Shih-chen, so it is probably the same play seen by K'ung, though he records the author as Lung Kai-an. Yang-chou-meng (A Yangchow Dream) was written by Yü-ch'ih-sheng, the artistic name of Yueh Tuan (see note 50).

24. K'ung just missed meeting Hung Sheng (1646-1704), the other great dramatist of this time with whom he has often been paired by Chinese critics. In 1689, the year K'ung returned to Peking, Hung departed the capital in disgrace after being dismissed from the Imperial Academy due to a performance of his Ch'ang-sheng-tien (Palace of Eternal Youth) on a day of mourning for the Empress Hsiao-i. See Ch'en, Hung pai-hsi/78-82.

25. Ku Ts'ai, courtesy name T'ien-shih, artistic name Liang-ch'i meng-o chü-shih, is briefly mentioned in Ch'ü-lu 5. See Lu, hsi-ch'ü-shih/97-98.

26. K/370. K'ung gives the name of this play as Ch'u-tz'u-p'u in a 1694 poem, regretting that the Nan-ya troupe deleted the act "Chao-hun (Summons of the soul)." However, in a preface to Hsiao-hu-lei, he refers to the play as "Li Sao (Encountering Sorrow)." See K'ung, Hsiao-hu-lei/18b.

27. The date given by Ku Ts'ai in this postscript to T'ao-hua-shan is the one generally accepted by scholars. However, in a preface to Hsiao-hu-lei, K'ung recalls the date as 1696. See K'ung, Hsiao-hu-lei/7a.

28. See K'ung, Hsiao-hu-lei/7a.

29. K'ung, Hsiao-hu-lei/13b.

30. T/5.

31. See Aoki, hsi-ch'ü-shih 1/390; Lu, hsi-ch'ü-shih/97-98; Wu, hsi-ch'ü kai-lun 2/31.

32. Ku wrote a conventional prologue act to the play while K'ung himself also wrote two prologues--a set of arias entitled "Po-ku hsien-ch'ing (Musings on Ancient Thnings)" and four arias in the "Che-ku-t'ien (Partridge in the Sky)" form. (Rpt. K/412-15) Thus, one cannot only compare an example of Ku's individual style but see that K'ung was capable, to some degree, of writing arias on his own.

33. See Wang, Yin-lu 2, 3. The art of composition and scoring was primarily transmitted through an oral tradition and written discussions of it are far from systematic or complete. For recent collections of some of the important Ming and Ch'ing treaties, See Chung-kuo ku-tien hsi-ch'ü, also Ku-tien hsi-ch'ü sheng-yueh.

34. Huang, Ch'ü-hai 29/1396-99.

35. See "Pien-chi (Chronology)". Reprinted in K'ung, Hsiao-hu-lei/9a-13b.

36. Information regarding the figures and events of the play may be found in Chiu-t'ang-shu (Old T'ang History), Hsin-t'ang-shu (New T'ang History), Tzu-chih t'ung-chien

(Comprehensive Mirror for Use in Government), T'ang-shih chi-shih (Anecdotes about T'ang Poetry), and T'ai-p'ing kuang-chi (Anthology of the T'ai-p'ing Era) as well as the other sources K'ung indicated in his prefaces.

37. See Collingwood, The Idea of History/231-49 for a discussion of the autonomy of the historian as he creates an imaginary picture of the past through selection, construction, and criticism of source material.

38. Among other innovations are three prefaces in addition to "Pien-chi" including "Se-mu (Dramatis Personae)," which contains a list of the major characters and short, biographical comments. There are also four introductory acts rather than the usual one, a set of arias to introduce the entire play, and a division of the play into two parts at Act 20.

39. CTS 7/4821. The use of "P'i-p'a-hsing (The Lute Song)" was a popular subject for dramatists since the Yuan. See Birch, "Ming Ch'uan-ch'i"/221-29.

40. Wu, hsi-ch'ü kai-lun 3/31.

41. Aoki, hsi-ch'ü-shih 1/390.

42. K'ung, Tao-hua-shan-chu 1/10.

43. K'ung, Hsiao-hu-lei/6b.

44. After K'ung's death, "Little Thunderclap" passed to one of his sons. An old maidservant sold it to a Circuit Intendant, Wang Tou-nan, for ten piculs of wheat. Wang then presented it to another K'ung, the Prefect K'ung Ssu-yuan. In the late nineteenth century, it was obtained by Liu Shih-heng (1875-1926), who considered it among his finest possessions, naming his studio, "Hsiao-hu-lei-ko (Pavilion of the Two 'Thunderclaps')." The noted painter and translator, Lin Shu (1852-1924), was invited to make illustrations and a gathering was held in which poems celebrating the instruments were collected. These were published in Shuang-hu-lei pen-shih (On the Two

'Thunderclaps') in 1911. The illstrations have been reprinted in Liu's Nuan-hung-shih edition of Hsiao-hu-lei. Kuei, Hsiao-hu-lei-chi."

45. Rpt. in K'ung, Hsiao-hu-lei adden./1a-16b. The metrics and musical score were revised by Wu Mei and Liu Fu-liang respectively. Wu also completed the second act, which was apparently in a fragmentary state.

46. Jen-jui-lu (A Record of Senior Citizens) in one chüan is dated October 25, 1698, and was published by Chang Ch'ao in the second series of Chao-tai ts'ung-shu, together with Down from the Mountain. Reprinted in K/481-85.

47. P/1, 5.

48. Little is known of Wang Shou-hsi except for the information K'ung provided. See T/5-6.

49. Ting Chi-chih, named Yin, was the most celebrated K'un-ch'ü actor during the late Ming and early Ch'ing in Nanking. Yü Huai mentions him performing in the company of the storyteller Liu Ching-t'ing and noted musicians. He lived well into his nineties and formed friendships with such poets as Ch'ien Ch'ien-i, Kung Ting-tzu, and Wang Shih-chen, all of whom wrote a number of pieces to him over the years. Ting was able to accumulate considerable wealth and purchased a mansion by the riverside in Ch'in-huai, where he hosted literati gatherings. In Scene 8, "Nao-hsieh (Commotion by the Riverside)," K'ung dramatizes an incident where the Fu-she holds a gathering at Ting's pavilion as Juan Ta-ch'eng's boat inadvertently sails near, only to turn and flee so as to avoid the wrath of the activists. Ting appears elsewhere in the play as a denizen of the pleasure quarters and as a member of the coterie surrounding Li Hsiang-chün. Yu, Pan-ch'iao 3/17, 19; K'ung, T'ao-hua-shan-chu 1/104, 133.

50. Yueh-tuan (1671-1704), also Yun-tuan, courtesy name Cheng-tzu, artistic name Hung-lan chu-jen, also Chang-po

shih-pa-lang, also Tung-feng chü-shih, also Yü-ch'ih-sheng, was from Hu-chou (modern Wu-hsing), Chekiang. He was a member of the Ch'ing imperial family, beiang a great-grandson of the dynastic founder, Nurhaci. A cultivated poet, Yueh-tuan was a noted patron of Chinese literati. He sponsored the compilation of the widely-read manual, Nan-tz'u ting-lu (A Collection of Southern Aria Forms) and wrote a drama, Yang-chou-meng (A Yangchow Dream), which K'ung viewed. In 1698, just around the time that K'ung was collaborating with Wang Shou-hsi, he was demoted from his rank as a prince but continued to maintain an establishment. He published two poetry collections titled Yü-ch'ih-sheng-kao (Writings by the Scholar of the Jade Pond) in 1695 and 1704. Hummel, Eminent Chinese/934; Wu, Ku-ch'ü/184.

51. Aoki, hsi-ch'ü-shih/384-87; for a complete translation of the play see K'ung, The Peach Blossom Fan (Ch'en, Acton and Birch, trans.).

52. K'ung wrote six prefaces in all, dating from the completion of the play in 1699 to the first printed edition in 1708. These are reprinted in T/1-25. In addition, some of the K'ang-hsi editions contain "eyebrow" comments by K'ung dispersed throughout the text.

53. See K'ung, "T'ao-hua-shan fan-lieh (Methods of The Peach Blossom Fan)." In T/11.

54. The following sources are listed in "T'ao-hua-shan k'ao-chü (Bibliography of The Peach Blossom Fan)." (1) Anon., "Chiao-shih (A Woodcutter's History)," an historical chronicle; (2) Hou Fang-yü, Chuang-hui-t'ang wen-chi, his collected prose works printed in 1656; (3) Hou Fang-yü, Ssu-i-t'ang chi (Collected Works from the Hall of Four Contemplations), his collected poetry appearing around the same time as the above; (4) Chia K'ai-tsung, "Hou fang-yü-chuan (Biography of Hou Fang-yü)," written by his friend

and editor of his collected works; (5) Ch'ien Ch'ien-i, Yu-hsueh-chi (Succeeding Accomplishments), the second poetry collection by one of the great writers of the seventeenth century who was also a prominent official serving both the Ming and Ch'ing; (6) Wu Wei-yeh, Mei-ts'un-chi (Collected Works of Wu Wei-yeh), the prose and poetry by one of the leading late Ming activists and early Ch'ing "survivors," printed in 1668-69; (7) Wu Wei-yeh, Sui-k'ou chi-lueh (An Account of Bandit Pacification), the title was often confused with that of another, Lu-ch'iao chi-wen (An Account by a Retired Rustic), whose authorship has been questioned. However, the content of the latter work, which contains accounts of the leading figures of the Nanking Restoration, is more relevant as source material and was probably the one consulted by K'ung; (8) Yang Wen-ts'ung, Hsun-mei-t'ang-chi (Collected Works from the Hall of True Beauty), the poetry and prose of the Late Ming painter and official; (9) Mao Hsiang, T'ung-jen-chi (Poems by My Friends), essays and poems by friends of the eminent aesthete and "survivor," printed in 1673; (10) Shen Shou-min, Ku-shan ts'ao-t'ang-chi (Collected Works from the Grass Hut on Mt. Ku), the collected works of an influential member of the Fu-she in Nanking; (11) Ch'en Wei-sung, Hu-hai-lou-chi (Collected Works from the Hall by the Lakes and Seas), the collected prose by one of the early Ch'ing's great writers who was the son of Ch'en Chen-hui, printed in 1686-89; (12) Kung Ting-tzu, Ting-shan-t'ang-chi (Collected Works from the Hall on Mt. Ting), the collected works of the celebrated seventeenth century poet, printed in 1673; (13) Juan Ta-ch'eng, Shih-ch'ao ch'uan-ch'i (Dramas from the Stone Den), dramas written by the noted exponent of T'ang Hsien-tsu's style from 1629 to 1644, of which K'ung cites two: Shih-tso-jen ch'un-teng-mi (Recognition of Ten Errors or Riddles on Spring Lanterns) (1633) and Yen-tzu-

chien (The Swallow Note) (1642). The preface is reprinted
in T/15-21. For studies of the historical background and
sources of K'ung's drama, see Struve, "History;" also "The
Peach Blossom Fan."

55. The actual leaders of the group supporting Prince
Lu (1618-62) were former Vice-President Ch'ien Ch'ien-i,
President of the Censorate Chang Shen-yen (1577-1645),
Vice-President Lü Ta-ch'i (Metropolitan Graduate, 1628),
Grand Supervisor Chiang Yueh-kuang (d. 1649), and Secretary
Lei Yen-tso (d. 1645). It was Lü in particular who was
associated with the manifesto against Prince Fu (d. 1646)
known as the "Ch'i-pu-k'o-li (Seven Vices of Prince Fu)."
These were: intriguing for the succession, lack of filial
piety, cruelty, interference in government, poor education,
lust, and drunkeness. Ma Shih-ying, however, argued that
Prince Fu had precedence over Prince Lu genealogically.
For historical views of the debate over the enthronement,
see Wu, Lu-ch'iao/1-2; Hsu, Hsiao-t'ien/201-2; Li Yao, Nan-
chiang i-shih (A History of the South). Quoted in K'ung,
T'ao-hua-shan-chu 1/205-6.

56. The "Ssu-chen (Four Commanders)" were Huang Te-kung
(d. 1645), stationed at Lu-chou, Anhwei; Kao Chieh,
stationed in Yangchow; Liu Tse-ch'ing, stationed in Huai-an
Kiangsu; and Liu Liang-tso (d. 1667), stationed in Lin-
huai, between Honan and Anhwei. Together with Tso Liang-yü
and Shih K'o-fa, they were the major defenders of the
Nanking Restoration.

57. For historical narratives of the death of Shih K'o-
fa, see Ming-shih 274/7022-23; Wu, Lu-ch'iao/16; Hsu,
Hsiao-t'ien/453-54.

58. Liu Ching-t'ing (c.1587-c.1668) was originally
named Ts'ao Kuo-ch'un and was born in T'ai-chou, Kiangsu.
His family had declined in status and his father became a
money-lender. Like his brother, Liu Ching-t'ing studied

storytelling but apparently often got into trouble with the
law and fled when he was about 15 years old to avoid
arrest. At some point, he is supposed to have changed his
name to Liu after sleeping under a willow tree. Liu Ching-
t'ing moved on to Hsu-i, Anhwei, where he devoted himself
to the art of storytelling under the guidance of a scholar,
Mo Hou-kuang. Mo advised Liu to approach performance as
personal cultivation and to achieve his ambition in his
stories. After perfecting his technique, Liu went to
Yangchow, Hangchow, Soochow, and then to Nanking where he
became the most famous storyteller of the time. He was
appreciated not only for his original interpretation of
such stories as "Wu Sung Fights the Tiger" and episodes
from the Sui-T'ang cycle but for his authentic and frank
personality. He was the guest of such elite officials as
Grand Minister of Mount Fan and Grand Councilor Ho Wen-
tuan. Liu frequently performed in Ch'in-huai and
associated with well-known stars of the theater such as
Chang Yen-chu and Shen Kung-hsien. Liu's fame rests not
only on his storytelling but on his activities in the
historical events of the period. Perhaps his most
rewarding patron was Tso Liang-yü, to whom he was
introduced around 1643. Tso's army was stationed in Anhwei
and Liu was invited to a banquet at his camp. Tso
supposedly placed swords outside the tent to frighten the
guests and was much impressed by Liu's fearlessness. He
kept Liu in his camp as an advisor, consulting him on the
most secret matters. Although Liu was barely literate,
Tso, who was himself from low origins, trusted him more
than the scholars who served as secretaries. Liu is said
to have personally executed soldiers disloyal to Tso and
advised Tso to march on Nanking to overthrow Ma Shih-ying
and Juan Ta-ch'eng. When Liu would visit Nanking, he would
be treated with great respect because of his powerful

influence over Tso. However, his political influence ended precipitously with Tso's death in 1645 and the fall of Nanking to the Manchus that same year. Reduced to poverty, he once again traveled about as a professional storyteller. At one point, he was a "pure guest" at Ma Feng-chih's camp. The latter was a military leader who had surrendered to the Manchus. Liu was treated as a performer rather than an advisor and soon left in discontent. His last years were spent traveling to places such as Peking, Yangchow, Lu-chou, and back to Nanking. He is known to have lived until 1668, when he was 82 years old. See Hung, Liu Ching-t'ing; Ch'en and Yang, Liu Ching-t'ing. For an eyewitness description of one of Liu's performances, see Chang, T'ao-an/67.

59. Tso Liang-yü (1598-1645), courtesy name K'un-shan, was born in Lin-ch'ing, Shantung. Although he had little formal education, he distinguished himself in military campaigns and gained the patronage of Hou Hsun, the father of Hou Fang-yü. He rose to command a major army during the rebellions of Chang Hsien-chung and Li Tzu-ch'eng, gaining victories and suffering defeats as he fought them in Shensi, Honan, Anhwei, Hukuang, and Szechuan. As the Ming declined, Tso was one of the generals who became increasingly independent and was courted by Ming authorities. He became Junior Guardian of the Heir Apparent and in 1644 was made an Earl. Around that time, he established headquarters in Wuchang, Hukuang, up the river from Nanking, and joined his army of 800,000 men with loyalist elements in supporting the Nanking Restoration. Relations with the court were never smooth, however, and a march on Nanking for food supplies was barely averted through the intervention of Hou Fang-yü. In April, 1645, Tso's opposition to the Ma-Juan regime led to his issuance of a manifesto to purge those close to the throne, and he

moved on the capital. This caused Ma to shift one of the Four Commanders, Huang Te-kung, to block Tso, thereby fatally weakening the line of defense against the Manchus. Tso died suddenly on April 29 and his son, Meng-keng (d. 1654), was subsequently defeated by Huang. Ming-shih 273/6987-98; Hummel, Eminent Chinese/761-62.

60. For a plot summary of Shih-ts'o-jen (Recognition of Ten Errors) and Yen-tzu-chien (The Swallow Note), see Huang, Ch'ü-hai/531-34, 525-31, respectively. For critical discussions, see Aoki, hsi-ch'ü-shih/304-10, Strassberg, "The Authentic Self"/78-81.

61. A description of a "ho-tzu-hui (hamper party)" was written by the painter Shen Chou and reprinted by K'ung's friend, Yü Huai in Yü, Pan-ch'iao/22-23.

62. Ironically, one of K'ung's precursors for the use of a storyteller to present a unifying vision of the play was Juan Ta-ch'eng himself, who employed a palace balladeer in the final scene of Shih-ts'o-jen to sing a set of arias unraveling the embroglio of the plot. Other examples which may have influenced him are the characters Ts'ao Shan-ts'ai in Wu Wei-yeh's Mo-ling-ch'iu (Autumn in Nanking) and Li Kuei-nien in Hung Sheng's Ch'ang-sheng-tien (The Palace of Eternal Youth).

63. Kao Chieh (d. 1645) was born in Min-chih, Shensi, and was a fellow local of Li Tzu-ch'eng, with whom he was allied in rebelling against the Ming during the 1630s. He absconded with Li's wife and surrendered to the Ming in 1635; thereafter, he aided government forces in suppressing his former comrade, rising to the rank of general in 1643. After suffering a serious defeat that year, he retreated from battle and began plundering the countryside in Shansi. Kao was appointed one of the "Four Commanders" in the Nanking Restoration and assigned to the wealthy city of Yangchow as headquarters. However, his reputation as a

plunderer was such that the population resisted his entrance. At the same time another general, Huang Te-kung, opposed awarding the city to Kao. Through the mediation of Shih K'o-fa, Kao agreed to move to nearby Kua-chou and later undertook an important expedition north to defend the Yellow River. There, he incurred the enmity of the local commander, Hsu Ting-kuo, whose wife had Kao killed in his sleep after a banquet. The death of Kao Chieh, followed by the surrender of Hsu to the Manchus, dashed the hopes of the Nanking Restoration for a recovery of the north and opened the way southwards for the Manchu invasion. Ming-shih 273/7003-6; Hummel, Eminent Chinese/410-11; Wu, Lu-ch'iao/20-24.

64. See chapter 3, note 56.

65. See K'ung, "The Peach Blossom Fan: Scene 4." Strassberg, trans.

66. For a discussion of the character of Yang Wen-ts'ung, see Wang, "Yu li-shih jen-wu."

67. The absence of the conventional reunion act was one of the features of The Peach Blossom Fan most widely noted by traditional critics. Yet popular sentiment for a comic resolution was such as to prompt K'ung's friend, Ku Ts'ai, to write another ending which he titled, "Nan-t'ao-hua-shan (A Southern Version of The Peach Blossom Fan)." K'ung was less than enchanted with this and later wrote, "the style is both refined and delightful, in the manner of T'ang Hsien-tsu, but though he may have supplied wht I left out, it rather makes me look like an old reprobate. Need I yield to him?" (T/7). Ku's scene has not survived and most critical opinion has tended to support K'ung. See Aoki, hsi-ch'ü-shih/389-90; Wu, hsi-ch'ü-shih 3/31, Liang, Ch'ü-hua/371.

68. "Tao-hua-shan kang-ling (The Organizing Principles of The Peach Blossom Fan)" is reprinted in T/22-25.

69. An interesting opinion of this scene was expressed by the modern critic Wang Kuo-wei, who was one of the first to recognize The Peach Blossom Fan as a monument of "transcendental spirit (yen-shih chieh-t'o chih ching-shen)" in Chinese literature, along with the eighteenth century novel Hung-lou-meng (The Dream of the Red Chamber). However, he compares the final enlightenment of K'ung's play unfavorably with that of the character Chia Pao-yü in the novel, stating that the play's is induced externally by Taoist Chang, while Pao-yü's is presented as occurring within the character's psychological development. This is a somewhat unfair comparison, for Chinese drama, lacking a strong tradition of extensive inner monologue, presents change in the mode of visible stage action while narrative by its nature is more capable of interior points of view. See Wang, "Hung-lou-meng"/253.

70. As an official of the Board of Rites in the Imperial Temple of Nanking, The Old Master may have been based in part on the dramatist's relative, K'ung Shang-tse. K'ung gives ample hints that the figure is an imaginary self-portrait though. The character first appears as a 97-year-old "survivor" in the prologue, set in September 1684. His lofty sentiments lauding the peace and prosperity of the K'ang-hsi reign remind the reader that this was the date K'ung lectured to the Emperor in Ch'ü-fu during the latter's Southern Tour. Yet another bit of esoterica is in the final scene dated November 1, 1648. The Old Master, upon meeting the hermits Liu Ching-t'ing and Su K'un-sheng, reveals that the feast day of the God of Wealth to whom he has just sacrificed is the same as his own birthday, which is also the date of K'ung Shang-jen's birth. For a discussion of The Old Master and K'ung's innovative use of the formal conventions of the fu-mo role and the prologue scene, see Kalvodovna, "Ch'uan-ch'i."

71. Among these was Wang Nan, courtesy name Mu-an, who served as Senior President of the Censorate under K'ang-hsi. In February 1700 he borrowed a copy and, during the Lantern Festival (March 5), staged a performance of Scene 23, "Chi-shan (Sending off the Fan)" by the Chin-tou (Golden Wine Cask) troupe from Anhwei, which had belonged to the late Li T'ien-fu (1635-99), Grand Secretary of the Wu-ying-tien Throne Hall. T/6.

72. K'ung recorded that he had lost track of whomever he had lent his own copy out to and was forced to borrow one from the household of a Governor, Chang P'ing-chou. T/6.

73. T/6-7.

74. The Chi-yuan (Sojourn Garden) was located in Hsia-hsieh (Lower Cross) Street and was originally the villa of Li Wei (see note 75). T/9.

75. A reference to Li Wei (1625-84), courtesy name Ching-yü, also T'ai-shu, artistic name T'an-yuan, also Chü-wu chü-shih, was born in Kao-yang, Chihli (modern Hopei). A Metropolitana Graduate in 1646, he entered the Han-lin Academy and quickly rose to Grand Secretary of the Pao-ho-tien Throne Hall by 1658. He was a close advisor to K'ang-hsi during the Wu San-kuei Rebellion and served as editor of various official compilations, retiring with the title of Grand Tutor of the Heir Apparent. Ch'ing-shih-kao lieh-chuan 37/1045; Hummel, Eminent Chinese/493-94.

76. An allusion to the descendents of Wang Tao (267-330) and Hsieh An (320-85) of the Chin, who were noted for their aristocratic way of life during the Southern Dynasties.

77. For statements of this view, see Meng, hsi-ch'ü-shih 2/364; Iwaki, "Kaisetsu" 2/533; Chao, "Lun k'ung shang-jen"/155; Ma, "K'ung shang-jen"/133.

78. See Ch'en, "yin-shih pa-kuan."

79. K/324.

80. See Li Kung (1659-1733), "Chi k'ung tung-t'ang an-t'ang t'ung ch'en hsin-chien, wan chi-yen, wu ching-an, ts'ao cheng-tzu, ch'en chien-fu, shao wei-jen chi-hsi fen-fu te-'yuan'-yun. (A Poem Using the Rhyme 'Yuan' Written at Gathering at K'ung Shang-jen's Waterside Studio where Ch'en Hsin-chien, Wan Chi-yeh, Wu Ching-an, Ts'ao Cheng-tzu, Ch'en Chien-fu and Shao Wei-jen were Present".) In Li, Shu-ku ts'ung-shu 2 (Yen-li ts'ung-shu ed). Quoted in Ch'en, nien-p'u/89.

81. T/6.

82. See Wang, Yin-lu 4/26b; Wu, Ku-ch'ü/184.

83. See Struve, "The Peach Blossom Fan"/108-14. For some of K'ang-hsi's view of the Ming, see Spence, Emperor/86-89, 144.

84. K/389.

85. K/363. The Tuan-wu Festival on the fifth day of the fifth lunar month recalls the suicide of the poet Ch'ü Yuan (c.343-290 B.C.).

86. Wang Yuan (1648-1710), courtesy name K'un-sheng, artistic name Huo-an, was born in Peking to a member of the Ming Imperial Bodyguard who sought refuge in a Buddhist monastery after the Manchu invasion. In 1660, the family moved to the Yangchow area, where Wang Yuan studied and developed an interest in military subjects. Although he lacked an advanced degree, he served in an editorial capacity on the Ming History project from 1685 to 1691 along with another friend of K'ung's, Wan Ssu-t'ung (1638-1702). Afterwards, Wang earned his living as a tutor to wealthy families and as a secretary to high officials. He gradually found it useful to obtain the provincial graduate degree, which he did in 1693, although his loyalist sympathies kept him from serving the Ch'ing. During the early 1700s, he formed a friendship with the philosopher Li

Kung in Peking which resulted in their collaboration. It was at this time that he met K'ung Shang-jen with whom he shared a common interest in empirical studies. He met Li's teacher, Yen Yuan, in 1703 and became his pupil. For the remaining years of his life, Wang was a leading exponent of that philosopher's activist and pragmatic theories. Ch'ing-shih-kao lieh-chuan 267/1471; Hummel, Eminent Chinese/842-44.

87. Wang, Chü-yeh-t'ang wen-chi 16. Quoted in Ch'en, nien-p'u/85. The Chin-t'ai (Golden Terrace) was a Peking landmark located outside Chao-yang-men (Gate Facing the North).

88. Liu Ch'i, courtesy name Ch'ing-ts'en, artistic name Yü-feng, was from Chu-ch'eng, Shantung. He became a Metropolitan Graduate and served as Prefect of P'ing-yang, Shansi, from 1705 to 1709. He is recorded as a compassionate official, popular for his acts of charity. Later he served as Judicial Commissioner of Kiangsi. P'ing-yang fu-chih 20/28a (Ch'ien-lung ed.). Quoted in Ch'en, nien-p'u/90.

89. K'ung wrote one preface, "T'ao-hua-shan hsiao-yin (A Brief Forward to The Peach Blossom Fan)" dated April 1699, immediately after the play's completion. "T'ao-hua-shan hsiao-chih (A Note on The Peach Blossom Fan)" is dated April-May 1708; "Tao-hua-shan pen-mo (All About The Peach Blossom Fan)" is undated but clearly written for the printed edition since it contains the anecdote about T'ung Che-ts'un. Several other prefaces are undated. These have been reprinted in T/1-25. In addition, the original edition contained other prefaces, afterwords, critical remarks, and poems which K'ung states he had collected from readers of the manuscript, including a preface by Ku Ts'ai. See T/7. For more bibliographical information, see Ch'en, nien-p'u/141-46.

90. P'ing-yang fu-chih (Gazetteer of P'ing-yang) in 36 chuan was begun in 1707 and finished a year later. The other editor was Liu Ch'i. See Ch'en, nien-p'u/92, 112.

91. Liu T'ing-chi, courtesy name Yü-heng, artistic name Tsai-yuan, was a member of the Chinese Bordered Red Banner. Beginning as an Honorary Licentiate, he served as prefect in several localities, distinguishing himself in the areas of famine relief, river control, education, and judicial administration. He eventually reached the office of Judicial Commissioner of Kiangsi but was demoted over an affair to Intendant of the Huai-yang Circuit. He was an accomplished writer, and his poems were collected in Ko-chuang-chi (Collected Works from Ko Village) and his prose in Tsai-yuan tsa-chih (Random Notes by the Garden Denizen), to which K'ung contributed a preface and a short entry on Stonegate Mt. (K/492-95). Min, Pei-chuan 17/1a-b; Chang, Kuo-ch'ao shih-jen 13/12b-13a.

92. For a study of the life and writings of Po Chü-i (772-846) see Waley, Po Chü-i; the poetry of Lu Yu (1125-1210) has been translated in Watson, The Old Man. See Chao, Ou-pei 6/78-97.

93. Chi, ssu-k'u ch'üan-shu 37/4074.

94. K/491-93.

95. For bibliographical information on Ch'ang-liu-chi (Poems from a Lingering Stay), see Ch'en, nien-p'u/114-15.

96. For a discussion of this phrase in connection with the didactic view of poetry, see Liu, Chinese Poetry/67ff.

97. Chin, Chin-hsiang-shuo/4b-5a; 13a-b; 22a. Chin Chih, courtesy name Hsiao-an, artistic name Tai-ch'iu lao-jen, was from Shan-yin (modern Shaohsing), Chekiang. Chin first met K'ung at poetry gatherings in Yangchow in 1687, and thirty years later visited him in Ch'ü-fu. He arrived in September 1717, escorting bones of relatives to be reinterred in the south, and renewed their friendship.

Among the works Chin wrote was a gazetteer of Shantung, a
miscellany titled <u>Chin-hsiang-shuo</u> (<u>Pocket-sized
Reminiscences</u>), as well as a number of poetry and prose
collections. Ch'en, <u>nien-p'u</u>/99-100.

98. Sun Pin and P'ang Chüan were military strategists
during the Warring States Period. They both studied under
Kuei-ku-tzu but later became adversaries by serving rival
lords. <u>Shih-chi</u> 65/2162.

BIBLIOGRAPHY

Aoki Masaru (Ch'ing-mu Cheng-er). Ch'ing-tai wen-hsueh p'ing-lun-shih (A Critical History of Ch'ing Literature). Ch'en Shu-nu, trans. Taipei: K'ai-ming shu-tien, 1969.

_____ Chung-kuo chin-shih hsi-ch'ü shih (A History of Recent Chinese Drama). Wang Ku-lu, trans. Taipei: Shang-wu yin-shu-kuan, 1965.

_____ "Yōshū ni atari hi no ko shūjin" (K'ung Shang-jen's Days in Yangchow)." In Aoki masaru zenshū 2/478-90. Tokyo: Shunjūsha, 1971.

Atwell, William S. "From Education to Politics: The Fu-she." In De Bary, ed., The Unfolding of Neo-Confucianism/333-65.

Birch, Cyril. "Some Concerns and Methods of the Ming Ch'uan-ch'i Drama." In C. Birch, ed., Studies in Chinese Literary Genres. Berkeley: University of California Press, 1974. 220-58.

Birch, Cyril, ed. Anthology of Chinese Literature: I. New York: Grove Press, 1965.

Bretschneider, E. "Botanicum Sinicum." Journal of the Royal Asiatic Society, North China Branch (new series) 25(1890-91)/1-468.

Brewitt-Taylor, C.H. Romance of the Three Kingdoms. Rutland, Vermont: Charles Tuttle, 1959 (rpt. of 1925 ed.).

Brunnert, H.S. and Hagelstrom, V.V. Present Day Political
Organization in China. Taipei: Wen-hsing shu-chü, 1963
(rpt. of 1911 ed.).

Busch, Heinrich. "The Tung-lin Shu-yuan and Its Political
and Philosophical Significance." Monumenta Serica
14(1949-55)/1-163.

Bush, Susan. The Chinese Literati on Painting. Cambridge:
Harvard University Press, 1971.

Cahill, James. Fantastics and Eccentrics in Chinese
Painting. New York: Asia House, 1967.

_____ Hills Beyond a River. New York: Weatherhill,
1976.

_____ "The Early Styles of Kung Hsien." Oriental Art
(n.s.), 16:1 (Spring 1970)/51-71.

Cahill, James, ed. The Restless Landscape: Chinese Painting
of the Late Ming Period. Berkeley: University Art
Museum, 1971.

Chang Ch'ao, ed. Chao-tai ts'ung-shu: i-chi (A Collection
of Literature of Our Age: Second Series). Shih-k'ai-
t'ang, 1833 (rpt. of 1700 ed.).

Chang Ch'i-yun. K'ung-meng sheng-chi t'u-shuo (Photographs
of Sites Connected with Confucius and Mencius).
Taipei: Chung-hua wen-hua ch'u-pan shih-yeh-she, 1960.

Chang Ching. Ming-ch'ing ch'uan-ch'i tao-lun (An
Introduction to the Southern Drama of the Ming and
Ch'ing Dynasties). Taipei: Tung-fang shu-tien, 1961.

Chang Chung-yuan. Creativity and Taoism. New York: Harper
& Row, 1963.

Chang Keng. Kuo-ch'ao hua-cheng-lu (Biographies of Ch'ing
Painters). Ts'ui-wen shu-chü, 1739 (preface).

Chang Tai. T'ao-an meng-i (Dreamlike Memories from the
Studio of Relaxation). Taipei: K'ai-ming shu-tien,
1957 rpt.

Chang Wei-ping, ed. Kuo-ch'ao shih-jen cheng-lueh (Biographies of Ch'ing Poets). Taipei: Ting-wen shu-chu, 1971 rpt.

Chang Yin-lin. "Shuang-hu-lei ying-pen-pa (Comments on Photographs of the 'Two Thunderclaps')." Shih-hsueh yü ti-hsueh 2 (July 1927)1-2.

Chao Chih-pi, P'ing-shan-t'ang t'u-chih (An Illustrated Guide to Famous Sights on the Way to the Hall Level with the Peaks). Taipei: Wen-hai ch'u-pan-she n.d. rpt. of 1789 ed.

Chao I. Ou-pei shih-hua (Chao I's Essays on Poetry). Peking: Jen-min wen-hsueh ch'u-pan-she, 1963 rpt.

Chao Li-sheng. "Lun k'ung shang-jen ai-kuo-chu-i te she-hui ken-yuan (On the Social Basis of K'unag Shang-jen's Patriotic Thought)." In Ch'en, et al., Ku-tien hsi-ch'ü/142-56.

Chao-ming t'ai-tzu (Hsiao-t'ung), ed. Wen-hsuan (Literary Anthology). Taipei: Wen-hua t'u-shu-kung-ssu, 1964 rpt.

Chaves, Jonathan. "Some Relationships between Poetry and Painting in China." In J. Watt, ed. The Translation of Art. Hong Kong: Chinese University, 1976. 85-91.

Ch'en An-na. T'ao-hua-shan ch'uan-ch'i chih yen-chiu (Research on The Peach Blossom Fan). In Ch'ü-hsueh chi-k'an. Taiwan: Dept. of Chinese Literature, Taiwan Provincial Normal University, 1964.

Ch'en Chih-hsien. "Kuan-yü t'ao-hua-shan te i-hsieh wen-t'i (On Some Problems in The Peach Blossom Fan)." In Yuan-ming-ch'ing er-chi/320-31.

Ch'en Chih-hsien et al. Ku-tien hsi-ch'ü yen-chiu lun-chi (Essays on Traditional Chinese Drama). Hong Kong: Hung-chih shu-tien rpt., n.d.

Ch'en Hao. Ch'ueh-li-chih (Gazetteer of Ch'ü-fu). 1585 (rpt. of 1505 ed.).

Ch'en Huan-ho, ed. Yang-chou ts'ung-k'o (Anthology of Works on Yangchow). Yangchow, 1934 ed.

Ch'en Ju-heng. Shuo-shu shih-hua (A History of Oral Narrative). Peking: Tso-chia ch'u-pan-she, 1958.

Ch'en Ju-heng and Yang T'ing-fu. Ta-shuo-shu-chia liu ching-t'ing (The Great Storyteller Liu Ching-t'ing). Shanghai: Ssu-lien ch'u-pan-she, 1954.

Ch'en Shih-k'o, ed. K'ung-tzu chia-yü shu-cheng (Anecdotes About Confucius with Commentary). Shanghai: Shang-wu yin-shu-kuan, 1939.

Ch'en-shu (Ch'en History). Yao Ssu-lien ed. Peking: Chung-hua shu-chü, 1974 ed.

Ch'en Wan-nai. Hung pai-hsi hsien-shang nien-p'u (A Chronology of Hung Sheng). Taipei: Wen-shih-che ch'u-pan-she, 1971.

_____ K'ung shang-jen yen-chiu (Research on K'ung Shang-jen). Taipei: Shang-wu yin-shu-kuan, 1971.

_____ K'ung tung-t'ang hsien-sheng nien-p'u (A Chronology of K'ung Shang-jen). Taipei: Shang-wu yin-shu-kuan, 1973.

_____ "Lun k'ung shang-jen 'yin-shih pa-kuan' i-an (On K'ung Shang-jen's 'Retirement from Office')." Ku-kung-wen-hsien 1:2 (March 1970)/35-41.

_____ Yuan-ming-ch'ing hsi-ch'ü-shih (A History of Drama During the Yuan, Ming and Ch'ing Periods). Taipei: Shang-wu yin-shu-kuan, 1966.

Ch'en Wen-shu. Chin-ling li-tai ming-sheng-chih (A Record of Famous Historical Sights in Nanking). Nanking: Han-wen shu-chü, 1933.

Cheng Chang-yun. Yang-ch'eng hsun-nan hsu-lu (Additional Biographies of Yangchow Martyrs). In Ch'en, Yang-chou/693-740.

Cheng Chao-ching. Chung-kuo shui-li-shih (A History of River Control in China). Changsha: Shang-wu yin-shu-kuan, 1939.

Cheng Ch'iao. T'ung-chih (A Comprehensive Record). Shanghai: Shang-wu yin-shu-kuan, 1930 ed.

Cheng Cho-lu. Shih-t'ao yen-chiu (Research on Shih-t'ao). Peking: Jen-min mei-shu ch'u-pan-she, 1961.

Chi Yun, ed. Ho-yin ssu-k'u ch'üan-shu tsung-mu t'i-yao chi ssu-k'u wei-shou shu-mu chin-hui shu-mu (Combined Reprint of the Catalog of the Four Treasureis, Catalog of Works Not Included in the Four Treasuries and Catalog of Forbidden Books). Taipei: Shang-wu yin-shu-kuan, 1971 rpt.

Chia K'ai-tsung. "Pen-chuan (Biography of Hou Fang-yü). In Hou, Chuang-hui-t'ang/1a-2b.

Chiang-tu hsu-hsien-chih (Supplement to the Chiang-tu District Gazettee). Taipei: Ch'eng-wen shu-chü, 1960 (rpt. of 1883 ed.).

Chiao Hsun. Chü-shuo (Remarks on Drama). In Chung-kuo ku-tien hsi-ch'ü 7/73-220.

_____ Han-chi (A History of Ancient Yangchow). In Ch'en, ed. Yang-chou 3, 4.

Ch'iao Meng-fu. Yang-chou-meng (A Yangchow Dream). In Ts'ang Chin-shu, ed., Yuan-ch'ü-hsuan (An Anthology of Yuan Drama).

Ch'ien Ch'ien-i. Mu-chai yu-hsueh-chi (Succeeding Accomplishments).

Ch'ien I. Nan-pu hsin-shu (New Accounts from Southern Regions). TSCC ed.

Ch'ien I-chi. Pei-chuan-chi (Collected Biographies). Kiangsi shu-chü ed., n.d.

Chien Su-tzu. Tung-hsien-chuan (Biographies of Taoist Immortals). In Yen I-p'ing, ed., Tao-chiao yen-chiu

tzu-liao ti-i-ch'i (Research Materials in Taoism: 1).
Taipei: I-wen yin-shu-kuan, 1974, 1-52.

Chin Chih. Chin-hsiang-shuo (Pocket-sized Reminiscences).
In Kuo-hsueh hui-k'o (Collectanea of Sinological
Works)/3525-72. Taipei: Li-hsing shu-chü, 1964 rpt.

Ch'ing-shih-kao (Draft History of the Ch'ing Dynasty).
Chao Er-hsun et al., eds. Hong Kong: Hsiang-kang wen-
hsueh yen-chiu-she rpt. of 1928 ed.

Ch'ing-shih lieh-chuan (Biographies from the Ch'ing
History). Taipei: Chung-hua shu-chü, 1962 rpt.

Chiu-t'ang-shu (Old T'ang History). Liu Hsu, ed. Peking:
Chung-hua shu-chü, 1975 ed.

Chou I-pai. Chung-kuo hsi-ch'ü-shih (A History of Chinese
Drama). Peking: Chung-hua shu-chü, 1953.

_____ Chung-kuo hsi-chü-shih chiang-tso (Lectures on
the History of Chinese Drama). Peking: Chinese Drama
Publishing Co., 1958.

Chou Jung. "Tsa-i ch'i-chuan liu ching-t'ing (Thoughts on
the Remarkable Story of Liu Ching-t'ing)." In Ssu-ming
ts'ung-shu I:3 (Collectanea of Mt. Ssu-ming). Taipei:
Chung-kuo wen-hua hsuan-yuan, 1966 rpt.

Chou Liang-kung. Tu-hua-lu (A Record of Paintings Seen)
(postscript 1673). TSCC ed.

Chu Hsieh. Chin-ling ku-chi ming-sheng ying-chi (A Photo
Album of Famous Historical Sights in Nanking).
Shanghai: Shang-wu yin-shu-kuan, 1936.

_____ Chin-ling ku-chi t'u-k'ao (Maps of Historical
Sights in Nanking). Shanghai: Shang-wu yin-shu-kuan,
1936.

Ch'üan-t'ang-shih (Complete Poems of the T'ang). Peking:
Chung-hua shu-chü, 1960 ed.

Chuan, T.K. "Wei Chung-hsien." T'ien Hsia Monthly 3:4
(1936)/330-40.

Ch'ueh-li kuang-chih (A Gazetteer of Ch'ü-fu). 1870 (rpt. of 1673 ed.).

Ch'ung-k'an chiang-ning fu-chih (Reedition of the Chiang-ning Gazetteer). 1880 (rpt. of 1811 ed.).

Chung-kuo ku-tien hsi-ch'ü lun-chu chi-ch'eng: 1-10 (A Collection of Treatises on Traditional Chinese Drama). Chung-kuo hsi-ch'ü yen-chiu-yuan, ed. Peking: Chung-kuo hsi-ch'ü ch'u-pan-she, 1959-60.

Chung-kuo ming-hua-chia ts'ung-shu (Famous Painters in Chinese History). Hong Kong: T'ai-p'ing t'u-shu kung-ssu, 1970.

Collingwood, R.G. The Idea of History. London: Oxford University Press, 1946.

Crawford, Robert. "The Biography of Juan Ta-ch'eng." Chinese Culture 6:2 (March 1965)/28-105.

_____ "Chang Chu-cheng's Legalist Thought." In De Bary, ed., Self and Society/367-414.

Crawford, Robert et al. "Fang Hsiao-ju in the Light of Early Ming Society." Monumenta Serica 14:2 (1956)/303-27.

Creel, H.G. Confucius and the Chinese Way. New York: Harper and Row, 1960.

De Bary, W.T. "Individualism and Humanitarianism in Late Ming Thought." In De Bary, ed., Self and Society/145-247.

De Bary, W.T., ed. Self and Society in Ming Thought. New York: Columbia University Press, 1970.

_____ The Unfolding of Neo-Confucianism. New York: Columbia University Press, 1975.

Dolby, William. A History of Chinese Drama. London: Paul Elek, 1976.

Dubs, Homer. "Did Confucius Study the Book of Changes?" T'oung Pao 22 (1928)/82-90.

Fan Ning. "T'ao-hua-shan tso-che K'ung Shang-jen (K'ung Shang-jen, the author of The Peach Blossom Fan)." In Yuan-ming-ch'ing er-chi/381-87.

Fang Pao. "Pai-yun hsien-sheng-chuan (Biography of Mr. White Clouds)." In Wang-ch'i hsien-sheng ch'üan-chi (Collected Works of Fang Pao). SPTK ed. 8/2a-b.

Fong Wen. "The Orthodox Master." Art News Annual 33 (1967)/33-39.

_____ "Tung Ch'i-ch'ang and the Orthodox Theory of Painting." National Palace Museum Quarterly 2:3 (1968)/1-26.

Frankel, H. "Poetry and Painting: Chinese and Western Views of Their Convertibility." Comparative Literature, 9:4 (1957)/289-307.

_____ "The Plum Tree in Chinese Poetry." Asiatische Studien 6 (1952)/88-115.

Frye, Northrop. Anatomy of Criticism. New York: Atheneum, 1969.

_____ A Natural Perspective: The Development of Shakespearan Comedy and Romance. New York: Harcourt, Brace and World, 1965.

Fu, Marilyn and Shen. Studies in Connoisseurship. Princeton: The Art Museum, 1973.

Fu Pao-shih. Ming-mo min-tsu i-jen-chuan (Biographies of Ming Loyalist Painters). Hong Kong: Li-wen ch'u-pan-she, 1971 rpt.

_____ Shih-t'ao shang-jen nien-p'u (A Chronology of shih-t'ao. Hong Kong: Lung-men, 1970 rpt.

Fung Yu-lan. A Short History of Chinese Philosophy. Derk Bodde, trans. New York: Free Press, 1966 rpt.

Giles, Lionel. Strange Stories from a Chinese Studio. Taipei: 1967 (rpt. of 1908 ed.).

Goodrich, L. Carrington and Fang, Chaoying, eds. *Dictionary of Ming Biography*. New York: Columbia University Press, 1976.

Han-shu (History of the Former Han Dynasty). Pan Ku, ed. Peking: Chung-hua shu-chü, 1962 ed.

Hashimoto Jun. *Ō Gyoyō*. Tokyo: Kanshi taikei 23, 1966.

Hegel, Robert E. *The Novel in Seventeenth Century China*. New York, N.Y.: Columbia University Press, 1981.

Hightower, James R. *The Poetry of T'ao Ch'ien*. Oxford: Oxford University Press, 1970.

Ho Ping-ti. "The Salt Merchants of Yang-chou: A Study of Commercial Capitalism in Eighteenth Century China." *HJAS* 17 (1954)/130-68.

Ho Wai-kam. "Tung Ch'i-ch'ang's New Orthodoxy and the Southern School Theory." In C. Murk, ed., *Artists and Traditions*. Princeton: Princeton University Press, 1976. 113-29.

Holzman, D. *La Vie et La Pensée de Hi K'ang*. Leiden: Brill, 1957.

_____ *Poetry and Politics: The Life and Works of Juan Chi*. Cambridge: Cambridge University Press, 1976.

Hou Fang-yü. *Chuang-hui-t'ang-chi* (Collected Works from the Hall of Heroic Regrets). SPTK ed.

_____ *Ssu-i-t'ang chi* (Collected Works from the Hall of Four Contemplations). SPPY ed.

Hou-han-shu (History of the Latter Han Dynasty). Fan Hua, ed. Peking: Chung-hua shu-chü, 1962 ed.

Hou Wai-lu, ed. *Chung-kuo ssu-hsiang t'ung-shih* (A Comprehensive History of Chinese Thought). Peking: Jen-min ch'u-pan-she, 1957.

Hsia, C.T "Society and Self in the Chinese Short Story." In Hsia, *The Classic Chinese Novel*. New York: Columbia University Press, 1968. 299-321.

_____ "Time and the Human Condition in the Plays of T'ang Hsien-tsu." In De Bary, ed., Self and Society/249-90.

Hsieh Kuo-chen. Ch'ing-ch'u nung-min ch'i-i tzu-liao ch'i-lu (Source Materials on Peasant Rebellions in the Early Ch'ing). Shanghai: Jen-min ch'u-pan-she, 1957.

_____ Ming-ch'ing chih-chi tang-she yun-tung k'ao (Research into Political Activism in the Ming-Ch'ing Period). Taipei: Shang-wu yin-shu-kuan, 1968 rtp.

Hsin-ch'ü-yuan (A New Garden of Drama Treatises). Jen Chung-min, ed. Taipei: Chung-hua shu-chü, 1967.

Hsin-t'ang-shu (New T'ang History). Ou-yang Hsiu and Sung Ch'i, eds. Peking: Chung-hua shu-chu, 1975 ed.

Hsu Nai. Hsiao-t'ien chi-nien (A Chronology of Years that Were Lean). Taipei: T'ai-wan yin-hang, 1962 rpt.

Hsu Shih-ch'ang. Ta-ch'ing chi-fu hsien-che-chuan (Biographies of Eminent Ch'ing Officials in the Capital). Tientsin: Hsu Clan, 1917 ed.

Hsu Wei. Nan-tz'u hsu-lu (Discussions on Southern Drama). In Chung-kuo ku-tien hsi-ch'ü 3.

Hu Chieh-chih. "Hou ch'ao-tsung kung-tzu-chuan (Biography of Hou Fang-yü)." In Hou, Chuang-hui-t'ang/1a-3a.

Hu Hsiang-han. Chin-ling sheng-chi chih (A Record of Famous Sights in Nanking). Shanghai: Hu ed, 1926.

Hu Shih. "The Establishment of Confucianism as a State Religion," Journal of the North China Branch of the Royal Asiatic Society, 60 (1929)/20-41.

Huang Lan-p'o. Shih-t'ao hua-yü-lu i-chieh (Commentary and Colloquial Translation of Shih-t'ao's Hua-yü-lu). Peking: Ch'ao-hua mei-shu ch'u-pan-she, 1963.

Huang Pin-hung and Teng Shih, eds. Mei-shu ts'ung-shu (Anthology of Treatises on Art). Shanghai: Shen-chou kuo-kuang-she, 1947 rpt.

Huang Wen-yang. Ch'ü-hai tsung-mu t'i-yao (Plot Summaries of Dramas). Hong Kong: The Sinological Suppliers, 1967 rpt.

Huang-fu Mi. Ti-wang shih-chi (A Record of the Early Emperors). Shanghai: Shang-wu yin-shu-kuan, 1936 ed.

Hucker, Charles. "The Tung-lin Movement of the Late Ming Period." In J. Fairbank, ed., Chinese Thought and Institutions. Chicago: University of Chicago Press, 1957. 132-62.

Hui Tung, ed. Yü-yang shan-jen ching-hua-lu hsun-tsuan (Commentaries on Selected Poems by Wang Shih-chen). SPPY ed.

Hummel, Arthur. Eminent Chinese of the Ch'ing Period. Washington: U.S. Library of Congress, 1943.

Hung Huang. Ming Drama. Taipei: Heritage Press, 1966.

Hung Shih-liang. Liu ching-t'ing p'ing-chuan (A Critical Biography of Liu Ching-t'ing). Shanghai: Ku-tien wen-hsueh ch'u-pan-she, 1956.

Ishikawa Jun et al., eds. Bunjinga suihen 1: Ō I (Selected Works of Literati Painters, Vol. 1: Wang Wei). Tokyo: Chūō kōronsha, 1975.

Iwaki Hideo. "Kaisetsu (Comments)." In Tanaka, ed., Gikyoku-shū 2/525-55.

Jung Chao-tsu. "K'ung shang-jen nien-p'u (A Chronology of K'ung Shang-jen)." Ling-nan hsueh-pao 3:2 (1934)/1-86.

Kalvodovna, Dana. "On the Chinese Ch'uan-ch'i Drama," Acta Universitatis Carolinae Philosophica et Historica 5 (1969)/57-71.

Kao Che. "Shih-t'an tao-hua-shan ch'ing-chieh te t'i-lien (On the Development of the Plot in The Peach Blossom Fan)." In Wen-hsueh i-ch'an ts'eng-k'an No. 12. Peking: Chung-hua shu-chü, 1963. 78-89.

Kao Ch'i. Hsin-ch'uan-ch'i-p'in (A New Evaluation of Southern Drama). In Chung-kuo hsi-ch'ü lun-chu 6/265-76.

Keng Hsiang-yuan. K'ung shang-jen t'ao-hua-shan k'ao-hsu (Research into K'ung Shang-jen and The Peach Blossom Fan). Graduate thesis, Taipei: National Cheng-chih University, 1971.

Ku Ch'i-yuan. K'o-tso ch'ü-yü (Drama Criticism by a Spectator). In Hsin-ch'ü-yuan/160-87.

Ku-tien hsi-ch'ü sheng-yueh lun-chu chi-ch'eng (A Collection of Treatises on the Music of Traditional Drama). Taipei: Hsueh-hai ch'u-pan-she, 1971.

Kuei Fu. "Hsiao-hu-lei-chi (On 'Little Thunderclap')." In K'ung, Hsiao-hu-lei/91a-92a.

K'ung Chi. Sheng-men li-chih (Ceremonial Rituals of the Confucian Shrine). Ch'ü-fu: Yen-k'an-t'ang, 1893 rpt.

K'ung Chi-fen. Ch'ueh-li wen-hsien-k'ao (Anthology of Documents on Ch'ü-fu). Taipei: Chung-ting wen-hua ch'u-pan kung-ssu, 1967 (rpt. of 1762 ed.).

K'ung Fu. K'ung-ts'ung-tzu (Confucius and His Disciples). SPPY ed.

K'ung Shang-jen. Hsiang-chin-pu (A Catalogue of My Art Collecting Pleasures). In Huang, Mei-shu ts'ung-shu, 1st series 7:2:8.

_____ Hsiao-hu-lei ("Little Thunderclap"). Nuan-hung-shih 1913 ed.

_____ Hu-hai-chi (Collected Works from the Lakes and Seas). In K'ung Shang-jen-chi (Collected Works of K'ung Shang-jen) Taipei: Shih-chieh shu-chü ed., 1964 rpt.

_____ K'ung-tzu shih-chia-p'u (Genealogy of the K'ung Clan). Taipei: Kuo-li chung-yang t'u-shu-kuan, 1969 (rpt. of 1684 ed.).

_____ K'ung Shang-jen shih-wen-chi (Collected Works of K'ung Shang-jen). Wang Wei-lin ed. Peking: Chung-hua shu-chü, 1962.

_____ Ta-hu-lei (Great Thunderclap). Nuan-hung-shih, 1913 ed.

_____ T'ao-hua-shan (The Peach Blossom Fan). K'ang-hsi, ed.

_____ T'ao-hua-shan (The Peach Blossom Fan). Wang Chi-ssu and Su Huan-chung, eds. Peking: Jen-min wen-hsueh ch'u-pan-she, 1959.

_____ T'ao-hua-shan-chu (The Annotated Peach Blossom Fan). Liang Ch'i-ch'ao ed. Taipei: Chung-hua shu-chü, 1955 rpt.

_____ The Blood-stained Fan (Scenes 10,11). H.C. Chang, trans. In H.C. Chang, trans., Chinese Literature: Popular Fiction and Drama. Edinburgh: Edinburgh University Press, 1973.

_____ The Peach Blossom Fan (T'ao-hua-shan). Chen Shih-hsiang, Harold Acton, Cyril Birch, trans. Berkeley: University of California Press, 1976.

_____ The Peach Blossom Fan: Scene 4." Richard Strassberg, trans. Renditions 8 (1977)/115-22.

_____ Tōkasen (The Peach Blossom Fan). Iwaki Hideo, trans. In Tanaka, ed., Gikyoku shū/284-524.

_____ Tōkasen (The Peach Blossom Fan). Kon Tōkō, trans. In Shina bungaku taikan: 4, 5 (Chinese Literature Series). Tokyo: Shina bungaku taikan kankō-kai, 1926.

_____ Tōkasen (The Peach Blossom Fan). Shiotani On, trans. In Kokuyaku kanbun taisei. Tokyo: Kokumin bunko kankōkai, 1921-22.

_____ Tōkasen (The Peach Blossom Fan). Yamaguchi Tsuyoshi, trans. Tokyo: Shunyōdō, 1926.

K'ung Yuan-ts'o. K'ung-shih tsu-t'ing kuang-chi (Gazetteer of the Ancestral Home of the K'ung Clan). Taipei: Shang-wu yin-shu-kuan, 1966 (rpt. of Mongolia, 1207 ed.).

Kuo Mao-ch'ien. Yueh-fu shih-chi (Anthology of Yueh-fu Poems). SPPY ed.

Kuo Shao-yü. Chung-kuo wen-hsueh p'i-p'ing-shih (A History of Chinese Literary Criticism). Taipei: Shang-wu yin-shu-kuan, 1970 rpt.

Legge, James. The Chinese Classics 5: The Ch'un Ts'ew with the Tso Chuen. Taipei: Wen-hsing shu-tien, 1966 rpt.

Li Chi. The Travel Diaries of Hsu Hsia-k'o. Hong Kong: The Chinese University of Hong Kong, 1974.

Li Ching-yeh. Ch'ü-fu hsien-chih (Gazetteer of Ch'ü-fu). Taipei: Ch'eng-wen ch'u-pan-she, 1967 (rpt. of 1935 ed.).

Li Chu-tsing. A Thousand Peaks and Myriad Ravines: Chinese Paintings in the Charles A. Drenowatz Collection. Anscona: Artibus Asiae, 1974.

Li Huan. Kuo-ch'ao ch'i-hsien lei-cheng: ch'u-pien (Biographies of Ch'ing Statesmen: First Series). Taipei: Wen-hai ch'u-pan-she, 1965 (rpt. of 1890 ed.).

Li-shih-chü lun-chi (Essays on Historical Drama). Hsi-chü-pao pien-chi wei-yuan-hui, ed. Shanghai: Shanghai wen-i ch'u-pan-she, 1962.

Li Tao-yuan. Shui-ching-chu (Water Classic). Peking: K'o-hsueh-yuan, 1955 ed.

Li T'iao-yuan. Yü-ts'un ch'ü-hua (Li T'iao-yuan's Remarks on Drama). In Hsin-ch'ü-yuan/343-66.

Li Tou. Yang-chou hua-fang-lu (The Painted Boats of Yangchow) (Preface, 1796). Taipei: Shih-chieh shu-chü, 1963 rpt.

Li Yü Hsien-ch'ing ou-chi (Random Thoughts from My Leisure Moments . In Chung-kuo ku-tien hsi-ch'ü 10/1-115.

Liang Chang-chü. Lang-chi ts'ung-t'an (A Compendium of My Notes). In Ch'ing-tai hsiao-shuo pi-chi-hsuan i-chi (Selected Random Notes of the Ch'ing Period: Second Series). Chiang Yu-ching, ed. Taipei: Shang-wu yin-shu-kuan, 1972.

Liang Ch'i-ch'ao. Intellectual Trends of the Ch'ing Period (Ch'ing-tai hsueh-shu kai-lun). Immanuel C.Y. Hsu, trans. Cambridge: Harvard University Press, 1970.

Liang T'ing-nan. Ch'ü-hua (Remarks on Drama). In Hsin-ch'ü-yuan/342-66.

Lippe, Aschwin. "Kung Hsien and the Nanking School: I." Oriental Art (n.s.) 2:1 (Spring 1956)/21-29; "Pt. II," ibid. 4:4 (Winter 1958)/159-70.

Liu Chieh-p'ing. Ch'ing-ch'u ku-tz'u li-ch'ü-hsuan (Selected Ballads and Popular Songs of the Early Ch'ing Period). Taipei: Cheng-chung shu-chü, 1968.

_____ Mu-p'i san-k'o ku-tz'u (Ballads by "The 'Wood-and-Leather' Wanderer"). Taipei: Cheng-chung shu-chü, 1954.

Liu Hsieh. The Literary Mind and the Carving of Dragons (Wen-hsin tiao-lung). Vincent Shih, trans. Taipei: Chung-hua shu-chü, 1969.

_____ Wen-hsin tiao-lung (The Literary Mind and the Carving of Dragons). Taipei: K'ai-ming shu-chü, 1969 rpt.

Liu I-ch'ing. Shih-shuo hsin-yü (New Anecdotes of Social Talk). Peking: Chung-hua shu-chü, 1962 ed.

Liu, James J.Y. The Art of Chinese Poetry. Chicago: University of Chicago Press, 1975.

Liu Shih-heng. Shuang-hu-lei pen-shih (All About the Two Thunderclaps). In Chang Yen, Sun Hsieh-ting, Lung Yun-chai, Wang Chieh-ch'en, eds., Chü-ch'ing ts'ung-shu (Compendium of Assembled Rooms) 1919 ed.

Liu T'ieh-yun.   Lao-ts'an yu-chi (The Travels of Lao
    Ts'an).   Shih-chieh shu-chü, 1976 ed.

_____   The Travels of Lao Ts'an.   Harold Shadick,
    trans. Ithaca: Cornell University Press, 1952.

Lo Kuan-chung.   San-kuo yen-i (Romance of the Three
    Kingdoms). Hong Kong: Chung-hua shu-chü, 1973 ed.

Lu Ch'ien.   Ming-ch'ing hsi-ch'ü-shih (A History of Ming-
    ch'ing Drama). Hong Kong: Shang-wu yin-shu-kuan, 1961.

Lü T'ien-ch'eng.   Ch'ü-lu (Rules of Drama).   In Chung-kuo
    hsi-ch'ü lun-chu 6/201-65.

Lynn, Richard J.   "Orthodoxy and Enlightenment: Wang Shih-
    chen's Theory of Poetry."   In De Bary, ed., The
    Unfolding of Neo-Confucianism/217-69.

_____   Wang Shih-chen As a Poet and Critic.   Ph.D.
    dissertation, Stanford, 1970.

Ma Yung.   "K'ung shang-jen chi-ch'i tao-hua-shan (K'ung
    Shang-jen and his Peach Blossom Fan)."   In Ch'en, Ku-
    tien hsi-ch'ü/127-41.

Mackerras, Colin.   The Rise of the Peking Opera.   Oxford:
    Clarendon Press, 1972.

Mao Chin.   Liu-shih-chung-ch'ü (Sixty Plays).   Taipei:
    K'ai-ming shu-chü, 1960 rpt.

Mao, Lucien, trans.   "A Memoir of Ten Days' Massacre at
    Yangchow." T'ien Hsia 4:5 (May 1937)/515-37.

Meng Yao (Yang Tsung-chen).   Chung-kuo hsi-ch'ü-shih (A
    History of Chinese Drama).   Taipei: Wen-hsing shu-tien,
    1965.

Miao Yueh.   Tu mu-chuan (A Biography of Tu Mu).   Peking:
    Jen-min wen-hsueh ch'u-pan-she, 1977.

Min Er-ch'ang.   Pei-chuan chi-pu (Addendum to the Collected
    Biographies).   In Chin-tai chung-kuo shih-liao ts'ung-
    k'an (Collectanea of Modern Chinese History Materials).
    Shen Yun-lung ed. Taipei: Wen-hai ch'u-pan-she, 1973
    rpt.

Ming-shih (Ming History). Chang T'ing-yu et al., eds.
Peking: Chung-hua shu-chu, 1974 ed.

Mote, F. "The Transformation of Nanking." In G. Skinner,
ed., The City in Late Imperial China. Stanford:
Stanford University Press, 1977. 100-53.

Nagel's China. Geneva: Nagel Publishers, 1974.

Needham, Joseph. Science and Civilization in China: 4.
Cambridge: Cambridge University Press, 1971.

Ni Hsi-ying. Ch'ü-fu t'ai-shan yu-chi (A Travelogue of
Ch'ü-fu and Mt. T'ai). Shanghai: Chung-hua shu-chü,
1931.

Nienhauser, Wm., et al. Liu Tsung-yuan. New York: Twayne
Publishers, 1973.

Ōbayashi Shōgen, ed. Togyūzo kunchū (The Ten Ox
Illustrations with Commentary). Kyoto: Kichūdō, 1966.

P'an Hsiang. Ch'ü-fu hsien-chih (A Gazetteer of Ch'ü-fu).
Taipei: Hsueh-sheng shu-chü, 1968 (rpt. of 1774 ed.).

Pan Tze-yen, trans. Reminiscenses of the Studio of Shadowy
Plum-blossoms (Ying-mei-an i-yü). Shanghai, 1931.

Peterson, Willard. Bitter Gourd: The Life and Thought of
Fang I-chih. New Haven: Yale University Press, 1978.

P'u Sung-ling. Liao-chai chih-i (Strange Stories from a
Chinese Studio). Shanghai: Chung-hua shu-chü, 1962 ed.

Shan-tung t'ung-chih (Gazetteer of Shantung). Shanghai:
Shang-wu yin-shu-kuan, 1934 (rpt. of 1915 ed.).

Shen Te-ch'ien, ed. Ch'ing-shih pieh-ts'ai-chi (Selected
Poems of the Ch'ing Period). Peking: Chung-hua shu-
chü, 1975 rpt.

Shen Te-ch'ien and Chou Chün, eds. Ming-shih pieh-ts'ai
(Selected Poems of the Ming Period). (Preface 1738.)
Shanghai: Shang-wu yin-shu-kuan, 1934 rpt.

Shih-chi (Historical Records). Ssu-ma Ch'ien, ed. Peking:
Chung-hua shu-chü, 1975 ed.

Shih-san-ching chu-shu (The Thirteen Classics: Texts and Commentaries). Taipei: I-wen yin-shu-kuan, 1965 (rpt. of 1815 ed.).

Shih Shu-i. Ch'ing-tai kuei-ko shih-jen cheng-lueh (Biographies of Women Poets during the Ch'ing). Taipei: Ting-wen shu-chü, 1971 rpt.

Sirén, Osvald. Chinese Painting, Vo. 5: The Later Ming and Leading Ch'ing Masters. London: Lund Humphries, 1958.

Spence, Jonathan. The Death of Woman Wang. Middlesex, England: Penguin Press, 1979.

_____ Emperor of China. New York: Knopf, 1974.

_____ Ts'ao Yin and the K'ang-hsi Emperor. New Haven: Yale University Press, 1966.

_____ and Wills, John, ed. From Ming to Ch'ing: Conquest, Region and Continuity in Seventeenth Century China. New Haven: Yale University Press, 1979.

Ssu-pu pei-yao (Reeditions of Important Works in the Four Libraries). Shanghai: Chung-hua shu-chü, 1927-36.

Ssu-pu ts'ung-k'an (Collected Reeditions of Works in the Four Libraries). Shanghai: Shang-wu yin-shu-kuan, 1929-36.

Strassberg, Richard. "The Authentic Self in 17th Century Drama," Tamkang Review 8:2 (October 1977)/61-100.

_____ "K'ung Shang-jen and the K'ang-hsi Emperor," Ch'ing-shih wen-t'i 3:9 (November 1978)/31-75.

_____ "The Singing Techniques of K'un-ch'ü and Their Musical Notation," Chinoperl Papers 6 (1976)/45-81.

Struve, Lynn. "History and The Peach Blossom Fan." Chinese Literature: Essays, Articles, Reviews Vol. 2, No. 1 (January 1980)/55-72.

_____ "The Peach Blossom Fan as Historical Drama." Renditions 8 (Autumn 1977)/99-114.

<u>Ta-ch'ing sheng-tsu jen-(k'ang-hsi)-huang-ti shih-lu</u> 3 (<u>Veritable Records of the K'ang-hsi Emperor</u> 3). Taiwan: Hua-wen shu-chu, 1963 rpt.

Tai Ming-shih. <u>Yang-chou shou-ch'eng chi-lueh</u> (<u>The Defense of Yangchow</u>). In Ch'en, <u>Yang-chou</u>/453-77.

<u>T'ai-p'ing yü-lan</u> (<u>The T'ai-p'ing Encyclopedia</u>). Li Fang, ed. Peking: Chung-hua shu-chü, 1960 ed.

Tanaka Kenji, ed. <u>Gikyoku-shū</u> (<u>Anthology of Chinese Drama</u>). Tokyo: Heibonsha, 1971.

T'ieh Pao, ed. <u>Pa-ch'i t'ung-chih</u> (<u>Biographies of Manchus in the Eight Banners</u>). Taipei: Hsueh-sheng shu-chü, 1968 (rpt. of 1799 ed.).

T'ien Lan-fang. "<u>Hou ch'ao-tsung hsien-sheng-chuan</u> (Biography of Hou Fang-yü)." In Hou, <u>Chuang-hui-t'ang</u>/1a-2b.

Ting Chung-hu, ed. <u>T'ao yuan-ming-shih chien-chu</u> (<u>Commentary Edition of the Poems of T'ao Yuan-ming</u>). Taipei: I-wen yin-shu-kuan, 1974 rpt.

Trevor, M.H., trans. <u>The Ox and His Herdsman: A Chinese Zen Text</u>. Tokyo: Hokuseido Press, 1969.

Tsen Chung-mien. <u>Huang-ho pien-ch'ien-shih</u> (<u>A History of the Yellow River</u>). Peking: Jen-min wen-hsueh ch'u-pan-she, 1957.

Tseng Yung-i. "<u>T'ao-hua-shan 'ai-chiang-nan' ch'u-tz'u te tso-che wen-t'i</u> (On the Problem of the Authorship of the 'Lament for South' Aria in <u>The Peach Blossom Fan</u>)." <u>Hsien-tai hsueh-yuan</u> 106 (January 1973)/23-5.

Tsui Shu, <u>Shu-ssu k'ao-hsin-lu</u> (<u>Research on Confuciuss</u>). TSCC ed. <u>Ts'ung-shu chi-ch'eng</u> (<u>Compendium of Collectanea</u>). Shanghai: Shang-wu yin-shu-kuan, 1935.

Tuan An-chieh. <u>Yueh-fu tsa-lu</u> (<u>Miscellany of Music</u>). TSCC ed.

Tung Pi. "<u>Lun k'ung shang-jen te shih ho shih-lun kuan-tien</u> (On K'ung Shang-jen's Poetry and Poetic Theory)."

In Wen-hsueh i-ch'an ts'eng-k'an 12. Peking: Chung-hua shu-chü, 1963. 143-53.

Wakeman, Frederick. "The Price of Autonomy: Intellectuals in Ming and Ch'ing Politics." Daedalus 101 (Winter 1972)/35-70.

Waley, Arthur, trans. The Book of Songs (Shih-ching). New York: Grove Press, 1960.

_____ The Life and Times of Po Chü-i. London: Allen and Unwin, 1949.

Wang Chi-lieh. Yin-lu ch'ü-t'an (Chats on Drama from the Earthworm Hut). Shanghai: Shang-wu yin-shu-kuan, 1934.

Wang Fu-chih, et al. Ch'ing-shih-hua (Ch'ing Poetry Criticism). Shanghai: Chung-hua shu-chü, 1963.

Wang Hsiu-ch'u. Yang-chou shih-jih-chi (A Record of Ten Days of Slaughter at Yangchow). In Ch'en, Yang-chou 6.

Wang Huan-piao, Ming hsiao-ling-chih (A Guide to the Tomb of Ming T'ai-tsu). Nanking: Chung-shan shu-chü, 1934.

Wang I. "Yu li-shih jen-wu tao hsi-chü jen-wu ts'ung t'ao-hua-shan chung te yang lung-yu shuo-ch'i (From Historical Character to Dramatic Character: A Discussion of Yang Wen-ts'ung in The Peach Blossom Fan)." In Li-shih-chü/315-26.

Wang Kuo-wei. Hung-lou-meng p'ing-lun (A Critique of the Dream of the Red Chamber). In Hung-lou-meng yen-chiu tzu-liao hui-pien (Collection of Research Materials on the Dream of the Red Chamber). Taipei: Ming-lun ch'u-pan-she, 1971. 244-65.

Wang Shu-nu. Chung-kuo ch'ang-chi-shih (A History of Chinese Courtesans). Taipei: Huan-yü ch'u-pan-she, 1971.

Wang Tseng-fang, ed. Chi-nan fu-chih (A Gazetteer of Tsinan). Taipei: Hsueh-sheng shu-chü, 1968 (rpt. of 1840 ed.).

Wang Ying-k'uei. Liu-nan sui-pi (Random Notes of Liu-nan). In Pi-chi ts'ung-pien. Taipei: Kuang-wen Book Co., 1969.

Watson, Burton. The Old Man Who Does as He Pleases. New York: Columbia University Press, 1973.

_____ Records of the Historian. New York: Columbia University Press, 1969.

Watters, C. A Guide to the Tablets in a Temple of Confucius. Shanghai: American Presbyterian Mission Press, 1879.

Wen Jui-lin and Li Yao. Nan-chiang i-shih (A History of the South). Taipei: T'ai-wan yin-hang, 1963 rpt.

Whitfield, Roderick. In Pursuit of Antiquity. Princeton: The Art Museum, 1969.

Wilhelm, Helmut. The I Ching or Book of Changes. Princeton: Princeton University Press, 1967.

Wright, Arthur R. The Sui Dynasty. New York: Knopf, 1978.

_____ "Sui Yang-ti: Personality and Stereotype." In A.F. Wright, ed., The Confucian Persuasion. Stanford: Stanford University Press, 1960. 47-76.

Wu Ch'i. Yang-chou ku-ch'ui-tz'u-hsu (Prefaces to Songs on Scenic Spots in Yangchow). In Ch'en, ed., Yang-chou 5.

Wu Ching-tzu. Ju-lin wai-shih (The Scholars). Hong Kong: Chung-hua shu-chü, 1973 ed.

Wu Mei. Chung-kuo hsi-ch'ü kai-lun (A General Discussion of Chinese Drama). Hong Kong: T'ai-p'ing shu-chü, 1964 rpt.

_____ Ku-ch'ü ch'en-t'an (Worldly Chats on Drama). Taipei: Kuang-wen shu-chü, 1962 rpt.

_____ Shuang-ya ch'ü-pa (Wu Mei's Remarks on Drama). In Hsin-ch'ü yuan/631-702.

Wu, Nelson. "Tung Ch'i-ch'ang (1555-1636): Apathy in
Government and Fervor in Art." In A. Wright and D.
Twitchett, eds., Confucian Personalities. Stanford:
Stanford University Press, 1962. 260-93.

Wu Wei-yeh. Lu-ch'iao chi-wen (A Hermit's History).
Taipei: T'ai-wan yin-hang, 1961 rpt.

_____ Mei-ts'un chia-ts'un chia-ts'ang-kao (The
Collected Works of Wu Mei-ts'un). SPTK ed.

Wu, William. "Kung Hsien's Style and His Sketchbooks."
Oriental Art (n.s.) 16:1 (Spring 1970)/72-80.

Yao Hsieh. Chin-yueh k'ao-cheng (Records of Recent
Dramas). In Chung-kuo ku-tien hsi-ch'ü 10/1-321.

Ying Shao. Feng-su t'ung-i (Encyclopedia of Cultural
Matters). SPTK ed.

Yü Huai. Pan-chiao tsa-chi (Random Notes from the Planked
Bridge). TSCC ed.

Yuan Hung-tao. Yuan Chung-lang ch'üan-chi (The Complete
Works of Yuan Hung-tao). Taipei: Wei-wen t'u-shu ch'u-
pan-she, 1976 rpt.

Yuan-ming-ch'ing hsi-ch'ü yen-chiu lun-wen chi (Collected
Studies on the Drama of the Yuan, Ming and Ch'ing
Periods). Peking: Tso-chia ch'u-pan-she, 1957.

Yuan-ming-ch'ing hsi-ch'ü yen-chiu lun-wen er-chi
(Collected Studies on the Drama of the Yuan, Ming and
Ch'ing Periods: Second Series). Peking: Jen-min wen-
hsueh ch'u-pan-she, 1959.

Yuan Shu-ting. Ch'ü-fu yu-lan chih-nan (A Traveler's Guide
to Ch'ü-fu). Ch'ü-fu: Hui-wen-t'ang, n.d.

GLOSSARY-INDEX

Aoki Masaru 青木正兒 , 242

Autumn Maiden 秋娘 , 233

Ballads: by Chia Fu-hsi, 34-36, 39; by K'ung Shang-jen, 165-67; see also P'i-pa, "Pity the South"

Book of Changes, The 易經: 152; K'ung's lecture on, 76-77, 87-89; and Confucius, 326n139; hexagrams drawn by K'ung Shang-jen, 330n153, 331n156

Chang Ch'ao 張潮, 366n50

Chang Fei 張飛 , 263

Chang Hsien-chung 張獻忠 , 29, 190

Chang I 張怡 , 205-8, 251, 271-72, 396n152

Chang P'eng 張鵬 , 76, 336n9

Chang P'eng-ko 張鵬翮 , 81, 343n27

Chang Shih-chen 張士甄 , 116, 348n69

Chang Tai 張岱 : in Ch'ü-fu, 6-10; in Yangchow, 133, 196, 298n22

Chang-tsung 章宗 , 94

Chang Wei 張薇 , see Chang I

Chao Er 趙二 , 232

Chao Meng-fu 趙孟頫 , 170

Cha Shih-piao 查士標 , 170, 173-75, 381n89

Chen 眞 (authenticity), 146

Ch'en Chen-hui 陳眞慧 , 136, 137, 246, 247, 248, 251, 368n51

Cheng Chu 鄭注 , 232-34, 239

Ch'eng-i 誠 意 (making the will sincere), 42

Cheng Kuang-yeh 鄭光業 , 233-35, 238, 240

Cheng-se 正 色 (Principle Beauties), 270

Ch'eng-tsung 成 宗, 22

Cheng Ying-ying 鄭鶯鶯 , 226, 232, 234-35, 239, 241

Ch'en Hou-chu 陳後主 , 192, 392n136

Ch'en Hsiu 陳 秀, 162

Ch'en Tzu-ang 陳子昂 , 243-44

Ch'i 氣 (Power), 271

Ch'i 奇 (unique), 266, see also Ch'uan-ch'i

Chia Fu-hsi 賈鳧西 , 33-40, 313n100-4

Chia K'ai-tsung 賈開宗 , 258

Chiang Ching-ch'i 蔣景祁 , 224, 400n11

Ch'iao Chou 譙 周, 7, 299n23

Ch'iao Meng-fu 喬夢符 , 123

Chieh-shan 介 山, 80, 112, 340n20

Ch'ien Ch'ien-i 錢謙益 , 259

Chien-se 間 色 (Intermediaries), 271

Chien-wen 建 文 , 43

Chih-kuo 治 國 (ruling the nation), 236

Chin Chih 金 埴, 284, 417n97

Chin-fen 金 粉 (golden powder), 192

Chin Fu 新 輔 , 119-20, 208, 211, 214, 350n6,7

Ching-hsing 經 星 (Warp Star), 271

Ch'ing-i 清 逸 (pure ellusiveness), 381n89

Ching-pu 經 部 (Regulators), 271

Ching-ssu 敬 思 , 49, 50, 57, 324n132

Ch'in-huai 秦 淮 , see Nanking

Ch'in Kuang-i 秦光儀 , 33

Ch'in-shih 秦 氏 , 30, 112, 217, 312n91

Ch'in Shih-huang 秦始皇 , 14, 302n41

Ch'iu Shih-liang 仇士良 , 232-34, 238, 241, 242

Ch'i-yun sheng-tung 氣運生動 (kinesthetic representation of Nature's vital spirit), 168

Cho Er-k'an 卓爾堪 , 172, 380n88

Ch'ou 丑 (clown), 262

Chou Liang-kung 周亮工 , 176, 179, 384n100

Ch'ü 曲 , 228, 254

Ch'uan 傳 (transmitting), 266, see also Ch'uan-ch'i drama

Ch'uan-chi drama 傳 奇 , 225, 230, 252, 254, 266, 268

Ch'üan Te-yü 權德興 , 232-3, 238

Ch'ü Chiu-ssu 瞿九思 , 24, 312n84

Ch'ü-fu 曲 埠 : description of, 1-10; K'ang-hsi Emperor's
    visit to, 75-116; present state of, 291-4, 295, see
    also K'ung Clan

Chu Hsi 朱 熹 , 19, 28

Chu I-tsun 朱彝尊 , 217

Chü Jan 巨 然 , 168, 386n108

Ch'ung-chen 崇 禎 , 194, 195, 249, 251, 256, 271

Chung-ch'i 中 氣 (Central Powers), 271

Chung Yu 鍾 繇 , 172

Chun-yü Fen 淳于芬 , 162, 164

Ch'u Sui-liang 褚遂良 , 172

Ch'ü Ta-chün 屈大均 , 201, 282, 396n149

Confucian Grove 孔 林 :   description of, 6-7, 10, 14,
    297n11; K'ang-hsi's visit to, 102-8; present state of,
    291-2

Confucianism: early growth of, 1-16; "ancient texts", 17,
    99, 303n50; ritual, 23-7, 74, 326n140; K'ung Shang-
    jen's attitude towards, 40-3, 320n114; music theory,
    190-91, see also K'ung Clan, "Pragmatist" Movement

Confucian Shrine: origin of, 14; political and economic
    growth of, 17-21, see also Confucian Grove, Confucian
    Temple

Confucian Temple 孔 廟 :   description of, 5-6; steles
    located in, 5, 94-5, 302n43-51; ritual ceremonies at,
    23-7; K'ang-hsi's visit to, 79-101; present state of,
    292-3, 297n11

Confucius 孔 子 :　in Ch'ü-fu, 6-7, 10, 12-14, 99; statues and portraits of, 6, 13, 91-2, 344n33; attitude towards ritual, 23,99, 311n75-83; quotations from, 39-40, 327n145; in The Peach Blossom Fan, 273; biographies of, 301n36; and The Book of Changes, 326n139; and Tzu-lu, 332n159

Courtesan Quarters:　in Yangchow, 124-5, 132-3; in Nanking, 196; see also Li Hsiang-chün, Glistening Maiden, Nanking, Yangchow

Dodo 多 鐸 , 258

Drama, see Ch'uan-ch'i, K'un-ch'ü, K'ung Shang-jen, Historical Drama, "Little Thunderclap", Theatre, The Peach Blossom Fan

Duke of Chou 周 公 , 4, 102, 296n10, 347n55

Duke of the Sagely Posterity 衍聖公 :　history of, 21-3, 308n70-4, see also K'ung Te-ch'eng, K'ung Yü-ch'i

Duke Shang 殤 公 , 12

Empirical Studies Movement 考證學 :　K'ung Shang-jen's attitude toward, 42, 72, 235

Extraordinary Events Whereby I Came Down from the Mountain, The 出山異數記 , 74-116, 335n7

Fan Ch'i 樊 坼 , 176, 383n99

Fang Hsiao-ju 方孝儒 , 201, 444n148

Fang I-chih 方以智 , 136, 137, 368n51

Fang Pao 方 苞 , 206, 397n154

Fang Wen 方 文 , 177, 385n102

Fan Hua-po 樊花坡 , 227, 402n20,21

Fei Mi 費 密 , 190-1, 391n130

Feng-chih ta-fu 奉直大夫 (Great Officer with Direct Access to the Throne), 10, 313n98

Feng Meng-lung 馮夢龍 , 166

Feng-tiao 風 調 (personal tone), 372n61

Fiyanggū 費揚古 , 80, 342n24

Fo-lun 佛倫, 208, 398n155

Four Commanders 四鎮, 257, 263, 408n56

Fragrant Lady, see Li Hsiang-chün

Fu 賦, 155, 254

Fu-ch'ai 夫差, 123

Fu-mo 副末, 273

Fu-she 復社 (Restoration Society), 177, 194-95, 197-98, 246, 247, 248, 256, 259, 269, 273, 393n140

Gazetteer of P'ing-yang, A 平陽府志, 417n90

Genealogy of the K'ung Clan 孔子世家譜, 72-73, 235, 335n1

"Genius and Beauty" 才子佳人, 260, 264, 269, 270

Glistening Maiden 潤娘, 233-35, 238, 239-40

Great Learning, The 大學; K'ung Shang-jen's lecture on, 76-77, 81-83, 86

"Great Thunderclap" 大忽雷 : musical instrument, 226, 243, 404n44; drama by K'ung Shang-jen, 243-44

Han Kao-tsu 漢高祖, 15-16, 302n43, 303n46

Han Huang 韓晃, 226, 227, 232

Han Wei 韓魏, 162

Han Wu-ti 漢武帝, 16, 303n49, 328n148

Harmonizing Below the Palanquin 輦下和鳴集, 224-25

Historical drama: K'ung Shang-jen's dramas as, 235-36, 251-74; 403n35, 36, 406n54, 415n83

Ho 何, 12, 300n32

Ho Hsun 何遜, 155, 158, 376n72

Hortensia Temple 瓊花觀, 156, 159-60, 187-90, 390n124

Ho-se 合色 (Unifiers), 271

Ho-tzu-hui 盒子會 (hamper party), 261, 411n61

Hou Fang-yü 侯方域, 136, 137, 246-51, 256, 258, 259, 260, 261, 263, 265, 269, 270, 271, 366n51

Hsiang Yü 項羽, 15, 302n43

Hsia-pi 狹筆 (fine manner of painting), 173

Hsieh-i 寫意 (free-style of painting), 171

Hsing-ch'ing 性情 (natural   sensibility),   141,   144-47,
    373n66

Hsing-ling 性靈 (personal nature), see Hsing-ch'ing

Hsing-lu sheng-tien 幸魯盛典 (The Imperial Visit to Ch'u-
    fu), 321n116

Hsiu-shen 修身 (personal cultivation), 236

Hsu Hsia-k'o 徐霞客 , 48, 323n127

Hsu T'ing-hsi 徐廷璽 , 80, 211, 341n22

Hsu Wei 徐渭 , 39, 315n108

Huang Ch'ao Rebellion 黃巢亂 , 54, 327n143

Huang Kung-wang 黃公望 , 54, 172, 178, 326n142

Huang Te-kung 黃得功 , 271

Huang Yun 黃雲 , 137-38, 139, 215, 364n50

Hu-ch'in 胡琴 , 226

Hu-lei 忽雷 , 226-27

Hung-jen 弘仁 , 173, 175

Hung-kuang 宏光 , 192, 195, 249, 250, 251, 256-58, 259,
    268, 271, 277

Hung Sheng 洪昇 , 402n24

Imperial Academy 國子監 , 16, 20, 21, 43, 114, 115, 193,
    217

I-p'in 逸品 (untrammeled painting), 173

Isangga 伊桑阿 , 80, 119, 340n19

I-yang 弋陽 , 34, 131-32, 252, 360n39, 41

Juan Ta-ch'eng 阮大誠 ; 369n52; as dramatist, 132, 136,
    240, 411n62; as politician, 177, 194-95, 197-98; as
    character in The Peach Blossom Fan, 247-49, 251, 256-
    61, 263-65, 267-74

Jun-se 潤色 (Supplements), 271

K'ai-yin-pu 凱音布 , 211

K'ang-hsi 康熙 : visit to Ch'ü-fu, 75-116; river control
    policy, 119-21, 208-14; second Southern Tour, 210-14;
    attitude toward The Peach Blossom Fan, 277

Kan-lu Rebellion 甘露亂 , 226, 234, 241, 242

Kao Chieh 高 傑 , 258, 263-64, 411n63

Kao Shih-ch'i 高士奇 , 80, 100, 108, 342n23

Ko-wu 格 物 (investigation of things), 42

Ku Hsien-ch'eng 顧憲成 , 194

K'un-ch'ü 崑 曲 , 131-32, 197, 228, 245-46, 259, 357n30, 359n36, 37, 38, see also Theatre

K'ung An-kuo 孔安國 , 16, 297n16, 303n50

Kung-ch'e 工 尺 , 230, 246

K'ung Chen-cho 孔眞灼 , 80, 343n26

K'ung Chen-fan 孔眞璠 , 28-29, 312n89

K'ung Ch'eng-t'i 孔承倜 , 27-28, 312n87

K'ung Ch'eng-tz'u 孔承次 , 27-28, 312n85

K'ung Clan 孔 氏 :   early history of, 11-17, 302n45, 46; economic growth, 17-19; education, 19-21, 306n63; offices and titles, 21-23, 306n64-67; southern branch, 22, 309n71; present state of, 291-94; genealogy of, 308n70-74, see also Confucian Grove, Confucian Shrine, Confucian Temple, Genealogy

K'ung Chü 孔 聚, 15, 302n44

K'ung Fu 孔 鮒 , 14-15, 99, 297n16, 300n24, 302n40

Kung Hsien 龔 賢 , 170, 175, 176-85, 383n97, 385n101, 103, 386n105

K'ung Hung-chieh 孔弘頎 , 27, 312n86

K'ung Jen-yü 孔仁玉 , 22, 308n69

K'ung Ko 孔 絅 , 37, 301n37

K'ung Kuang-ssu 孔光嗣 , 21, 307n68

K'ung Jung 孔 融 , 17, 302n45, 304n52

K'ung Mo 孔 末 , 21-22, 308n68

K'ung Shang-jen 孔尙任 :   early years, 10, 27-49; attitude toward Ming loyalism, 29, 198-208; as connoisseur, 31, 136-37, 169-70, 191, 225-28, 284, 313n95, 392n133-35, 400n2; and The Peach Blosssom Fan, 33, 137, 198-99, 244-77, 281-82, 284;   attitude toward education, 40-42, 43; toward Confucianism, 41-42, 320 n114; travel to Tsinan, 43-48; poems by, 43-47, 72, 121, 134, 135, 151-62, 165, 166, 174, 175-76, 179, 183-84, 185, 187-88, 200-1, 202, 206-7, 212, 215, 218-19, 220, 224, 227, 278, 285-86, 288-89; travels on Stonegate Mt., 49-70, 71-72, 285-89; as editor of Genealogy and A New Gazetteer, 72-73; as master of Confucian ritual, 74, 282; as lecturer and guide to K'ang-hsi, 75-15; as Erudite of the Imperial Academy, 115-117; in Peking, 115-17, 217-25; as river control official, 117-18, 121, 172, 208-15; and the theatre, 127-28, 227-28, 274-75, 276-77, 281, 358n31; in Yangchow, 133-91, 208-10, 214-15; as host, 134-39, 172, 187-90, 376n76; poetry criticism, 138, 140-41, 145-51, 283-84; poetry collections, 139, 224-25, 283; friendships with painters, 167-87, 214, 377n80; and music theory, 190-91, 227-28, 229; in Nanking, 192-208; second meeting with K'ang-hsi, 212, 214; as dramatist, 225-77; and musical instruments, 225-28; resignation from office, 275-79; later years, 280-89; descendants, 292; other names, 300n27

K'ung Shang-li 孔尚立 , 79, 81, 87, 115, 337n13

K'ung Shang-tse 孔尚則 , 32-33, 36, 313n98

K'ung Sheng-yu 孔聖佑 , 53, 326n141

K'ung Te-ch'eng 孔德成 , 293

K'ung T'eng 孔 騰 , 16, 303n48

Kung-tiao 宮 調 , 230

K'ung Ting-tzu 龔鼎孳 , 217, 259

K'ung Tuan-ts'ao 孔端操 , 22, 309n73

K'ung Tuan-yu 孔端友 , 22, 309n71

K'ung Wen-na 孔聞訥 , 28, 312n88

K'ung Yen-chih 孔衍誌 , 73, 217

K'ung Yen-nien 孔延年 , 16, 304n50

K'ung Yen-p'u 孔衍譜 , 73, 217

K'ung Yen-shih 孔衍栻 , 51, 217, 324n135

K'ung Ying-ta 孔穎達 , 17, 304n53

K'ung Yü-ch'i 孔毓圻 : 42, 320n116; as host to K'ang-hsi, 75-115 passim, 211, 229

K'ung Yü-t'ing 孔毓廷 , 80, 93, 343n25

K'un-ts'an 禿 殘 , 171

Kuo Hsiu 郭 琇 , 208, 398n156

K'uo-pi 闊 筆 (broad manner of painting), 173

Kuo Tuan 郭 鍛 , 233, 240

Ku Ts'ai 顧 彩 , 228-30, 242, 243, 245, 274, 402n25, 412n67

Lan Ying 藍 英 , 186, 250-1, 389n121-23

Late Ming romanticism: in Nanking, 195-98; in The Peach Blossom Fan, 264, 269

Lei-ch'i 淚 氣 (Evil Powers), 271

Li 禮 (ritual): 23-27, 74, 311n75-83, 326n140; in The Peach Blossom Fan, 273-74 see also Confucianism

Liang Cheng-yen 梁正言 , 232-33

Liang Ch'i-ch'ao 梁啓超 , 72, 242

Liang Hou-pen 梁厚本 , 232-35, 239, 241

Liang Shou-ch'ien 梁守謙 , 232-33, 238

Li Chen-li 李貞麗 , 197, 246, 247-8, 250, 393n144

Li Chih 李 贄 , 39, 315n108

Li Hsiang-chün 李香君 (Fragrant Lady), 33, 197-99, 246-51, 260, 261, 264-67, 268, 269-70, 271, 393n143

Li Hsiu-lang 李修郎 , 228, 402n22

Li Hsun 李 訓 , 234, 238

Li Kung 李 塨 , 276, 415n80

Li Mu-an 李木庵 , 276

Li Po 李 白 , 64, 333n161

Li Tou 李 斗 , 126

"Little Thunderclap" 小忽雷 : musical instrument, 226-28, 229, 404n44; drama by K'ung Shang-jen, 229-42, 401n16

Li Tzu-ch'eng 李自成 , 29, 205, 249, 263

Liu Ch'i 劉 榮 , 281, 282, 416n88

Liu Ching-t'ing 劉敬亭 , 33, 36, 246, 247, 249, 251-52,
    258-9, 260, 261-2, 271, 408n58

Liu Pei 劉 備 , 263

Liu T'ing-chi 劉廷璣 , 282-83, 417n91

Liu Tsung-yuan 柳宗元 , 48, 234, 238, 323n128

Liu Yü-hsi 劉禹錫 , 205, 234, 238

Li Wei 李 蔚 , 275, 414n75

Li Yü 李 漁 , 240

Lü-lü kuan-chien 律呂管見 (Theory of Pitch in Confucian
    Music), 320n115

Lu Yu 陸 游 , 283, 417n92

Manchu Conquest; of Ch'ü-fu, 28-29; of China, 31-32, 195;
    of Yangchow, 122, 187, 354n14; of Nanking, 199-205,
    251; of Peking, 205, see also Ming loyalism

Man of Ch'i, The 齊人章 , 36

Mao Hsiang 冒 襄 , 136-37, 220, 363n50, 370n53, 54

Mao Tan-shu 冒丹書 , 137, 364n50

Ma Shih-ying 馬士英 , 136, 195, 249, 251, 256-57, 263, 269,
271, 272, 274, 370n52

Mei Ch'eng 枚 乘 , 155

Mei-yuan 莓 垣 , 49-50, 58, 70, 324n132

Mi Fei 米 芾, 94, 173, 180, 345n36

Mingju 明 珠 , 80, 90, 103, 108, 112, 208, 338n17

Ming loyalism: in Ch'ü-fu, 29; in Shantung, 32, 313n96; in
    Yangchow, 122, 160, 187; in Szechuan, 190; in Nanking,
    195, 199-205; in Peking, 205; see also Chia Fu-hsi,
    Huang Yun, K'ung Chen-fan, Kung Hsien, K'ung Shang-
    jen, Manchu conquest, Mao Hsiang, Teng Han-i, Shih
    K'o-fa

Ming T'ai-tsu 明太祖 : 18, 193; tomb of, 201-2, 204, 212

Min I-hsing 閔義行 , 191, 392n132

Music Master Departs for Ch'i, The 太師摯適齊 , 36

Nanking 南 京: restoration of the Ming in, 136, 137, 177,
    192, 195, 198, 254-74, 406n54-57; school of painters,

176, 383n98; <u>Manifesto</u>, 177, 195; description of, 192-205; Ch'in-huai quarters, 195-97, 199-201, 203, 246, 247-48, 393n142; K'ang-hsi in, 211, see also K'ung Shang-jen, The Peach Blossom Fan

<u>New Gazetteer of Ch'ü-fu</u>, A 闕里新誌 , 73, 335n3

Ni K'uang-shih 倪匡世 , 365n50

Ni Tsan 倪 瓚, 172, 173, 175, 177

Old Master of Ceremonies, The 老贊禮 , 252, 272-74, 413n70

<u>Organizing Principles Behind The Peach Blossom Fan, The</u> 桃花扇綱領 , 270-71

Ou-yang Hsiu 歐陽修 , 156, 159

Painting: relationship with literature, 167-68, 376n75; "eye area" of, 168; southern tradition, 168-9; "professional amateur", 169; K'ung Shang-jen's friendships with painters, 167-87, see also Tung Ch'i-ch'ang, Nanking

<u>Peach Blossom Fan, The</u> 桃花扇 : origins of story, 33, 137, 185, 197-99, 205-8, 245; painters represented in, 185-6; comparison with "Little Thunderclap", 242; creation of, 244-46; plot of, 246-52; prefaces to, 244-45, 254, 266-67, 275, 281, 406n52,53, 412n68, 416n89; critique of, 252-74; contemporary judgment of, 274-77, 281-2, 414n71; first printed edition of, 282; <u>Southern Version of</u>, 412n67, see also K'ung Shang-jen

P'ei Tu 裴 度 , 234

Peking 北 京 : K'ung Shang-jen's attitude toward, 141; fall of, 195, 205; K'ung Shang-jen in, 115-16, 217-25

<u>Pien</u> 變 (transformation): in literature, 145; (metamorphosis) in painting, 178

Pi Mao-k'ang 畢懋康 , 109, 347n66

<u>P'ing-t'ien-hsia</u> 平天下 (pacifying the world), 236

<u>P'i-pa</u> 琵 琶 , 226, 227, 233

"Pity the South" 哀江南 , 34, 36

Po Chü-i 白居易 , 232-35, 236, 238, 283, 417n92

Poems from a Lingering Stay 長留集 , 283, 417n95

Poems from the Lakes and Seas 湖海集 , 139, 224

Poems from the Waterside Studio 岸堂稿 , 225

Poetic theories: metaphysical, 138, 221-3; of K'ung Shang-
    jen, 139-51; "pragmatic", 149-50, 223, 225, 322n122,
    417n68, 69, 375n70; orthodox, 283-84; didactic,
    417n96, see also Hsing-ch'ing

Po-yü 伯 魚 , 5, 7, 99, 297n15

"Pragmatist" Movement 載道派 , 149-50, see also Poetic
    theories

Prince Chao-ming 昭明太子 , 160, 163

Prince Fu 福 王 , see Hung-kuang

Prince Kung 恭親王 (Ch'ang-ning 常 寧), 112, 348n67

Prince Lu 路 王 , 256

P'u-ch'ü 譜 曲 (scoring of dramatic arias), 230, 403n33

Rainbow Bridge Garden 虹 橋 , see Red Bridge Garden

Recognition of Ten Errors 十錯認 , 259, 411n60

Record of Senior Citizens, A 人瑞錄 , 244, 405n46

Red Bridge Garden 紅 橋 , 127, 134, 161, 163, 357n29

Ricci, Matteo, 193

River control: Ch'ing policy toward, 118-21, 208-14, 350n3,
    6, 351n7, 353n12; late Ming policy toward, 349n2, see
    also K'ang-hsi, K'ung Shang-jen

Romance of the Three Kingdoms, The 三國演義 , 263

Romantic comedy: K'ung Shang-jen's dramas as, 236, 260-74

Salt Merchants: in Yangchow, 125-27, 128, 357n28, 358n32

Samha 薩穆哈 , 80, 120-21, 341n21

Se 色 (Beauty), 270

Sha-ch'i 殺 氣 (Destructive Powers), 271

Shen Chou 沈 周 , 172, 464n61

Sheng-men li-yueh-chih 聖門禮樂誌 (Ceremonial Music of the
    Confucian Shrine), 320n115

Shen Han-kuang 申涵光 , 149, 223, 373n69

Shen-yun 神 韻 (spiritual resonance), 221-22

Shih 詩 poetry, 228, 230, 254

Shih K'o-fa 史可法 , 122, 157, 160, 195, 198, 249, 256-58, 263-64, 271, 274, 353n13, 408n56

Shui-hsing 水性 (watery nature), 270

Silda 席爾達 , 79, 80, 338n16

Songs of the South 楚辭譜 , 229, 403n26

Stonegate Mt. 石門山 , 1, 49-70, 175, 229, 295n2, 323n129, 335n169

Su K'un-sheng 蘇崑生 , 36, 197, 246, 248, 250-52, 260, 264, 271

Su Tung-p'o 蘇東坡 , 156, 159, 167-68

Sui Yang-ti 隋煬帝 , 123, 156, 159, 332n53, 355n16

Sun Ch'üan 孫權 , 192

Sung Che-tsung 宋哲宗 , 18

Sung Chen-tsung 宋眞宗 , 18, 94, 105, 328n147

Sung Hui-tsung 宋徽宗 , 93, 328n147

Sung Lien 宋濂 , 24, 312n84

Sun Tsai-feng 孫在豐 , 77-78, 80, 100, 108, 117, 121, 208, 211, 337n12

Swallow Note, The 燕子箋 , 247, 259-60, 267-68, 411n60

Tai Pen-hsiao 戴本孝 , 170, 171, 175-76, 382n94

T'ang Hsien-tsu 湯顯祖 , 197, 228, 259, 264-65, 267

T'ang Hsuan-tsung 唐玄宗 : 101; poem by, 346n53

T'ang Pin 湯斌 , 120-21, 352n11

T'ang Te-tsung 唐德宗 , 226, 232

T'ang Wen-tsung 唐文宗 , 226, 235, 238, 241-2

Tan-p'u heng-yen 澹圃恒言 (Enduring Words from Placidity Patch), 39, 314n107

Tao 道 (the Way), 148-49, 152, 157, 160, 221, 254, 270, 271

Tao-chi 道濟 , 170, 171-73, 174, 378n83, 380n84, 86

Taoist Chang 張道士 , see Chang I

T'ao-shu 套數 (set of aria forms), 230

T'ao Yuan-ming 陶淵明 , 58, 323n131, 330n155

Teng Han-i 鄧漢儀 , 138-39, 212, 214, 321n117, 364n50

Theatre: in Yangchow, 127-32, 357n30, 358n32-35; in Peking, 227-28, 274-75, 276-77, 402n22; in Nanking, 359n37, see also K'un-ch'ü

Theory of Pitch in Classical Music 律呂管見 , 191

Thousand Peaks and Myriad Ravines, A 千山萬壑 , 178-79, 181

T'ieh Hsuan 鐵鉉 , 43-44, 322n119, 120

Tien 典 (allusiveness), 222

T'ien Wen 田雯 , 149, 223-24, 245, 373n69

T'ien Yang 田仰 , 249, 250

Ting Chi-chih 丁繼之 , 245, 259, 405n49

Ting Yeh-ho 丁野鶴 , 39, 318n109

"Transcendant spirit" 厭世解脫之精神 , 413n69

Tsa-chü 雜劇 , 230

Ts'ai I-so 蔡益所 , 251

Ts'ai Wang-nan 蔡綱南 , 276

Tseng-tzu 曾子, 6, 14

Tsinan 濟南: K'ung's journey to and early poems on, 43-48; later journey to, 282

Tso-ch'ü 作曲 (composition of dramatic arias), 230, 403n33

Tso Liang-yü 左良玉 , 248, 249, 251, 258-59, 263, 271, 410n59

Ts'ui Wei-ya 崔維雅 , 120, 351n8

Tsun-ching 尊經 (textual authority), 42

Tsung Yuan-ting 宗元鼎 , 139, 371n61

Tu Fu 杜甫: poems by, 53, 58, 67-68, 325n137, 330n154, 334n167, 337n14

Tu-ku Yü 獨孤郁 , 232, 233

Tu Mu 杜牧, 123-25, 134, 158

Tu Li-niang 杜麗娘 , 264-65

T'ung 通 (universality), 270

T'ung Che-ts'un 佟蔗村 , 282

Tung Ch'i-ch'ang 董其昌 , 136-37, 168-69, 170, 173, 176-77, 178, 376n78

Tung Chung-shu 董仲舒 , 161, 163

Tung-lin 東 林, 194, 241, 256, 393n138

Tung Yuan 董 源, 168, 179, 386n108

Tz'u 詞, 228, 230, 254

Tzu-kung 子 貢, 7, 92, 104-5

Tzu-lu 子 路, 57, 63, 328n150-52, 332n159

Tzu-ssu 子 思, 7, 302n39

Wang Ch'i 王 歧, 162

Wang Ching 王 荆, 162

Wang Hsi 王 熙, 80, 89, 90, 98, 100, 108, 112, 114, 211, 339n18

Wang Hsi-chih 王羲之, 189

Wang Hui 王 翬, 170, 174, 220, 377n81, 378n82

Wang Kai 王 概, 178, 386n106

Wang Ken 王 艮, 320n114

Wang Kuo-wei 王國維, 413n69

Wang Meng 王 蒙, 172

Wang Shih-chen 王士禎, 134-35, 137, 140, 150, 161, 163, 219-23, 277, 279, 361n41, 362n45

Wang Shih-min 王時敏, 170

Wang Shou-hsi 王壽熙, 245

Wang Wei 王 維, 167-68, 218, 223, 327n146, 332n158

Wang Yang-ming 王陽明, 27-28, 380n114

Wang Yuan 王 源, 279, 415n86

Wei Chung-hsien 魏忠賢, 194, 241, 247, 259, 393n139

Wei-hsing 緯 星 (Woof Star), 272

Wei Liang-fu 魏良輔, 131, 359n36

Weng Shu-yuan 翁叔元, 116, 348n73

Wen-jou tun-hou 溫柔敦厚, (mild, tender, sincere and profound), 283-84

"Wood-and Leather" Wanderer, The 木皮散客, see Chia Fu-hsi

Woodcutter's History, A 樵 史, 255

Wu Ch'i 吳 綺, 151, 375n71

Wu Mei 吳 梅, 242, 404n42

Wu Pin 吳 彬, 175

Wu P'ing-shan 吳平山 , 157

Wu Wei-yeh 吳偉業 , 240, 258, 259

Wu Ying-chi 吳應箕, 246, 247, 248, 251

Yangchow 揚 州 : description of, 122-35; painters in, 169,
      171, 173, 177; dramas about, 228, 402n23; in The Peach
      Blossom Fan, 257-58, see also K'ung Shang-jen, Theatre

Yang Wen-ts'ung 楊文驄 , 33, 176, 185-86, 198, 246-51, 261,
      268, 269-70, 274, 388n120, 412n66

Yen Ku-ku 閻古古 , 39, 318n109

Yen Yü 嚴 羽, 221

Yin-yang 陰 陽 , 270

Yü 禹 , 151-2

Yuan Chen 元 稹, 234, 238

Yuan Hung-tao 袁宏道 , 39, 145, 316n108, 373n67

Yü Ch'eng-lung 于成龍 , 121-2, 208, 211, 352n9

Yü-ch'i (Excess Powers) 餘 氣 , 271

Yü Chin-ch'üan 余錦泉 , 128

Yueh-tuan 岳 端 , 245, 402n23, 405n50

Yü Huai 余 懷 , 197, 199-200, 220, 394n145

Yü Min 于 敏 , 233

Yung-lo 永 樂 , 43, 193, 201, 321n118-19

Yu shih-men-shan chi 遊石門山集 (Wandering on Stonegate Mt.),
      49-70, 335n169

Yü T'i 于 頔 , 233